The Path I Trod

The Path I Trod

THE AUTOBIOGRAPHY OF

TERENCE V. POWDERLY

EDITED BY HARRY J. CARMAN

HENRY DAVID AND

PAUL N. GUTHRIE

AMS PRESS
NEW YORK

AMS PRESS, INC.
New York, N.Y. 10003

INTRODUCTION

O N JANUARY 22, 1907, Terence Vincent Powderly wrote to a friend, "This is my birthday, I am fifty-eight years young today. Tomorrow I begin to write a partial autobiography. . . . I have not been understood by many and I want to prepare this to leave this after me so that I shall be able to give a reason for what I did even tho my lips be sealed. . . . No one knows what my motives were but me, and I am going to tell why I did certain things so that my real self will be known by those who care to read of it." During the seven years preceding 1921 he devoted much time to his autobiography, and by the spring of that year it apparently assumed satisfactory form. After that date, as far as it can be discovered, he made no significant changes in the manuscript here published for the first time as *The Path I Trod*.

This title is Powderly's, for on a discarded page of the manuscript he noted that "These are the concluding lines of a chapter on McKinley, whom I worked with from 1877 to the time of his death in 1901. They were written in 1917, and some day may be published in my book: 'The Path I Trod.'"

In a letter to John E. Barrett, dated January 15, 1889, Powderly sketched his life in the following words:

I am credibly informed that I was born January 22, 1849 at Carbondale, Pa. Went to school until thirteen when I was employed by the D. & H. Canal Co. to guard a point where a number of switches were placed to prevent any tampering with them. At fourteen was employed by the same company as car examiner and at seventeen was apprenticed to the Machinist trade in the shops of the D. & H. company. Served out my three years and came to Scranton at 20 and was employed by the D.L. & W. Co. in the locomotive shop. Joined the Machinist and Blacksmiths Union in 1871, was elected president of the subordinate union to which I belonged in 1872. Was married in 1872 and in 1873, some three weeks after Jay Cooke's failure was discharged because of my activity in union matters. Went west, worked in Galion O. and Oil City Pa. Came back to Scranton and in 1875

was employed by the L. I. & C. Co. in the erection of the Steel Works of
that Company. When the machinery was all in I went to work for the
Dickson Co. at the Cliff Works where I continued until for want of orders
that company suspended all its employees in April 1877.

Was elected Mayor of Scranton Feb. 19, 1878, again in 1880 and again
in 1882. Was nominated by the Greenback Labor party for Lieut. Gov. in
1882 but declined the nomination.

Joined the Knights of Labor in 1876 although I was sworn in in 1874.
In February 1877 District Assembly No. 5 was organized in Scranton. I
was elected Corresponding Secretary and held the position until the spring
of 1886 when my duties as G.M.W. took me away from home so much
that I could not attend to it. In 1878 all of the various parts of the Knights
of Labor were called together at Reading Pa. There we found another District Assembly No. 5 and we surrendered our right to the number and
took 16.

Was elected General Worthy Foreman of the Order at St. Louis January
1879 and in September of that year was elected G.M.W. The term was for
one year until 1886 was reelected each year until 1887 when no election
was held, the term having been extended the year previous to two years.
Salary for the first four years was $400. out of which I paid all my expenses
as G.M.W. and devoted what was left to the building up of the Order. In
1883 the salary was increased to $800 in 1884 to $1,500 and in 1886 to
$5,000. At the last session of the General Assembly the salary was again
fixed at $5,000 but informed the convention that I would draw but three
thousand for the year and if at the next session they considered that I had
earned the other two thousand they could dispose of it there.

In 1885 we had about 80,000 members in good standing, in one year the
number jumped up to 700,000 of which at least four hundred thousand
came in from curiosity and caused more damage than good.

Was elected at Indianapolis to represent the K. of L. at the Worlds Fair
at Paris next summer. The Order was invited to send a representative by
the French syndicates and Deputies of Economics.

There, I believe I have touched on the important events in my life. I omit
all mention of my personal beauty and accomplishments as well as a great
deal of truthful detail which if it reached the ear of the public might oblige
me to fortify my house and wear a sheet iron, boiler plate coat when on the
street. If you happen to be in possession of any of these damaging facts please
smother them for the good of the community at large; the example might be
bad you know.

To John Swinton, Powderly's physical appearance was strik-
ingly at odds with that of his fellow labor leaders. "English
novelists take men of Powderly's look for their poets, gondola

scullers, philosophers and heroes crossed in love," he wrote in *John Swinton's Paper*, October 17, 1886. Swinton reported that Powderly was at this time "a slender man, under average height with mild blue eyes behind glasses. Blond mustache hides his mouth and bends down to below his chin. Light brown hair in curves that are neither waves nor curls rests on his coat collar, heavy behind but almost burned away at the top. . . . He looks and behaves like a man of good breeding, accustomed to the usages of society, but is unlike the average labor leader in appearance."

Powderly remained General Master Workman of the Knights of Labor until 1893, when he resigned at the Philadelphia General Assembly rather than continue as chief officer of the Order with a General Executive Board antagonistic to his policies. The General Assembly had previously cleared him of the personal charges brought against him, and he was elected over his objections. In the following year, however, he was expelled from the Order on the ground that he had refused to turn over certain of its properties to the officers who succeeded him. Reinstated as a member of the Knights of Labor by the Birmingham General Assembly in 1900, he joined Local Assembly 4896 in Washington, D. C. In 1894 he became a member of the bar in Scranton, Pennsylvania, and three years later he was admitted to practice before the Supreme Court of Pennsylvania. In 1901 he was granted the right to practice before the Supreme Court of the United States.

President McKinley appointed Powderly Commissioner-General of Immigration in 1897, and he held this post until he was removed by President Theodore Roosevelt on July 2, 1902. The President's action grew out of a controversy concerning the official behavior of the Assistant Commissioner of Immigration at the Port of New York. Later the President learned that the accusations leveled against Powderly in the course of the controversy were unfounded, and in 1907 he issued an executive order setting aside the civil service rules so that he could name Powderly Chief of the Division of Information in the Bureau of Immigration. The first step in President Roosevelt's *amende honorable* had come a year earlier, when Powderly was appointed special representative of the Department of Commerce and Labor to study the causes of emigration from Europe to America. In the course of his investigation of the problem, Powderly visited the British Isles, Germany, Holland, Belgium, France, Austria-Hungary, and Italy. Between 1902 and 1907 he participated in several business ventures, none of which was very profitable. He was president of the Black Diamond Coal Company, the Washington representative of the General Lubricating Company of Philadelphia, and conducted a real estate business in Washington. In addition he did considerable writing for magazines and government officials. Powderly held the post of Chief of the Division of Information of the Bureau of Immigration until 1921, when he was named a member of the Board of Review of the Bureau. Between that date and his death, June 24, 1924, he also served as Commissioner of Conciliation in the Department of Labor.

In 1872, Powderly married Hannah Dever, who died in 1901, and eighteen years later he married Emma Fickenscher who had been his invaluable secretary when he was at the head of the Knights of Labor. Mrs. Powderly died February 24, 1940, at the age of eighty-four, in Washington, D. C.

Powderly obviously designed his autobiography as a vindication of his public life and work. During the 'eighties he was the outstanding figure on the American labor scene. Labor leaders of equally significant and lasting influence experienced comparatively little of the fame, notoriety, adoration, and detestation which he enjoyed. Powderly headed the Noble Order of the Knights of Labor for fourteen years during a period which witnessed radical changes in America's industrial and social order. These transformations were reflected in the structure, program, leadership, and the phenomenal growth and decline of the Knights. In the life of the American labor movement, the 'eighties were years of crisis. When workers literally poured into the Order to produce a membership of over 700,000 in 1886, it seemed to many, for a moment, that labor was on the point of fashioning an instrument for dealing with an industrial capitalist society in process of growth and consolidation. From the vantage point of the present, the significance of the Knights seems essentially threefold; as the champion of the idea of solidarity ("An injury to one is the concern of all"); as the last important manifestation of middle-class reform philosophies in the American labor movement; and as an organization which educated the American public in the importance of organized labor.

As General Master Workman of the Knights, Powderly was a storm center in the camp of organized labor. He was attacked from all sides—by trade-unionists, fellow Knights, employers, reformers, politicians, and clerics. Since then he has been sharply handled by students of American labor history, with the result that the popularity which he won and the degree to which he was a characteristic product of his milieu have been somewhat obscured.

The Path I Trod is more than Powderly's justification of his life and work. As a self-revealing portrait of a man and his times it is an important addition to the source literature of American labor history. Students of that field, in general, and the editors, in particular, owe a great debt to Mrs. Emma F. Powderly. Not only did she make available for study and publication her husband's autobiography, but she also turned over to the editors Powderly's letter files. These include his official orders, dispensations, circulars and the like, perhaps some 75,000 letters, post cards and telegrams to and from Powderly, and letters of Uriah S. Stephens for the years 1878-79. Most of this rich source material for a crucial and fascinating phase of American labor history has never before been examined or published. It is the present plan of the editors to publish at least one volume of selected Powderly letters in the near future.

The editors have sought to present Powderly's autobiography essentially as he wrote it. His inconsistencies in punctuation have been corrected, however, and considerations of space dictated the deletion of some twenty-five thousand words. Wherever omissions have been made they are indicated by ellipses. Beyond that there is no departure from the original text. In every case the material left out is either without significance or appears elsewhere in the volume. Nothing has been deleted that throws light on Powderly as labor leader and as man, or that modifies Powderly's delineation of himself and his times.

Lastly, the editors are grateful to all those who, in any way, have aided in the publication of this autobiography. They are especially indebted to the Columbia University Council for Research in the Social Sciences for financial assistance.

H. J. C.
H. D.
P. N. G.

CONTENTS

The Path I Trod

Chapter One

THE START, WITH SOME ADVANTAGES

All men of whatsoever quality they be, who have done anything of excellence, or which may properly resemble excellence, ought, if they are persons of truth and honesty, to describe their life with their own hand. . . . BENVENUTO CELLINI.

PERHAPS Cellini was right when he said that, but it is not of record that he expressed an opinion as to who should decide what the principal events of a man's life consist of. What may appear to be an event of prime importance to one individual may be only secondary or no interest at all to others. It might happen, too, that an event of great moment would be based on an apparently unimportant happening—such as being born for instance, an event of which little notice is taken at the time of birth, unless the child is equipped with six toes on each foot, some other mark of distinction, or is a million-dollar baby. . . . I didn't have six toes, and if my parents had wealth they concealed it from me; neither did I differ much from other babies of my sex.

As some of the principal events of my life may be due to unconsidered trifles, I shall tell you about them as I proceed and shoulder upon you the burden of responsibility in judging of their importance.

Many of my principal events have become history through pens that took their coloring from friendship, enmity, jealousy, partiality, or prejudice; some of my friends saw in me a demi-god and said so, my enemies, equally as truthful perhaps, from their viewpoint, saw only a demon, and not only said so but kept repeating it. I was not good enough to be the former or bad enough to be the latter and tried to strike a mean between such opposites. It does not do, therefore, to take the historian too seriously; at best he but weaves the warp of fancy into the woof of fact and gives us the web called history.

Every now and then we read obituaries in which the departed is treated to flattery, praise, disparagement or censure according to the religious bias, political partisanship, or dyspeptic lens used by the writer in viewing the merits or demerits of deceased.

That it may come to him who reads in my own writing, I shall take the liberty of anticipating the obituarian by having my say first.

Born without previous notice, and when I wasn't expecting it, I didn't note the date until reminded of it later. With defective vision to start with I didn't see many of the bad or cruel things transpiring around me. I began to catch things early. The first was scarlet fever, after that came measles; the former deprived me of the use of one ear, in consequence, I did not hear half of the disagreeable things that others had to listen to. In addition to these advantages, I was born of poor but Irish parents and that made up for a whole lot.

Before their marriage my father and mother were Terence Powderly and Madge Walsh; after marriage they were one, and I always held to the belief that my mother was the one. She was to me, anyway.

Shortly after his marriage, in 1826, my father shouldered a gun, which he borrowed from a neighbor, walked through the wide open gateway leading to Lord Cunningham's estate, and shot a hare. For so doing he was arrested, tried, and found guilty on three counts in the indictment, to wit: carrying a firearm without warrant of law, trespassing on a gentleman's estate, and willfully, deliberately, and with malice aforethought taking the life of a hare. I submit to the dispassionate and unbiased reader that he was obliged to carry the gun without warrant of law, for the English code denied to Irishmen the right to carry firearms, and since he had no estate of his own to shoot a hare on, he had to shoot him on another man's land or not shoot him at all. Instead of dismissing him with a vote of thanks for not shooting the landlord, they sent him to Trim jail for three weeks. Trim is the county seat of Meath County, Ireland.

On regaining his liberty he determined to leave Ireland, and becoming enthusiastic over the prospect he addressed this remark to my mother: "Let us leave this damn country and go to America where a man may own himself and a gun, too, if he wants to."

After an eight weeks' trip across the Atlantic in the *Royal George*, which was crowded to her capacity by twenty-three passengers, all of them first class, they landed at Montreal, Canada. They went up the St. Lawrence River on a smaller boat to Ogdensburg, New York, where they arrived July 27th, 1827. The day before they landed my oldest sister was born on the boat. They reached Ogdensburg, New York, early in the morning, a fortunate circumstance for them, since it gave my father all day to look for work. He had with him, when he stepped on American soil, my mother, the baby and one English shilling. He was fortunate in coming as early as 1827, for at a later period I might, as Commissioner-General of Immigration, be obliged to deport him as likely to become a public charge. The shooting of that hare might influence me some, too, and perhaps I might consider him undesirable. However, being six feet two inches tall, built in proportion to height and capable of doing his own thinking, he could and did take care of himself and a few others.

So far as known, he was the first Powderly to emigrate to America. He came from Ireland. The first of his ancestors to land in Ireland came from France shortly after the revocation of the Edict of Nantes in 1685, and, being a Huguenot, he found the climate of England more healthful and conducive to longevity than that of France. He was Hugo Poudrele. He went to Canterbury, where he met and married an English girl and shortly after crossed over to Ireland where he settled in Drogheda. The Irish have made changes for the better all over the world, and I think they improved the spelling when they first wrote the name as it came through my father to me.

My father worked for nearly two years with a farmer at Ogdensburg, and having saved a little money removed to Carbondale, Pennsylvania, where he arrived June 15, 1829. Not a wheel was turning on a passenger train and there wasn't a locomotive running in the United States at the time, so he and my mother walked part of the way along the trail blazed by the Indians a few years before when they came down to Wyoming to lay the foundations for the monument that now stands where they massacred and scalped the New England settlers and others who had built homes along the Susquehanna.[1] Sometimes they were taken aboard of a hay wagon by a farmer who was going their way, and when they reached a stage route between villages they made use of a stage. In this way they covered the distance, some 200 miles, between Ogdensburg and Carbondale. It was not Carbondale then, just a level spot along the Lackawanna River between the blue fringed ranges of the Moosic spur of the Alleghenies. The level, and mountains too, were covered by dense forests. With his axe my father assisted in chopping down the trees from which the first church in that part of the state was built. The roof was made of the limbs and bark of the hemlock, maple, and oak trees used in its construction. When it rained during time of service the congregation, although made up of strictly temperate people, was obliged to get wet. That church was dedicated to no particular form of worship. First come first served. Being a Catholic, my father hoped the first clergyman to come to the place would be a Catholic priest, but was doomed to disappointment, for it was a Presbyterian minister who first visited Barrendale as the place was then called.

All who lived there attended church that day, my father among the number, and when the congregation was dismissed it hung around to interview the clergyman and hear the news from the outside world. . . . The minister who was enroute to Albany from Philadelphia was expected to tell his hearers, among other things, about some of the shortcomings of dwellers in the cities and towns he passed through on his way to them. . . .

The only vehicle of transportation they had was the wheelbarrow. Encouraged by its successful use, the Delaware and Hudson Canal Company selected my father as its representative to go to Bethany, which is in Pennsylvania, fifteen miles away, to purchase a mule or a horse. He selected a horse, although he

[1] The Wyoming Valley "massacre" occurred in 1778. Led by Tories, Indians lay waste to the valley and killed many women and children.

could have procured a mule for less money. He, with rare fore-sight, realized that capital is always timid. It was not only timid then but scarce, and D. & H. stock wasn't quoted on the market at $156 a share. Had he bought a mule and the mule should balk, as mules do sometimes for they seem possessed of human intelligence in that respect, the operations of the company would come to a standstill during the mediations of the mule.

Anthracite was then under discussion as radium is now and about as little known.[2] The Delaware and Hudson Canal Company, now the Delaware and Hudson Railroad Company, had just discovered coal in Carbondale and were making preparations to ship it to market. They purchased a locomotive in England (the *Stourbridge Lion*), had it shipped over, and on its arrival at New York City transported it to Honesdale by the canal route. It was the first locomotive to stand or run on a track in the United States.[3] It did more standing than running, for it was as heavy as seven tons, and the consensus of opinion seemed to be that no track could stand such a weight. It made its first trip on August 8 or 9, 1829.

Naturally great excitement prevailed in the neighborhood when it was announced that a rival to the company horse was to draw the new cars from the mountain top to the canal at Hones-dale. Four cars were built. They were considered mammoth affairs; they would hold all of two tons of coal each. These cars, the first loaded with anthracite in Northeastern Pennsylvania, were built by a carpenter in the employ of the Delaware and Hudson Canal Company, named Thomas Mullen. By the way, Mullen and his wife were among the twenty-three passengers that came over from Ireland on the *Royal George* in 1827. My father asked him for, received permission to, and did load these cars, the first to leave Carbondale over the gravity road then being con-structed. This road consisted of levels, grades, and planes. Hemp ropes, operated by stationary engines, were used on the planes;

[2] This is somewhat misleading. Anthracite was known and used sometime be-fore this, but on a very limited scale because of the absence of proper furnaces, stoves, and transportation difficulties.

[3] It was preceded by the experimental locomotives of Oliver Evans and James Stephens.

horses drew the cars on the levels, and on the grades they went without horses or engines. My father accompanied the train he loaded over the planes to the summit; but the locomotive failed to fulfill the expectation of its owners in that it could not make the full distance of ten miles owing to a bridge or two that spanned the track.

My father, though not a doubting Thomas so far as the locomotive was concerned, returned to Carbondale with his confidence in the horse unshaken. He bought a few horses himself later and with their help did good service for the company.

With the building of the railroad, sixteen miles long, from Carbondale to Honesdale where it connected with the canal, the route was opened between the upper anthracite fields and New York City. . . .

It is as well to be born in the first chapter as elsewhere, and, though I have only secondary evidence as to the fact, believe it happened as related to me afterwards by my mother, who said the doctor found me in an old hollow log and, as our house happened to be nearest to the log in question, he wrapped me up in his cloak, carried me to the house and left me with mother. That happened on the morning of January 22, 1849.

Just a word about our house and then I'll pass on. It was a frame building of six rooms. Unmatched boards to which wall paper was attached on the inside and siding on the outside made up the wall part; no laths, no plaster, and when the wind blew the house would rock as well as the cradle. This rocking tore the wall paper apart and when it snowed the beautiful snow would lay in streaks across the bed clothes in the morning. It was only when our folks grew somewhat haughty and purse proud that we had rag carpet for the floors in sitting room and bed rooms.

I was the eleventh of twelve children, all but one born in Carbondale. The ratio was two boys to each girl. Though of slight build as a boy I always presented the appearance of being quite stout owing to the clothes I wore. . . . My mother would reduce the length of the outgrown trousers of my older brothers, but— for want of time—left the other measurement about the same. I had a greater variety of clothing and of more ample dimensions than any of the others. It was a girl who came after me, and in the matter of clothes she had to shift for herself, mine wouldn't answer; anyway they wouldn't fit anyone when I became charitable enough to want to give them away.

I was twelve years old before I donned a suit of clothes made specially for me and of material that hadn't been sampled and tried out by one of my older brothers. The clothes I formerly wore fit me so much that those who saw me in my first owny own suit didn't recognize me, or else thought I wasn't well and was pining away.

Chapter Two

BEGINNING MY EDUCATION

WHAT I HAVE TOLD YOU up to this time was based on hearsay, but my informants were "upright, credible" people and I regard their statements to me as accurate, or reasonably so. What is to follow shall be a record of events in which I participated, or to which I was a witness.

Several important things happened to me before I was seven years old, but similar things happen to most boys, so I'll not burden you with them.

The circus didn't travel by rail in the fifties, it came by wagon route and we called it the "overland" circus. On the morning of circus day the boys would go to meet it, starting about five o'clock. My mother wouldn't permit me to accompany the other boys, and as a consequence I didn't have a chance to run alongside of the elephant to get a close view of him. I had heard that elephants were fond of potatoes and one day determined, in the interest of science, to test the matter. On a sunny circus morning I annexed about a half peck of potatoes, cut each one in two, and carried them out to the fence fronting the road. Jack Clark, a neighbor's boy of about my age, assisted me in my pursuit of knowledge. He could see when the elephant came close enough, I couldn't, and, anyway, my mother wouldn't let me pass the fence line. It was understood that when the elephant reached a point near our gate Jack was to throw a few potatoes in front of him and then scatter them on a line leading up to the fence on which I was perched with a quantity of potatoes in my clothes to hand out to the trunk bearer when he came near enough. Elephants do like potatoes. When Columbus—that was the elephant's name—got a whiff of the first potato, he stopped, picked it up, and, packing it away in his trunk, began a search for more. He found them; his investigations led him directly to where I was sitting on the fence. I recall that at our first meeting I was a trifle reserved and bashful, but as I handed out the potatoes the reserve wore off and we became more intimate. When the supply of potatoes was exhausted the elephant passed his trunk gently around my shirt in search of more. Although he was an immense animal and could easily have separated me from the fence and damaged me, he was very gentle. His gentility was in marked contrast with the course mother pursued toward me after the circus passed by. For a time I regretted that the elephant hadn't taken me away with him. My mother didn't appear to be a bit interested in the theory that elephants are fond of potatoes. No great stride in progress or discovery was ever prosecuted without entailing suffering or hardship on the discoverer. . . . Elephants just love potatoes. The keeper of that animal couldn't move him from the spot in front of our fence while I was demonstrating my theory. The language he—the keeper—used was vigorous and lurid enough to move mountains and bore no resemblance to anything I had ever heard in church; it didn't move the elephant. . . .

My father was a pronounced Democrat, my mother a pronounced abolitionist. . . . When the Buchanan-Frémont campaign of 1856 was in progress I had attained an age that entitled me to be termed reasonable; seven is the age of reason in some, while one hundred and seven would be about right for others. . . .

The echoes of the Lincoln-Douglas debates had about died away. The debates between my father and mother, for and against slavery, were still on. I had to listen to them and naturally became much interested; having faith in my mother I took her side of the question. On the morning of election day, after father had started for the polling place, I asked mother when she intended going. She smiled as she said: "I have no right to, I am not a man and only men vote." That answer did not appeal to me as a good and sufficient reason why she should not vote. I was not a woman, I was seven years old, had attained the age of reason and knew it. I resolved to vote for my mother and going to the polling place, half a mile away, asked a man who was peddling tickets from a cigar box to give me a Frémont ticket. He gave me one, a bunch of them, and, going to the window where the tickets were handed in, [I] attempted to reach up to pass my ballot through the aperture to the election board inside. I was not tall enough and a bystander lifted me up. A man inside asked who I was going to vote for. Because I believed in it and to impress my father, who stood close by chatting with some friends, I shouted "I'm going to vote for Frémont." That shout was my undoing; the son of the proprietor of the hotel where the voting was done, some three years older than I and four sizes bigger, whom I shall call Mike, because that was his name, met me on my way home and proceeded to change my politics, beginning with my head to which he added a new bump or two and a pair of dark rims to wear round my eyes for a while. His arguments were forceful but not convincing. That was my baptism of fire. From that day to this I have been a believer in, and an advocate of, equal suffrage.

The thrashing he gave me that day and some that he contributed later had a sobering influence on me so I may as well tell about them now. I spent a couple of years in the "Little Red School" before going to work and fell desperately but not hopelessly in love with one of the girls who attended. She was a year or so older than I but that made no difference. It happened that Mike was in love with her also. The demon of jealousy took possession of him, and he availed himself of every opportunity to humiliate me in her eyes. Her name was Kittie. One day at recess I was talking to Kittie on a serious matter and, being very nearsighted, had to get quite close to see her. . . . I stood rooted to the spot, or thought I did until Mike stole up behind me, broke the thread of my remarks, and tore me loose from the soil with a ten hundred and fifty volt kick. It hurt my feelings, it hurt me, it humiliated me beyond expression, for Kittie was considering a proposal of marriage which I had just tendered her. I was nearly ten years old, and, having read love stories in the old New York *Ledger*, knew how to select a few well chosen remarks for such an occasion. The *Ledger* never related an account of a lover having the romance kicked up into his hat though, and in the absence of such detail I treated Mike to a surprise party. Though of slight build and nearsighted, I was quick in my movements. I gave Mike a good, swift thump on the nose, turned and ran away. He, as I expected, started in pursuit. When he was within arm's length, I threw myself on my hands and knees; he couldn't stop and passed abruptly over me, landing on his head. I lost no time in straddling his chest and, plying my fists with rapid and telling effect, soon made his face unpresentable. . . .

Seven years later I was a brakeman on the Delaware & Hudson gravity road, running what was known as the switchback train. It consisted of about twelve or fourteen empty cars which ran by gravity down the mountain side, making stops in switches at intervals. One day when my train stopped in a switch, Mike got aboard. I chatted with him until the train passed into the next switch. Fastening the brakes securely, I addressed Mike somewhat like this: "You used to thrash me at school, do you think you can do it now?" He promptly answered in the affirmative. We selected a place under the trees, took off our coats, and—but why harrow your feelings with detail. He never gave me so sound a thrashing as he did that day. We rode together to the end of the route, shook hands, and parted. I don't remember seeing him again until one day in 1905 when, on a visit to Carbondale, a prematurely aged man, wasted by sickness, hobbled up to me, grasped my hand, and, after making himself known—for I did not recognize him—said: "Terry, can you forgive me for the way I treated you at school and for that unmerciful beating I gave you on the switchback?" Placing my hand on his shoulder I answered him: "I have nothing to forgive. I have never avenged a personal injury in the whole course of my life. I do not now and never did carry resentment beyond the day of its birth. I owe more to you than any other man not related to me. I have traveled much and have worn many hats; if ever one of these hats began to get pinchy or too small for my head, all I had to do to reduce the swelling would be to think of how you took the conceit out of me the last time you prescribed for me. There's nothing to forgive, Mike, I owe you only gratitude and blessings."

I admit that at school I often resolved to murder him but could not decide on the exact method of his execution or on a plan that would punish him sufficiently. . . .

I have heard it said that the oldest child of a family has the hardest time of it. I never was the oldest child of any family so I don't know about that. I was the eleventh, almost the shake of the bag, and know that my childhood was not a picnic.

My father spent no time in saloons; my mother did not go to the movies, and when my brothers came from work they, as a rule, remained home in the evening. Up to the time they married and left home they had to account to mother for every minute, after work hours, spent out of her sight. After supper (we didn't call it dinner up in Pennsylvania unless we ate it at noon time), I helped mother to wash, dry, and dispose of the dishes, pots, and pans. We used no side dishes, and so it did not take long to get the dishes done. Sometimes I would give them a lick and a promise, but that only lengthened the task; she would make me do it all over again.

There were no coal breakers then. Anthracite was delivered in lumps just as it came from the mine, few of them smaller than one's head. I was the coal breaker for our family. Each day, after the chamber work for the cows and horses was done, I had to break the coal to be used for the next twenty-four hours. I was taught how to do everything around the house as well as to mend my own clothing. I have not forgotten how yet. In cooking I seldom had to consider the construction of fancy dishes. Enough beef and pork would be salted down in the fall to last all winter. We grew our own potatoes and other vegetables. In addition to my knowledge of housekeeping I was educated in the rudiments of farming on a garden plot of about two acres. Corn, cabbage, potatoes and various kinds of garden truck were grown. When the harvest season came I did my full duty at that time too.

Corn-meal mush, or stirabout, was a favorite dish with my father. I have heard people go into raptures over what they called the nutritious and delicious corn-meal mush. They did not have to eat it as regularly as I did or work so hard to grow it. In addition to my other accomplishments, I could churn and make butter.

It is in no spirit of boasting that I tell of my youthful accomplishments. I did most of these things because the hand that rocked the cradle that I was swayed in ruled the part of the world that I was brought up in; it held the scepter too, and as it was sometimes a broom stick and at other times a switch, I, as in duty bound, did what I was bidden—when I could not dodge it.

Baseball, as now known, was not in the curriculum, so we played "two old cat." I took part in the game, sometimes as batter but oftener as batted. When batting, the ball would get so close before I could see it that I often missed it. When catching, the ball seldom missed me, it would slip through my hands and catch me somewhere between my forehead and chin, or amidships between chin and feet. I did not know I was nearsighted. . . . How could I know there were different kinds of vision? I had heard of and read about stars, but was skeptical; I could not see them. One evening, when I was eighteen years old, I tried on a pair of glasses, and for the first time saw the different stars and constellations outlined against the blue. I can feel the awe and wonder of that hour now. . . .

I don't know that it snowed any more when I was a boy than it does now, but snowstorms seemed to adhere to a more rapid schedule, and as to quantity the allowance was most generous. Ninety days of good sleighing every winter was about the thing then. When it snowed it did it with reckless abandon, and I had to shovel paths to the barn, coal shed, and road. We had no streets, just roads and paths. On many occasions I tunneled snow drifts to the barn and coal house. Three and four feet of snow on the level was not unusual after a storm. We had a neighbor who took a deep interest in other folks' business and talked about it in a way that did not always win their approval. Once he invaded a snow tunnel I had constructed just to see how our cows were getting along; it led to the stable. He was interested in cows, too. I saw him go in. The tunnel fell on him as he was coming out. It was my tunnel, it would have to go some time. I wasn't grieving about it, but my mother, who happened to see the how and why of the tunnel's destruction, called me to account. I didn't have to plead guilty; she knew I was. She had often told me the same thing before, but never in so forceful and impressive a manner as on that occasion, when she said: "You must never lift a hand to an aged person, be respectful to every one, particularly those who are older than you, and never refuse or fail to answer a civil question asked of you by one who needs information. Never let me catch you doing the like of that again." She never did. When duty called and I had anything like that, or nearly like it to perform, I first ascertained that she didn't command a view of the situation. I can't say that I obeyed my mother on all occasions, but I tried. Somehow I always thought she enjoyed seeing the tunnel fall on that old snoop. . . .

We had no gas—illuminating gas I mean; kerosene hadn't been discovered;[1] our principal illuminator was the tallow candle. When the beef was salted down in the fall, the tallow was rendered and stored away in pans for use during the winter. In addition to my other accomplishments I made the candles as required. . . . I said the candle was the principal illuminator; the other was a fire of anthracite, not the kind of stuff they sell you now, but the real thing. Before that fire I have seen my father and three or four of my brothers reading many a night. There was always mending to do, and by the same light, reinforced by the candle, my mother would cover the rents and tears of the day.

Flags were not so easily obtained then. As a boy, the flag of our country meant a whole lot to me. It was part of my mother, part of me. She used to cut out the stripes and stars and sew them together into my flag. I have owned a flag ever since I was knee high to a grasshopper, but not one have I ever possessed that did not impart to me a blessing from my mother, for she always blessed it and me when she made one for me.

When the uncivil war broke out—now don't contradict me, it was an uncivil war—I went out to the woods back of the house, cut a straight sapling, trimmed it and climbing to the top of the house nailed it at the peak above the kitchen. Then I nailed to it my mother's flag and mine. When wind and rain tore it to shreds, she made another and I nailed that to the mast in place of the old

---

[1] Kerosene was discovered in 1852 by Abraham Gesner, a Canadian geologist. In 1853 Gesner introduced its use into the United States.

one. My father didn't quite favor my cutting away the shingles to make room for the flag pole, but his objections did not count. . . . He was as devoted to the flag as I could be, but I think he would have spared the shingles and selected another place for the pole. . . .

A company of Carbondale troops were coming home after Antietam was fought. Two of my brothers were in the company. My mother and most of our neighbors went to the station to see them disembark. Although I had been at work some two years, a holiday was proclaimed in honor of the return of the troops, and I was detailed to stay home and cook dinner. Everybody and everything was full of enthusiasm, even the pot I was watching bubbled over. It swung on a crane and in my haste to pull it from over the fire, [I] upset the frying pan. I was barefooted, the hot gravy fell on one of my feet, scalded it badly, and I took no further part in the reception.

I was laid up for several days. I bear scars of that conflict yet, and have never applied for a pension. I know I deserve one, but the consciousness of that fact and the additional fact that I kept the flag flying over our house from Sumpter [sic] to Appomattox is my reward.

I wasn't quarrelsome, I was not big or strong enough to be, with any show of success, but somehow seemed to get into a number of scraps and nearly always got the worst of it, physically; the other fellow didn't make an ostentatious display of his person when hostilities ceased. On one occasion my mother, who did agricultural work at times, was thrashing me and my father rescued me, not as hurriedly as I could wish however. I explained to him that it had to be a fight or a foot race and I didn't run even though the other boy was larger than I. Then he said: "I don't think your mother is punishing you for not running. I don't want to learn of your provoking a quarrel with anyone, but never let me hear of your running away from anybody." He never did.

Chapter Three

I JOIN A TRADE-UNION AND
AM BLACKLISTED

CHILD LABOR LAWS were not on the statutes when I was growing up,[1] and if they had been my mother would have repealed
them so far as I was concerned. She made me work the first day I
was able to do anything, kept me going when there was anything
to be done, made no allowance for overtime, and if I didn't do it
right the first time she had a most persuasive and convincing way
of causing me not to forget next time. It was quite appropriate,
therefore, that my first job (it would be called situation or position now) should be to attend a switch on the Delaware and
Hudson Railroad. . . .

. . . Let me say here that no boy or girl was ever spoiled by
useful labor performed under the watchful eye of a loving mother.
I know it didn't hurt me any to learn the things she taught, and,
thanks to her, there aren't many things to be done around a house
that I cannot do. She didn't spoil the rod through failure to employ it. I kept my own counsel and remained silent on a lot of
things or she would have used it oftener. . . .

I was thirteen years old when I shifted the scene of my activities to the railroad and began to work for wages. It became my
duty to turn a switch and allow what was called the "No. 1 train"
to pass from the main track to a siding that led to a coal chute.
How could I see this train coming when so nearsighted? I didn't

[1] Even at the cost of spoiling Powderly's pleasantry, it should be noted that
this is not correct. A Maine statute of 1848 prohibited the employment of children under sixteen for more than ten hours a day. In the 1850's, Ohio, Connecticut, and Rhode Island limited the hours of children in industry by statute. This
early legislation and the provisions for enforcement were very inadequate.

have to see it. That train was made up of empty cars and with my one good ear it was easy to detect the difference between the sounds made by empty and loaded cars. "No. 1 train" was the only one of its kind, so I just turned the switch when the rattle of an approaching train of empty cars smote my ear. . . .

Attending the switch claimed my attention but a few months. I aspired to higher pay. Some might say a higher field of labor; I could say the same if I wanted to lie. I may lie before I get through with this recital, but just here don't [sic] seem to me to be a good place to do it. I wanted a higher wage and got it when I became car examiner. After that I became a car repairer. Then I shipped before the mast as a brakeman in charge of that switch-back train where Mike and I exchanged uncivilities. . . . The switchback track consisted of short steep grades down the mountain side. At the end of each grade the train ran into a switch in which the track was laid to an ascending grade which was the beginning of the run down to the next switch. After running into and out of five switches, the train slowed down at the terminus, and on stopping my train I would ride up the planes to the starting point. These switches would hold sixteen cars between switch and head block, but no one ever brought more than thirteen cars into a switch without bumping the head block or failing to clear the switch. I started with ten cars, and hearing a good report from them—for I couldn't see—I increased the number until I could bring fourteen cars in and out of the switches. I am proud of that achievement yet, that's why I like to tell it. I made ten runs a day; with an extra car each trip I brought sixty cars more than anyone else through every week. . . .

The machine shop was located at the terminus, and while waiting for a train to take me back to the starting point, I put in my time prowling round looking at the machinery; I decided to become a machinist. I had higher aspirations of course, but that would do for a starter. I became the subject matter of a legal instrument in which my father and the master mechanic were the parties of the first and second parts. In that document I promised to be a good boy and due diligence exercise, in consideration of which James Dickson,[2] the master mechanic, obligated himself to initiate me into "the arts and mysteries" of the machinist trade. I entered upon the duties of an apprentice on August 1, 1866. By James Dickson I was duly and truly prepared to travel in foreign countries and earn journeyman's wages. Dickson served his time in the old country as an apprentice under George Stephenson, the inventor and builder of the first locomotive, and worked on its construction. Stephenson gave to Dickson, when his term expired, a number of machinist tools of his own make. Among them was a pair of four-inch calipers. Dickson loaned these to me, I used them during my apprenticeship, and on its expiration he presented them to me with his blessing. Through the hands of James Dickson they passed from George Stephenson to me so you needn't wonder that I prize them highly. A kinder man or a better mechanic I never met than James Dickson; he was a strict disciplinarian and whenever he saw me indulging in anything not specified in the articles of indenture or the statute in such case made and provided, I was punished. He didn't punish me often—my works of mischief were performed when he wasn't looking. . . .

One of the first tasks assigned to me was to take the old locomotive, *Stourbridge Lion,* apart. It had been standing back of the machine shop for a number of years; the company wishing to utilize the space it occupied, sold the boiler to a Carbondale foundryman who made use of it for many years; it is now in the National Museum, Washington, D.C. The wheels and frame on which the boiler rests are not the originals. These I took apart in 1866 and saw them go to the blacksmith shop to be forged over into something new.

In those days an apprenticed machinist had to learn how to forge and temper the tools he worked with. He was taught how to operate lathes, planing, slotting and such other machines as were then in use. He fitted the parts at the bench and then assembled them together as one complete whole whether locomotive or stationary engine.

James Dickson was a hardheaded, softhearted Scotchman who

---

[2] James Dickson apparently came to America from England in 1832, and, after living in Toronto, Canada, finally settled in Carbondale in 1836.

thoroughly understood his business and human nature. He was no task master, yet every man and boy in his employ would cheerfully remain on duty until all hours of the night at his request. He never discharged anyone. The shop bell would ring for five minutes at seven A.M. and one P.M. to assemble the shop force for duty. At quitting time, twelve noon and six P.M., a few taps of the bell would suffice. One of the peculiar things about that bell was that I could hear it distinctly the first tap at twelve and six, but when it continued ringing for five minutes morning and noon the sounds it made were scarcely audible. The intent in ringing it five minutes was to call the workmen together; the stopping at the end of five minutes was supposed to be a signal to go to work, but it didn't always have that effect. One day after the bell had tolled the accustomed five minutes and the shop clock had continued on for five or ten minutes, Mr. Dickson came into the shop and found a group of the men—and one boy—discussing perpetual motion. A French machinist, who had given some thought to the subject and had constructed a model which he intended having patented, was eloquently telling what perpetual motion would do when Mr. Dickson tapped him on the leg with his cane and said: "We have perpetual motion now, you see it in the movements of the sun, moon, and stars, you feel it when day changes to night, but man will never invent any other kind until he is able to lift and hold himself out at arms length by the coat tails so high that his feet won't touch the ground. There is another kind of motion though, and I advise each one of you to make it toward your machines and benches." . . .

I suppose every apprenticed machinist has played the same tricks as I did and has had the same tricks played on him as I had, and since the cause of religion will not be promoted by discussing them, I'll just tell you about a miracle I performed. There weren't so many holidays as now, New Year's Day had no special significance to us then, and the shop bell rang out on that day, unless it fell on Sunday, just as on other days. I had no authority vested in me to proclaim a holiday, but did the best I could. Taking with me a pail of water on the evening of December 31, 1867, I climbed up to the belfry, after the echoes of the quitting-time ring had ceased. Turning the bell upside down, I poured the water into it, then held the clapper in the middle until a coating of ice had formed. The thermometer was—well never mind, I don't know where it was that night—I only know it was bitter cold and that I stayed by the bell until the water was frozen thick enough to hold the clapper. It took something over an hour; the doors and windows of the shop were fastened. It wouldn't do to let the watchman see me passing through the shop, so I slid down to the edge of the roof at a corner, climbed out over the cornice, and went down the rainpipe. The bell didn't ring next morning. I was on hand though and saw the bell ringer pull the rope and go through the motions. He produced no sound, but amid the crash of machinery and whirring of belts he didn't know it. Mr. Dickson came hurriedly into the shop about 7:30, hunted up the bellman and berated him for not ringing the bell, he protested that he had done so, and I bore witness to the fact. . . . Mr. Dickson told us to go with him to the belfry, we did and found the cause of the bell's silence. We looked all round for some evidence to indicate how the bell could accumulate ice when it hadn't rained and hadn't been turned upside down. Nothing in the way of a prop was visible. Sitting on the railing of the belfry, Mr. Dickson looked steadily at me with, I think, a twinkle or two in his eye and said: "By jocks, that's a miracle, it didn't rain last night and had it done so it wouldn't rain up. If it could rain up it wouldn't stick and freeze round that bell clapper. It's a miracle."

During the forenoon he called me into the office and when the door was fastened he said: "Take a chair." There wasn't a chair in the office; he used an empty nail keg for a seat when at his desk. I sat on another keg, and, drawing his keg chair up close, [he] looked me straight in the eye as he said: "How the devil did you work that miracle?" . . . I told him how I did it. He seemed puzzled and then came back at me this way: "I have been to see the night watchman and he says that no one came in or went out of this building after six o'clock; how did you manage that?" He was skeptical until I took him to where I descended to earth after working the miracle and pointed out the tracks I made in the snow, and . . . fitted my shoes into the prints they made the night before. On the way back to his office he instructed me to go through the shops and tell all the hands that they need not report for duty in the afternoon, that it would be a half holiday. . . .

During the year 1869 the anthracite mines of Pennsylvania were idle for many months during the summer and fall. As much of our work in the machine shop depended on the operation of the mines, the continued idleness of the miners necessitated the laying off of many shop hands. My term of apprenticeship having expired on August first of that year, I was among the number relieved of duty. This occurred at the close of business August 15. I secured employment in the machine shops of the Pennsylvania Coal Company at Dunmore, Pennsylvania, and a short time after went to work as a journeyman in the machine shops of the Delaware, Lackawanna, and Western Railroad Company at Scranton, Pennsylvania.

While the miners' suspension (they did not call it a strike that year) was in progress, I heard frequent comments on and criticisms of it among workmen not engaged in the mining business. As a rule these comments and criticisms were not partial to the miners. The other workmen seemed to regard the miners as enemies. There was no union among machinists or other shopmen in Carbondale or Scranton.

In some vague sort of way it impressed me that there was something wrong in the labor world when so little sympathy was expressed by workingmen generally for the striking miners.

Early in September, 1869, while I was employed at Dunmore, an explosion occurred in the mines at Avondale some twenty-three miles south of Scranton. On the 9th, a day or two after the explosion, I went to Avondale and for the first time saw and heard John Siney,[3] then the moving spirit of the Miners and Laborers' Benevolent Association,[4] who came from his home at St. Clair in Schuylkill County to lend his effort in behalf of the stricken people of Avondale.

[3] John Siney, perhaps the outstanding figure in the early history of organization among the coal miners, died in 1880.
[4] The Workingmen's Benevolent Association of Schuylkill County, a miner's union, was founded by John Siney in 1868, and legally changed its name in 1870 to the Miners and Laborers' Benevolent Association.

. . . Siney . . . was the first man I ever heard make a speech on the labor question. I was just a boy then, but as I looked at John Siney standing on the desolate hillside at Avondale, with his back toward a moss grown rock the grim, silent witness to that awful tragedy of ignorance, indifference, thoughtlessness, and greed, and listened to his low, earnest voice, I saw the travail of ages struggling for expression on his stern, pale face. I caught inspiration from his words and realized that there was something more to win through labor than dollars and cents for self. I realized for the first time that day that death, awful death such as lay around me at Avondale, was a call to the living to neglect no duty to fellow man. John Siney gave expression to a great thought at Avondale when he said: "You can do nothing to win these dead back to life, but you can help me to win fair treatment and justice for living men who risk life and health in their daily toil." The thought expressed in that far away time became my thought. . . . But I'll say no more about Avondale or Siney here; let's get back to where we were when that explosion shook the hills of Avondale.

My first inquiry on returning to Dunmore was whether there existed a union or brotherhood among [the] men. I found no trace of such a thing, and the same was true of Scranton where I went to work in December of that year. One could read the papers of that day from one end of the year to the other, and if they found any reference to a labor organization it was one of abuse, ridicule, or scorn. No one connected with organized labor dared to allow his name to appear publicly as a member. The blacklist would be employed and idleness, poverty, destitution, and perhaps death would be the reward of open identification with a labor union in that era.[5]

One day I saw a notice in a Philadelphia paper of a meeting of a molders' union. I wrote, care of the paper, to the secretary of the union asking if he knew anything about a machinists' union and received a prompt answer to my letter and inquiry. Yes, there was a Machinists and Blacksmiths International Union[6] with

[5] This should be taken with the traditional grain of salt.

[6] International Union of Machinists and Blacksmiths of the United States of America.

headquarters at Cleveland, Ohio. I induced a shopmate of mine to write the president of the Machinists and Blacksmiths Union for information as to how a local body could be organized. My handwriting at that time wasn't of the Spencerian order, and anyway I had such bad spells every time I tried to write that I feared a communication from me might not make a good impression. That's why I used a proxy. A prompt reply gave me the needed information. In a couple of weeks an organizer came to Scranton and "Subordinate Union No. 2 of Pennsylvania" was established. I was not permitted to join because I was not old enough. When I attained the proper age, Union No. 2 had lapsed, and over a year passed before it was revived. In November, 1871, I was admitted to membership in the union. The following year I was elected secretary. I had learned how to write some. Then they insisted on electing me president, and though I had never, up to that time, mustered up courage enough to make a motion I became the presiding officer. So that I might have a working knowledge of the law I studied the constitution and by-laws so well that I could repeat every section and article in the little book. Then I procured a copy of Cushing's Manual and endeavored to know what it was all about. I extricated myself from the tangles of parliamentary law when I was told that it was "the essence of common sense"—and when I realized that common sense is the most uncommon kind of sense, I thought I knew why Cushing's Manual was invented.

Right here is a good place to remark that at a public meeting one night Tom Foley was, much to his dismay, called on to preside over its deliberations. His name wasn't Foley, but he still lives, is moderately healthy, has a string of relatives, all descendants of Irish kings and warlike in disposition, so to spare their feelings and mine too, I'll call him Foley. Tom took the chair and after an attempt to thank the meeting for the honor conferred asked what they wanted to do. Two men were nominated for secretary of the meeting. Let us call them McGrath and Rubenstein. When the nominations were made Foley said: "come up Rubenstein and be the secretary." Several protests were voiced but Foley silenced the protestants by saying "Rubenstein will do this business all right, he won't dare do anything else for he's the only Jew in the house and anyway there's Irish enough on this platform now to keep the peace." Exasperated by Foley's high handed procedure, a member moved: "that in our future deliberations we be guided by Cushing's Manual." Everyone present who thought, or wanted others to think, that he knew something about parliamentary law shouted: "I second the motion." It looked unanimous to Foley who slowly rose to his feet, walked to the edge of the platform, and solemnly announced: "When yez selected me to be yere president I thought ye meant it, but before I'm warm in me sate ye make a motion to be guided be Cushins Manyel. Now I don't know Cushins Manyel, he may be a rale fine man but I give yez distinctly to understand that the minute Mr. Cushins Manyel steps up on this platform Mr. Foley steps off." Thus reassured the meeting proceeded to business. . . .

On September 19, 1872, I joined another union with a membership of two when Hannah Dever and I were married. That union followed an understanding that perfect equality should exist between us, there would be but one treasury, that each should have equal right to it, that liberty of action and speech should always prevail between us. For nearly thirty years we lived up to that compact. We had trials, vicissitudes, struggles, poverty, and destitution at times, but never an angry word did either hear from the other. . . .

The financial depression of 1873, known as Jay Cooke's panic, spread ruin throughout the United States. Workers were discharged everywhere and hundreds of thousands of industrious men were reduced to penury through unemployment.

The master mechanic of the shop I worked in frequently invoked my aid in securing good machinists or blacksmiths through our union, and I was astonished when, one Saturday night shortly after the panic began, he called me into his office and told me that I was not to report for duty on Monday. He frankly said he bore me no ill will, but that he had his orders and was obliged to carry them out. As near as I can remember he said: "You are the president of the union and it is thought best to dismiss you in order to head off trouble."

I was asked by members to call a special meeting of the union that action on my case might be taken, but I refused. At the next regular meeting the matter came up, but I protested against any action looking toward a strike and succeeded. The other members of the union who had been dismissed were reinstated. I was not. Then my eyesight failed, and for a few weeks I was almost totally blind. On recovery I began a tramp through some of the western states in search of work.

In the hope of finding employment in Canada, I invaded that country in the winter of 1873-74, and walked the ties from Windsor, Ontario, to Buffalo, New York, a distance of two hundred and fifty miles. Occasionally I earned a quarter or half dollar, shoveling snow. I may add that snow was my principal diet but I do not recommend it as either fattening or nutritious.

Once I earned seventy-five dollars for chaperoning a drove of pigs to town for a farmer—I know I earned seventy-five dollars, but received only seventy-five cents. My intimate association with pigs on that occasion was an education. I learned to know that not only has a pig a will of his own but several of them, and each separate will influences him to start, regardless of destination, in different directions at one and the same time. . . .

I have read stories written by men who became tramps "for the fun of the thing" or to learn something of tramp life from experience. They undoubtedly learned a great deal but they did not acquire a knowledge of what a real tramp meets on his journeyings. Only the man who stands utterly alone, friendless, moneyless, ill clad, shelterless and hungry, looking at the sun sinking red in a mid-winter snow, can know what it is to be a real tramp. That experience was mine, through no fault of mine. I have sampled in all its awful reality the desolation and misery of tramp life that at times, during blinding storms of sleet and snow, seemed to shut out all sight and sound and hope of God.

Before I forget it let me say that when I left the employ of James Dickson at Carbondale he gave me the only recommendation he had ever written. Through the rains and winds and snows of my tramp life I carried that recommendation as a benediction and a prayer.

Chapter Four

STUDYING LABOR AND HUMAN NATURE

EVERY NOW AND THEN I think of something I should have told you in the first or second chapter, so don't mind if I go back there occasionally. It may happen also that in relating one incident others directly connected therewith are brought to mind, and memory, that invisible record on which man's acts are inscribed, gets busy. It's remarkable how one thing brings up another, as the old woman said after she swallowed a spoonful of ipecac.

In telling you of my discharge in the fall of 1873, it called to mind the means resorted to in securing an advance in wages in the early part of that year. It used to be the custom in those days for machinists, not held back by home ties, to lend an attentive ear to the call of the wanderlust when the blue birds ventured north in the spring. In our shop were quite a few who had intimated to me that they would like to "go west" or somewhere with the opening of warm weather. It was true also that the sentiment in favor of an increase in wages was practically unanimous. The matter came up in our union and after a lengthy discussion it was resolved as the sense of the meeting that we demand an increase in wages. Coupled with the demand was a threat to strike in case the increase was refused. I didn't like the word demand or the threat to strike. In the union we had less than a third of those eligible to membership. After some persuasion on my part the union agreed to allow the motion to lie on the table until the next meeting. I made a canvass of the shop, ascertained that about twenty-five mechanics intended to quit and seek work elsewhere. I asked each one not to give in the usual notice to quit. . . . The plan agreed on was to go singly to the master mechanic, ask for an advance in wages and, on refusal, to give notice to quit at the expiration of the seven days agreed upon. This agreement was like polish on a shoe, good only on one side, for when the master mechanic wanted a man to quit a minute's notice would suffice. When some ten or twelve had asked for an increase and, meeting with refusal, had given notice to quit, Mr. Dawson showed signs of weakening. It had been arranged that when this happened I was to go to him. I did, and when I stated my purpose in calling he said: "You too! well I'll advance your wages ten per cent but don't tell any one what I give you." When I entered the shop the next one to approach me and inquire what luck I had was Barney T——. In answer to his inquiry I said: "I had a satisfactory talk with Mr. Dawson, he asked me not to tell any one what he gave me and I shall not. Go to him when the proper time comes and I think you'll be satisfied." Barney had not been scheduled to approach Mr. Dawson immediately following me but he butted in and went direct to the office of the master mechanic. Years after I learned that he misrepresented me to Mr. Dawson that day. Barney was rather disappointed on seeing a notice of a ten per cent advance in wages posted that afternoon, for he was of a roving disposition and just wanted an excuse to leave town. He used to change his Post Office address very often and usually about the time his rent fell due.

During my tramp life I, as previously stated, passed through Canada in the dead of winter. Napoleon's march through the snow from Moscow wasn't a circumstance to what I went through in Canada. . . . I found nothing of a permanent character to do there and returned to the United States early in 1874. I secured employment at Galion, Ohio, and was thinking of settling down there when the master mechanic asked me one day if I hadn't worked in Scranton, Pennsylvania, for a man named Dawson. I of course answered in the affirmative. Next day I was discharged and again took up my tramp. I learned afterwards that this man and Mr. Dawson were friends and in correspondence with each other. It seems my name occurred in this correspondence.

Early in May I reached Oil City, Pennsylvania, by the tie route and recognizing the hailing sign of the Machinists and Blacksmiths Union as displayed by Charles Neidich the foreman of the

Oil Creek and Allegheny River R. R. Shops, I made myself known as a member of the union and was assigned to duty at my trade. I remained in Oil City for six months, and was recalled to Scranton to take up the work of fitting and installing coal-breaker engines and machinery.

The first Bessemer steel mill in northeastern Pennsylvania was in course of construction in Scranton that year; they had gone along far enough to fit and install the machinery. An advertisement for a machinist who knew how to work to drawings caught my eye, and I was selected to do the work. I had been there for about two weeks when Mr. Dawson passed through the mill one day and in less than an hour I was dismissed from the service of the Lackawanna Coal and Iron Company. I at once went to the general manager, W. W. Scranton . . . who gave me the position, and told him what happened. He inquired why I had been discharged from the employ of the D. L. & W. R. R. Company; I told him it was on account of my being president of the union. He asked me if I was president then. I answered in the negative, but in order to be fully understood told him that I was at that time secretary. His next question was: "If I reinstate you will you resign from the union?" My answer to that was: "I am insured for one thousand dollars in the union. I cannot afford any other insurance. If I resign and am killed in the employ of this company, will it pay my wife one thousand dollars?" He looked steadily at me awhile and said: "Go to the mill and tell Davidson to set you to work."

When the machinery was all in place, the mill in operation and making steel, I, through Mr. Scranton, secured employment at the Cliff Locomotive works of the Dickson Manufacturing Company. One day while rebuilding a Lackawanna locomotive, Mr. Dawson passed through the shop, saw me, and I was called into the office, paid off, and sent adrift. I at once saw Mr. Scranton who effected my reinstatement. I was placed in charge of a department and remained in the employ of the Dickson Manufacturing Company until, through lack of orders, the shops were closed on May 31, 1877.

From the day Walter Dawson discharged me in 1873 to the

time I left the employ of the Dickson Manufacturing Company in 1877, he was instrumental in having me dismissed from four machine shops, and prevented me from securing employment in any shop in Scranton immediately following my first dismissal. I make this statement on the strength of his own admission to me some years later.

I could find nothing to do in, or around Scranton, following the closing down of the locomotive works. Horace Mann says, "The common school is the republican line of fortification."[1] Let me supplement that by saying that the education received in the public school is the ammunition to be used in holding the fortifications against the assaults of the enemy. With a view to storing away some ammunition I went to school during the summer of 1877. I also took active part in building up the Order of [the] Knights of Labor in Luzerne County; Lackawanna County, which divided Luzerne in 1878, hadn't arrived yet. I'll tell you about that later, and stay with Mr. Dawson awhile. Early in July, 1877, a strike broke out on the B. & O. at Martinsburg, West Virginia, and spread through Pennsylvania until it reached Scranton. On July 22, 1877, one hundred and twenty-six locomotives, the property of the Pennsylvania Railroad, were burned in the round houses at Pittsburgh. Shortly after twelve o'clock noon, the 23d, a crowd gathered in front of the Western Union bulletin board on Lackawanna Avenue, Scranton, to read an account of the burning of the engines. Mr. Dawson, on his way home to lunch, stopped to read the bulletin. He could get no nearer to it than the curb owing to the throng. He was a small man, not much bigger than a pint of cider and was standing on tiptoe, craning his neck to get a view of the bulletin when I arrived on the scene. I did not notice Dawson until I saw Jack M——, a workman who had recently been laid off by Dawson, stoop down and pick up a good-sized cobble stone from the gutter. He stepped in behind Dawson, raised his hand, and was about to bring the stone down on Dawson's head when I caught his wrist, drew his hand down, and,

[1] This statement appears almost in the form Powderly gives it in "The Necessity of Education in a Republican Government," the third of a series of seven lectures which Horace Mann delivered before various county conventions of Massachusetts.

without attracting any attention, as I thought, pulled Jack away
and into a narrow court adjoining the Second National Bank.
Then I asked him what he was about to do. He said he had intended knocking Dawson's brains out. He was under the influence
of liquor, and, though he was quite ugly at the time, yielded to my
advice to carry the matter no further. When I requested that he
turn the stone over to me he said, "You have a damn sight more
cause to break his head than I have." I soothed him some by saying, "Yes I know I have, and since it's my job you have no right
to do it; give the stone to me." He did, I threw it away and
walked Jack off home. Though I didn't know it at the time, that
was a good political move on my part; I made a friend by it, and,
when I ran for mayor the following spring, that friend not only
voted for me but induced others to do so. He was an official of the
bank, was leaning out of a window just above us when Jack and I
had our interview, and a witness to everything said or done. He
was a friend of Dawson's and told him all about it.

I saw no more of Mr. Dawson for many years. In the meantime he had severed his connection with the Delaware, Lackawanna, and Western Railroad Company, and, after spending
some time at his old home in England, had returned to the United
States to settle up his affairs. One day in 1895 he walked into my
law office in Scranton, and, after surveying two or three men who
were present, asked if Mr. Powderly was in. He didn't recognize
me at first. He had some legal business to transact and asked me
to attend to it for him, saying also: "I need the service of an honest lawyer, and learning that you were practicing law come to
you." To my question as to whether he thought I'd fill the bill he
said: "I know you are honest and if you are as good a lawyer as
you were a machinist you'll do."

I took the case, carried it to successful issue, and purposely said
nothing about a fee until I turned the papers over to him. When
he asked what my fee was, I remarked that I hadn't thought of it
in connection with his matter for I felt repaid in having him come
to me. He wouldn't have it that way and paid me a liberal fee. He
seemed inclined to talk and I gave him the opportunity by inviting
him to my home that evening. There he told me that he always

liked me but that it was his duty to report everything to his superiors. The fact that I was president of the union militated
against me and caused those "higher up" to regard me with suspicion. The part I played in securing the advance in wages went
against me also. He said that Barney told him I had boasted of
getting a raise in pay; he also informed him of all I had done, and
a lot more than I ever thought of doing, as well as everything
that transpired in the union. He concluded his remarkable statement by saying: "When Mr. Seymour told me of how you prevented that man from knocking me on the head I felt worse than
I can describe."

.Many men, aware of the treatment I received at the hands of
Walter Dawson, have asked me why I did not avenge the wrongs
he inflicted on me. I am not aware that he did inflict wrong on
me. . . . I did some good through being blacklisted. It made me
more than determined to perfect an organization that would
render blacklisting impossible; it made me mayor of Scranton
where I learned that we are all good and bad instead of good or
bad. It taught me how to put myself in the place of the vilest,
filthiest, lowest-down tramp that comes to me for help. It taught
me when men were brought before me for trial how to pierce the
veil between cause and effect, between motive and act; it enabled
me to come down from the bench as a magistrate, a representative of the law, and before the bar of my own heart and conscience
place the prisoner then before me on the bench in my stead. I
never passed on evidence given in trials before me without asking
of myself what I would do were I in that man's place. . . .

I tell you until you attain the faculty of placing your own brain
in the other fellow's head and thinking with it as he would think
in the environment surrounding him, you are not fully qualified to
sit in judgment on other men. Oh, yes, I know what the law says
and I have profound respect for the law, particularly when it is
the voiced expression of a people's calm, deliberate judgment.
The law is not everything though and cannot cover all things. It
fixes one penalty for every offense no matter though the offenders
differ from each other in temperament and environment as widely
as the seasons. . . .

No, you cannot judge all men by the one standard, any more than you can make shoes for all of them on the same last. No law that ever darkened white paper in the printing can lay down a rule of conduct for all men to follow alike.

I'll tell you by and by how I passed on about a thousand charges of petty offenses committed by boys and girls who were brought before me for trial during the six years that I held the position of committing magistrate. I never fined one, I never tried one, I never lectured one or wrote the name of one of them on a court docket.

Before I forget it let me suggest a rule which if followed by every man and woman will help a great deal: If you owe a man a dollar, pay it; if you owe him a grudge, forget it, and always be kind.

I'll admit that when I was feasting on snow up in Canada during the winter of 1874 I did entertain homicidal thoughts about Walter Dawson, but when I saw that stone about to descend on his head all my resentment vanished before the picture of the suffering and agony that stone would fling into the hearts of those who loved Jack M—— and Walter Dawson.

Then think of Mr. Dawson coming to me after the lapse of years, employing me as his attorney, telling me why I was black-listed, and renewing our old-time friendship. Wasn't that compensation for all the suffering I endured? . . .

Chapter Five

I MEET JOHN SINEY AND JOIN THE KNIGHTS OF LABOR

A SHORT TIME AGO I briefly referred to my admission to the Machinists and Blacksmiths Union, and, since you are interested in my labor work, let me tell what it was that influenced me to join the union and take so deep an interest in it.

I had no more cause for complaint of ill-treatment in the shop I worked in than hundreds of other young men, and had I considered my own selfish interests alone it is quite likely I would never have affiliated with any labor organization.

When on that September day at Avondale I saw the blackened, charred bodies of over one hundred men and boys as they were brought to the surface, when I saw a mother kneel in silent grief to hold the cold, still face of her boy to hers, and when I saw her fall lifeless on his dead body, I experienced a sensation that I have never forgotten. It was such a feeling as comes to me whenever I read of death in the mines or on the railroad.

Then when I listened to John Siney I could see Christ in his face and hear a new Sermon on the Mount. I there resolved to do my part, humble though it might be, to improve the condition of those who worked for a living. Of course I had no plan, the germ of brotherhood was just quickening to life in me and I had no idea of what I ought to do to help, to be of use to others. Whatever of success I achieved in after years, I can truthfully assert that its bedrock was not cemented in selfishness; self-interest and my work in the union and Knights of Labor lay in directions diametrically differing from each other. Nor was I a reformer, for of all ill-used, ill-fitting, and undeserved terms, reformer, it seems to me, takes rank with the worst. Men claiming to be reformers came to me by the hundred to enlist my aid, or that of the Knights of Labor through me, in some project that at first seemed worthy, but a half hour, or an hour's talk—for I listened to all of them—disclosed the microbe of personal feeling and ambition, hate or greed, that hoped to grow big and powerful with a little help from me. Whenever I hear a man proclaim himself a reformer I look for a motive. In a majority of cases it may be found rooted in revenge, disappointment, or greed. I never was a reformer and always objected to being called one. If I had the right to give myself a name, I would call it equalizer. The scales didn't tip even, the pendulum didn't swing with steady stroke between capital and labor, between employer and employed. I saw that something was wrong, but didn't realize that long centuries of ownership in men who worked had begotten feelings of caste, pride, intolerance, and even hatred in the breasts of many of the employers of labor in that day.

Then, when I considered the utter indifference to the material welfare of their employees manifested by the employing classes, I asked myself if Christianity was still alive, for every mother's son of the men who employed labor was a Christian. Then, too, the church of that period favored the rich and well-to-do as against the poor if the acts and utterances of many of its foremost spokesmen meant anything.

When a workman was injured in shop, mine, or on the railroad, the claim agent of the employing company would at once present himself with an instrument of agreement for the injured man and his wife, if he had one, to sign. By the terms of this instrument the company would be released from all responsibility in consideration of the payment of a few dollars. Let me tell you of one such case out of the hundreds I witnessed. A coal miner, a neighbor of mine, had his back injured through a fall of a rock in the darkness of the mine. The claim agent called to see him; he asked for time to consider and sent for me. He had a wife and children, his means were meager. I advised against signing a release, and here is what he said: "I am buying this house from the company. If I don't sign this release, I can never get a day's work under that company or any other round here, for if I get well I'll be blacklisted. When my next payment on the house falls due, or the interest is not paid we'll be thrown out on the street. With no work, no money, no friends, what will my wife and my babies do?" I called on his pastor, endeavored to arouse his sympathy and have him intercede with the company officials in behalf of the injured man. He told me to mind my own business. I afterward obtained evidence to prove that the company which employed James S—— had contributed liberally to the building of the church of which that man was pastor. . . .

I saw workmen robbed through company stores. I was obliged to submit to being robbed too, and know that I paid exorbitant prices for necessities, in some cases fifty per cent more than I would have paid elsewhere. Injustice in the levying and collection of rents and taxes, filching men's labor through company-store practices, mortgaging the bodies and souls of living men through small pay enforced by the blacklist, and other wrongful acts done the workers by professed Christians without one word of protest against the evils or a word of comfort to the oppressed by Christian ministers or men of influence and standing, convinced me that "they who would be free themselves must strike the blow"; that if abuses were to be abolished the workers themselves would have to abolish them. Do it individually they could not. Working shoulder to shoulder in organization, not of one calling but all callings, appeared to me to be the only hope.

As I gave time, thought, and study to the question of industrialism and the abuses that had grown with it (or should I say clung to it), I realized that many of the hurts the workingman suffered from were self-inflicted. Intemperance was a curse to labor; poverty, loss of self-respect, loss of standing in the community, and other evils entailed on workingmen came to them largely through intemperance. As I dived beneath the surface, I found that liquor, though not listed among articles sold in company stores, masqueraded as "sundries" on the pass books in which company-store purchases were entered. Following it further, I discovered that liquor was carried into the mine and drunk there; it was carried out on the railroad and drunk there to the risk and danger of fellow worker and traveling public. I found that the practice of fee-ing petty bosses for favors shown to certain workmen in mine, shop, and elsewhere was indulged in to an alarming degree.

Strange as it may appear to you, the industrious, faithful, sober workman stood less chance of promotion at that time than the grafter, perhaps I should say graftee, who greased the itching palm of some petty foreman or superintendent for leave to earn his daily bread.

That I might be of use in ridding the world of labor of its manifold burdens is why I became a member of Machinists and Blacksmiths Union on November 21, 1871. I have told you that I became the secretary and later on the president of the Scranton branch, Union No. 2, of Pennsylvania. I carried a clear card with me during my tramp life, and at Oil City I deposited the card in, and became a member of Union No. 6 of Pennsylvania. In later life I was charged by many with being an agitator; some of my friends in defending me against assault denied that I was an agitator; they were wrong, I was an agitator and as such did all that lay in my power with voice and pen to agitate against the injustices practiced on workingmen and women.

I was wholly impartial in that agitation for I was as severe on the worker for what he did to wrong himself and [his] fellows as on the unjust employer who ill-treated his employees. Yes, I was an agitator. Danger, perhaps death, lurks in the stagnant pool, but stir it, agitate it that the danger may be known and its consequences avoided.

During all the years I was General Master Workman[1] of the Knights of Labor I had a picture above my desk representing the world's greatest, most sublime agitator. He whose heart, moved to indignation and pity, condemned the wrongs inflicted on the toiling poor by the rich and powerful. Did they not call Him an agitator when they said: "He stirreth up the people." Did He not pay the penalty for being an agitator when they pressed the thorns

[1] Until 1883, the name of the office was Grand Master Workman. In a letter to John Law, "Grand Master K. of L. Africa," January 13, 1892, Powderly wrote: "When the General Assembly of the K. of L. was instituted we designated our officers as 'Grand Officers.' Five years after in our General Assembly we decided that the word grand smacked too much of aristocracy and we changed it to general and since then our officers are known as General Officers."

into His flesh, and nailed His hands and feet to the cross? Had
Christ sanctioned or condoned the practices of the rich and great
do you suppose He would have been crucified? Had He looked
on in silence and uttered no protest against wrong do you believe
He would have ascended the cross as He did? Christ, if I read
Him aright, did not die for the unjust rich man any more than
He did for the lazy, poor man. He lived and worked for the industrious poor, for them He agitated, for them He died. He
could have lived and been honored by the rich of that day. He
elected to die rather than pay such a price for life. . . . One day
in a pessimistic mood I wrote these two lines and placed them on
that picture, at the foot of the cross:

> Work for self and humanity honors you,
> Work for humanity and it crucifies you.

I was an agitator. Perhaps I was not wise or prudent in all my
agitating but my purpose was to ameliorate conditions that in
some instances seemed intolerable. Bear in mind the laborer of
that period was not the well-read, self-reliant, sober, independent
man you recognize in the workingman of today. There were but
few national trade-unions that could boast of a membership of
over fifteen or twenty thousand.[2] For the most part men were not
organized at all, and as a consequence agitation was a vital necessity. When through my agitation abuse came to me from press,
pulpit, and those I tried to serve, I could always look on the picture of the crucified Christ and find consolation in the thought
that a divine example had illuminated nineteen hundred years of
the world's history, that it shone as bright as on its first day, and
that duty to fellow men called for agitation in their interests. I
agitated and am vain enough to believe I did some good by causing the people to see things they never saw before, and set them
to thinking of how the abuses pointed out to them could be corrected. During all the years of this agitation I was never for a

[2] There are no trustworthy statistics on trade-union membership for this period.
According to John R. Commons and Associates, *History of Labour in the United
States,* 2 vols., New York, 1921, II, 46-48, there were thirty-two national and international trade unions on the eve of 1873, with a total membership of about
300,000, of which perhaps a half-dozen had 15,000 or more members.

moment actuated by hatred of, or opposition to, the employing classes as such. The injustice they practiced, sanctioned, or condoned was what I agitated against.

But I am digressing. As a member of the union I was called on to make a few remarks occasionally and in that way acquired the faculty of thinking while standing and soon learned how to make a short speech without getting flustered too badly. I always was, and am now, quite nervous in starting a talk.

I wrote articles for our trade journal and the daily press on the subject of organization. I wrote verse at times too. The latter always appeared over a nom de plume; I recall that as a wise precaution when I consider the quality of the poetry the Muse was instrumental in making me responsible for; I never like to shirk a responsibility, and am grateful that I can charge that poetry up to a Muse. . . .

Early in August, 1874, Union No. 6 elected me its delegate to a district meeting of the unions of Pittsburgh, Oil City, Meadville, and Franklin, all in Pennsylvania. This district meeting was held at Franklin, September 2, and I was there named as the delegate to represent the district in the general convention at Louisville, Kentucky, September 16. At that convention I was honored by the president, John Fehrenbatch,[3] in being placed on the Committee on Finance.

Let me say a word about Fehrenbatch. He was a man of marked ability and sterling integrity. He stood so far in advance of the rank and file as a wise, farseeing leader of men that he suffered the fate of many who went before and of others who followed him, in being misunderstood. I was led into the error of criticizing him harshly by representations made to me by an "old head" in the organization and have been heartily sorry for it ever since. I learned to appreciate John Fehrenbatch's fidelity and wise leadership long before I became the recipient of kicks when I thought I had earned bouquets.

At the convention in Louisville I unconsciously became one of

[3] John Fehrenbatch was active from 1872 on in the movement to form a national federation of trade-unions. In 1876 he was elected to the Ohio legislature, and two years later he assumed a federal post.

the first, if not the very first, advocate of the referendum in the United States. So anxious was I that every member should be induced to take a deep interest in the organization and know everything pertaining to it that I presented a resolution reading as follows:

Resolved: That all amendments to the constitution be separately submitted to each subordinate union for their approval or disapproval.

That's not grammatical, I know, but those who heard it understood what I meant and that's what I desired as a starter. I had never heard of the referendum but that's what I aimed at. We had the initiative then, for all laws or amendments to law saw their initial prompting in a subordinate union, but that which would serve or please one union might be of no use to, or bear heavily on, another. To have all pass on what one proposed was why I advocated the referendum in 1874. I had read that Giuseppe Mazzini's motto was "one for all and all for one"[4] and believed, as I do now, that it wouldn't be a bad thing to enact legislation with that idea in mind.

One of my first moves on joining the union was to attempt to pry the gates ajar so as to allow boilermakers to enter. I talked on it and wrote about it but was completely squelched when a committee, reporting on a resolution I had offered, solemnly declared it to be the sense of the meeting that: "The boilermakers owing to their untidy habits and lack of neatness in dress would reflect no credit on our order through affiliation with it. Your committee therefore are obliged to report unfavorably on the resolution."

A notice had been served on every member that action was to be taken on my resolution and a full attendance was the result. No evidence of a sense of humor was manifested when the chairman went on to say that when the day's work was done and the boilermakers had occasion to leave home after supper, they did so in the same garb as that in which they had toiled during the

---

[4] These are, apparently, not Mazzini's exact words, but he frequently expressed the idea in somewhat similar language.

day in the shop. His remarks I cannot quote, but the report appears on the minutes just as I give it.

I became indignant when he made his report, and that indignation didn't abate any when the vote showed less than a dozen noes as against some hundred and ten ayes on a motion to adopt the report. Held down by parliamentary usage, I couldn't say the things I wanted to say so I said nothing. I gave vent to my feelings in another way; going to the secretary's desk I obtained a piece of paper, and when the order of new business was reached I expressed my thought in these lines:

> Aristocrats of labor, we
>   Are up on airs and graces,
> We wear clean collars, cuffs, and shirts,
>   Likewise we wash our faces.
>
> There's no one quite so good as we
>   In all the ranks of labor.
> The boilermaker we despise,
>   Although he is our neighbor.
>
> The carpenter and molder too,
>   The mason and the miner,
> Must stand aside as we pass by,
>   Than we there's nothing finer.
>
> But some day, some how, things will change,
>   Throughout this glorious nation,
> And men of toil will surely meet
>   In one great combination.

Noticing that I had gone to the desk and was writing something, the members present expected a new resolution on the subject, and remained to hear it, so quite an audience greeted my outburst. Right here I ought to write "Applause," for they did applaud heartily, and when a motion prevailed to inscribe my lines on the records of the meeting, I knew I was forgiven. . . .

While the Knights of Labor were then secretly working their way to light and a world's recognition, I had never heard of that Order. What I had in mind was the Industrial Brotherhood which I joined and became an organizer of on June 4, 1874. I have told about that society in *Thirty Years of Labor*,[5] and shall merely say in passing that it was the intention of those who founded the Industrial Congress, and later the Industrial Brotherhood,[6] to bring the scattered, weak and defenseless trade unions of that day into closer affiliation and cause the membership of each to devote time and study to social, economic, and political questions as well as those pertaining to their trade relations.

One day in 1874 I was delegated to attend an anti-monopoly convention at Philadelphia and while there met a number of men prominent in the labor movement, among them one William Fennimore[7] of that city. One evening he invited me to his room, locked the door, and told me to kneel down. I thought he wanted me to join him in prayer, and refused to kneel until he captured me with a little soft solder by saying I was just the kind of young man he was looking for. He had sounded me, liked my sentiments—such as they were—and desired that I join an order that had for its object the recognition of the rights of all who toiled, etc. I knelt and then took an oath to foster, cherish, and further the "Noble and Holy Order of the * * * * * " as the Knights of Labor was then called. As I recall it, Mr. Fennimore did not then tell me the name of the organization or impart to me any of the secret work of the same. I had informed him of my membership in the Industrial Brotherhood, that I was deputy president for western Pennsylvania, and that John Siney, who was present at the meeting, was the deputy president for the eastern part of the state.

[5] *Thirty Years of Labor, 1859-1889*, Philadelphia, 1889. A "revised and corrected" edition appeared the following year.

[6] Following the dissolution of the National Labor Union in 1872, there were several attempts to form national labor organizations. The Industrial Congress, almost purely trade union in character, was an outgrowth of a convention of trade-union delegates, July 15, 1873. The Industrial Brotherhood, a secret labor organization, fused with the Industrial Congress in 1874, contributing to the Congress its name, ritual, and constitution. The Congress became less strictly trade unionist in program and concerns after this date. Neither could withstand the adverse conditions of the depression years, and both organizations ceased to exist after the 1876 Congress.

[7] William Fennimore became a member of the first assembly of the K. of L. in January, 1870, about a month after its establishment, according to *Thirty Years of Labor*, pp. 76-77. See, however, John R. Commons and Associates, editors, *A Documentary History of American Industrial Society*, 10 vols., Cleveland, 1911, X, 19, which implies he was a member in 1869.

I had organized branches of the Industrial Brotherhood in Oil City and Pittsburgh before returning to Scranton in the fall of 1874, but from that time on kept up a search for the Knights of Labor and was not successful until a shopmate, in the Cliff Locomotive Works of Scranton, invited me to a "labor lecture" to be given on the evening of September 6, 1876. I presented myself at the designated place, accompanied my friend to the hall and was mystified when we were ushered into a small room and told to wait awhile. Soon after a man wearing a black gown and mask came out to question us. He appeared to be more satisfied with our answers than I was with his appearance, for I had no thought of joining a society of any kind that night.

Local Assembly No. 88 of the Knights of Labor, composed of stationary engineers, was in session. My name had been proposed for membership, acted on favorably, and in the manner described I had been brought forward for initiation. I was under the impression that the friend who accompanied me was being received exactly as I was, and until he congratulated me at the end of the initiation ceremony I did not suspect anything to the contrary. It was the practice at that time to sound a man before presenting his name, then to propose and ballot for him without his knowledge or consent. If elected, he would be brought to a meeting at the appointed time by his proposer who, if the candidate did not answer the questions satisfactorily, would depart with him and he would be none the wiser as to whether his friend was a member.

Local Assembly No. 88 was instituted May 15, 1875, and, being composed of stationary engineers in and around the mines, workmen of other callings were not admitted to membership until the parent body at Philadelphia granted permission to take in miners, laborers, and other classes of workmen in the summer of 1876. The officers of Local Assembly No. 88 had been notified that I had been pledged to the principles of the Order, but were not personally acquainted with me. A relative of the shopmate who proposed me was a stationary engineer and member. Through him my friend was admitted and instructed to bring me forward for initiation.

Prior to my admission to the Knights of Labor I had a little time for rest and recreation. After September 6, 1876, I knew no waking hour that I did not devote, in whole or part, to the up-building of the Order. That you may form an idea of what the organization of the Knights of Labor aimed at, I'll tell you some-thing about how men were initiated at that time. Since radical changes have been made in ritual and initiatory ceremonies of the Order, it can do no harm, and may do good to tell you how men were admitted to membership in 1876. Women were not granted the right of membership until 1881.[8] In fragments our ceremony of initiation has been published. Whenever parts of our secret work were given publicity we professed ignorance of the matter, or else denied that there was any truth in the publication. I feel that you will find much to commend and but little to take excep-tion to in what I am about to tell you. Bear in mind that every word was written and the whole ritual prepared by men who were ardent trades-unionists who knew what sort of treatment condi-tions then called for. They were not theorists even though they placed their ideals so high that all could not reach them. They worked with hand and brain, they knew the needs of labor and the duties which men of all ranks owed to each other. Note the firm, manly, just tone of the ceremony, and you may admit that those who gave the Knights of Labor being were safe, sane, prac-tical, God-loving, patriotic men who would place humanity above wealth, and do but simple justice in the transition. . . .

When you look round you today you see a host of young men just broken loose from college, filled with knowledge gleaned from books, writing, talking, vociferating, exasperating, and bleating about the coming revolution which the toiling masses are prepar-ing to precipitate. With no practical knowledge of actual condi-tions, relying on what they read or are told, they mistake the lighting of a match for a conflagration. To them the illumination caused by the pyrotechnic lightning bug becomes as portentous of evil as the real lightning's lurid flash.

The workingmen, especially the organized workingmen of the

---

[8] The first women's local assembly was organized in Philadelphia in September, 1881. The entrance of women into the Order had been an issue since 1879. It was not until 1882, however, that the General Assembly formally permitted females six-teen years and older to be initiated into the Order.

United States, are not planning a revolution. They of all people are most concerned in the perpetuity of our institutions, and don't forget that when it becomes necessary to defend this nation from invasion or foreign meddling, the workingmen may be depended on to do as they have always done. Don't understand me as saying that they regard all our institutions as perfect or that all our laws are just and equitable. They don't favor many of the judicial interpretations given these laws either, but they are not going to smash the dishes and break up housekeeping just because the cook spoils a meal or two. No indeed. In the case of the cook they'd induce her to change her methods; if she didn't they'd change the cook.

Notwithstanding all this, revolutions, peaceful or murderous, may come, but they won't be cut-and-dried affairs. Revolutions are not manufactured or made to order; they are never successfully planned or deliberately entered upon; they do not come at the bidding of one man or one set of men; they grow and then come. . . .

But this isn't telling you about the Knights of Labor.

Chapter Six

HOW ORGANIZING WAS DONE BY
EARLY KNIGHTS OF LABOR

THE FIRST LOCAL ASSEMBLY of the Knights of Labor was organized in 1869; its existence was kept a profound secret from all who were not members. Its name, objects, and methods of procedure were never spoken even in whispers, beyond the door of the Assembly Hall. The difference, except as to secrecy, between the early Knights of Labor and a trade union was that only those working at a definite trade could become members of a union of that trade, while men of all callings, with a few exceptions,[1] could join a mixed assembly of the Knights of Labor. From 1869 up to 1878, the Knights of Labor had no platform, preamble or declaration of principles, and the extreme secrecy surrounding its movements gave to organizers a latitude of expression in explaining the purposes of the order that was limited only by the imagination of the organizer. I sat in a local assembly of the Knights of Labor prior to 1878 and listened to an organizer —called preceptor in those days—portray the wonderful results to follow the establishment, by the Knights of Labor, of the "rule of perfect equality among men" when that organization became strong enough to successfully champion the cause of oppressed humanity. . . .

[1] With the organization of the General Assembly in 1878, membership qualifications were changed. In addition to workers, persons who had been wage-earners were also admitted to the Order, but they were not to exceed in number one-fourth of the membership of the local assembly. Bankers, lawyers, doctors, and those who sold liquor or made their living by its sale, however, were excluded. In 1882, a local assembly was permitted, by a decision of Powderly, to admit a "capitalist," if it wished. In this year, too, the age limit, which had been 21, was reduced to 18. In 1884, the age limit for new members was further lowered to 16, and the prohibition against doctors removed. Professional gamblers and stockbrokers were also excluded from membership at this time.

Traveling slowly, building carefully, and working silently, it would take many years to build up an organization of sufficient strength or importance, numerically or otherwise, to command attention on the part of workers or employers. When you reflect that each man had to be sought out, questioned, or sounded as to his views, and then balloted for separately before being admitted to membership, you will realize that the battlements of the fortress of organized greed were in no immediate danger of crumbling before the assaults of organized labor.

. . . .

I visited local assemblies of the Knights of Labor in Massachusetts, West Virginia, and in western Pennsylvania prior to the organization of the General Assembly at Reading in January, 1878, and found a babel of opinion being erected on a base of misunderstanding. Each officer of importance interpreted according to his lights, and though each man may have been honest enough, the lights were of many colors and of kaleidoscopic movement.

To change all of this, bring order out of chaos, unite the widely separated parts of the society, and direct the movement along well-defined, harmonized lines was why local assembly and district assembly pooled their issues in a General Assembly at Reading, Pennsylvania, on January 1, 1878.

The ceremony of initiation in use when I became a member, and as we found it at the meeting in Reading, was vastly different from that in use today and much longer. A great deal of the old work has been retained, though it is not imparted to the candidate as formerly.

It should be understood that the member who then proposed a man for membership had previously discussed labor matters with him and had ascertained what his opinion was concerning the propriety of establishing a secret society having the improvement of labor conditions as its prime object.

With the founding of the General Assembly at Reading in 1878 and the adoption of the declaration of principles of the Industrial

Brotherhood,[2] the remnants of which merged into the Knights of Labor, we had something to hold out to workingmen as a bid for their support.

To the Knights of Labor, all who toiled might find entrance and a welcome. The scavenger doing his work on the street was admitted on exactly the same terms of equality as the highest priced or most skilled artisan. The name of the Order was never printed and seldom spoken. Only in the assembly was it mentioned and then only that the newly initiated might know the name of the Order he had joined. On all other occasions written or oral, it was referred to as the "*****s."

When a candidate was presented for initiation,[3] he was asked three questions. First: "Do you believe in God, the Creator and Universal Father of all?" Second: "Do you obey the Universal Ordinance of God, in gaining your bread by the sweat of your brow?" Third: "Are you willing to take a solemn vow binding you to secrecy, obedience, and mutual assistance?" On receiving affirmative answers to these questions the applicant would be admitted and initiated. If he declined, he would be pledged to secrecy as to all he had seen and heard and respectfully dismissed.

After the first part of the oath of secrecy had been administered, special emphasis would be laid on the following, which constitutes the real pledge and which the candidate would be called on to repeat as spoken by his instructor:

I do truly and solemnly promise strictly to obey all laws, regulations, solemn injunctions and legal summons, that may be sent, said or handed to me.

I do truly and solemnly promise that I will to the best of my ability, defend the life, interest, reputation and family of all true members of this Order, help and assist all employed and unemployed, unfortunate or distressed Brothers to procure employment, secure just remuneration, relieve their distress and counsel others to aid them, so that they and theirs may receive and enjoy the just fruits of their labor and exercise of their art.

[2] The preamble and platform adopted by the K. of L. in 1878 were derived with modifications from the constitution of the Industrial Brotherhood. For a comparison of the two, see Norman J. Ware, *The Labor Movement in the United States, 1860-1895*, New York, 1929, Appendix I, pp. 377-380. Powderly, it should be noted, was a delegate and an organizer in the Industrial Brotherhood.

[3] For a complete manual of the initiation ceremony, see Commons and Associates, *Doc. Hist.*, X, 19-24.

During the administration of the oath the entire membership would stand in a circle with hands joined. This circle typified the unending bond of fraternity in which it was intended the Order would ultimately hold all workers.

The presiding officer of the local assembly was known as Master Workman, the next in order was the Worthy Foreman. The Master Workman, after the oath had been administered, would direct that the candidate be taken to the "base of the sanctuary there to receive the instructions of the Worthy Foreman."

Here it is well to tell you that in the language of the Order of Knights of Labor the meeting room was called the sanctuary. . . . The Worthy Foreman when the candidate came before him would say:

In the beginning God ordained that man should labor, not as a curse, but as a blessing; not as a punishment, but as a means of development, physically, mentally, morally, and has set thereunto his seal of approval in the rich increase and reward. By labor is brought forth the kindly fruits of the earth in rich abundance for our sustenance and comfort; by labor (not exhaustive) is promoted health of body and strength of mind, labor garners the priceless stores of wisdom and knowledge. It is the "Philosopher's Stone," everything it touches turns to gold. "Labor is noble and holy." To glorify God in its exercise, to defend it from degradation, to divest it of the evils to body, mind and estate, which ignorance and greed have imposed; to rescue the toiler from the grasp of the selfish is a work worthy of the noblest and best of our race. Without your seeking, without even your knowledge, you have been selected from among your fellows, for that exalted purpose. Are you willing to accept the responsibility and trusting in God and the support of sworn true *****s, labor with what ability you possess, for the triumph of these principles among men?

You will take note of the language of the charge of the Worthy Foreman. When speaking of the "Philosopher's Stone" he says that "everything it touches turns to gold." The word "gold" was used for over eight years or from November, 1869, until the General Assembly was organized at Reading, Pennsylvania, in January, 1878. At that first session of the General Assembly I was a member of the committee on law. I was at the time a candidate for the office of mayor of Scranton on the Greenback-Labor ticket. As a loyal believer in the greenback, I deemed it my duty to give gold no quarter. I made it my business to appear before the committee on secret work and recommended that the word wealth be substituted for gold in the Worthy Foreman's charge. The recommendation was adopted and ever since the word wealth appears where the word gold was formerly used.

No, it was not contempt for gold that caused me to suggest the change. They say that it is familiarity which breeds contempt, and I had never been on familiar enough terms with gold to entertain contempt for it. My thought was to teach our members that wealth stood for more than gold. When you read my explanation of the characters on the emblem of the "Philosopher's Stone Degree" you will understand why I suggested the change.

The candidate, on answering affirmatively, was then conducted to and introduced to the Master Workman "as a fitting and worthy person to receive the honor of fellowship in this noble and holy order."

No officer of the Knights of Labor ever occupied a seat on a platform or on an elevation above the members. Officers, to give an object lesson in equality, sat on a level with all others in a sanctuary.

The Master Workman standing at the "capital," as the stand in front of him was called, would take the novitiate by the hand and say:

On behalf of the toiling millions of earth, I welcome you to this Sanctuary, dedicated to the service of God, by serving humanity. Open and public associations having failed, after a struggle of centuries, to protect or advance the interests of labor, we have lawfully constituted this Assembly. Hid from public view, covered by an impenetrable veil of secrecy, not to promote or shield wrong doing but to shield ourselves and you, from persecution and wrong by men in our own sphere and calling as well as others out of it, by endeavoring to secure the just reward of our toil. In using this power of organized effort and coöperation, we but imitate the example of capital heretofore set in numberless instances. In all the multifarious branches of trade, capital has its combinations, and whether intended or not, it crushes the manly hopes of labor and tramples poor humanity in the dust. We mean no conflict with legitimate enterprise, no antagonism to necessary capital, but men in their haste and greed, blinded by self-interest, overlook the interests of others and sometimes even violate the rights of those they deem helpless. We mean to uphold the dignity of labor, to affirm the nobility of all who live in accordance with the ordinance of God, "in the sweat of thy brow shalt thou eat bread." We mean to create a healthy public opinion on the subject of labor (the only creator of values or capital), and the justice of its receiving a full, just share of the values or capital it has created. We shall with all our strength support laws made to harmonize the interests of labor and capital for labor alone gives life and value to capital, and also those laws which tend to lighten the exhaustiveness of toil. We shall use every lawful and honorable means to procure and retain employ for one another, coupled with just and fair remuneration, and should accident or misfortune befall one of our number, render such aid as lies within our power to give without inquiring his country or his creed. Without approving of general strikes among artisans, yet should it become justly necessary to enjoin an oppressor, we will protect and aid any of our number who thereby may suffer loss and as opportunity offers, extend a helping hand to all branches of honorable toil. Such is but an epitome of our objects. Your duties and obligations, your privileges and benefits you will learn as you mingle with and become acquainted in the noble and holy Order of the ***** of *****. Conduct our Brother to the V. S. at the centre who will instruct him in the workings of an Assembly when in session.

The "V. S.," or Venerable Sage, was the officer who instructed the newly admitted member in the secret work of the Order, such as the grips, passwords, and how to tell when an assembly of the Order would be in session.

. . . I shall briefly tell you of the opening and closing ceremonies so that when you learn of some of the things that happened to me afterward you will be familiar with them. The "open service" was quite lengthy when fully gone through with, and it was not unusual to open and close by "proclamation." The Master Workman, for want of time or other reason, was authorized by law to omit the opening and closing. It was done when the Master Workman called the members to their feet by giving three raps of the gavel and when a circle had been formed round the center, the Master Workman would say: "And now by the power in me vested I declare this Assembly opened (or closed) by proclamation."

It is to a part of the closing service I wish to direct your attention. At the conclusion of the business of the meeting the Master Workman, if the assembly was to be closed in due form, would assemble the members in a circle round the center. At the center would be a square altar stand or small table with an open copy of

the Holy Scriptures in view. When all would be ready the Master
Workman would say: "Assume the attitude of devotion."

Each member would then reverently bow his head and the
Master Workman would continue:

> Father of all, God of love, we render thee
> hearty thanks for Thy goodness. Bless all our
> acts; may all our work begun, continued and
> ended, redound to Thy glory and the good of
> man.

Each member would then say "Amen" or else repeat these
lines:

> God of the granite and the rose,
>   Soul of archangel and the bee,
> The mighty tide of being flows,
>   Through every channel, Lord from Thee.
> It springs to life in grass and flowers,
>   Through every grade of being runs;
> 'Til from creation's radiant towers,
>   Thy glory flames in stars and suns.

> God of the granite and the rose,
>   Soul of archangel and the bee,
> The mighty tide of being flows,
>   Through all thy creatures, back to Thee.
> Thus round and round the circle runs,
>   Infinite sea without a shore,
> 'Til men and angels, stars and suns,
>   Unite to praise Thee, evermore.

Pay particular attention to that last verse and see if it savors of
pantheism. You'll understand the significance of this reminder
later on.

The anteroom of a Knight of Labor meeting place was known
as "vestibule," and placed on the outer door would be a globe
which symbolized the field of our operations. On entering the
vestibule the member saw a triangular altar, red in color, with
a closed copy of the sacred Scriptures thereon. Resting on the Bible
would be a box containing a number of blank cards. It was one
of the aims of the Order to cause every member to know how to
"write his name in full" on one of those cards and pass it in

through the wicket to the Inside Esquire, who would read the name aloud that all might know who was in waiting. That card had a far deeper significance than to apprise members of who sought entrance. Some of the "evils to body, mind, and estate" came through ignorance, and we intended that every member should at least know how to write his own name instead of being obliged to make his mark in the presence of witnesses who might deceive him as to the purport of the instrument he signed. I had the evidence of over one hundred men in Scranton that the lesson taught by that card, one of the first card systems, influenced them to take a course in writing so that they could not only write but read their names and other things beside.

I have quoted from the old secret work to indicate that when a man stood before the altar in an assembly of the Knights of Labor and drank in the lessons running through the lines spoken by the officers, he realized that something more was expected of him than to allow others to do his future thinking for him. He heard a direct appeal to his intellect and heart, an appeal which, though it came to him in a low subdued tone of voice, was an impressive message of love for fellow man. It inspired me in that faraway time and abides with me now as a sublime truth coming to me through the years from Calvary.

When the vast columns of industry were initiated in the Order of the Knights of Labor, it was a pooling of heartbeats and throbbing intellects. In the old days we studied only our rights; in this organization we were to understand that while we had rights to battle for, we owed duties to our fellow men as well. We could claim no right for self that did not carry with it an obligation and a call to do our duty by and to others.

I admit the odor of the old order of things clung to us then. We hadn't learned to specialize for the day of the individual workshop, and jack-of-all-trades was not so far back of us in time. . . . It had not dawned on us that in the march of industry the chasm between the all-round workman and the specialist was opening wider and yet more wide every year. Muscle-saving, brain-impelling machinery was displacing the handicraftsman everywhere and in every line of endeavor. So compelling and rapid were the strides of inventive genius that even while we were demanding recognition for him who earned his bread through the sweat of his face, the machine was being installed which called for little or no expenditure of sweat. It was ordained perhaps that in the Knights of Labor the workers of America should receive their first education in specializing. We admitted all men[4] and taught them the significance and value of organized, coöperative effort. Workers who up to that time dreamed that their callings could not be classed as skilled were taught to know that there is no unskilled labor. . . . All trades, all callings came into the Knights of Labor, and, catching the inspiration born of touching elbows in a common cause, they called their fellow toilers together to meet with them at the dawn of the day of specialty. We believed one man to be as good as another and entitled to the same "rights, privileges, and benefits" in life. Maybe we placed a too implicit faith in what the Declaration of Independence held out to us. Perhaps some lingering, belated wind from the scenes of the early days of the French Revolution carried to our minds the thought that equality could be won, so far as rights and duties went, without reddening our record with a single drop of human blood. . . .

The current of thought and interest in human betterment flowed in sluggish channels and was recorded by faint, irregular pulse beats. We did not, could not, realize how quickly the piling of wealth in the laps of a few would change the whole complexion of our economic affairs. Many of those now known as multimillionaires were then laying the foundation of their colossal fortunes on the bodies and souls of living men. The workmen of Pittsburgh and crimsoned Homestead were pouring their sweat and blood into the crucible from which came, as at the bidding of a magician's wand, the millions, their millions, that one millionaire is now so lavishly and yet so cautiously, giving away to every one save those whose labor created them and whose reward was the hot-scalding water on that July day in 'ninety-two, mingled with their tears and the tears of their widows and orphans

[4] See footnote 1, p. 47.

after earth had made its last payment to them in closing over their tired, worn, senseless clay.[5]

When we vitalized and gave to the world the declaration of principles of our old Industrial Brotherhood we held out the chart of truth as we saw it. For doing so we were derided, sneered at, ridiculed, laughed at, and when we caused this nation to stop and think, those who were aiming at making everything subservient to wealth and corporate power changed their attitude and began to abuse us.

Read that once despised preamble and then read the messages of the Presidents of the United States to Congress for the last two decades. Turn to the statutes of the United States and of the various states and stamped there—indelibly it may be—you'll find plank after plank of the platform of the Knights of Labor. We did not live or speak or work in vain.

Within one week after my admission to Local Assembly No. 88, I had spoken to at least twenty-five machinists concerning the Order. I brought the matter before the Machinists and Blacksmiths Union No. 2 and inside of six weeks an assembly of machinists was organized. I didn't want the place, but they made me Master Workman. One of my first acts was to bring forward the question of organizing the boilermakers. We could at that time admit all grades of workmen to a craft assembly as sojourners. That is, they would remain as sojourners until a sufficient number of their own trade to make an assembly would be initiated. One of the boilermakers I proposed was a tall, gaunt Irishman whose love for his fellow men was like the never-dying perfume of earth's sweetest flower. When Hugh Murray for the first time heard the Master Workman in closing the assembly say: "And now by the power, etc.," he whispered to me, "I tell ye Terry, the Irish are at the top, middle, and bottom of everything good. It must have been an Irishman who wrote that or he'd never say, 'and now be the powers I'll close the assembly.' "

We had no organizers, paid or otherwise. Every member car-

---

[5] The reference is to Andrew Carnegie and to the bitter Homestead strike of June 29—November 20, 1892, which spread to Carnegie mills in Pittsburgh and Duquesne.

ried a message to his fellows, and in a short time assemblies began to grow and flourish all through. the coal fields. Five assemblies were sufficient to constitute a district assembly and on February 24, 1877, a sufficient number of local bodies united, through their delegates, in District Assembly No. 5. The number was changed to 16 a year later after the General Assembly was organized at Reading. . . .

I was elected corresponding secretary of District Assembly No. 5, and at once entered on the work of extending it throughout the United States. My wide acquaintance in the Industrial Brotherhood and Machinists and Blacksmiths Union, through their leading men, gave me an advantage others did not possess. I made the best of it by corresponding with all of them. Such information as I could legitimately impart I gave to my correspondents. Frederick Turner,[6] Secretary of District Assembly No. 1 of Philadelphia, Charles H. Litchman,[7] of a local assembly at Marblehead, Mass., and one or two others were working along the same lines that I followed. Between us we brought the scattered threads of the Order together at Reading, Pennsylvania, January 1, 1878, and there the General Assembly of the Knights of Labor began its national and international existence and work.

In a short time the membership in Luzerne County grew to

[6] Frederick Turner, born in England in 1846, came to the United States when he was ten, and became a goldbeater by trade. Beginning in 1873 he organized local assemblies of goldbeaters in Philadelphia, New York, and Boston. He served as secretary-treasurer of the Knights of Labor and on its General Executive Board.

[7] Charles H. Litchman, 1849-1902, worked as a salesman, studied law, and tried his hand at business before he became prominent in the labor movement. While holding office as National Secretary and International Grand Scribe of the Knights of St. Crispin, he was chosen General Secretary of the K. of L. in exchange for bringing the shoemakers into the Order. During the next fourteen years he held office on and off in the Order to the accompaniment of much criticism. His conduct as General Secretary was marked by inefficiency, financial difficulties, and some questionable money and business manipulations. When he gave up the office for the second time he was under sharp fire. His great preoccupation during these years and afterward was with politics. He was at different times an independent, a Republican and a Greenback Laborite. Greenback-Labor votes elected him to the lower house of the Massachusetts legislature for one term. He later returned to the Republican fold, and at the close of the century attained some measure of importance in the party. In a letter to John W. Hayes, January 13, 1889, Powderly wrote: "Do not do as Charlie used to do . . . [when revoking the commission of an organizer] and say that 'acting by and under the authority of the General Master Workman, I do hereby sever your head from your insignificant neck.' Let him have the real cause. . . ."

over 18,000, and, strange to say, not a word of our movements or existence appeared in the press. ·

Minooka is a small town just beyond the limits of Scranton, to the south. From where I lived to a small hall in Minooka was about five miles. One afternoon in February, 1877, Peter Mullen, who lived in Minooka, came to my house and mysteriously whispered that he would have about fifty men together in a hall in Minooka at eight o'clock that night; he invited me to come down and organize an assembly of the Knights of Labor. I assured him I would be there, he went his way, and early that evening I started for Minooka. There were no trolley cars then, the steam cars were not running on a schedule adapted to my requirements, so I walked. . . . I reached Minooka on time, organized the assembly with Mullin's[8] help. . . .

It was about eleven o'clock when the meeting closed and I started home. The sky was overcast . . . when we entered the hall; it was snowing and blowing when I began my walk to Scranton. Owing to financial differences between the gas company and the city government the streets of Scranton were not lighted that night and hadn't been for months. Apparently everybody in Minooka had gone to bed for I saw no windows lighted up. I had to cross a large field to make the railroad which led to Scranton and was the most direct route. It seemed to me that field had increased its acreage between eight and eleven o'clock, for it took a very long time to reach the down-hill part that led to the railroad. When I did reach the railroad there was no sign of a station in sight. I expected to walk anyway and started. In a short time I heard the soft, regular exhaust of a fan engine and about the same time fell into a cow pit in the track. I suppose you know what a cow pit is, so there's no use in describing. . . . I struck my head against the planked side of the pit, and was so stunned that I remained several minutes in a semi-unconscious condition. Then I heard an exhaust much different from that of the fan engine. A freight train was close by, limping its way south. I calculated that I wasn't strong enough to pull myself out of the pit and remained there until a train of about twenty cars passed over me. I imagined all sorts of things happening to me. First the engineer might pull

[8] The variation in the spelling of the name is in the original manuscript.

the ash pan open and let some hot coals down on me; he didn't. Then what if an axle would break. I thought of all the things that could, but didn't, happen [to] that train. It seemed an eternity until the rumble of the last car began to lose itself in the snow and silence. I looked for a place in the planking to catch the toe of my shoe and found one side of the pit was open. I could at any time have walked out and spared that train crew the unknowable horror of running over a man. I went to the fan engine house, and was told I was about seven miles from Scranton. Part of the time I must have been walking in a circle in that expansive field and went south instead of toward home. Looking at my watch I saw it was past one o'clock. The engineer, proffering the hospitalities of his "shanty," was known to me, and I concluded to keep him company until daylight rather than continue my walk and run the risk of discovering more cowpits. The engineer, Harry Gordon, was obliged to remain awake to attend to the fan which pumped good air into, and foul air out of, the mine. I couldn't sleep and utilized part of the time in initiating Gordon into the mysteries of the Knights of Labor.

.   .   .   .

I tell you of this happening that you may know something about the hardships endured by the pioneers of the labor movement. We walked, daylight and dark. We ate, not when we were hungry, but when and where we could get it. We shared our homes, tables, and beds with each other. I often had two or three Knights of Labor with me over night. We slept in shanties, ash pits, freight cars, or wherever night caught us after our work. Why did we do it? Because it was necessary and we wanted to be of use. . . .

We have been compared to the early crusaders, but I cannot think of a comparison less fitting. A crusader is, or was, a fellow who dressed himself up in a suit of sheet iron clothing, pulled an iron skillet over his head, drew on a pair of steel, knuckle-jointed gloves, climbed up on a horse that always looked too fat to run, set a crowbar-looking thing called a lance into a metal-lined pocket in the saddle, and, in company with a lot of other animated hardware stores rode out of town "on their gaily caparisoned steeds" in the direction of the Holy Land to rescue the tomb of the

Saviour. I can't think of anything more idiotic than a crusader going to rescue the tomb of One who everywhere throughout the world is filling, not a tomb, but the throbbing hearts and brains of those who love the humanity for which He died. . . .

The Knights of Labor aimed at rescuing man himself from a tomb, the tomb of ignorance. The aim was to roll away the stone from that tomb that he might know that moral worth and not wealth should constitute individual and national greatness.

Teachers of the people were then belying the Christ they professed to represent in proclaiming that God had ordained that certain men should be born and remain hewers of wood and drawers of water and that certain other men had been created and commissioned by the Almighty to be their masters by divine right. It was the rule then, with honorable exceptions of course, when men went on strike to be told from the pulpit that "they should be content to live in that sphere in life to which it hath pleased God to call them." I couldn't believe in such a doctrine and believe in God at the same time, so I held steadfastly to my faith and belief in God.

The great strike of 1877 in Pennsylvania made victims of hundreds of Knights of Labor, who left the state and went in all directions carrying with them no murderous lance; neither were they dressed in garments of steel. They were clothed in righteousness, and bore in their hearts and minds God's high and holy command: "Love your neighbor." Perhaps we did not always give the public to understand that love of neighbor was our aim for we had to strike, boycott, and do other things not supposed to be in accord with the Ten Commandments. But remember that for the first time in human history labor, in the last quarter of the nineteenth century, stood at least partially solidified, partially organized, and partially united in opposition to a power that had its origin in the first lockout, on the day that Adam and Eve were locked out of that rather exclusive garden in which fruit was grown with apples a specialty. That power was greed, century-fortified, steel-armored greed, and you must not blame us for striking against it now and then or for using other harsh methods. . . .

Chapter Seven

THE PHILOSOPHER'S STONE

WHEN THE FIRST SESSION of the General Assembly adjourned at Reading, Charles H. Litchman, the newly elected Grand Secretary, and Thomas P. Crowne[1] were designated to proceed to Philadelphia and install Uriah S. Stephens[2] as Grand Master Workman. Mr. Stephens was obliged to leave the General Assembly before it adjourned and was elected during his absence. I accompanied them to Philadelphia, and after the installation of Mr. Stephens a general discussion took place as to the future of the Order. Among other things the designing of a seal came up for consideration, and a proper motto to encircle it was to be adopted. After several suggestions had been made I fished from my pocket a clipping which I had cut from a paper some days before. It read: "THAT IS THE MOST PERFECT GOVERNMENT IN WHICH AN INJURY TO ONE IS THE CONCERN OF ALL." The author's name was not given but it struck me as being just right. It appeared to please the others and was adopted without question. Mr. Stephens, who was a Greek scholar, said that it was from the writings of Solon, the Greek lawgiver. Ever since then it has done duty among millions of men and women as a slogan during strikes, lockouts, and boycotts. When the Order began to grow in numbers and men were discharged for activities as Knights, they invariably asked for assistance on the ground that "an injury to one is the concern of all." My aim as General Master Work-

---

[1] Thomas P. Crowne, a Brooklyn shoemaker, was chairman of the first Executive Board set up by the first General Assembly.

[2] Uriah Smith Stephens (1821-82), by trade a tailor, was active in politics before he and eight former members of a garment cutters' union organized the first assembly of the K. of L. He was less a trade unionist than a humanitarian idealist who sought to unite all workers into a single "brotherhood." This is clearly evident in some two hundred Stephens letters found among Powderly's correspondence.

man was to keep before our membership the thought that they should labor for the perfecting of a government in which an injury to one would be the concern of all. It often happened that the concern of one was made the occasion of an injury to all.

At that meeting Mr. Stephens invited me to his home, where I again met Mr. Fennimore, who four years before had sworn me in as a Knight of Labor. During my visit Mr. Stephens conferred on me the Philosopher's Stone degree. It was the intention to establish that as a degree to be conferred for meritorious conduct in the field of labor. I trust to memory to recall Mr. Stephens' words as he conferred the degree, for nothing was ever written or printed concerning it. . . .[3]

You find on the lower half of this plate, and beneath the tree, three numbers; they differ on each emblem; no two are, or can be, alike for these numbers relate to the personality and membership of the possessor of this emblem.

The number to the left signifies that that is the number you bear on the Master Workman's roll book in your assembly. The number to the right is that of your local assembly while the one at the bottom is the number of the district assembly to which your local assembly is attached. These numbers serve a useful purpose; should accident or misfortune befall you and the power of speech fail you, a member of this degree would instantly know, on examination of this emblem, who stood before him and claimed his counsel or aid.

In addition to the characters already explained you will find on either side of the triangle and at its base other letters to which deep significance was attached. They are S., O., A. They stand for Secrecy, Obedience, and Assistance. Secrecy concerning everything seen, heard, or done in a local assembly or any other body of the Knights of Labor. Obedience to lawful commands issued by competent authority under law conferring the authority. It was not to be a blind obedience but one that would be rendered pursuant to law or rule made by the majority. Assistance "is to be given to him whose claim is that he needs." I take pride in

[3] For Powderly's report of Mr. Stephens' words, see Appendix I, pp. 429-430.

acknowledging the authorship of that definition. The saying is not original with me but . . . at my suggestion it was approved and adopted by the first G. M. W., of the K. of L. If a brother stood in need of food, fuel, clothing, comfort in words or act, in advice or direction, "render such aid as lies within our power to give without inquiring his country or his creed."

EMBLEM OF THE PHILOSOPHER'S STONE DEGREE

I give here a representation of both plates. These plates are enclosed in crystals in the shape of hemispheres and when pressed together form one united whole. You will notice that the numbers are 1, 222, and 16. My number on the Master Workman's roll book was 1, the number of my assembly was 222, and the number of the district assembly to which 222 was attached was 16. A brother of the Philosopher's Stone degree on examination of the emblem attached to my watch chain would know that Number 1, of Assembly No. 222, of District Assembly No. 16, stood before him.

The work of the Philosopher's Stone degree was never completed by giving it a place in the printed secret work of the Order, and, so far as I know, was imparted to but eleven men.

During my incumbency of the office of General Master Workman, I conferred the Philosopher's Stone degree upon but three members, although I had been authorized to bestow it upon those worthy to receive it.

When I became G. M. W., in September, 1879, the district assembly had no ritual. Delegates from local assemblies were admitted rather informally; they were ushered in without ceremony of any kind, nothing was said or done to impress them with a sense of the importance of their new surroundings. One of my first duties was to prepare a ritual containing rules of admission and conduct after admission for the delegates. I shall not trespass on your time by repeating all the ritual contained, but shall ask you to carefully read what the District Master Workman said on receiving new members. I do not recall that when I read that address for the first time in District Assembly No. 3 of Pittsburgh, anyone present objected or offered to amend or change it. I read from the manuscript just as I had written it, and give it just as I read it then and as it has stood ever since.

In the beginning of creation, it was ordained that all things tangible should have certain qualities. In some, form and size. In others, strength, weight, density, and ductility. In others, color, flavor, nutrition, and warmth. In *all*, purity and plenty in their order. These qualities determine their fitness for the use of man, and by them he can decide, with the certainty of nature's laws, their intrinsic value. But ignorance and greed have established other standards in the world. While nature and industry may create in plenty, false distribution withholds and causes artificial scarcity and famine. Greed adulterates and idleness gambles in the products of toil and grows rich off the necessities of the producers. Rare gems and precious metals have been made the representative of "labor done." These have been supplemented by paper credits, thus rendering the world's labor susceptible of manipulation by the idle few, and making it possible, through want, to reduce the worker to actual slavery. What the world calls "hire" is only "wages slavery." While machinery should be the only slave of man, to do his work and lighten his toil, capital can and does monopolize machinery, thereby depriving labor of its God-ordained increase, dictating its remuneration, riveting more firmly the chains of oppression, and rendering it almost impossible for the toiler to participate equally in the occupation of the soil and the elements of natural wealth. To pause in his toil, to devote time to his own interest, to gather a knowledge of the world's commerce, to unite, combine, and cooperate in the great army of peace and industry, to nourish and cherish, build and develop the temple he lives in, is the highest and noblest duty of man to himself, to his fellow man and to his Creator.

We welcome you to the army of peace, where we bring the producer and the consumer together, render useless the mere handler or jobber, and save the extortion of the speculator, the drone and the non-producer. Here we are taught to use the five avenues of the soul, the God-given senses, to acquire wisdom for the benefit of man. We shall use the five elements of nature— land, air, light, fire, and water—the God-given wealth of the world, to produce the materials that promote the happiness of all. We shall assert our right to the five mechanical powers, all embraced in the word "machinery," to do our bidding, assist our labor, and lighten the burden of our toil. We affirm that five days in the week are sufficient for industrial pursuits, and shall therefore labor to bring the time when there shall be five days in the week for labor, and two days for rest—one for God and the other for humanity.

As I look back to the day I wrote that and think through the years to now I am more impressed with these words than when I wrote them: "While nature and industry may create in plenty, false distribution withholds and causes artificial scarcity and famine. Greed adulterates and idleness gambles in the products of toil and grows rich off the necessities of the producers." . . .

There were those in the Knights of Labor who affected to believe that I was not fit to be General Master Workman because I did not know what the founders of the Order had in mind when they adopted certain emblems and sign language. I determined to give them something to think about and so prepared an explanation of our signs, seals, and other things. When the old story of my lack of knowledge was repeated at the Philadelphia session of the General Assembly in 1884, I asked that body to go into secret session and listen to me while I explained things to them. They were dumbfounded, and when I finished reading, they adopted, unanimously too, a motion to approve of what I had read, adopt it as a whole, and circulate it throughout the Order. The impression the carpers got was that I had sat at the feet of the founders and drunk in the lessons I had read to them. The truth is, and now for the first time I say it, every paragraph, sentence, line, and word in that explanation was conjured up and written by me between daylight and daylift of one twenty-four hours in my home in Scranton, and my only prompter was a dictionary which I consulted occasionally to find a word that I was not in the habit of using. So successfully did I disguise my vocabulary that up to this hour I have not been suspected of being the sole author of "The Explanation of the Signs and Symbols of the Order."[4]

This "Explanation of the Signs and Symbols of the Order,"

[4] The text of the "Secret Circular" and an illustration of "The Great Seal" will be found in Appendix II.

together with constitution and ritual, or A. K., were printed in French, German, Italian, Lithuanian, Polish, and several of the languages spoken in Russia. Assemblies of the Order flourished in Great Britain and Ireland, in France, Belgium, Italy, and as far away as South Africa. Though no local assemblies of Knights of Labor exist in any of these countries now, the principles of the Order still live and continue to inspire men and women to strive for the betterment of industrial conditions. . . .

Chapter Eight

SOMETHING OF MY POLITICAL ACTIVITIES

I BECAME A POLITICIAN in a personal way in 1870 when I cast my first vote for a county ticket that had been organized and nominated by the laboring men of Luzerne County. I had nothing to say for, or anything to do with, that party then except to vote the ticket. In 1872 I joined a Republican Grant and Wilson club and on election day voted for General Grant. That was the first President of the United States I voted for. I took part in one parade with the Grant and Wilson club, carried a torch through the streets of Scranton, wore a shoulder cape that should have been a mackintosh, for the man to the rear of me in the procession emptied the oil from his lamp on my clothing, ruining my coat and trousers. When we massed before the grand stand, had given three cheers and a tiger for somebody, the chairman introduced a man wearing a lot of auburn hair and a loud voice who began in the usual taffy-dispensing way to compliment the horny-handed sons of toil for their manly independence and sturdy patriotism. We cheered, and that encouraged the idiot to go on to tell us a lot of things about ourselves that we should have recognized as lies had we not been full of enthusiasm and coal oil. Then he told of what General Grant did to lick the rebels and wound up in a peroration full of perspiration and references to Appomattox. I had no better sense, politically, at the time than to think he was a wonder. I didn't know until I got home about the coal oil on my clothing. . . .

When 1876 came round I was a member and president of a Greenback-Labor club. I didn't know so much about the currency question but had an opinion or two on labor matters. We had three hundred members in the club, and as I think back over it I am persuaded that over two-thirds of them just joined the club to sit down somewhere and rest; they didn't do anything else. I was so enthused that I began to pity Tilden and Hayes for how bad they'd feel the morning after election to see Peter Cooper swept into the White House by a tremendous majority. I had no ambition looking toward a cabinet or ambassadorial position under Cooper, but I prepared a telegram of heartfelt congratulations to send him just the moment I learned of his election. I held that telegram several days, hoping the returns would show up differently, and then sadly abandoned the idea—the time wasn't opportune.

The majority of the Greenback-Labor club resided in the district I voted in, and I expected to read of a good majority for Cooper and Cary the morning after election. Just three votes appeared in the Greenback-Labor column to the credit of the Cooper and Cary electors.[1] At first I was indignant, for I was morally certain that there were more Greenback-Labor votes polled. After a while I wondered how the election board missed the three votes and hadn't counted them for one of the other fellows. It was disclosed to me then that it wasn't because of a lack of votes we didn't carry the district, but because, being new and inexperienced, we hadn't selected the right kind of counters to sit on the election board. Yes, it is a fact that one of the members of the election board explained to me that on such occasions as an election it was customary for the board to credit as many votes as might be necessary in that district to the Democrat ticket, it being "naturally Democratic," and that there was no sense in throwing good votes away on weak, foolish, unknown, and unnecessary third parties. I began to think some more and to make inquiries in other districts. I discovered that the same practice prevailed in many of them and was not confined to one party. Having votes cast for a man didn't mean that they would be counted for him. The disclosures made to me horrified me.

Luzerne County had eighteen thousand men organized in the

[1] The Greenback vote in Pennsylvania was 7,187; the vote for the entire country was 81,740 out of a total of almost eight and one-half-million votes cast.

Knights of Labor. There was to be a full county ticket elected in November, 1877. After one of the sessions of District Assembly No. 5 adjourned one night, I asked the delegates to remain. They did, and then I made my first political speech. After recounting what I had learned about politics and told of the necessity for honest elections, after warning them that no workingman or poor man could aspire to office under the conditions then prevailing, I suggested that they, in their separate localities, discuss the advisability of putting a county ticket in the field, that we select men to be appointed by the court to be watchers on the inside of the polling booths, and that all the rest of us should be watchers on the outside so that the vote of every citizen should be counted for the man it was intended for. I wound up with this statement:

If we find that the ballot boxes have been stuffed as on previous elections and ascertain the identity of the scoundrels who do it, let us hang every one of them. Murder may be committed in the heat of passion, robbery may be committed because of poverty, other crimes may be committed against the person through passion, but the man who defeats the will of the people at the ballot box is worse than murderer, burglar, thief, and raper combined, for he strikes at the foundations of civil government and is deserving of death once his guilt is established.

I don't know that I would talk that way now but I meant it just as I said it then, and feel just that way yet. In some way my speech gained publicity and the papers of both parties attacked me as a man of incendiary tendencies. I said nothing for publication but quietly organized a movement looking to the holding of a county nominating convention; it was successful. The convention met in Pittston on September 11, 1877, a full ticket was nominated, a platform adopted, and the campaign was on.

I was not a delegate to the convention. I thought it best not to go. My fear was that I might be nominated for some office, and [I] didn't wish to identify my position as secretary of District Assembly No. 5 with politics. I drew up the platform, entrusted it to James Mitchell[2] who was a delegate, and, without changing word or sentiment, it was unanimously adopted.

Poor as church mice, how could we provide funds to run a

[2] James Tyndale Mitchell, (1834-1915), a Pennsylvania jurist, edited the *American Law Register* and was elected to the state Supreme Court in 1888.

campaign? We didn't; we expected those nominated to work for the people if elected, and we shouldn't expect them to pay assessments. I was made a member of the county committee.

Nicholas Kiefer, a Knight of Labor and a printer, agreed to print the tickets for the cost of ink and paper. Up to that time the old parties printed five tickets for each voter in order to allow for waste. The matter of tickets was left to me, and I had but two tickets printed for each voter. Then I instructed the Knights of Labor throughout the county that I had done so and that they should see to it that wasting of tickets should be cut down to the minimum. I had the tickets, when printed, taken to my house, where members of my family and neighbors cut, folded, and tied them in bunches. There was no secret or blanket ballot then. Each candidate's name and the office he was nominated for appeared on a separate slip and [this] was so folded as to show only the title of the office and not the name of the candidate. That part of the ticket was folded so as to hide the name from view.

Those tickets were taken to all parts of the county by men who walked. I carried some to Carbondale, sixteen miles away to the north, and Wilkes-Barre nineteen miles to the south.

On election day we had our election overseers, appointed by the courts, on the inside of the polling booths, and eighteen thousand, earnest, honest, determined workingmen stood round the polls throughout the county. All day long, from seven to seven, these men stood guard, many of them without a bite to eat, and not one received a cent for service rendered.

The result of that election, a Waterloo for the two old parties,[3] is written on the records of old Luzerne County, but the heroism, self-sacrifice, devotion to principle, and priceless fidelity of the workingmen is a story that never has been and never can be told in such a way as to reflect on the men of this hour the glory of that day in 1877 when the prayer "God give us men" was answered.

Every vote was counted for the man and party it was intended for; there was no ballot box stuffing and no necessity for hanging

[3] This is exaggerated, but Greenback-Labor candidates did capture the following Luzerne county offices: sheriff, recorder, coroner, commissioner, surveyor, auditor. The Greenback-Labor ticket was responsible for a serious decline in the Democratic vote, and enabled the Republicans to run ahead in the county.

anybody. For the first time in Pennsylvania the call of the political boss fell on deaf ears, the shackles of partisanship were broken, and the thin edge of the wedge of independence inserted between the citizen and his old party affiliations.

The ballot boxes from all over the county were taken to the courthouse at Wilkes-Barre for storage and safe keeping. A detail of one hundred Knights of Labor stood guard around the courthouse from Tuesday, the day of election, until Thursday when the official count was completed by the judges of the court. Nine hundred other men stood ready throughout Wilkes-Barre to respond to a prearranged signal in case of an attempt to enter the courthouse by unauthorized persons. We were as determined that there would be no tampering with the returns as we were that there should be no stuffing of ballot boxes. I was one of the hundred to guard the courthouse. I brought rope with me.

About December 1, 1877, I wrote to Oil City for the purpose of securing employment, received an encouraging answer and was told to hold myself in readiness to go on or before the first of January. On the 19th of December I received a letter from the superintendent of the open shops in Oil City notifying me to come on when ready, that a place was awaiting me. That afternoon I placed my resignation as corresponding secretary of District Assembly No. 5 in the hands of Joshua R. Thomas, the preceptor and organizer of the district with instructions to lay it before the next meeting. On the morning of the 20th I bought my ticket and had my trunk taken to the railroad station intending to take the westbound night train for Oil City.

A city convention of the Greenback-Labor party had been called for the 20th of December, the day I was to leave for Oil City. I had nothing to do with calling the convention. As a matter of fact I had endeavored to postpone the convention until about the middle of January. I had an experience during the fall campaign that caused me to believe that a committeeman's life was not a happy one, and, fully expecting to be one of the committee, if I remained in town, I had hoped to shorten the period of worry and anxiety by deferring the holding of the convention. Being busy arranging my affairs preparatory to leaving town that night,

I did not go to the convention, and about three o'clock that afternoon Hank Canavan and Hugh Murray called at my house to
inform me that I had been nominated for mayor by acclamation.
It did not surprise me, for I had heard a whisper of my probable
nomination and promptly told my informants that I didn't want
the office anyway for I didn't think I knew enough to be mayor.
Every office that I ever held in the Machinists and Blacksmiths
Union, the Industrial Brotherhood, and the Knights of Labor
came to me unsought, but I accepted them cheerfully, willingly,
and worked as hard as a man could in each position to fulfill all
requirements. I didn't want to be mayor, the thought of being so
appalled me. I was a student in, but had not yet graduated from,
the school of hard knocks. The mayor of Scranton was, at that
time, clothed by law with the powers of a committing and civil
magistrate, something like [a] police judge. I had never witnessed the holding of court, had never heard an oath administered except the impromptu kind we used in the machine shop
when things went wrong. The committee insisted on my going
to the convention and I did. On the way over I busied myself
framing a speech declining the nomination. As I was entering the
hall a man standing near the door remarked loud enough for me
to hear him: "He'd make a hell of a mayor." That man must have
been a mind reader, for that is just what I was saying about
myself. Whenever I say anything derogatory of myself I can take
it complacently, but it's different when a party of the second part
talks that way. I was running that remark over in my mind when
I entered the convention. Instantly every man rose to his feet,
began to cheer and hurrah for "our next mayor." I was escorted
to the platform and introduced to the convention by the pre···ding
officer.

I am very sorry I cannot give you an idea of my popularity by
telling you how long the applause continued. When it ended I
faced the convention and as promptly accepted the nomination
as if I had been hankering for it all the time. I'd show that fellow
whether I'd "make a hell of a mayor" or not.

I was elected, and one of the first men I appointed to the police
force was Patrick Golden, the man who made the remark I over-

heard on entering the convention. Whether I made that kind of a mayor or not he made one of the best police officers the city of Scranton ever had. But I'm getting ahead of my story.

I was nominated for mayor, accepted the nomination, and was sworn not to withdraw from the contest until the verdict at the ballot box was in, that I was not running and would not run in the interest of any other party or person, and that if elected my sole duty and effort would be to serve the people of Scranton as mayor without fear or favor. To all of this I said amen, and that minute began a campaign which did not end until seven o'clock on the evening of election day, Tuesday the 19th of February, 1878.

Sometime in the early part of January, the members of the campaign committee discovered that I was not a politician of the wire-pulling, vote-corralling variety, and informed me that I would have to meet the voters where they congregated. Don't run away with the idea that they wanted me to go to church. They said that on former occasions it was the custom for candidates to visit saloons throughout the city and be "hail fellows well met" with the citizens who frequented such places. At first I demurred; they insisted and after urgent persuasion I agreed to do as suggested. I am glad I did, for I learned something that I hadn't heard of at school and you don't find in books.

I had never been in a saloon, had never even tasted anything with alcohol in it so far as I knew. It was planned that in company with members of the committee I should make the rounds of the principal saloons of the city and endeavor to secure votes by ministering to the spirituous wants of the citizens I would meet in these places. The first saloon we entered was in a section of the city known as Pategonia. We found it full of thirsty patriots who flocked round us at once and began to tell how much they thought of me and how eager they were to vote for me. I, endeavoring to follow instructions given by the committee, sidled up to the bar, leaned my elbow on it and was about to say "What'l ye have" or "What do you want" or something like that when a tall, angular-looking man walked up to me, took my hand in his and began to squeeze it. His grip was viselike, and as he gripped he thrust his thumb nail into the back of my hand and began to twist it round as far as it would go. He drew the first blood. In a maudlin voice he began to tell me I was no politician, that it was doubtful if I'd be elected because I hadn't been out setting 'em up every night. I stood it some time and when others crowded round and shouted: "Speech, speech," I made a short speech. It was my first speech in that campaign and the last one I made in a saloon. The sight of that man inspired me. A part of his supper that had escaped destruction at meal time clung to and mingled with the beer suds that moistened about a pint of riotous-looking sunburned whiskers that camped on his chin. When he talked, or tried to, he squirted liberal quantities of a mixture of beer and tobacco gravy into my face. His clothing, which was unclean, untidy and unsanitary, looked as if it had been spread over him with a hay fork. I experienced a feeling of loathing, not because of what he said, what he did, or how he looked, but because he called himself a workingman and as such demanded of me to supply beer to him in exchange for his vote. I despised myself for placing it in his power to tender such an insulting offer to me by going there to meet him. Then I made my first public speech in the mayoralty campaign of 1878. It wasn't very long and it won't bore you if I repeat it. I said:

You say I am not a politician, you are mistaken. I am a politician but not the kind you have been accustomed to meeting in such places as this. As a politician I am a living protest against the beer-swilling, back-biting, hand-wringing, saloon-haunting practices of the old time politicians, and if the men of Scranton demand of me to do as the citizen debauching politicians of the old parties have done in the past, I don't want to be your mayor; I'll stop running, and you may all go to hell.

Of course consternation prevailed. I didn't wait to observe it, for I at once left the place and went home.

I had no supporters among the daily papers. A reporter for one of them overheard my speech and without quoting it all said my language was unfit to print and that "Powderly assured those who offered to vote for him that if elected they might go to hell." Editorially I was roasted in about a half column of mock sympathy for the honest workingmen I had wheedled into nominating me. It was pure demagoguery from end to end.

Having no great moral prop in the shape of a daily paper to lean on, I wrote a circular and had it given out all over the city. The campaign committee tried to choke me off but to no avail. Let me quote from that circular.

I did not want or seek the nomination for mayor. I accepted it not to do as others did before but to do the best I knew how to give Scranton an honest administration. I intend, if elected, to pay every citizen a full equivalent for voting for or against me by doing my duty as mayor fearlessly, faithfully and as well as I know how. I intend to remain sober all the time so that I shall know what I am doing. No man, whether he votes for or against me, has any right to expect more than that from me.

My work has been and shall be a protest against the practices which reduced that man to, and below, the level of a common beggar. Capable of earning good wages, at his trade (he was a stone mason), he practically offered his vote to me for beer. I can find no language severe enough to properly characterize the habit men have fallen into of going to saloons to offer their ballots, our ballots, in exchange for a drink of beer, rum or a cigar. The right to vote was won for us on many a hard-fought field by our revolutionary fathers and should be held so sacred that conscience alone should direct its course. It should be cast for the man or principles, or both, that appear best for all the people. If you think I am that man and represent such principles, vote for me. Whether you vote for me or not do not ask me to solicit votes in exchange for beer, rum, or vile cigars.

I am sorry I told that man to go to hell, not so much on his account as my own. I became indignant at the sight of a man with marks of labor on his calloused hands degrading himself and asking me to become a party to his degradation. Perhaps I should have said something else to bring him to a true realization of what he, and those congregated there, were doing to make themselves slaves to liquor and political boss rule. If I pay for a vote in beer or cigars the man I buy from has no further claim on me. I intend that every citizen of Scranton shall have the right to come to me and demand of me to set the name of Scranton right before the country. I'll do that if elected but I shall not go to another saloon to buy votes or debauch voters.

I was as roundly abused for what I said in that circular as for telling the man to go to hell. He didn't go there, he is in Scranton yet and I am told he has never been seen in a saloon or under the influence of strong drink since. He called on me to apologize for what he did. I wouldn't let him and was imprudent enough to ask him to prune his whiskers; then he offered to trim me. I reasoned him out of that frame of mind and we effected a compromise on the whisker question which has staved off hostilities ever since.

The Democrats and Republicans united in a citizens' party, nominated for mayor a prominent man, a Civil War veteran and a splendid citizen. On February 19 I was elected,[4] on April 1 I was sworn in as mayor and then the trouble began.

The chief of police, P. DeLacy, a Democrat and an uncivil war veteran, was also a member of the Democrat city committee. I was importuned by members of my own party to remove DeLacy and put a labor man in his place. I refused to do so unless they produced a better man, or one equally as good as DeLacy. I also informed them that as a currier his record on the labor question was straight. Perhaps I was partial to DeLacy on three counts. He had been a captain of infantry in the army during the uncivil war; he was a temperance man; and, though he had nothing to do with selecting the place, I gave him full credit for good intentions in being born in Carbondale, my native city. I didn't remove him and have always been glad of it, for the whole United States could produce no better chief of police or more honorable man than Captain DeLacy. It was DeLacy who won the battle of Gettysburg. He was too modest to claim the credit for it but I know from the way he talked about it and the many descriptions he gave me of the battle that he must have done it.

A number of the "best people" of Scranton held a meeting, by invitation, to discuss the feasibility of removing from the city. I say best people because they admitted that they were the best. Of course there were other best people there but they weren't wealthy. It was decided at the meeting—which, by the way, was opened with prayer by Dr. Logan, pastor of the First Presbyterian Church—that property was not safe in Scranton with a mayor of communistic tendencies in the chair. I would be quite likely to break out and head a mob of riotous workingmen at any time, etc. When told of it I said nothing, didn't want to express an opinion until I felt certain about the communistic tendencies. I had never heard of them before and hunted for a dictionary. It wasn't so bad after all. A communistic tendency isn't such a bad thing to have if one is good enough to be a communist in spirit and practice as well as profession. I wasn't a communist, and,

[4] Powderly was elected by a majority of 500.

therefore, didn't have the symptoms, or tendencies the best people suspected me of harboring.

One night about 10:30 on my way home I met a man in soldier's uniform, with a rifle on his shoulder, parading in front of the bridge across the Lackawanna river. I stopped to question him when he ordered me to move on. I told him who I was, and then he informed me that he had been ordered out by Major Boies. I went back to the office, called in the chief of police, directed that he take a squad of patrolmen and arrest every man found under arms and patrolling the streets. He did, and after three or four had been locked up the Major called me up to ask me why I did it. I told him these men were inciting to riot by parading around with firearms; they had no right to do so and I simply complied with my oath of office in removing them from harm's way. He said his reason for ordering them out was because of rumors of a socialist uprising in Chicago and feared it might affect Scranton. I then informed him that I was peace officer of the city, that I would hold myself responsible for the good order of our citizens, and, if I couldn't preserve order with the forces at my command I'd call on the sheriff of the county. If we couldn't maintain order, we had the right to call on the governor of the state for the armed forces of the commonwealth, but until that time no armed men would walk the streets of Scranton, for I'd lock every one of them up as fast as he began operations. He learned that I was in earnest, and on his personal assurance that the militia men would go home, I released them. There was no other uprising that night.

After observing me for some time the best people came to the conclusion that I was tame enough to eat bread out of their hands and relinquished the idea of leaving town. If I had been gifted with the real-estate broker instinct, see what a harvest I could have reaped by keeping up a communistic bluff and have a partner get options on the properties they would have sacrificed.

The pendulum swung to the other extreme in a short time, and instead of regarding me as no good the best people began to think I was extra good. A city as large as Scranton was at that time, about 75,000 inhabitants, is apt to have some houses of unquestioned immorality in it; Scranton had its share. One day eleven men, many of them ministers of the gospel, called on me at the mayor's office. They represented the temperance, moral, and religious sentiment of the community and stated that they had called to invoke my active aid in suppressing the social evil in the city.

If you have ever had experience on or with committees, you have observed that a spokesman is usually selected to state the aims and objects of the movement; then every other member of the committee will chip in his quota of talk whether it be relevant or the reverse. Every one of the eleven made a speech, and, as was to be expected, the discussion took a wide range. The social evil and everything relating to it in the way of sin and iniquity came in for denunciation and execration as each one wound up his peroration. It was an enthusiastic manifestation of virtuous indignation. I knew we had good people in Scranton, but didn't feel sure they were quite so good until eleven of the cream of our social life told me they were the best kind of men. I listened without comment until the last of the eleven lapsed into silence and then asked if anyone else had anything to say. Of course there wasn't anyone else to talk. I didn't know but what some of them might wish to start over again. They seemed to be satisfied with their effort. I thanked them for calling and after a few preliminary remarks said that I would be glad to act on their suggestion. This is what I told them:

I am in accord with your sentiments as expressed by your chairman and others. It shall be my aim to rid Scranton of every house of ill-fame, but I'll need a lot of help. I hope I may count on your coöperation and aid. I shall drive every female prostitute out of the city or at least prevent her from following her calling here. If you gentlemen will help me it can and shall be done.

They unanimously, even vociferously, pledged me their hearty assistance. Then I went on to say:

I shall take it on myself now to answer for every female prostitute in Scranton and assure you that she will no longer do business here if you gentlemen will answer for the male prostitutes of your congregations and the community by assuring me that they will hereafter refrain from visiting and patronizing these women. It ought to be easy for you to do this in your collective capacity, eleven in number, since I, just one individual, am willing to, and feel quite hopeful of being able to, do as I have promised to do.

You can go a great way in the direction of ridding our city of this nuisance if you will urge your parishioners and friends to cancel their leases with the women who rent these houses, or else refuse to renew the leases when they expire and assist the women in these resorts to secure other employment. I am not asking you gentlemen to do as much as I promise you that I shall do. Between us I feel that we can accomplish a great deal of good.

That was in 1878, and, if I am credibly informed, Scranton has quite a few houses of the ruby light variety yet. I frequently met members of that committee of eleven afterward, but so far as I am aware they haven't effected any material change in the moral atmosphere of Scranton.

The mayor's office and the city lockup were about two blocks apart. It was the custom when arrests were made during the night to bring the offenders through the streets to the courtroom in the morning in the mayor's office. I had part of the floor space in the lockup enclosed within a railing and each morning held court there. Such prisoners as were in durance were not subjected to the humiliation of being scoffed and jeered at on their way through a public thoroughfare to the courtroom.

After a short time I began to feel a bit ashamed of Carbondale. The drunks and disorderlies made inquiries, on sobering up, concerning the mayor and his antecedents. On learning that I was born and raised in Carbondale they invariably gave that city as their birthplace or residence when questioned for docket entries in court. They expected I would be lenient with a fellow townsman. One day a robust, healthy-looking man, who had been boisterous while drunk the night before, came before me for a hearing. After making the proper entries and ascertaining that he too was from Carbondale I imposed this sentence on him: "That you, Jack Robinson, be taken from this courtroom to the Delaware and Hudson railroad station, placed on a train thereat, and sent to Carbondale where you are to spend six months at such labor as you may find to do in that city." He went to Carbondale. The daily paper of that city criticized me, mildly though, for making a penal colony of my native city. Robinson, glad to get off so easy, resented the fling at me by taking up his residence in Carbondale. He remained more than six months, he's there yet, and turned out to be a well-behaved, sober, industrious and orderly citizen. He is more orderly now than ever; he is in the cemetery having died in 1910, leaving after him a family that any man might be proud of.

We hear and read a great deal now about juvenile courts, the moral uplift of youthful sinners, and how very essential it is that minor offenders, being amateurs in crime through lack of experience, should have courts of their own and be tried in a way calculated to keep them from contact with older and more hardened offenders. Elaborate plans are being outlined and put in practice in our large and small cities to save, reform, or correct the evil tendencies of boys and girls in whose lives the germs of crime have begun to sprout. . . . Philanthropists, humanitarians, settlement workers, and bughouse reformers get busy devising plans to manufacture new court machinery to plane off the rough edges, sandpaper the moral fiber and varnish over the ascertained delinquencies of the children, many of whose lapses may perhaps be traced to the lurid accounts published broadcast of how the morals or immorals of their predecessors detected in iniquity were laundered, starched, and ironed out in a juvenile court while the Honorable Knowall Buttinski and Mrs. Morality Uplift sat on a bench with the judge, took a deep interest in the proceedings, asking questions of the youthful prisoners. While this was going on, the newsboys outside the courtroom may have been shouting out the red headlines in a yellow press so loud that the young offender could hear his name coupled with the philanthropic people who sat on the bench with the judge. All about crime and how to commit it in such a way as to enlist the interest of the goody-goods of society with more money than sense is served up in daily paper and monthly magazine. I have an idea that all of the publicity and a great deal of the procedure and practice in our juvenile courts could be dispensed with to the benefit of society at large.

My incumbency of the office of mayor of Scranton covered a period of three terms of two years each. I take great pride in telling that I was mayor for three terms, for no other mayor served three terms.

During the six years I held the office a number of boys and girls were apprehended and brought before me for trial. I never gave a public hearing to any of these cases, and no docket entries were made of any save the few whose offenses were of so grave a character as to remove them from the jurisdiction of the municipal court.

The first youthful offender brought before me for trial was a boy eleven years old charged with disorderly conduct. He had failed to return to school after recess and had thrown stones at another boy, smaller than he, for some taunting remark. He looked frightened but defiant, and his clothing was rather untidy. I took notice of his quick movements, the shape of his head and hands and hastily arrived at an opinion that his offending was just surplus energy going to waste.

I called him inside the bar enclosure to the private office which opened therefrom, told him I was too busy to hear his case then but in a few minutes would be ready for him. I handed him a pencil and a few sheets of paper and told him he might occupy his time while waiting in writing, drawing, or reading. Privately I questioned the officer as to the extent of the damage inflicted on the other boy and ascertained that his exterior had not been marred by contact with the stones thrown at him. In a short time I went into the private office and engaged the lad in conversation. He was bright, alert, and intelligent. I noticed that he had made some pencil marks on a sheet of paper, but did not touch or refer to it at first. His name, age, residence, names of parents, and some other questions were asked and answers noted. I remarked that the officer who arrested him told me who he was and where he lived. I had an object in that. If he thought that I knew all about him he wouldn't be apt to tell me any falsehoods. Boys are just like men, when they do lie they feel that they have to stick to it. I am not prepared to go as far as the psalmist who anticipated [Theodore] Roosevelt by a few centuries in saying that "All men are liars." Most of us are though, and it is best to keep the temptation to lie in the background.

I questioned the boy about a number of things before referring to his trouble and discovered that his ambition was to become a locomotive engineer when he grew up. I was right at home on that subject, and in a short while he thawed out and asked me a few questions about the construction and running of locomotives. When we got around to it I said:

We have had such a long and interesting talk that it has grown late and I won't have time to hear your case today; come here at eleven o'clock next Saturday morning and be sure not to tell anyone you were arrested. I'll make no entry of the case until we talk it over again. Ask the boy you had the trouble with to come with you. In the meantime try your hand at making a better drawing of an engine than this and let me see what you can do Saturday.

.　　.　　.　　.

Saturday morning he was promptly on hand. Hands, face, and shoes were shined up; his clothing was neatly arranged and he seemed to be quite chummy with the little fellow who accompanied him. He had a roll of paper which he appeared to be anxious that I should examine first thing. I did, and for a time all three of us were absorbed in a pencil sketch of a locomotive which he had been working on. I knew he would rather talk about throwing reverse levers than stones, but we got around to that, too. The boys agreed that inasmuch as no one but us three and the officer knew anything about it, the boy the stones missed wouldn't press the matter if I would overlook it that time. I thought it over awhile and finally said:

You two boys are friends and I suppose always will be. Perhaps after all he didn't mean to hit you when he threw stones at you, and since you are not inclined to press the matter I'll do nothing further about it. I ask you to come in to see me once in a while Saturday mornings when you have time and your mother don't need you to run errands or do something around the house. If you find time to make drawings of locomotives or anything else I would like to see them. If you become an engineer you'll need an education, and it would be as well not to miss an hour at school hereafter.

I had an idea that boy would arbitrate his difficulty with the smaller one when I dismissed him the first day and judging that he might prefer making pictures to reading I gave him the opportunity. . . .

I have told you about that case somewhat in detail so you may know how I managed the boys and girls who came into my court. There were hundreds of them, and I can recall but two cases where they ever came before me charged with a second offense.

I didn't attempt to awe or frighten them by looking solemn or severe. I met them as though they had just dropped in for a chat. I was frank with them, gained their confidence, put them on their honor, kept track of them by having them report to me without their knowing that they were doing so, for they all regarded their calls at my office as a favor to me. It was a matter of pride with them too, for they did their best to show me how well they could do the things we were all so interested in.

Didn't this take a lot of time? Of course it did, but not near so much as if I went through the forms of law in giving each one a trial. I violated no law in doing as I did. The mayor was expected to use common sense on all occasions and that's what I tried to do.

. . . .

Though a few girls were brought up for trial, I had no trouble with them. I would not have girls taken before a man for trial, I mean first offenders. A woman who could be a girl with girls should hear such cases. I managed other cases on a plan not laid down in the statute or court rules. One morning a tall, heated-up, angry man walked in and said he wanted to swear out a warrant for a neighbor of his. My caller and I had worked together in the shops of the Lackawanna Company some years before. I knew the man for whom he demanded the warrant also. It seems that old and prolific source of trouble, the line fence, caused the row. They had fallen out over the exact location of a post hole. While Hugh and I were discussing the matter, the party for whom the warrant was desired walked in. His name was Ned. I bade him good morning and asked what I could do for him, he said: "I want a warrant for that fellow there," pointing at Hugh. Hugh was over six feet tall, Ned was a little over five feet. Both were Irish. Hugh was usually easygoing and good-natured; Ned was as scrappy as a hen guarding a brood of chickens. I said: "This is fortunate. Hugh wants a warrant for you also. I shall not have to waste time sending an officer to arrest either of you. Just be seated while I make out the papers." Ned sat down facing Hugh, I left them glaring at each other, went to the desk and began to attend to some deferred business. After staring at each other for about ten minutes they became fidgety. Hugh finally asked if the warrants weren't ready. Then I left the bench, came out to where they sat, and remarked: "I have not made the warrants yet. To do so means costs for one or both of you. No matter which I decide in favor of, the other will take an appeal to a higher court. If the judge does not take the case from the jury and divide the costs between you, he may direct the jury to do so, and you men haven't fifteen or twenty dollars to pay into the court. You are neighbors, never had trouble heretofore, that fence is not being built. Why don't you save time and money by shaking hands, calling the trouble off, and going home to renew your work on the fence."

Hugh said: "All right Mayor, I'll do as you say, but if I had five minutes at Ned I wouldn't want the law on him." Ned bristled up, took a step nearer Hugh and snapped out: "I wouldn't want five minutes at you." I called the day officer, told him to let down the latch on the door, draw the blinds on the windows, and then open the folding doors to a large room adjoining the courtroom. Then I invited the combatants into this room, asked them to remove their coats and get ready. "Get ready. What for?" was the question that came simultaneously from both.

"Why Hugh said he'd be satisfied with five minutes at you. You say you don't need five minutes to do him up. I don't know anything about the rules of the prize ring but I'll stand behind one of you, the officer behind the other and we'll see fair play; get ready. It will be the cheapest way out of the trouble and you'll have to settle it this way or shake hands like sensible men and go home to attend to that fence."

Hugh extended his big, boilermaker's fist, Ned shoved his little bunch of nerves and muscles in it; as he did so he said: "There's me hand Hugh, but I declare to me God I'd rather give ye a wallop of it along side the jaw. The mayor wants us to make peace though, and peace it is." . . .

Some three weeks later I met Ned on the street, he rushed up to me and blurted out: "Did you hear about Hugh, he died this morning and I'm awful glad." I was shocked and indignant. I thought a great deal about Hugh and the idea of a man carrying resentment beyond the grave as Ned evidenced by his unkind remark was more than I could stand, so I said: "You unfeeling little wretch, how can you talk that way about the death of Hugh ———?" Then the significance of his words dawned on him and he hastily corrected himself thus: "Oh, ye don't understand me. I'm grieved to the heart at his death, but I'm glad we aren't inimies as we would have been only for you and what ye done to make us friends again. That's why I say I'm glad." . . .

While the mayor received a salary, he was entitled to certain fees, but I never collected any. I seldom imposed a fine, preferring that the offender retain the money to pay his debts with.

One Saturday about one o'clock I saw a man I had worked with in the mills go into a saloon across the street from the mayor's office. I sent the day officer over telling him to whisper to Billy C——— that the mayor wished to see him in his office. Soon after Billy came in. He was in working clothes. It was pay day at the works, and I thought he hadn't had time to go home with his money before entering that saloon. He asked why I sent for him, and I inquired how much money he had about him. Instantly his hand shot down into his pocket and out came a roll of bills. I took them, counted eighty-three dollars and a half, placed the money in an envelope, put it in the safe and shut the door. Billy, astonished and angry, asked why I did that. My answer was: "That's what your fine amounts to." "Fine for what?" came his question. "For getting drunk," I said. "I'm not drunk." "No, not yet, but you were going to get drunk." Then he exploded: "Heavens and earth, mayor, surely you can't fine a man for going to get drunk." All I said to that was: "Well don't you see that I've done it."

He then became abusive, and I reminded him that I might lock him up for contempt of court, told him to go home and come to the mayor's office that evening with his wife. He left the courtroom swearing vengeance on the mayor. I detailed one of the police officers to walk after him and tell Mrs. C——— to come with him that evening. They came at the appointed time. Each one showed anger and resentment.

I took the money from the safe, counted it, handed it over to Mrs. C——, and, placing a receipt for the amount before them, asked that they affix their signatures to it. That done I said:

"About one o'clock today the firm of which you are a partner, Mrs. C——, was on the verge of bankruptcy. I appointed myself receiver of the assets, which I have just turned over to you. Some months ago Billy lost his month's pay in a saloon. The saloon-keeper says he didn't take it, and I believe him. A man whom I suspect of being a pickpocket was in the saloon when Billy lost his money. I have no evidence to proceed on or that man wouldn't be at large. He walked into the saloon after Billy today, and that is why I fined him $83.50.

"Hereafter, Billy, when you draw your pay go home with it first, turn it over to Mrs. C——, and if, in your sober senses, you feel that you can afford to waste a dollar or two for liquor, take that much and no more. You'll find it ample to make a fool of yourself with. Don't go into a saloon again with your whole month's pay in your pocket." Mrs. C—— and Billy left the office after extending their hearty thanks and blessings for the $83.50. I felt far richer than if I had kept the money; perhaps the amount wasn't large enough to tempt me to keep it.

.   .   .   .

I had given much thought and study to the tax levies of Scranton, and discovered that, although my predecessors in the mayoralty had collected thousands of dollars in fines, they were never considered, or, if they were, such consideration was not manifest in the tax duplicates in the shape of reduction in the citizens' taxes. . . . I discovered also that those who paid fines were poor men whose misfortune rather than criminal instinct threw them into the clutches of the fining power. For being drunk a man could be fined anywhere from one to ten or more dollars. The circumstances sometimes governed, but usually the culprit was fined about as much as the magistrate could find in his clothes. I studied the drink habits and prevalence of thirst among our citizens as well as a temperance man could, with the result that I determined not to fine a man for being drunk, or drunk and a little disorderly, if I could avoid it. The men brought before me for drunkenness were, for the most part, hard-working, industrious citizens who on drinking more than was good for them became unsteady of foot and perhaps loud of voice. They were, as a rule, apprehended in, or after leaving, the saloon, and, having no restraining hand or head to guide them, fell into the clutches of the law as represented by a policeman. The saloon then was regarded as the poor man's club. He could afford no other, and for partaking too liberally of its offerings he might be arrested, locked up, and either fined or given a term in jail. I discovered that others drank to get drunk too, some of our "best people" in fact. They had liquor by the case sent to their homes, they drank it in their clubs and on quite a few occasions some real good people smashed each other's heads and hats in these clubs and other places I could name. On such occasions there would be some friend or acquaintance present to stop the row and send the offender home in a cab instead of being run in to the station house by the minions of the communistic mayor who might not appreciate the fact that he would be dealing with a representative of the "best people" when the case came on for trial in the mayor's court.

The workingmen who came before the mayor charged with drunkenness were heads of families as a rule. They owed the grocer, shoemaker, or tailor perhaps. If I fined them I would be making the city of Scranton no richer, and would be depriving the drunkard's wife and family of part of their livelihood; I would be making it harder for them to pay their debts. Instead of fining them I usually emptied their pockets of all the money they had [and] placed it in a sealed envelope in the safe. I required the man to accompany his wife to the mayor's office, where, on signing a receipt, jointly, I would turn the money over to the wife.

Men who in previous years had asked for assistance from the poor board had their pride touched to such an extent by my treatment that they quit drinking and supported their families instead of turning them over to the town to do it for them. I believed then and do now that I saved money for the taxpayers of Scranton by not fining her citizens for the same kind of lapses that wealthier men were guilty of but escaped detection under cover of a fashionable club. . . . But better far than money, the self respect of the offenders was preserved.

When I was nominated for mayor the second time my political enemies contrasted the amounts turned into the city treasury in fines by my predecessors with the amount turned in by me. One writer plainly intimated that I had pocketed the fines. It happened that the young man's father had worked with me at one time. We were on very friendly terms. I then held the joint receipt of the young fellow's father and mother for about eighteen dollars that I had saved up from the father's earnings by not fining him one day when he appeared before me charged with drunkenness. I saw the father, explained the matter, and left it to him to cause his son to make the proper correction of the record; he did.

Attacked by other writers, I wrote out a statement of what I had done, wound up with this paragraph, and published it.

The people of Scranton now know just how much I collected as fines, how much I turned in and why I didn't collect more money in fines. They may verify what I here tell them by an examination of my dockets. If I am reëlected I shall continue to pursue the same course and shall not turn the money of any man into the city treasury as a fine when it should be devoted to the payment of his just debts.

I was reëlected and did as before. I continued the same policy during a third administration of the office of mayor.

The work of uplifting society was not fashionable then, and I did not have the aid of any organized body but the Knights of Labor in my practical work of "spreading sweetness, goodness, and light." The self-annointed, personally appointed censors of our morals who are now devoting time, talk, and other people's dollars to scavenger work in the slums, alleged social betterment, community welfare with an occasional excursion into the realms of the latest outlet for virtuous strenuosity, white slavery, weren't agitating the atmosphere then in vociferating against the practices in the train of which many modern evils follow. I can name the fathers of some present-day reformers who were engaged in exploiting the workers and contributing the money so acquired to the building and upkeep of churches without giving a thought to those whose labor provided the funds they were expending and whose homes they may have been pauperizing.

Understand me fully. I did not treat all offenders alike. First offenders may never be second offenders if they are treated properly and their better natures are appealed to and touched. There are some natures that kindness does not appeal to. I was not an "uplifter." My idea was to reach the individual before he went down to a point from which he needed uplifting. . . .

I endeavored to approach every trial with an open mind and so far as I could, to put myself in the place of the defendant. . . . I wasted no sympathy on the undeserving once I became convinced they were undeserving. To such the full penalty of the law was meted out, and they were told just why I did it. . . .

I am persuaded that the uplifters, the sympathizers with criminals, and the apologists for those who commit crime should either be excluded from courtrooms or silenced while there.

The field of real reform is so large that the reformer need not invade the precincts of a courtroom to do good if he is so inclined. I long ago came to the conclusion that the most successful reformer is the one who earnestly undertakes to reform, and succeeds in reforming, himself. Too many "go in for reform and uplift" because it is a fad. . . .

I had no set rule or cut-and-dried plan to follow as mayor. I didn't know any more than to greet every day's sun after it arose without going away from my work to meet it. I judged what I found of good and bad without looking for worse. The fact that men and women who weren't any better than the law allowed, when I was mayor, and came before me to certify to that fact, became sober, industrious, respected members of society and still call me their friend as a result of our day in court together is the one bright spot in my mayoralty life that never grows dim.

The fact that the indebtedness of the city of Scranton was greatly reduced during my incumbency of the office of mayor was not due to me, although I helped some. We had competent, trustworthy men as controller, city solicitor, treasurer, and city clerk. These officials gave their time and best thought to the financial affairs of the city. It is true that I as mayor had to sign all appropriation bills and that I scrutinized each item carefully, but I never found any of them incorrect, unnecessary, or exorbitant.

The city councils were, for the most part, composed of good hardheaded citizens who hadn't learned that in a few years a new word would, with every right of entry, appear in the dictionary with a new meaning. Graft then had to do with horticulture or floriculture; it has another and a different meaning today.

My chief cause of complaint against the councils was because of their economical way of doing things. On taking up the duties of mayor, I found the city without a seal or a board of health, although the law creating the city called for both. Between sessions of councils I consulted many members about the necessity for a seal. They said: "Go ahead and get one, we'll honor the bill of course." I designed a seal; had the proper inscription circling a representation of a stone bridge with a locomotive on it and a coal breaker. It was all typical of the city and very neatly arranged. When the firm sent the seal to me they sent with it a bill for fifty dollars. I at once paid the bill and sent it to the councils with my approval, expecting to be promptly reimbursed. They laid the bill on the table, appointed a committee to talk to me about it and find out if it was worth the money and why I hadn't obtained the consent of the councils before purchasing it. I explained that the time for making estimates was a long way off, that need for the seal was imperative, and that I had consulted all the council men I could reach and received their approval before ordering it. That committee appeared satisfied with my action, the seal, and the price. They reported to [the] councils and in doing so said that the seal was paid for and there need be no haste displayed in reimbursing the mayor. If anyone should tell you that I have no interest in Scranton you may say that I still own its official seal for at last accounts it was still in use. . . .

The charter of the city called for a board of health. The statute provided for one, but the city authorities never established one until I took the matter up and pressed it so persistently that the councils finally passed an ordinance establishing the board and defining its duties.[5] The mayor was ex-officio chairman of the board of health, and in conjunction with Dr. William E. Allen, a member of the board, we drew up the rules and regulations to govern its activities. The fact that these rules are still in force speaks well for the foresight and ability of Dr. Allen, for he had most to do with their preparation.

The temptation to narrate many incidents, humorous, serious, and pathetic, is great, and, since I can resist anything but temptation, I am entitled to commendation for not inflicting a number of them on you. I've told you sufficient to enable you to form an estimate of my fitness for the office. I made a good mayor, I'm sure of it, but if you need additional evidence go to Scranton and ask those who knew me as mayor. If they don't bear out what I tell you—well, they are not as truthful as I give them credit for being, that's all.

I'll tell you of two happenings before leaving the mayor's office. One day in June, 1878, an officer came into the courtroom with a small-sized, nervous-looking man he had apprehended for peddling on the streets without a permit. The man's face attracted my sympathy at the first glance. The features were clear cut, sharply outlined and expressive of determination and will power. To me he looked hungry and his looks didn't belie him. I asked what he had been peddling, he said: "Soap." "Why didn't you apply for a permit before beginning operations?" was my next question. "I didn't know anything about a permit or that it would be necessary. I don't want to beg. I need money to buy food and lodging. Just had a trifle, with it I bought some soap and began to sell it when I was taken before you. I want to earn what I eat and that, may it please your Honor, is why I sold soap. I had no money to pay for a peddler's permit or license, even if I had known that such a thing would be necessary."

It was about noon, we chatted awhile, and during our talk I learned that he was a Virginian, born and raised in Brunswick

[5] This was done in 1878.

county, that he had been in the Confederate army, had been at work in the North until his health gave way, was working his way back home, and here's where I found him. I invited him to lunch, he accepted, and I took him home with me instead of to a restaurant. Our folks had never seen a real, live rebel, and I wished to let them look on one. I forgot to say that while he was in the courtroom some one went away with his basket of soap. I never tried to find out who took it, for I gave the one who abducted it credit for good intentions. A man who will steal soap must intend to lead a clean life.

I gave him a permit; he started out with a new outfit and a request to make my office his headquarters, particularly on rainy days.

One day I called Chief DeLacy in and introduced him to Mr. Crane as a veteran of the Civil War. They shook hands warmly. DeLacy asked: "What regiment were you in, comrade?" I don't remember the number but it was a Virginia command. DeLacy looked the man over critically and then extending his hand again said: "That was a hell of a regiment. We had no end of trouble with it. Sit down and let us talk about it." I laid down the club I had provided before the introduction. I didn't know just what form the hostilities would assume and deemed it prudent to take no chances. Those two men wasted more good paper making sketches of the field where the battle of the Wilderness . . . was fought than would pay for all the soap Crane missed selling by reason of the discussions.

DeLacy invited Mr. Crane to address his Grand Army Post; he did and lived to tell the tale. If I am not mistaken that was the first time a Confederate soldier addressed a body of Union veterans. After that occurrence I began to suspect our Scranton G. A. R. men of being a dirty lot. They would go home two or three times a week with their pockets full of soap, and Crane did a rushing business in army circles.

If you have never listened to an old veteran of the Civil War talk, just hunt one up and have him tell you about it. You needn't ask him to tell about any one but himself, that will be enough. If he was a Federal soldier, you'll wonder the war lasted half as long as it did. If he is a Confederate, you'll wonder why it ever stopped.

.   .   .   .

One day Crane came into my office, his face radiant and happy. He held out a letter to me. In it I read that a sum of about nine thousand dollars had fallen to him and he was requested to return to his home and settle up things. We parted, and at parting he took a gold ring from his finger, with his name inscribed on the inside, and placed it on one of mine. I told him I never accepted presents. His face clouded a bit, then brightened up again as he said: "This is not a present, or of the present, this is unending and for all time. Won't you wear it and make me happy in the thought that something of mine is near you?" How could I refuse? I didn't, and not for one hour has that ring been absent from the place on the little finger of my left hand where Harry D. Crane placed it with his blessing on that October day in 1878.

. . . The circus parade, from the bespangled queen of beauty sitting sideways on a white pony in gaudy trappings, attended by a retinue of bashi-bazouks, Turks, or Corconians [Khoi-Khoins?] riding high-stepping Arab steeds—bred in old Kentucky—all the way through the line of rumbling animal cages to the tootful, if not tuneful, steam calliope, has always attracted me. . . . I have the same desire to crack peanuts and sit close to the ring on the inside of the tent when the "elephants go round and the band begins to play" as I did when I got my first look at wonderland in old Dan Rice's show.

You must not blame me, then, for taking a good and long, if not longing, look at the flags atop of the tent of Coup's circus while on my way to the mayor's office on the morning of August 4, 1879. The flags of all nations, blown by a stiff breeze from the west, were in plain view. I stopped to take a good look and saw just one little, greasy-looking American flag competing, in the wind flapping, with the ensigns of several foreign lands along the rim of the main tent, while up at the top, above all else, swung a brand-new British flag, or Union Jack. When I reached the mayor's office I wrote the following note and sent it by one of the day police officers to Mr. Coup:

MAYOR'S OFFICE
AUGUST 4, 1879

W. C. COUP, ESQ.,
DEAR SIR:

This morning in the arrangement of the flags over your pavilion the British flag was the highest. If you raise the flags after the rain ceases, you will take the precaution to place the American flag in its proper position, that is: *above all others*, for no other flag can float above it in this city.

Very respectfully yours,
(*Signed*) T. V. POWDERLY
MAYOR

That letter was entrusted to a German policeman who had just returned to Scranton after serving several years in the regular army of the United States. I could have sent it by an Irish officer just as well, but I only wanted the British flag taken down and not the tent. I therefore deemed it prudent and diplomatic to arrange the matter with Mr. Coup through a neutral power. I told Jacob Goerlitz to hand the note to Mr. Coup or his manager. He did. I had no press agent in that transaction except Mr. Coup. He gave my letter out for publication and with it one of his own. In the absence of an evening paper he had a circular distributed through the city. It had my letter and his reply, the latter as follows:

SCRANTON, AUGUST 4, 1879

HON. T. V. POWDERLY, MAYOR
DEAR SIR:

I am in receipt of your note of this morning, calling my attention to the placing of the British flag at the top of the pavilion. That was an oversight on the part of one of our employees who could not find the large American flag we always use on such occasions.

I have purchased a new American flag and you will find it in its proper place, viz: "above all others," this afternoon and evening.

I thank you for calling my attention to this matter and herein invite you and all the other good people of Scranton to attend our afternoon and evening performances. I promise them a treat in the shape of a real American show under one of the best American flags I could find in Scranton.

I am sir,

Respectfully yours,
(*Signed*) W. C. COUP

It was the most natural thing in the world for me to write that letter. Yes, I was patriotic but I wasn't parading my patriotism. That letter meant just what it said and all it said. . . . I have, all down the years that have slipped away since August 4, 1879, refused to take part in demonstrations where the American flag wasn't first, foremost, and highest.

Was I commended for what I did? Did any man or set of men publicly take the ground that I did the right thing that morning? Not one. I was ridiculed through the press and from the pulpit. A clergyman, commenting on the incident the following Sunday, said among other things: "No defence of our glorious flag is required at the hands of an importation whose name is Terence."

. . . . .

The Scranton papers did not refer to the matter editorially or otherwise. One of them, the Scranton *Republican* of August 12, 1879, quoted the following from the *Evening Chronicle* of Pottsville, Pennsylvania:

Mayor Powderly, of Scranton, having noticed through his greenback spectacles that the English flag at Coup's circus floated higher than the stars and stripes, emulated the monkey that climbed the tree and wrote to Mr. Coup about it, requiring him to arrange his flags so that the American flag would float "above all others" in Scranton. This is an exhibition of patriotism which should never be forgotten. We would advise the people of Scranton to at once erect a monument to Mayor Powderly, surmounted with the eccentric agitator's statue with the American flag in one hand raised "above all others," which others should be placed in the left hand. These, with a copy of his Shenandoah speech pinned to his left lapel and the traditional knife in his boot, with its accompanying motto, should complete the figure. The people of Scranton could then afford to bid the mayor a last farewell, and it would be money in Mr. Coup's pocket to shoot the white whale, burn that mummy of a devil fish, and tote Powderly around in their stead.

The writer of that intended it to be funny, even humorous. I have no doubt he laughed over it when he wrote it. The *Evening Chronicle* of Pottsville was at that time controlled body, boots, and breeches by Franklin B. Gowen, president of the Philadelphia and Reading Co. The Shenandoah speech referred to was delivered at Columbia Park, Shenandoah, on July 23 of that year. It was a Knights of Labor gathering I spoke at. The *Chronicle* garbled my words, distorted my advice to the miners assembled at the meeting, and, by reason of its inaccuracy, drew down on my head the wrath of a number of Roman Catholic priests who took the statement of the *Chronicle* at its face value. Since I shall tell you all about that at another time I'll not bother you with the details now.

Other papers referred to the flag incident in a sneering way. I was charitable enough to ascribe their allusions to me as the output of political envy and took no public notice of their attacks or insinuations. I was in politics then; anything I might have said would not be regarded as wholly free from political buncombe or flapdoodle. . . .

One Sunday afternoon in Chicago I stood on a street corner watching a procession of alleged socialists going out to the lake front to hold a meeting. A man at the head of the procession carried a large, blood-red flag. Somewhere along in the line I saw a marcher carrying a small American flag fastened to his umbrella with the stars turned down. I walked alongside of him a short distance and called his attention to the improper position of the flag. I was under the impression that he did it through ignorance. He told me to go to hell. . . .

Next morning I called on Mayor Harrison, and during our interview he inquired if I had seen the procession the day before and what I thought of it. I expressed my sentiments freely and unreservedly and ended by saying, "such a procession as that couldn't parade the streets of Scranton with the stars and stripes behind the red flag and upside down at that." He smilingly asked what I would do to prevent it. Here is my answer: "I don't know just what I would do, but that procession would not insult our flag. The mayor would do his duty by demanding that due respect be shown our flag, and then, if that procession refused or failed to comply with his demand and persisted in going forward, it would do so only by passing over the dead bodies of the mayor and his police force. I don't know just what I would do."

The following evening I attended and spoke at a joint session of a number of local assemblies in Chicago. Several faces in the meeting appeared familiar to me and at first I could not place their owners. Finally it dawned on me that I had seen them pass before me in the parade of the day before. They were just the men I wanted to talk to. When my turn came and I had spoken for a few minutes, I referred to the socialist procession, in no very complimentary terms either, and among other things said this:

To my way of looking at things the man who is indifferent to the manner in which the American flag is treated should be living in another country than this. I do not refer now to the silk, the bunting, or other material of which it is composed, neither do I refer to its colors or their arrangement; what it stands for—and it stands for more than any other flag, ensign or banner on earth—is what every American should see between the stripes and interwoven around the stars when he looks at our flag. Notice how I say that, it is your flag and it is my flag, but far more than either—it is our flag. Every broad, majestic river, every tiny rivulet, every hill, mountain, and plain, every field of growing grain, every meadow that yields substance to cattle, every town, hamlet, city, and state, every mine and workshop, every mercantile and commercial establishment, every factory and railroad, every turning wheel of industry, every lathe and loom, every bit of parchment or paper or scroll of pen that records the progress of our country to higher altitudes in art, invention, science, literature, and handicraft, yes, every HOME in this broad land, loom up before the American who looks upon and reads our flag aright, for by the searchlight of patriotism he may see all of these and more in the sunlight of a world's promise of peace and prosperity to mankind as it radiates over land and sea from our flag.

When you translate our flag into language you read an inspiring, human document, written in the blood of men who loved liberty of act and conscience better than power or gold; a document written by the reflected light of the coming stars that glisten now upon its field of blue to illumine the pathway over which lovers of liberty throughout the world may travel toward the Democracy of the future in which Latin, Teuton, Celt, and Slav shall unite to proclaim liberty and brotherhood throughout the world and to all the men and women of earth.

While I am proud of being a native-born American and would not exchange my birthplace for any other on earth, I entertain no prejudice or feeling against any other American who may have been born in a foreign land. I have known and now know citizens born beneath alien skies whose patriotism equals that of any man born on the soil of America. My father, though of foreign birth, lived and died as good an American as any man I ever knew.

Shortly after landing at Ogdensburg, N. Y., in 1827, he declared his intention to become a citizen of the United States. Removing to Carbondale, Pennsylvania, before the expiration of five years, he applied for final naturalization papers there, and, since there was no Bureau of Naturalization to conduct proceedings, he failed of securing a certified copy of his first papers. As a consequence he had to start all over again. The distance from Carbondale to Wilkes-Barre is thirty-five miles. In the thirties of the last century a stage made semiweekly trips between the two places. Wilkes-Barre was, and is, the capital of Luzerne county, but being in a hurry my father walked fourteen miles over the mountains to Bethany in Wayne county, declared his intentions anew, and when the required period had elapsed he walked over again and carried back with him the document which made him "a free man, accountable to God and the United States without let or hindrance of any other government or country on earth." I quote his exact language as stated in my presence some years afterward.

Americanism is not a matter of birth; it is of the conscience and heart. He who on landing on the soil of the United States is imbued with a desire to live forever free from the rule or dictation of any foreign state, to respect and obey our laws, to sustain our institutions, to honor our flag and what it stands for, is American in his heart. When he holds his certificate of naturalization in his hand, he becomes the equal before the law of every other American. If he accepts that certificate with a reservation, mental or otherwise, he is not an American either in heart or conscience, and I would not permit such a man to enjoy the privileges of a free man. Something more than an oath before a magistrate of the law, something more than the testimony of witnesses that a man has resided for a stated time in a certain jurisdiction, something more than a knowledge of our language or ability to read and write it, should be demanded of the applicant for Americanization before a naturalization court. Schools of Americanization are being established and they are very good, but the man or woman on whom citizenship is conferred should stand in open court before the bar of public opinion, with his neighbors, his American neighbors, surrounding him, ready to meet every honest man who could challenge his right to that greatest of honors as to his sentiments toward our country and our flag. Every neighbor should be a character witness. If sentiments of loyalty to king, czar, foreign potentate, or government of any description could be testified to, if any slighting allusion to our country, its government, its institutions or its flag could be proved as indicative of the attitude of that candidate, then he should be denied admission to the American family. No man of foreign birth should be expected to banish love of native land from his heart, but love of native land and adherence to a foreign government, or power, differ materially. . . . Undying love for the institutions of the United States is what we expect from every man or woman who becomes American by naturalization.

As I write these lines the zenith of the year 1914 has been reached and passed. A conflagration of incendiary origin has burst into flame in Europe. A prince of the house of Hapsburg has been assassinated and that has been given as the cause of the war now in progress, but the train ignited by this match was laid after Sedan in 1871, and may be traced to the foot of every throne in continental Europe. Before 1871 the political history of Austria was traced in terms of deceit, deception, duplicity, treachery, and broken pledges. Germany has treated her treaty with Belgium as a "scrap of paper"; she learned how to treat treaties as nothings from Austria, for that government . . . during the wars with Napoleon, held no pledge as binding, no promise as sacred, no agreement as valid. . . .

I am personally acquainted with hundreds, yes thousands, of subjects of the Austro-Hungarian Empire and from their lips have heard the story of that government's treachery and underground work among them in the United States. Consular agents, clergymen, prominent men who represent the Austro-Hungarian countries, have been commissioned to use every influence they possess to cause immigrants from that empire to send every dollar they can spare from their earnings back home to be invested there. They are urged not to become citizens of the United States. The Slavic subjects of Francis Joseph have told me repeatedly that every influence known to craft and intrigue is used to prevent their Americanization. I am persuaded that when a Slav applies for citizenship, he does so as the result of conviction that this is to be his future home, that he has arrived at the conclusion that he will in future abide by our laws, live up to our ideals, and in reality be one of us. . . .

I am asked by our President to remain neutral, and I shall respect his wishes, for as an American I believe it to be my duty to stand behind him with all my power and influence. Mentally, however, I cannot remain neutral without doing violence to the promptings of my own conscience. I have no faith in the governments of Germany or Austria-Hungary. I fear that the flame now spreading throughout Europe shall continue to spread until it shall be extinguished in American blood. I hope we may be able to remain neutral; I fear that it will be impossible to do so.

When talking to my American brothers, of foreign birth, in the labor movement I have tried to point out the difference between the alien applying for naturalization and the American citizen. On landing in this country the immigrant is a subject and not a citizen. He is subject not to the will of a free people but to an individual who claims to hold him in subjection by power given from on high by divine right; he is a subject of one sovereign who claims the power and right to rule his body and his soul. All that the word implies is included in that one word: *subject*. The American is a citizen subject only to his God and his country; he is not subject to one sovereign but is himself one of millions of sovereigns who unite in making the law, in fixing the rule of action to be obeyed, and followed by all.

Chapter Nine

THE TELEGRAPHERS' STRIKE AND OTHER THINGS

THE MAN WHO TESTIFIES to his own acts is apt to be a biased witness. In all probability he will not be charged with using an impartial pen. It has been said by some, presumably, wise man: "Write not a man's deeds until he dies." I hope the man who unburdened himself of that weighty morsel of rot is still alive, and that he may live to recognize his utterance as arrant nonsense. Had he said: Judge not a man until he dies, he might lay claim to some wisdom. The man who accomplishes something is better qualified to tell how and why he did it than one who moves into the world after he dies and cannot of his own knowledge tell anything about it. The post-mortem chronicler of my acts couldn't possibly get the right view of me from any angle. He would have to look through my writings, speeches, and recorded doings so far as he could find them in public or private libraries. He wouldn't be able to tell why I wrote certain things at one time, certain other things at other times and did some things that seemed to be at variance with my utterances and writings. If this man never mingled with those who worked he wouldn't know that an officer of a labor organization cannot always cut across lots to get to a determinate spot. "Straight as an arrow" is true only while the arrow is passing through thin air. The moment the arrow strikes an obstacle in its flight, something happens to the arrow or the obstruction. In either event the arrow no longer goes straight and that holds true, whether the object in shooting it be accomplished or not. An actor in the world's swift-moving drama may be called a weathercock too, but that, if anything, is an argument in his favor, for the weathercock that doesn't yield to the changing winds is of no use as a weathercock. . . .

I am to tell you now of some of the things I did, or [that] happened to me, as General Master Workman of the Knights of Labor. To write the history of the Knights of Labor is an impossibility. Its history was the history of the day in which it moved and did its work. I am aware that some young men fresh from college have tried to write the history of the organization, but they failed. They applied logic and scientific research; they divided the emotions, the passions, and feelings of the members into groups; they dissected and vivisected the groups; they used logarithms, algebraic formulas, and everything known to the young ambitious graduate of a university. . . . They attributed to me certain motives, ambitions, and intentions that I never dreamed of. From where they sat, while writing, they endowed me with a firmness I never possessed or a weakness most unparalleled. Others claimed I was very inconsistent in many ways. These came nearest to being right; I was inconsistent. I changed my mind and my tactics frequently. Haven't you heard that "a wise man changes his mind often; a fool never"? Among the many names applied to me no one ever called me a fool—in my hearing—and I never read of it. Wasn't it Gladstone who said: "I'll say what I believe today though it contradict everything I said yesterday"? The only really consistent man I ever knew was an inmate of the asylum for the insane at Danville, Pennsylvania. He believed in the same thing all through his asylum days. He claimed to be King Charles the First and indignantly repudiated the rumor that he had been beheaded. . . .

I was called weak and strong, conservative and radical, steady-going and erratic, religious and irreligious, reverent and irreverent, and many other things. I was called a visionary oftener than anything else. . . . Perhaps there may have been ground for each statement, but on making a mental inventory of the men who charged me with these things I thought I detected symptoms in each of the very complaint he thought I was suffering from. The historian tries to cause you to see through his glasses, you know. We'll find what we hope to find, too, even if we have to invent it. So much by way of preparing your mind for a recital of a few things that I was concerned in during the time I was General Master Workman of the Knights of Labor.

At the second regular session of the General Assembly held in St. Louis, Missouri, January, 1879, I was elected Grand Worthy Foreman, the second place in the list of officers. At that session the time of holding the General Assembly was changed from January to September, and at the Chicago session held pursuant to that change I was elected to succeed Uriah S. Stephens, who was obliged to decline a reëlection owing to failing health. From September 5, 1879, until November 30, 1893, I was continued in the office of Grand (afterward changed to General) Master Workman.

When I accepted the office of G. M. W., at Chicago in 1879, it was with the intention of retaining the place a year or so. Just bear in mind that I was elected mayor of Scranton in February, 1878, and Grand Master Workman in September, 1879. You see the charge, so often repeated, that I made the Grand Master Workmanship a stepping stone to the mayoralty had no foundation in fact. . . .

After my election, and before I was sworn in as mayor, I passed an examination before the board of examiners of Luzerne County and was registered as a law student with Ira H. Burns, then city solicitor of Scranton. I devoted my spare hours to reading law until elected Grand Master Workman. On that day I closed my law books and they remained closed until December 1, 1893, when, on resigning as General Master Workman, I brushed the dust of fourteen years from them and resumed my studies.

The salary of Grand Master Workman from 1878 to 1883 was $400 per annum. As mayor my salary was $1500.

Quite a few people believe the officeholder banks all of his salary during his term and lives happily forever after. Others there are who regard the salaried officeholder as a culprit; they have been educated to look upon him as a robber anyway and do their best to rob him. . . . Not a week passed during my incumbency of the mayor's office that I didn't have to buy tickets for balls, picnics, raffles, excursions, church fairs, bazaars, and a number of other things. . . . Raffles seemed to be the favorite method of getting cash from me. Had I won all the pigs, turkeys, cows, horses, and shotguns that were raffled off and for which I bought tickets while mayor I could stock a good-sized farm and arm enough men to guard my investment. One month I saved the tickets I invested in, and, on deducting the amount paid for them from the salary I received for that month, discovered that the lowest wage I ever received as a machinist would have enabled me to save more money. . . .

One of the most respected citizens of Scranton, a man who lived and died in an odor of sanctity, doubly distilled, asked me once to contribute a certain sum to a church affair, and, when I told him I couldn't afford to do so, he said: "Oh! come now, put your name down, it won't come out of your pocket, you can get your hand in the city treasury any time you like."

I learned enough of politics to become convinced that the politician is just as honest as those who elect him. The day is coming when it will be just as unfashionable for the people to rob a public servant as for that personage to rob the people, and for fear I may not live to see that day, let me tell you now that I have done something to effect the change.

From September, 1879, to October, 1884, I turned the salary I received as Grand Master Workman back into the treasury of the Knights of Labor. I never received credit for this except in the General Assembly, and deem it but simple justice to the man I am writing about to make it plain that it was not the munificent salary that held me in office.

It never was the intention of those who founded and built up the Knights of Labor to resort to the strike as first aid in the settlement of differences between employer and employed. Don't forget that the founders were all trade unionists who had seen the futility of ill-advised, hastily begun strikes.

Here let me say that I don't know, and never knew, an officer of a labor organization who favors or favored the strike except as a last effort to effect a redress of grievances. The public has been educated to believe that labor leaders, as they are called, just glory in and fatten on strikes. Prior to my first election as

Grand Master Workman I declared my position on the strike question and stated that I would never favor a strike until I became convinced:

First: That the cause was just

Second: That every reasonable means had been resorted to to avert the strike

Third: That the chances of winning were at least as good as the prospect of losing

Fourth: That the means of defraying the expenses of the strike and assisting those in need were in the treasury or in sight of it.

I said it, and repeated it; I wrote and rewrote it so that our entire membership knew to a positive certainty just where I stood on that vital question. I didn't write or talk for public consumption that I might win public favor for the Order or myself. I meant every word of it. Our membership knew that I regarded the strike as a system of warfare, and that if I should be expected to make war the law should be complied with and the sinews of war provided prior to declaring war.

Where a strike was forced on us, as it frequently was, the case would differ from one in which we, as an organization, declared a strike. We would have to defend ourselves as best we could. In no such case did I ever fail, or refuse, to do every legitimate thing in my power to win a strike so forced on us.

Not once did I, during my fourteen years' incumbency of the office of General Master Workman, order a strike. I wish to make that so plain to you that I cannot be misunderstood, for I have been severely and unjustly criticized by our own members as well as others for ordering strikes that ended disastrously to the men.

I have also been charged with ordering off strikes at the wrong time, and those who made the charges were not slow to add that I had done so for a consideration and had sold the strikers out. . . .

The world has been educated by a not overscrupulous press to believe that every "labor leader," as officers of labor societies are called, fattens on strikes, revels in strikes, and goes out of his way to order strikes. The reverse of that is the truth. I do not know and never did know a labor officer who did not view the strike with gravest apprehension. Nothing can injure the conscientious officer of a labor organization more than to lose a strike unless it be to win one. If he loses he is sure to be charged with selling out, if he wins he'll be expected to keep on striking—and winning right along. Bad as it is to be charged with selling out a strike that one has ordered, it is terrible to have to bear the accusation of having sold out a strike he had nothing to do with.

While I never ordered a strike, I was directly responsible for the settlement of four hundred and eight cases of dispute between employer and employed in my fourteen years of stewardship, and was instrumental in the adjustment of some seven hundred other differences between workmen and employers. Some of the cases I settled were of grave importance.

My name was prominently associated with four or five large strikes that I had nothing to do with and appeared on the front page of the sensational press in large letters, while my real accomplishments were set down, when noticed at all, in some obscure part of the paper and printed in nonpareil type.

The telegraphers' strike of 1883, the strike on the Gould system in the Southwest in the spring of 1886, the packers' strike in Chicago in the fall of 1886, and the strike on the New York Central and Hudson River Railroad in 1890 were the ones that brought me into unenviable notoriety, and that in face of the fact that I had no act or word either in ordering three of these strikes on or off. I ordered the packers' Chicago strike off, though I had nothing to do with ordering it on. I would order it off under similar circumstances today but would do it in person and on the ground instead of at long range.

Local assemblies of telegraphers were organized during 1882 and the early part of 1883. They knew but little about the aims and purposes of the Order of Knights of Labor, and rarely visited the assemblies of other trades or callings. For the most part they were young, enthusiastic, and hopeful. So secretly did they prepare for a strike that not one of the general officers of the Knights of Labor knew of it until they had formulated their grievances, arranged for the day and hour to strike, and had presented their demands to their employers. This done, they notified me by means of a communication in which this passage occurs:

We are managing this matter ourselves, do not intend to involve the Order in it, and shall need no financial aid, for our strike will not last over forty-eight hours until our members will be called back to their keys again.

We deem it a courtesy we owe to you as head of our Order to acquaint you of these facts and to invite you to meet with us that we may explain in detail what our future plans are.

I accepted the invitation, went to New York, met the executive officers of the telegraphers, and heard what their "future plans" were. Their plans, as explained to me, were the hope of winning based on youthful enthusiasm, an utter lack of knowledge of the resources of the telegraph companies, and an equally lamentable lack of evidence concerning their own weakness. They also lacked organized experience and funds.

I did everything that lay in my power to cause them to revoke the strike order and defer action until the following year. I was afterwards criticized for my action but not by the telegraphers. Here is the plea I made to them:

I regret that you have taken this action without fully and freely conferring with your general officers. The General Executive Board, which numbers a telegrapher as one of its members, should have been consulted before you decided to strike. I hope you may see your way clear to recall the order you have sent out and postpone action until next year. I know that your members have a right to feel aggrieved, but the ills they complain of are the growth of years and can be endured a few months longer in order to insure success.

Next year will be presidential year; by the first or middle of July all of the parties shall have placed their presidential candidates in the field; the campaign will be opening, not only every American citizen but every reading man in the world will be anxious to obtain the news as it is clicked off from the keys held by your members. When that time comes present your demands. In the meantime the General Assembly shall have had opportunity to act on the matter and lay plans to assist you.

If you do this and fortify yourselves by carefully instructing your members how to proceed you may not have to do more than present your claims.

I take no stock whatever in your idea of winning in forty-eight hours. You have the strongest force in the United States to combat; it can summon millions to its aid and can enlist enough men and women to operate a sufficient number of keys to prolong the struggle.

You have done the wrong thing in holding out the hope to your membership of winning in forty-eight hours, for if you do not win in that time many will lose hope and go back to work. Think this over, recall your strike order and await the most opportune time you may ever have to secure what you seek and are so justly entitled to.

That's what I said, and that's what the Secretary of District Assembly No. 45 wrote down and inscribed in their minutes.

My suggestion appealed so forcibly to them that they went into executive session and considered it for over an hour. Then they told me they feared the effect of a recall of the strike order. They were not so sanguine of winning as was the convention that ordered them to strike. They struck that night, and every one knows the result. They did not win in forty-eight hours; the strike dragged on for weeks with men and women returning to their keys here and there at intervals. When finally it ended, disastrously to the strikers, its victims could be numbered by the score.[1] Sometime after the termination of the strike a man named Robert Harding stated through the public press that I had attended the convention of the telegraphers at which the vote to strike was passed, that I encouraged them to strike and promised them financial aid in carrying it on.

John S. McClelland, a member of the General Executive Board, a telegrapher, and familiar with all that had transpired, heard Harding's statement repeated in a telegrapher's local assembly and listened to some language about me that he knew was undeserved. He procured a copy of what I said to the Telegraphers' Executive Board and published it broadcast, adding that he did it as an act of justice to me and with the knowledge and consent of the officers of the Telegraphers' District Assembly No. 45. I doubt very much if that publication changed many minds. He who wants to think ill of a man doesn't want to hear anything to cause him to think well of him.

[1] For additional material on the strike, which, however, ignores Powderly's role and his meeting with the officers of D.A. 45, see Ware, *Labor Movement in the United States, 1860-1895,* pp. 128-31; George E. McNeill, ed., *The Labor Movement; the Problem of To-Day,* New York (1888), pp. 390-92.

That publication became the base of a severe criticism of me by the editorialists of the country, who saw, or affected to see, in what I said something diabolical, seditious, treasonable, and unpatriotic. I would paralyze the transmitter of news at the exact time that people were most in need of it. From the point of view of the man who makes news and wires it, from the point of view of the man who makes editorial on what the newsmaker sends over the wires, I was a rascal so fiendish as to deserve skinning, and they skinned me to a finish. . . .

I am writing this thirty years away from the day I gave that advice. I have since then struggled up the steep ascending grade of life, have passed the great divide that separates youthful enthusiasm from ripened judgment, and, as deliberately as I ever said anything, do I now say that word for word would I give the same advice today under like circumstances. I don't believe in war or in strikes, but if I must do either I'll hit my enemy at the most opportune time to knock him out with one well-delivered, well-timed blow. . . .

As Grand Master Workman I had no authority vested in me to interfere or act in any capacity in a strike. My connection with the telegraphers' strike was just as I have told you. I was called on just once during the strike but in a way that until now the public never heard of. One day when the strike had been in progress about a week or ten days, I was hastily summoned to New York City by McClelland, who met me at Hoboken on the arrival of my train, rode over on the ferry with me, and told me why he desired my presence.

From the beginning of the strike, headquarters had been kept open night and day in New York City for the use of the strikers and their sympathizers. At these meetings speeches would be made to keep up the spirits of the men and women on strike. Each evening a secret meeting of the Telegraphers' Assembly would be held and addresses would be made there also. The night before McClelland sent for me some pretty radical speeches had been made, and on adjournment one of the speakers selected three or four strikers, all men, to meet and confer with him. He told them that, reposing special confidence in them, he sought their coöperation in a plan to bring the strike to a speedy termination by striking terror to the heart of the telegraph company. Fronting the Western Union Building on Broadway was an immense pole which held the principal wires of the country on their way into the building. Destroy that pole, bring its lacing of wires down in confusion, and the strike would be won. Dynamite would do it; he would procure the dynamite, hand it over to them, and two days later, at 8:30 o'clock P.M. he would meet them at a designated spot and show them how to do the terror-striking act.

McClelland told me that one of the men had confided the details to him, that the explosive would be carried to the place in a box, and, though he had advised against carrying out the plan, they were determined to go through with it. What could be done to stop it, what would I advise? I didn't voice what came into my mind but said: "All right, you and I shall meet them and stay with them to see this thing out." He was usually very cool and easy-going but got somewhat excited, and urged that my idea was the wrong one. I said that perhaps it was, but I'd go through with it and he need not stay after he had introduced me to the prospective dynamiters. I added "there won't be an explosion." His reply was to the effect that he hoped not, that he would stay with me no matter what came of it. We met the three men; I was introduced and said to the man carrying the box: "We should not be seen hanging round here. Let you and I take this box to the Astor House; Mac will stay round here with the other boys until Mr. D. comes. Then with him on the ground come to the Astor House, and we'll bring the box down so he can show us how to use its contents." That was agreed to. I had previously written a note, sealed it, and placed it in the hands of the man it was addressed to at the Astor House. The young man, the box, and I occupied a corner in the parlor of the Astor House from about a quarter to nine until about ten forty-five. Then McClelland came in and announced that D. hadn't arrived, that the others had gone home disgusted and we might as well go home. I was stopping at the Astor House so I didn't have to go out of the hotel. Inviting them to my room I carried the box along and, the door locked, I looked McClelland straight in the face as I asked: "Did you really expect D. to come tonight?" He said yes, and all at once a light seemed to start up before his eyes. I suspected that the box might contain a few old boots, a horseshoe or two, and some other truck, but carefully handled it while undoing the wrapping. It was dynamite and enough of it to lift a good part of the lower end of Manhattan Island off its hinges. Carefully I restored it to its place in the box, rewrapped it, and in company with McClelland went to the foot of Barclay street, where we took the ferry boat for Hoboken. McClelland lived there. On the way we deposited the dynamite on the waters of the Hudson River and, for fear it wouldn't sink, we utilized as an anchor an iron bar that the ferry boat company may have been looking for ever since. Before parting from the other man, I secured his name and address. I asked him to go to D.'s house and if he was not there to ascertain where I might find him and report to me at ten o'clock the following day. At nine next morning he was on hand and reported that D. had gone away the day previous and was in Camden. I went to Camden, found him, and told him I intended to have him arrested. He laughed as he said: "I didn't give that stuff to them, some one else must have done so. Anyway you have destroyed it." I served notice on him not to again interfere in the affairs of the telegraphers and he didn't. . . .

Before leaving the hotel I secured the letter I had entrusted to the care of the clerk at the Astor House. The envelope bore this legend:

W. Van Benscoten, Esq.,
    Astor House
    If I do not call for this before morning, open it; otherwise hand it back to me.

(Signed) T. V. Powderly

The note inside contained this:

Friend Van Benscoten:
              A few men propose to do a desperate deed with dynamite; I intend to prevent it. I intend getting possession of the dynamite and should I be apprehended with it in my hands you will know what use to make of this. I shall ask you when I get hold of the dynamite to come to the parlor and see me holding it. The name of the promoter of the plan to use the dynamite is_____.

Should events necessitate your opening this you will say that John S. McClelland who accompanies me has nothing to do with the plan on foot. He called me in to prevent a crime and I intend to do so.

Sincerely yours,
(Signed) T. V. Powderly

On reading it over I believe I would write it differently today, but in that hurried hour I found no time to think or act otherwise.

You are asking why I did not leave the dynamite in the hands of those who carried it to the Western Union Building since I had no faith in D. putting in an appearance? Because I wasn't sure he wouldn't come. I also feared that on his failing to put in an appearance, the men might undertake to do the job themselves. I took no chances.

When I was in the parlor of the Astor House I had Mr. Van Benscoten come in for some purpose or other and while he was there I said: "Don't come too near me, I'm a dangerous character. I have a trunk full of dynamite here and it may go off."

He laughed as he eyed the box and after awhile left the room. The young man beside me grew very fidgety, but I assured him the best thing for us to do was to appear indifferent. I have always entertained a suspicion that he expected to see a couple of policemen walk in and arrest us.

Three years later Jay Gould made a remark in my presence that caused me to wonder why we weren't all arrested that night. But I'll tell you about that when I get around to the great Southwest strike.

I suppose you have been putting two and two together and have concluded that organized workingmen are all dynamiters and a bad lot generally. Well, we are not good enough to be saints or bad enough to pretend to be; but consider the millions on millions of workingmen in this country and from that number subtract the users or advocates of the use of dynamite, and then consider the thousands of clergymen in the country and the number who go wrong; the number of bankers we have in the United States and the number who fall by the wayside, and you'll realize that for the one fool workingman who uses dynamite and does harm with it, a hundred or more businessmen or professional men wreck banks, homes, heart ties, and the lives of other men. Don't forget either that they were workingmen who prevented the use of dynamite that night in 1883. Again, you should remember that the workingman has not had the advantages of training and education the others have been blessed with and as a rule when he does, or attempts, any desperate deed he is smarting under some real or fancied grievance that for the moment produces in his mind what in a wealthy man might be called a brain storm.

Chapter Ten

THE SOUTHWEST STRIKE AND ITS AFTERMATH

IT IS, OR WAS, well known that I not only did not favor the ordering of strikes, but opposed entering upon them until the depths of the last harbor of peaceful adjustment had been sounded. . . . I was as outspoken as I knew how to be on that question. Individuals criticized me for my views, but the general order of the Knights of Labor always approved of my position and by an overwhelming majority.[1] The individual critics said that strikes were beneficial, that they were educational, that they made for progress, that they would illumine a page in history for the workmen of future ages to read with profit and by which they would, or could be guided; also that if men and women suffered and starved for sake of a cause in the here and now it would rebound to the benefit of posterity. Then they would grow wise, and fling the old saw: "The blood of the martyr is the seed of the church" at me. I admitted that there was some truth in what they said, but maintained my position that the cause should be just, that everything consistent with honor should be resorted to to effect settlement before resorting to a strike, that the chance of losing was not greater than winning, and that the means to defray expenses should be in the treasury or in sight.

As to posterity, I believed then and do now that we shouldn't devote too much time to planning for its future. We of today are posterity; we are the posterity for which our forerunners made provision, or thought they did. If we carefully, wisely, deliber-

[1] Neither the rank and file nor important local and district assemblies consistently subscribed to Powderly's attitude on the strike. There was strife on this score within the Order, as well on the question of the control of strikes by the general officers and the establishment of strike funds.

ately, and successfully plan and execute for our forerunners' posterity we shall have done the best for the posterity that may one day be privileged to call us its forerunner.

I don't take much stock in that "blood of the martyr, seed of the church" story either. It is not of record that it was a martyr who originated it. The church that depends for its existence on a supply of martyrs' gore, that finds it necessary to moisten its roots in human blood, is in a bad business and ought to quit it. The church that cannot live and thrive on truth, justice, and love as its seed and has to depend on the sufferings of men whose blood must be shed for it will always need fresh supplies of blood, and it appears to me that as a blessing to humanity, outside of its preachers, it must prove a failure. . . .

Precious lives were lost in strikes; homes were wrecked and children deprived of education through strikes, millions of dollars were lost to labor through them, and in the main this great waste and loss could have been avoided. I could never rid my mind of the idea that in these avoidable strikes we were injuring posterity—our fathers' posterity.

I believe, however, that nothing is altogether lost in this world and in some way the misery, distress, privation, and hunger caused by strikes may have effected some good. . . .

Conditions change so rapidly that what we strike for and win this year may not be worth having next year. In the three hundred and sixty-five days of the year man can accomplish just so much. Today's loss can seldom be replaced by tomorrow's gain.

Memory is a treacherous thing too, and few workmen of 1914 remember, or have learned, anything about the strikes of the eighties. To satisfy myself on that score I visited the railroad yards in Wilkes-Barre one day while waiting for a train and, singling out a few men, engaged them in conversation about labor contentions, strikes, and such things. I just wanted to learn how much they knew of the lessons that come filtering down through the years. Inquiry concerning the strike of 1877, the telegraphers' strike of 1883, the Southwest strike of 1886, elicited no information. Then I asked if they had ever heard of a man named Martin Irons, but the blood of that martyr wasn't known to these members of the present-day church. I suggested the name of John Siney as one they would be likely to recall but they did not know him. I finally got around to my own name, and though all of them had heard the name, they had lost track of the man or what he stood for. . . .

I noticed as I passed along through life that the man who lost his wages, his home, or suffered other personal loss through a strike never enthused sufficiently over the "blood of the martyr, seed of the church" ointment when applied to his hurts to recommend it for use among those he cared for.

The great Southwest strike produced a number of martyrs— we knew them as victims—and if the awful sacrifices made by these men and women did any good for them or posterity I have missed reading about it.

The history of that strike has been written and may be found in the report of a Congressional Committee that went over the entire field of contention under the chairmanship of Hon. Andrew G. Curtin of Pennsylvania.

Before the midnight bell is tolled for me and there yet remain a few who may verify or contradict, let me set down "in my own writing" a brief recital of the part I took in a strike that convulsed society, disrupted industry and, for a time, paralyzed business along the lines of railroad known as the Gould system, in 1886.[2]

In 1885 the men on the Missouri-Pacific R. R. struck for redress of certain grievances, and were fairly successful. They, for the first time, were recognized in the making of an agreement to which they and the company were parties. . . . No one knows, no one may ever know, why that agreement was not lived up to by the subordinate officials of the railroad company. Here and there some act of petty tyranny on the part of a local foreman or superintendent would be complained of and go unredressed. Shop

[2] Compare Powderly's account of the Southwest strike which follows with Ware, *op. cit.*, pp. 145 *et seq.* The accepted version of Martin Irons's role in the strike (see below, pp. 120 ff) is completely at odds with Powderly's. There is good reason for accepting the latter's version. It is confirmed by letters in Powderly's correspondence and by independent evidence in a manuscript study of the Southwest strike, *A Frontier Strike,* by Ruth A. Allen.

discipline would be changed, wage scales altered and in such a way as to give the men cause to believe that a sinister purpose lurked beneath it all. The men were not well organized. The Knights of Labor as an order was weak numerically and only shopmen, car repairers and trackmen were represented, in the local assemblies. The engineers, firemen, switchmen and conductors were organized in the various railway brotherhoods. The members of these organizations, as individuals, professed sympathy for the Knights of Labor and unorganized men who were being subjected to injustice and annoyance right along. At various points along the system the hope was held out that if the shopmen would strike the members of the railroad brotherhoods would support them in the movement by refusing to operate trains if strikebreakers were called in to replace the men who went out.

Some local superintendents and foremen affected friendship for the shopmen and threw out hints that the company would yield quickly in the face of a strike.

In many local assemblies of the Knights of Labor were paid spies who reported every move to the company officials, and, to leave no doubt of their loyalty to the cause of labor, these men were loudest in denunciation of the practices of the railroad officials. In some cases they proposed measures which had for their purpose the provoking of a breach between company and men.

Everything that could be done to precipitate a strike before the men became thoroughly organized was resorted to. As the last straw, a member of the Knights of Labor named C. A. Hall, of Marshall, Texas, was discharged for absenting himself from the shop to attend a meeting of District Assembly No. 101, and this in face of the fact that Hall had been granted leave of absence by the very foreman who discharged him. Realizing that it was the intention to provoke a conflict, the Executive Board of District Assembly No. 101 sent to each local assembly a detailed account of the grievances the men complained of and asked for a vote on the question of striking as a means of redress.

The discharge of Hall did not originally figure in the list of grievances, but so well timed was his dismissal that to the public, which had to depend on a press at that time largely influenced by the corporations involved, it appeared that it was the paramount issue. Public opinion, that fickle jade, would not approve of stopping the traffic of a great railroad system because of the discharge of a single individual, and throughout this country the news was flashed that the strike was "all on account of a man named Hall." This was done to obscure the real issue, or issues, for there were many involved.

The first intimation that I received of a strike or trouble of any kind on the Gould Southwest system came in the shape of a telegram received on March 7, 1886—the day after the strike was ordered—from A. L. Hopkins, an official of the Missouri-Pacific Railroad Company. I was presiding over a meeting of the General Executive Board of the Knights of Labor in the Bingham House, Philadelphia, when the dispatch was handed to me; it follows:

NEW YORK, MARCH 6, 1886

T. V. POWDERLY, SCRANTON, PA.

Mr. Hoxie telegraphs that Knights of Labor on our road have struck and refuse to allow any freight trains to run on our road, saying they have no grievances, but are only striking because ordered to do so. If there is any grievance we would like to take it up with you. We understood you to promise that no strike should be ordered without consultation.

(*Signed*) A. L. HOPKINS

When that telegram was read to the board, one of them said the morning papers, which I had not seen, stated that a strike had been ordered "because of the discharge of a man named Hall"; with that and only that information before me I prepared and sent this reply to Mr. Hopkins:

A. L. HOPKINS, VICE PRESIDENT

M. P. R. R. Co., NEW YORK

Have telegraphed west for particulars. Papers say strike caused by discharge of man named Hall. Can he be reinstated pending investigation?

(*Signed*) T. V. POWDERLY

The Board at once wired Martin Irons[3] as follows: "What

[3] Martin Irons, an interesting example of frontier radicalism who merits far more attention than students of the American labor movement have given him, was born in Dundee, Scotland, in 1833, and came to America at the age of fourteen. He had had a wide range of experiences before he became a member and Master Workman of Local Assembly No. 3476 of the K. of L. in Sedalia, Missouri. Shortly afterward, he became chairman of the Executive Committee of District Assembly No. 101, made

caused the strike? Wire us full particulars at once." This reply was received on the 8th. "Violation of contract by company; look for letter."

On the 8th I received another message from Mr. Hopkins in this language:

Thanks for your message and suggestion. Hall was employed by Texas Pacific and not by us. That property is in the hands of the U. S. court and we have no control whatever over the receivers or *other* employees. We have carried out the agreement made last spring in every respect, and the present strike is unjust to us and unwise for you. It is reported here that this movement is the result of Wall Street influence on the part of those short of the securities likely to be affected.

(*Signed*) A. L. HOPKINS

At that time the General officers of the Knights of Labor had no power lodged in them by law to order a strike on or off, or to interfere in the internal affairs of a district assembly. Whenever the good offices of the General officers were invoked, it was, as a rule, after trouble began and not before. The law of the Order said: "A District Assembly shall have sole authority within its jurisdiction."

The local assemblies along the lines of the Gould system had, during the winter of 1885-86, organized District Assembly No. 101. When the incident to which Mr. Hopkins referred in the last thirteen words of his first dispatch occurred, the local assemblies of Knights of Labor along the Gould system of railroads were attached directly to the General Assembly or divided among three or four district assemblies.

A disturbance on the Missouri-Pacific system in 1885 brought Mr. Hopkins and me together in conference, and it was during that meeting I may have expressed the sentiment attributed to me in Mr. Hopkins's first dispatch. District Assembly No. 101, when

---

up of the employees of the Gould system. He played a leading part in the struggle of the workers against the Gould system, and responsibility for the Gould strike and its violence was universally placed upon his shoulders. He not only was vilified in the press, but also received very shabby treatment at the hands of his fellow workers and a great many Knights. Disillusioned and heartbroken, he left Sedalia after the strike, and dropped out of public view. He was a tired, unhappy old man long before his death in 1900. The ablest and fullest treatment of the Southwest strike and of Martin Irons is Ruth A. Allen's manuscript study, *A Frontier Strike*.

organized, had absorbed the local assemblies over which I, as General Master Workman, had previously had jurisdiction.

It was estimated that 48,000 men were employed along that system who were eligible to membership in the Knights of Labor. An examination of the records in our general office disclosed the alarming fact that less than three thousand members had been reported up to March 1, 1886, by the local assemblies which made up District Assembly No. 101. In the main these were raw recruits who were unacquainted with the aims and objects of the Knights of Labor. They had studied the constitution of the Knights of Labor only far enough to see that "A District Assembly had sole jurisdiction in its own territory." Having the authority to do so and not knowing that the system was practically unorganized, they voted to strike.

Perhaps I should qualify that statement or let Martin Irons do it. Who was Martin Irons, you ask? He was the chairman of the Executive Board of District Assembly No. 101. A Scotchman by blood, a nobleman by nature, a machinist by trade, a conscientious, honest man and though of slight build, a giant in opposition to what he believed to be wrong.

It developed the day after the strike broke out that the Gould system had been preparing for it and was fairly well supplied with men to take the places of most of the strikers. The company officials knew the numerical strength of the organization along its lines, and, while they had enough men to replace the Knights of Labor, they had not calculated on their unorganized employees striking in sympathy with the members of the Order.

As the strike progressed and the chances of winning it faded day by day, the Executive Board of District Assembly No. 101 invited the representatives of the other railroad district assemblies to a conference. The Wabash and Union Pacific systems were, or had been, organized. The former had in 1885 passed through a lockout which reduced the membership to almost nothing, so the main hope lay in the men of the Union Pacific system, District Assembly No. 82. A joint meeting was called for March 20 at Kansas City, Missouri. I was invited, went there, and attended the session. That was my first connection with the Southwest strike. The representatives of the Union Pacific system without hint or suggestion from me refused to engage in a sympathetic strike or place a boycott on freight delivered to them from the Gould system. Thomas Neasham, Master Workman of District Assembly No. 82, stated at the outset that his colleagues and he had agreed while enroute to Kansas City not to jeopardize their interests by violating their agreements in engaging in either strike or boycott in behalf of District Assembly No. 101. Martin Irons was present at that meeting. I met him for the first time that day, and have never seen him since parting from him that night. We occupied adjoining rooms at the same hotel, and spent the evening and early part of the night discussing the perplexities of the situation confronting us. From the lips of Martin Irons I heard a story that night which up to this hour I have not made public, although Irons placed no seal of secrecy on my lips. He left it to me to reveal or divulge as I saw fit. Since then, years after he became a wanderer and an outcast because of the part he played in that struggle, he related to others the facts he divulged to me at a time when the world of labor was being educated by an unfriendly press to believe we were enemies, that he was envious of me, was aspiring to supplant me as General Master Workman and that I was jealous of him. Let Martin Irons speak for himself and then judge for yourself whether a man who envied me would place himself in my power by such a revelation at a time when publicity of it would be most damaging to him. Judge also whether Martin Irons would have reposed such confidence in me had he borne me ill-will. Learn a little of the inside history of 1886 from lips now voiceless:

As you know, Powderly, I had a vote of the assemblies taken on our grievances, and the board met to count it. One member of the board opened the envelopes, counted the votes, and passed them across the table to another member for verification. I sat at the head of the table paying strict attention to the proceedings. I did not count the votes but relied on the statement made to me by my colleagues. The vote as announced to me was favorable to a strike by a large majority. When the total vote was tabulated I made this remark—"I'm sorry they did it for I fear we are not well enough organized yet—." Some days after in company with some members of a local assembly at Moberly one of them said that he distrusted their secretary and feared he was a tool of the company. He said that the secretary did not appear pleased when the vote of the local was against a strike. I remembered distinctly that when the vote of that local assembly was read off at the meeting of the Executive Board of 101 it was largely in favor of strike. I secured from these brothers a statement of how the vote stood.

At Moberly I heard a rumor which alarmed me to the effect that the members of my board had counted a majority for strike when such was not the case. I told a member of our board that I intended bringing the matter up at our next meeting and if I had been deceived I would call for another vote and in such a way as to get the truth no matter what happened to me. We met in St. Louis, in the Hurst Hotel. One of the members of the board invited me to his room saying he wished to consult me on important matters before the board met. When we got off the elevator at the top floor he led the way round to the rear end of the hotel and we entered a room which overlooked a back lot. I noticed him remove the key of the door from the outside, place it in the lock and turn the key after we entered. Then he drew a chair over to a table that stood in the center of the room, invited me to sit down, he taking a seat at the other side of the table. After a few minutes chat he pulled the table drawer out a bit, took out some manuscript, handed it over to me saying:—"read that Martin and sign it." You have seen the statement which I issued reiterating the strike order and affirming that it was legally ordered; well that is the paper he handed to me to sign. When I read it, he said that he heard I intended to have another vote taken and thought this would obviate necessity for it. I said: "Why man alive I don't know anything about this and won't sign it until I consult the board." It seems that while I was reading he pulled his gun and was holding it in his hand beneath the edge of the table. When I said I'd consult the board, he lifted the gun in sight aimed it straight at my head and said:— "Don't put your hands near your pockets, just sign that paper." I did not dare remove my hands from the table. I tried to reason with him but to no avail. He told me that a stranger to the hotel people had engaged that room the day before, paying in advance for a couple of days, had given him the key, that no one had seen us enter the room and if the chambermaid found my dead body next morning it would go out that Martin Irons had committed suicide. With that revolver staring me in the face I signed that paper for I resolved that once free from him I could do as I pleased but if he killed me I would be no better than so much dirt. Now Powderly, what would you have done?

My reply was: "Under so persuasive and convincing an argument as that I would have done just as you did, but why didn't you expose him to the board or have him arrested afterward."

His answer was: "I did not know which of the board stood in

with him, they were not all present; besides that man never left me, sleeping or waking for four days. If out of his sight a minute some one else spelled him off and I realized my death warrant would be sealed the minute I tried anything. In the meantime my letter had gone out to the public, the strike had gained such momentum, had taken in so many workers, had involved so many new issues that the original causes of the strike had been swallowed up and it would not only be useless but would look like treason on my part to do anything."

Martin Irons's course commended itself to my good judgment. He told me . . . how men were deserting at various points, how new men were being brought in as strikebreakers every day, how the members of the railroad brotherhoods had not lived up to their promises not to operate trains with strikebreakers, and that defeat sure and certain was staring them in the face. He asked if I could not secure an audience with Jay Gould when I went east and try to effect some settlement that would get the strikers out of the awful predicament they were in.

He told me the story of his struggle to keep the men from striking until they were better organized, of how newspaper reporters and others sought interviews with him and garbled his words. He told me that men in and out of the Knights of Labor urged him to announce himself a candidate against Powderly for General Master Workman. When he told me of this he added: "Don't believe the stuff that they make me say. I am not a candidate for G. M. W., I don't want a change in that office and I sincerely hope you don't believe what has gone out as purporting to come from me." I assured him that I had not been influenced by the rumors, and anyway he had as good a right to be a candidate for the place as I or any other Knight had. We parted that night with the firm resolve to do all that lay in our power to save as much of the wreck as we could and to keep up a bold front in doing it. While sitting on the edge of the depot stoop waiting for my train, he expressed himself in terms of bitter condemnation of the course pursued by members of the Brotherhood of Locomotive Engineers who had assured him personally that they would,

if a strike were ordered, help and encourage the Knights of
Labor:

They promised me not to pull a car that would be coupled, switched, or
handled in any way by a scab. They failed us in every particular and at every
point along the system. The local superintendents and foremen who expressed friendship for us and told our men the company couldn't stand a
strike were acting for the company to lead us on to strike.

Worse than all some of our own members, tried and trusted men as I
thought, have betrayed us and reported our every move to the companies. I
am sick at heart, for now they are damning me for bringing on a strike that
my best judgment opposed.

Powderly, go to Jay Gould and make any settlement short of absolute
condemnation of us and I'll ratify it.

We were together until my train pulled out. I stood on the rear
platform of the car and waved him a parting farewell. As I stood
in that fleeting moment looking backward I saw, and can see him
now, brush the tears from his eyes and with bowed head turn
toward Golgotha to pick up his cross, a cross which he carried
lonely and alone through long years of agony and ostracism, until
worn, weak and in pain he fell beneath it at Bruceville, Texas. . . .
I never saw him since. . . .

I stopped at Bloomington, Illinois, on my way east and when
at the station to take my train slipped on the depot platform and
fell; one of the baggage hands shoving a truck loaded with trunks
and satchels saw me fall, tried to steer his truck away from me
and in doing so dumped part of his load. A piece of baggage fell
on me, fractured three ribs on my left side, and inflicted some
painful bruises. . . .

I continued my journey to Scranton where I consulted Dr.
Allen, my family physician, who advised my remaining quiet for
a couple of weeks. I arrived home the afternoon of the 25th; I
had wired from Kansas City to our general secretary-treasurer,
Frederick Turner, to call a meeting of the General Executive
Board in New York City on March 27, and on that date I met
with the other members of the board in the Astor House. On assembling and after a brief consultation it was decided to seek an
interview with Jay Gould. With the exception of that part of the
statement of Martin Irons relating to the details of his signing a

renewal of the strike order under duress in the Hurst Hotel, I gave the members of the board a full statement of conditions as I found them. In addition to what Martin Irons told me, he had written me, dating his letter March 21, asking me to leave no stone unturned to put an end to the strike. From that letter I quote this paragraph. . . .

Men are being starved, others assaulted, lives are in jeopardy and property is being destroyed. Wires have been tapped and we are charged with it. I told you enough to convince you that we can't win, but neither of us can make that statement public. I am willing to accept the censure and abuse which must come when this strike ends so let it come before additional suffering is entailed on our struggling members. We must not think of ourselves or what may be said of us. For God's sake Powderly get to Jay Gould and try to convince him that he should give ear to the call of humanity. Do this and may God bless you.

I did, and while God may have included remembrance of that among the many blessings I was favored with, I for years received the curses of men who "knew not what they did." Hoping to shield Martin Irons, I assumed the sole responsibility for the effort I made at his request to interview Jay Gould in the hope of ending a most disastrous and unwise strike.

Shortly after the members of the board came together this letter was sent, by messenger, to Jay Gould at the Western Union Building a short distance from the Astor House:

MR. JAY GOULD
   Sir:
        The General Executive Board would be pleased to have an interview with you at your convenience today for the purpose of submitting the southwest difficulties to a committee of seven for arbitration, three of the committee to be appointed by yourself and three by the General Executive Board, the six to select the seventh member of the committee, their decision in the matter to be final. Should this proposition be acceptable, we will at once issue an order for the men to return to work.
        By order of the General Executive Board.
                                    (*Signed*) FREDERICK TURNER
                              SECRETARY-GENERAL EXECUTIVE BOARD

The last nineteen words of that letter would not have been written had it not been for the statements made to me, verbally and in writing, by Martin Irons, which I had communicated to the board. Under the circumstances we felt warranted in saying that we would order the strike off as indicated.

In his reply Mr. Gould said:

I have your note of this date proposing an interview between your executive committee and the officers of this company, for the purpose of submitting to arbitration by a committee of seven what you term the "southwest difficulties." You are doubtless aware that [in] negotiations which took place here last August between Mr. T. V. Powderly, General Master Workman, and associates, and the officers of this company, it was agreed that in future no strikes would be ordered on the Missouri-Pacific Railroad until after a conference with the officers of the company, and opportunity to adjust any alleged grievances. In view of this fact, attention is drawn to the following correspondence between Mr. A. L. Hopkins, vice president, acting for this company in my absence, and Mr. Powderly.

Here Mr. Gould quoted the telegrams, heretofore referred to, which passed between Mr. Hopkins and me, after which he continued as follows:

No reply to this message was received, but this company's request for a conference was ignored, and its premises at once invaded and its property destroyed by the men of your order in great numbers, who also seized and disabled its trains as they have since continued to do, whenever attempting to run. The Board of Directors of this company thereupon had a copy of the correspondence above given made and transmitted to Mr. H. M. Hoxie, the first vice president and General Manager at St. Louis, with instructions to use every endeavor to continue the operation of the road, and committed the whole matter to his hands.

Mr. Hoxie's overtures, made through the governors of Missouri and Kansas, who stated that they found no cause for the strike, were rejected by your order. These and the subsequent correspondence between him and Mr. Powderly are well known to you and Mr. Hoxie's course has been confirmed by the Board, and the matter is still in his hands. I am therefore instructed by the Board to refer you to him as its continuing representative in the premises.

I am directed to add in behalf of the Board that, in its judgment, so long as this company is forcibly kept from the control of its property, and from performing its charter duties, its business is done, if at all, not under conditions of law, which are common to all citizens, but only at the will of a law-breaking force. Any negotiations with such a force would be unwise and useless. Terms made with it would not be a settlement of difficulties, but a triumph of force over the law of the land. It would mean nothing in their judgment but new troubles and worse. This is the result of their experience.

In the meantime, the Governor's proclamation enjoins upon your men to return to duty, and this company's continued advertisement offers them employment on the same terms as heretofore. The Board further suggests that inasmuch as your order assuming in your communication responsibility for these men and power and control over them, the following from the proclamation of the Governor of Missouri is expressive of their duty and your own:

"I warn all persons, whether they be employees or not, against interposing any obstacle whatever in the way of such resumption, and, with a firm reliance upon the courage, good sense and law abiding spirit of the public, I hereby call upon all citizens to assist in carrying out the purposes of this proclamation; and I also hereby pledge the whole power of the State, so far as it may be lawfully wielded by its chief executive officer, to sustain the company and its servants in said resumption, and to restrain and punish all that may oppose it."

When this proclamation shall be obeyed and when the company's late employees shall desist from violence and interference with its trains, the Board hereby assures them that they will find themselves met by Mr. Hoxie in the spirit in which he had heretofore successfully avoided rupture and cause for just complaint, and in that just and liberal spirit, which should always exist between employer and employed.

By order of the Board.

Very respectfully yours,
(*Signed*) JAY GOULD
PRESIDENT MISSOURI-PACIFIC RY. Co.

In my quoting of the second telegram to me from Mr. Hopkins, on March 7 you will find the word "other" in italics; that I do to call your attention to the fact that in his quotation of that message the word "other" is omitted. Jay Gould was not present when Mr. Hopkins sent that telegram to me, or perhaps the latter would not, by implication at least, have claimed the receivers as employees of the Gould system.

A careful perusal of the letter of Mr. Gould shows that it was intended for public consumption. Worse than that, it contained statements which though unpalatable to our board were incontrovertible. The governor's proclamation was not based on what he knew of the real grievances of the men but on what officials of cities and towns and company officers along the railroad had told him. The men on strike were not interviewed or heard until the

Curtin investigating committee went over the Gould system to investigate the strike, its causes, and some of its effects.

On receipt of Mr. Gould's letter, which fell upon the board like a dash of ice water, the first impulse was to abandon further attempts to reach him, but, remembering my pledge to Martin Irons, I drew up and, with the approval of the board, sent the following:

NEW YORK, MARCH 27, 1886

JAY GOULD, ESQ.,
  PRESIDENT MISSOURI-PACIFIC RAILWAY CO.,
DEAR SIR:

We have received your reply to our communication of this morning.

The statements made in your reply are worthy of more consideration than can be given to them at this moment.

We are not in possession here of the telegrams or communications, or copies of the same, referred to in your letter.

We came here unprepared, with no thought of using them; and even though we had them here, the field that would be opened up for discussion would be so broad that it would take a great deal of time and space to cover it, as contained in your reply.

This would necessitate a review of the transactions of last year, beginning with the strike of 1885, continuing through the Wabash troubles, which brought on our meeting with you in August, down to the strike on the Texas-Pacific and its extension to the Missouri-Pacific lines. We consider that all this is unnecessary at this time. Public interest, the interests of both parties to this controversy, will not be served by a longer continuance of the strike, if there is a shadow of a chance to bring it to a speedy termination.

With that idea in view we prefer to let this discussion rest, and allow the matter to be decided on its merits by an impartial committee of seven, selected as indicated in our communication of this morning.

Let them proceed to adjust the difference, and having settled that matter, setting in motion the idle wheels and hands, we have no objection to that same committee reviewing our actions in the matter, and are willing to be judged, to receive censure at their hands, if necessary, for any shortcomings they may deem us guilty of.

The needs of the hour require that this strike terminate speedily; if that is done the other matters can be very readily attended to.

Very truly yours,
  (*Signed*) T. V. POWDERLY
    GENERAL MASTER WORKMAN
      KNIGHTS OF LABOR

Through William McDowell of Newark, N. J., a Knight of Labor who was acquainted with A. L. Hopkins, it was arranged that I was to meet Mr. Gould at his residence Sunday evening, March 28. There were present in addition to Mr. Gould, Mr. Hopkins and Mr. McDowell. The chair I sat in was placed so that my back was close to a heavy portiere; behind the portiere sat a stenographer taking notes. . . . Of this arrangement . . . I knew nothing . . . until Mr. Gould later on published a report of what transpired at our meeting.

Our conference lasted until close on to midnight. The whole field of contention was discussed. Mr. Gould, at times, condemned the strikers in severe terms, while Mr. Hopkins was at all times conciliatory. Gould's strongest point was that the General Master Workman or the General Executive Board could not control the members of local assemblies. The reason for this I explained, stating as I did so that I had the assurance of the chairman of the executive board of D. A. No. 101 that he would ratify such action as I might advise after our conference ended. With this understanding Gould withdrew his opposition to submitting matters in dispute to arbitration as well as to reinstating members of the Knights of Labor. We parted with the understanding that if the General Executive Board would telegraph Martin Irons to declare the strike at an end, he would wire Hoxie to reinstate the men in their old places regardless of their affiliation with the Knights of Labor and that disputed points would be submitted to arbitration.

On my way back to the hotel and in [the] presence of McDowell I sent this message by wire to Martin Irons:

Had conference with Gould, arbitration agreed upon, your wishes complied with, official message to follow in the morning.

On reaching the hotel I called the General Executive Board together, related what had transpired and, that fault of memory on my part might not mislead them, had Mr. McDowell verify the statement I made. A telegram was then prepared and sent to Martin Irons briefly reciting what had transpired and directing him to declare the strike at an end.

Next morning Mr. Gould wired Mr. Hoxie as follows:

In resuming the movement of trains on the Missouri-Pacific and in the employment of labor in the several departments of this company you will give preference to our late employees whether they are Knights of Labor or not, except that you will not employ any person who has injured the company's property during the late strike; nor will we discharge any person who has taken service with the company during the late strike. We see no objection to arbitrating any differences between the employees and the company past or present.

(*Signed*) JAY GOULD
PRESIDENT
MISSOURI-PACIFIC RAILWAY Co.

Those who imagine that the hours of an officer of a labor organization flow smoothly on in uninterrupted current have never been present at meetings such as we held in New York at that time. Standing in twos and threes at my bedroom door at all hours were reporters for newspapers, agents for stockjobbers, fake labor men who pretended to be members of organized labor and traded on their supposed intimacy with Powderly or some other member of the General Executive Board. Among my many callers were Wall Street men anxious to get even with Jay Gould for some offense, real or imaginary. . . . I was repeatedly advised to purchase the stock of the companies affected by the strike, hold it until the strike would be declared off, and then sell it at a profit. I did not then or at any time while I was General Master Workman buy, directly or indirectly, a share of stock or bond of and kind, neither did I ever consult or read or have any one do so for me, the stock reports. I have been told repeatedly, since resigning as General Master Workman of the Knights of Labor, that I could have become a millionaire through manipulation of the stock market, that I could have done it legitimately and that I neglected my own interests in not doing so.

Perhaps according to the code of ethics which prevailed in the business world of that day I was shortsighted in not availing myself of the many opportunities presented to me. . . . Of an investigating turn of mind, I would like real well to be a millionaire just to see how it would feel, but above that I always wanted, when looking in a glass to brush my hair or adjust my necktie, to see the reflection of an honest face instead of that of a self-seeker and a hypocrite. Not only did I not dabble in stocks but I accepted no gifts or favors from corporations or employers of labor while I was General Master Workman. In justice to them let me say that, though I would not have accepted them, they never offered me any.

When the telegram was sent to Martin Irons it was signed by Frederick Turner, as secretary of the General Executive Board. I was so besieged by reporters at the time that it was deemed best for him to sign it. I knew of it, and approved of it. Martin Irons accepted the telegram in good faith, but because it did not come from the General Master Workman one of the members of the Executive Board of D. A. 101 expressed doubts as to its genuineness and insisted on further delay. Hoxie did not relish the idea of being dictated to by Gould. The newspapers were full of lurid reports of what dire things the men would do if Knights of Labor were not first restored to their old places. A number of unlooked-for stumbling blocks impeded the progress of Martin Irons, who acted in good faith all the time, and the strike was continued. Martin Irons was censured for not insisting on "Knights of Labor first" in the reinstatement of the strikers. He was right in making no such claim, but he could not then explain why without exposing the weakness of his district assembly to the world. Fully four-fifths of the strikers belonged to no organization at all, and it would have been manifestly unjust to discriminate against them. . . .

On March 30 the General Executive Board had another meeting with Jay Gould. After a long and somewhat heated discussion I requested Mr. Gould to ask Hoxie to meet the General Executive Board or a committee of the striking workmen. Gould promised to do so, and a majority of the board went to St. Louis there to renew their effort to bring the strike to an end. I had some thirty other strikes or lockouts to look after, also a few broken ribs to patch up, and did not go to St. Louis. In but one capacity did I again have anything to do with the Southwest strike. The victims of that strike were many; they needed aid. I drew up an appeal for funds to relieve their distress, submitted it to the other members of the General Executive Board, received their approval, and on its promulgation $86,901.26 were subscribed by the general public and organized labor. Over one-half of that amount came from those who were not Knights of Labor or trades-unionists. Hon. David B. Hill,[4] then Governor of New York, sent me his check for two hundred dollars and a personal letter, requesting that his name be not made public. It cannot help or hurt him now to make the fact known, and in addition to say that he frequently favored me with his wise counsel during the days when prudent advisers were few and unwise ones numerous.

At times since then I have been accused of ordering the strike on and off for a money consideration. At other times Martin Irons was charged with being the offender. As I look back . . . I am inclined to think that I erred in remaining silent under the slanders heaped upon me. . . . My connection with that strike was just as I tell it. The course pursued by Martin Irons was as I give it to you. Loyalty to the labor movement sealed his lips and he suffered in silence to the end. It can injure no one now to tell the truth . . . about the why and wherefore of my connection with the Southwest strike. I did not order it on, I did not order it off; a full account of nearly every detail connected with it may be found in the Congressional report of the committee of Congress known as the "Curtin investigating committee." . . .

Those who sit snug and warm by a comfortable fire of an evening reading the daily paper may form opinions on fiction rather than truth; often they do when they read of the doings of members of organized labor. They do not know of the pits and mines laid in the path of the officer of a labor society, they do not reflect that he must rely on his own knowledge, judgment, or intuition in facing obstacles and cannot, as agents of corporations do, rely on advice given by well-trained, well-paid, experienced lawyers.

It is said that truth is mighty and shall prevail; but truth is a good deal like gunpowder or dynamite; it must be handled carefully, not recklessly, deliberately and not hastily. An economical use of truth at times is preferable to a lavish expenditure of it.

[4] David Bennett Hill (1843-1910) entered the United States Senate in 1892, after serving as governor of New York 1885-91.

Martin Irons and I knew where the weak places were in our organization, we knew they were far more numerous than strong ones. The truth was that we had no strong points of vantage in our favor outside of a fickle public opinion inclined to opposition to corporate power rather than friendship for the cause of the striking workmen. The daily press with few exceptions was against us. Public officials and politicians generally were with us to the door of the voting booth. . . . We had no influential friends; professional and business men were not in sympathy with us; the church was almost solidly arrayed on the side of wealth and power. To tell the truth, the whole truth, and nothing but the truth, would in all likelihood have deprived us of nearly every friend we had save God alone, and He, working so far away from us and through ministers who had their ears to the ground whereon the mighty and great did walk, was in danger of being misrepresented too. I know it is the fashion now for churchmen to profess friendship for labor and labor societies, but a Catholic priest, one of the bravest, noblest of men, was disciplined and deprived of his pastorate by his bishop because he espoused the cause of the striking men of the Southwest in 1886.

. . . . .

Chapter Eleven

THE CURTIN COMMITTEE, JAY GOULD, AND MARTIN IRONS

IT WAS AT THE REQUEST of President Cleveland that the Curtin investigating committee[1] was appointed.

When I was able to travel again, after the members of the General Executive Board went to St. Louis, subsequent to our last meeting with Jay Gould, I went to Washington, called on [the] Hon. Andrew G. Curtin,[2] whom I knew very well, and with him went to the White House, where he presented me to the President. Mr. Cleveland gave a patient hearing to what I had to say and then held a private consultation with Curtin. While walking from the White House to the street, Mr. Curtin told me that the President favored the appointment of the committee and would so intimate to the leaders in Congress.

Sometime after the strike ended I was in New York and as was my custom stopped at the Astor House. I couldn't go a hen's race in those days without an account of it appearing in the papers, and, when Mr. Gould noticed that I was in New York, he sent a messenger to the Astor House asking me to call on him. I accepted the invitation. The interview took place at his home and as before it was on a Sunday evening and in the same room. Mr. Gould noticed my careful scrutiny of the portieres and laughed as he said: "There is no one behind it tonight." His object in having me call was, as I at first thought, to upbraid me for some of the

---

[1] Its report is *Report of the House Select Committee on Labor Troubles in Missouri, Arkansas, Kansas and Texas*, House Doc., 49th Cong., 2d sess., 1886-87. No. 4174.

[2] Andrew Gregg Curtin (1817-94) was known as the "great war governor" of Pennsylvania. He served as minister to Russia (1868-72) and as a member of the House of Representatives (1881-87).

things I wrote about him during the strike. As near as I can recall his words they were:

You did me a grave injustice in charging me with these offenses. When you said I was a railroad wrecker you but repeated what men who opposed me in the Street said of me. When men tried to get the best of Gould and failed, they charged him with commission of offenses of which they were guilty. Mr. Powderly, I have learned to regard you as an honest man. I don't mind what Wall Street men say of me, but when you make charges against me it hurts. I expect it from them and [here he laughed] I guess I give them cause for grumbling. When you say anything the public will listen. I believe your desire is to promote the best interests of workingmen and I have thought so since one night during the telegraphers' strike in 1883 when you frustrated the designs of some hotheads who planned to blow up the pole carrying the lead wires into the Western Union Building.

I didn't ask you to come here to quarrel with you but to say that it is my ambition to build up a railroad system such as the world never saw before. You know I can't take it with me when I die and I don't want to. I want to leave it as a heritage to the American people. All I can get out of it is a place to sleep and my meals; what more can any one get? I don't believe the men are treated any worse on the Gould system than on other western lines but I am willing to abide by your decision in the matter. I'll have one of our best cars fitted out for you, stocked with everything you need, will provide typewriters and stenographers, or you may employ your own and I'll pay them. Go over our entire system, make such inquiries as you please and where you please. I'll give you a letter to our officials instructing them to deal frankly and fairly with you. Make inquiries of workingmen, business men, and professional men as to our treatment of our workmen. See if you don't find they are as well treated as the employees of any other system.

I was astonished at this statement, made in such an earnest manner, and deliberated quite a while before saying anything. I will confess I had but little confidence in Jay Gould; I had read so many bad things about him that I looked with suspicion on everything he said or did. In my dealings with him, however, I found him pleasant, exceedingly outspoken, and apparently candid. After thinking the matter over I said:

"I am thankful to you for this offer but cannot avail myself of it. Were I to do as you suggest and find that your men are treated as well as men in like callings on other lines I would so report. The moment that report gained publicity, your enemies and mine would say you had bought me up and the result would be injurious.

I shall ask you to notify your subordinates to deal candidly and freely with me, however, so that if I get the opportunity to do so I may prosecute an inquiry on my own account." This he promised to do and then he called his daughters into the room and introduced me as the man he had "so much trouble with a while ago." They received me very pleasantly and I, after taking my last look at Jay Gould, retired.

I began an inquiry into the condition of the workers along the Gould system but was never able to make a thorough investigation. I went far enough, however, to learn that there was much truth in what Gould told me. I found that division foremen and local bosses were not deterred by religious or conscientious scruples from inventing petty schemes and plans to oppress and humiliate the workmen. Through Sidney Dillon, counsel for the Gould system, I placed a memorandum setting forth what I had learned in the hands of Jay Gould. I never received an acknowledgment and did not expect to. Dillon afterward told me that Gould went over my memo with the general manager of the Southwest system, and quite a few local tyrants were removed or transferred along the Missouri-Pacific and other Gould lines. Whether my memorandum had anything to do with the changes which were made I never learned. . . .

I believe Jay Gould was in earnest when he said that it was his ambition to found a great system of railroads and leave it a heritage to the American people. I do not and did not approve of the methods he employed in carrying out his plans, but I know so little about his methods, and that little came to me, as it did to others, from his competitors and rivals in business, that I don't know how much of it to credit. I believe watering of stocks, sharp practice in dealing in stocks, and oppression of workingmen and women employed by corporations are wrong. How far Jay Gould entered into such transactions I do not know. The testimony on which he has been judged came largely from the lips of men who were engaged in playing the game with him and lost. Except in degree, he was no more to blame than they. He represented a system that I believed to be wrong, and that system is what I opposed. Notwithstanding all that transpired, or the press made me say, during that struggle I had nothing personal against Jay Gould.

[There is a story that] a man stopped over night at a little country hotel; the landlord assigned him to a bedroom that hadn't been occupied for several weeks. When he came down in the morning to wash at the pump, another guest, noticing blotches of blood on his face, asked what the cause was. He said he had spent the best part of the night fighting and killing bedbugs. On being asked why he did that, he remarked: "Well, now that I think it over I really don't know. I had nothing against the bugs, they were total strangers to me, wouldn't know one of them if I met him on the street. But it was the business they were in and the infernal way they did it that I objected to."

.   .   .   .

I remarked a while ago that I would have something more to say about Martin Irons. When the Southwest strike ended he was reproached for his failure to make a strike that was forced on him successful, he was reviled by those for whom he battled, and society at large . . . ostracized him. He was by trade a machinist and bore the reputation of being a good one. His picture, which the newspapers and mazagines sought and published in the days of his fleeting, though unsought, popularity, was kept for reference by master mechanics and superintendents of machine shops throughout the Southwest. When he applied for a job he was courteously received, patiently listened to, and politely dismissed with: "Sorry, but we have no vacancies and our waiting list is full."

Despairing of obtaining work at his trade, he sought employment as trackman, car repairer, section hand, street laborer, hotel porter and hostler, but everywhere he met with the same reception. He gathered a few pennies and opened a cigar stand in the hope that his old associates would patronize him; some did and paid for what they bought, others obtained credit and never paid their bills. He sought entrance to every honorable avenue through which he might walk in self-supporting independence. He found every door closed in his face. Weak, tired, moneyless, footsore, sick at heart and soul, he was forced to tell of his hunger and poverty to one who reported the fact to the police.

One day I picked up a paper and saw an account of the arrest, conviction and sentence of this "disturber of the peace," this "malefactor" whose real offending was his effort for human betterment. It said that when [he was] called for trial no attorney rose to plead his cause, no friendly hand came out of the gloom to touch his, and for want of money to pay the fine levied by the court he was sentenced to the rock pile there to wear the badge which ignorance and ingratitude imposed, the ball and chain. "Martin Irons in the chain gang, there's your labor agitator for you; now he's getting his just deserts," is what a man at my elbow said. I was away from home, had no money by me, so I wired a friend to pay his fine and send the bill to me; he and others appeared for Irons.

It was charged against me that I was unfriendly to Martin Irons, that I was jealous of him, that I feared him and disliked him. I believe you know from what I have already told you that there was no truth in these stories. . . . I don't know that any of those who became embittered against me because of these industriously circulated falsehoods ever troubled their heads about extending a helping hand to Martin Irons in his hour of need. Josh Billings said: "Human nature is mighty onhuman, awful deaf an' powerful nearsighted when a man needs a hand to pull him out of the ditch." . . .

I am not particular about changing opinions already set, neither do I feel that I need vindication of my course with regard to Martin Irons. I do want you to realize that the word friendship means something to me. That's why I tell you that I did just a little to pluck a thorn or two from the pathway of Martin Irons. When I reached home I wrote a letter of sympathy to him, and . . . mailed . . . him [a check]. . . .

In 1897, when President McKinley appointed me Commissioner-General of Immigration I had the giving of a few places not covered by civil service law or regulation. Ascertaining the address of Martin Irons and learning at the same time that he was in hard luck, I wrote him tendering one of the places at my disposal. . . . His reply . . . [was] a manly acknowledgment of a greeting over the miles from a brother. . . .

Martin Irons is dead . . . and men have grown eloquent in telling of his life and works. They did not know him at all. . . . No one can know the inner man outside of himself, but he won't tell all even if he knows and I am not sure that he does. We paint a character, but in selecting and mixing the colors we use the pigments of our imagination with the result that the portrait is largely what we wish it to be and not what the man really is, or was. . . .

Martin Irons was a student and an educated man. . . . Irons never learned the art of employing language to conceal thought, he used it to cause men to understand and succeeded.

He did not strive to build up a tower of numbers along the Southwest system when organizing the Knights of Labor; he endeavored to gather in the few who could think and plan rather than the many who didn't do either. If numbers mean anything, a well-populated pincushion can make a good show of heads, but when counted they would be only pin heads. To educate a few to go out and teach the many was his hope, but the needs of the men were pressing; Irons could not extend his vision to them and they could not wait, they could not wait. Perhaps it had to be that way.

.   .   .   .

Chapter Twelve

THE STOCKYARDS STRIKE

Now I SHALL TELL YOU of my connection with what was called the "Packers' Strike of 1886" in Chicago.[1] Perhaps as good an introduction as any would be a quotation from *The Story of a Labor Agitator*, published in 1903 by Joseph R. Buchanan.[2] Writing of my views on compelling members of the cigar maker's union, who belonged to the Knights of Labor also, to sever connection with that union or the Knights of Labor, he says:

At Richmond he [Powderly] was unequivocally with the anti-unionists. This was Mr. Powderly's first serious mistake as General Master Workman, though he had been criticised because of his course in the Southwestern strike and during the eight-hour movement of May 1, 1886. . . .

While the General Assembly was in session at Richmond the employees of the union stock yards at Chicago went on strike for the eight-hour day. Thomas B. Barry, member of the General Executive Board, was sent at once by the board to take charge of the strike. The twenty-five thousand strikers had the stock yards completely tied up, and it was known that the bosses were on the point of yielding, when a telegram from the General Master Workman dumped the fat into the fire. This telegram ordered the men to abandon their demands for an eight-hour day and to return to work. The strikers were dumfounded by what they considered the ill advised and inopportune act of the General Master Workman, and, when assured that there was no mistake about the order refused to obey it. Mr. Powderly then sent a message—open, instead of in cipher—to Mr. Barry, directing him, if the men refused to work, to take their charters from them. Barry was almost heart-broken. He withheld the Master Workman's telegram for two days, but it turned out that the bosses knew of Powderly's order

[1] For information on this much controverted strike and Powderly's role, see Ware, *Labor Movements in the United States, 1860-1895*, pp. 152-54; Commons, *History of Labour*, II, 418-20; *Proceedings of the General Assembly of the Knights of Labor of America, Held at Minneapolis, Minnesota, October 4 to 19, 1887* (1887), pp. 1477-99. Powderly's account is plainly one of self-justification.

[2] Joseph Ray Buchanan (1851-1924) was an able and characteristically western labor leader.

before Barry had read the message, and, realizing that the General Master Workman was playing their game, they adopted a resolution which said to the strikers, "You can return to work only on condition that you renounce your allegiance to the Knights of Labor." . . .

The only explanation ever offered of the General Master Workman's conduct in the Chicago stock yards strike was scarce an explanation at all, as it also needed explaining. Here it is: A Roman Catholic priest, the Rev. P. M. Flannigan, of St. Anne's Church, Town of Lake, Cook County, had written to Mr. Powderly urging him to call the strike off. Father Flannigan, claiming to know the sentiments of the packers, declared that they were fully determined not to work their plants on the eight-hour plan. He further declared that great hardships—perhaps destitution—threatened the families of thousands of the strikers, and, urging Mr. Powderly to put a stop to the strike, said, "In your whole life I do not think you will ever again have an opportunity of doing such a service to so vast a number as in this instance." At the time that letter was written, the shut-down in the yards and packing-houses was complete, and not an appeal for assistance had been received by the managers of the strike.[3]

In these lines Mr. Buchanan sets forth the gravamen of my offending in the stockyards, or packers', strike. I have too high a regard for Mr. Buchanan personally and for his sense of justice to believe that he would knowingly misrepresent me.

While his assertion that I was "unequivocally with the anti-unionists," at the Richmond session of the General Assembly may not appear to have anything to do with the stockyards strike, it was one of the feeders to the volume of abuse and vilification that came my way then and continued to come for many years after. I was not with the anti-unionists at Richmond or anywhere else, there or at any other time. Prior to the session at Richmond I wrote a letter to be read in all our assemblies warning them that other organizations were attempting to get control of the Knights of Labor and asking them, in selecting delegates to the convention, to "put none but Knights of Labor on guard at Richmond." Protectionists, Free Traders, Single Taxers, Socialists, Anarchists, Bellamyites, and Blatherskites as well as some trades-unionists had stated openly that it was their intention to capture the Knights of Labor at Richmond and make use of it as

[3] Joseph R. Buchanan, *The Story of a Labor Agitator,* New York (1903), pp. 316, 318-21.

a field for their propaganda. It was my aim to hold the Knights of Labor organization for Knights of Labor. . . . I took no part in the fight against the cigar makers union,[4] and did not believe the action in expelling them was lawful or warranted. As General Master Workman I rendered a decision setting forth the illegality of the action and asking our members not to take action on the vote expelling the cigar makers from the Knights of Labor. Certain Knights of Labor were bitter against trade-unionists; certain trade-unionists were bitter against the Knights of Labor. The cause or causes of this state of feeling extended far back of the Richmond session and have no place in this recital. . . . My action in the General Assembly at Richmond was not against the cigar makers union. I make that statement "unequivocally" and without reservation. Mr. Buchanan will admit, I think, that he did not feel overkind toward me at that session. We did not see much of each other, through no fault of mine, and it is quite probable that he would not have written as he did could he have witnessed and listened to the heated arguments between the opponents of the cigar makers union and me at Richmond. . . . Nothing that I could say or do at that session could have prevented the action taken but it served the purpose of those engaged in the strife to make me appear as an enemy of the cigar makers union, and, having the ear and ink of the press, they used both to color me according to their own views or wishes. The record at no point shows me an enemy to any trade-union; but I was a Knight of Labor and whether wise or unwise that was sufficient for me.

My "course in the Southwestern strike" was just as related heretofore . . . and the criticisms Mr. Buchanan heard were not from men who knew the real facts.

My action "during the eight-hour movement of May 1, 1886" had a bearing on the stockyards strike.[5] In 1885 the Federation

[4] The history of the complicated relations between the K. of L. and the cigar makers is treated fully in Ware, *Labor Movements in the United States, 1860-1895*, pp. 258-79.

[5] Compare the following with Ware, *op. cit.*, Chap. XIII; Commons, *History of Labour*, II, 375-85; Henry David, *The History of the Haymarket Affair*, New York (1936), Chaps. VII-VIII.

of [Organized] Trades [and Labor Unions of the United States and Canada] issued a call for a strike for the eight-hour day to begin May 1, 1886. In the early part of that year local assemblies of Knights of Labor began to spring up everywhere. So fast did the organizers send in applications for charters for local assemblies that I was called on by the General Secretary and General Executive Board to suspend organizing for thirty days. I was criticized for that action, too, but our general office was too small to hold the force necessary to open the envelopes and take care of the money sent in as charter fees. Lawyers, bankers, gamblers, and liquor dealers were prohibited from becoming members of the Knights of Labor, and yet organizers sent in applications by the hundred with the names of representatives of these callings on the roll as charter members. We at that time did not recognize "humanitarian" as a branch of labor; an organizer gave the occupation of one of the members applying for a charter as "humanitarian."

Others sent in the names of men who were known to be, or suspected of being, Pinkerton detectives. Had I given my reason for calling a halt on organizing other than I did, I would have warned every gambler, rum seller, and detective just how to escape detection and slip unobserved into the Knights of Labor.

A great many of the new assemblies began to pass resolutions favoring "Our General Master Workman's call for a strike for eight hours on May 1, 1886," and send them in to our general office.

Men were rushed into the Order so rapidly and with such slight preparation that they, in many instances, did not know but that the Federation of Trades and Knights of Labor were identical. Realizing that misunderstandings and trouble must inevitably follow through ignorance of the fact that the Knights of Labor had not set the first of May as the day on which to inaugurate a strike for eight hours, I prepared and issued a letter to our organization stating the facts. I did not say they should not strike for eight hours, but I did most emphatically say that if they did they should not do so under the impression that they were striking in obedience to any law, rule, or command of the Order of Knights of Labor. Furthermore they should not expect to get support, financially or otherwise, from the Knights of Labor. That is the action I was "criticized for during the eight-hour movement of May 1, 1886." I do not recall that I was criticized by anyone who had the interest of the Knights of Labor at heart or by any one who believed that our members and the public should know the truth. It was my duty to take the action I did take. I thought I did right then; I have no apologies to offer for it now.

It was that "eight-hour movement" that precipitated the stockyards strike to which Mr. Buchanan refers, but it did not happen as he relates it. What I now tell you can be verified from the record and by the speech of living men who were and are in possession of the facts.

When May 1, 1886, arrived no general strike for eight hours was undertaken, but the stockyard employees of Chicago struck for and gained the eight-hour day with ten hours pay. That was in May, 1886, and not "while the General Assembly was in session at Richmond" in October; nor is it a fact that the "bosses were on the point of yielding." They had yielded, had granted the demands of the workmen, and, had these same workmen followed my advice given in the summer of 1886, they, in all probability, would never have been called on to strike against a return to the ten-hour day on the eleventh day of October, 1886. Believing that unless competitors operated their plants on the eight-hour plan the Chicago packers would undoubtedly return, or endeavor to return to the ten-hour day, I, in July, 1886, while in Chicago, urged the employees of the packing houses to organize the employees of packing houses in Chicago and other cities with a view to securing uniformity of action between them and the Chicago institutions. I went farther than that; I offered to grant commissions to such organizers as they would recommend through their district assembly and afford them every facility to carry the work to successful issue. They appeared pleased with my suggestions and offer but never acted in the matter. I urged them once again in like manner and with the same result. In October, and while the General Assembly was in session at Richmond, the packers—who had assured their employees that they would willingly continue the eight hour a day policy if they brought the packing houses of other cities under like rules—gave notice of returning to the ten-hour work day. Before this, however, the Beef Slaughterers' Assembly arranged a scale of wages based on the eight-hour day, presented it to their employers; it was accepted and under it they—according to their own statement—"got along very well." On October 11, the employing pork packers posted notices of a return to the ten-hour day. The pork men immediately struck work, while the beef men in the employ of Swift, Morris, and Armour continued at work. The General Assembly was in session at Richmond, the Chicago representatives held a caucus, fixed on T. B. Barry, a member of the General Executive Board, as the man to go to Chicago, and next day brought the matter before the convention. That body, and not the General Executive Board as Mr. Buchanan says, voted to send Barry to Chicago. I was in the chair and being, on motion passed by the General Assembly, asked to state what powers Barry should be clothed with, rendered this decision:

That the member selected by the General Assembly to go to Chicago be clothed only with such power as will allow him to effect such a settlement with the packers of Chicago as will restore harmony to the now conflicting elements. But, in case of a failure to effect such a settlement, the Order, or any part of it, shall not be in any way involved or called upon for financial assistance. And inasmuch as the strike was not authorized by the Order, the Order must not be held responsible for it or its consequences. That the only connection this Order holds to the strike lies in the tender of its good offices toward effecting a settlement.

That's from page 175 of the printed record, of the proceedings of the Richmond session of the General Assembly; and many men and women who were present at that convention and heard that body unanimously adopt my decision as the rule of conduct for Barry to follow are still living to bear testimony to the fact that Barry went as the agent of the General Assembly and not of the General Executive Board, not to take charge of the strike, but to act as provided in that decision, which, by unanimous adoption by the General Assembly, became law.

In secret session the General Assembly learned from Chicago representatives that they were not all on strike in the stockyards and that it was mainly in the hope of preventing all from striking we were asked to interfere. Furthermore, it was also stated—not for public information though—that those on strike were for the most part not members of the Knights of Labor or any other labor organization.

Barry went to Chicago, not to take part in a strike for eight hours but in a strike against a return to ten hours, not as agent of the General Executive Board but as the representative of the whole General Assembly; not to do as he pleased but to do as he was instructed to do; not to add to the strike but to try and end it; not to "take charge of the strike" but to unite with others in helping to settle it.

When he got to Chicago he did not find that "the twenty-five thousand strikers had the stockyards completely tied up" but found the employees of Swift, Morris, and Armour and Company at work. Furthermore, he and the Master Workman of District Assembly No. 57, to which the few Knights of Labor in the stockyards belonged, were made acquainted with the real condition of affairs by the Master Workman and a committee of Cattle Butcher's Assembly No. 7802. In [the] presence of Mr. Barry the District Master Workman ratified the action of Local Assembly No. 7802 and signed "an order to Armour's men to stay at work until called upon to do something else." This is quoted from the record and must stand even though men saw fit to misrepresent the real condition of affairs. The District Master Workman was at that time the nominee of the United Labor party for sheriff of Cook County, Illinois. He had a perfect right to be a candidate for office but it was unfortunate that his candidacy occurred at that time. He was a delegate to the Richmond session and accompanied Mr. Barry to Chicago. I have never heard that Mr. Barry gave anyone to understand that he went to Chicago with full power to settle the strike, but the men were led to believe he had such power, the Chicago papers so reported, and he did not contradict the rumor. On October 15, the District Master Workman ordered the beef butchers to strike, and, believing that they had full power of the General Assembly of the Knights of Labor back of them, they quit work. That order to strike was issued with the knowledge of the man sent by the General Assembly to make peace. A committee from Local Assembly No. 7802 called on Mr. Barry and from the record I quote:

> Brother Barry before you left Richmond did the General Executive Board clothe you with power to settle this trouble. Answer: No, they merely sent me here as an angel of peace, with instructions not to involve the order in any way.
> Then they will not support the men in a move of this kind? Answer: No.

The men expressed dissatisfaction with the action taken, and telegraphed to me at Richmond explaining the real situation and asking for instructions. That message I never received. Nearly a year afterward I saw a copy of it in Chicago. Why, how, or by who it was suppressed or kept from me at Richmond I can only surmise but I do not know. Mr. Buchanan could not have known this, or he would have written differently.

The following day, October 16, Father Flannigan, referred to by Mr. Buchanan as furnishing the explanation for my calling the strike off, sent not a letter but a lengthy telegram to me at Richmond. . . . I give it in full, just as I gave it a year later to the General Assembly:[6]

"CHICAGO, ILL., OCTOBER 16, 1886

T. V. POWDERLY
GENERAL MASTER WORKMAN

In behalf of the twenty thousand employees at the Union Stock Yards and their families I send this telegram to say that something must be done, and done at once, or the misery and suffering that these people will endure in the near future will be fearful to contemplate. The packers are determined that under no circumstances can they afford here in Chicago to do

[6] In his annual address at the Minneapolis convention, Powderly said of this telegram:
"On the 16th of October, and while I was still absent from the General Assembly, a dispatch was received there and remained unnoticed until some weeks after the General Assembly closed. It was while examining the mass of letters, telegrams, and pamphlets that were sent to me at Richmond that I first read this telegram. . . .
"Had I noticed this dispatch while at Richmond I would have answered it from there, but it was weeks afterward before I came to see it, and before I came to it I had read in the papers that I had been influenced in my transactions by the church."
Proceedings of the General Assembly of the Knights of Labor of America, Eleventh Regular Session . . . October 4 to 19, 1887, p. 1479.

business on the eight hours a day basis when in all the rest of the country men work ten hours. While entirely willing to accept the shorter day just as soon as it becomes universal, so that all may be on the same level at the same time, they fully resolve to carry on their business. They are importing, and will continue to import, foreign workmen, and unless this matter is settled immediately this immense army of workmen, some have labored here many years, most of whom have their homes and families here, will find themselves replaced by others and never be taken back. You are known all over this country as a man of rare good judgment, cool and self-possessed, fair and judicious on every side, and I have no doubt that were you here you would settle this difficulty, so full of dreadful possibilities, in a very short time and settle it effectually. In your whole life I don't think you will ever again have an opportunity of doing such a great service to such a vast number of people. I believe it is your duty to do what you can in the interest of humanity and peace, and I am confident you will regard it in the same light. It is for this reason, and this only, that I send this message. I have been pastor of this church and in the neighborhood for many years. I know the condition of these people and I can clearly see the poverty and suffering and possible crime, that will surely follow in the wake of this strike if it be permitted to drift along to the inevitable catastrophe. Please answer.

P. M. FLANNIGAN,
ST. ANN'S CHURCH
TOWN OF LAKE

On Thanksgiving Day, November 25, 1886—mark the day— I opened a package of letters and telegrams that had been received by the General Secretary of the Knights of Labor in bulk from someone in Richmond, Va., who either held them, or obtained them, from someone who had possession of them from the time the General Assembly was in session in early October in that city. Father Flannigan's telegram, several other telegrams, and letters bearing on the strike which was then in progress were in that package and for the first time I saw that telegram from Father Flannigan.

Let us go back to Chicago the day Father Flannigan wired me. Mr. Barry, on or about October 19, called a number of the leaders in the strike together and told them he and the District Master Workman had decided to order the men "back to work on the ten-hour system, and that they continue to work until between the 7th and 10th of November when a spirit of discontent would be shown and the leaders would give the order and the men would strike but not allowed to get past the office when they would be ordered back to work at eight hours and nine hours pay."

A day or two following, Mr. Barry called a meeting of the men in Germania Hall, explained his plan, and stated that he: "did not have power to settle the trouble when he came but had since telegraphed and got it and that it might be necessary for them to go back to ten hours for a short time." He then ordered the pork men to resume work at ten hours, and the beef men at Armour's *at eight hours*. The strike at an end, the men returned to work on or about October 19, 1886. Barry came on to Philadelphia, and on October 22, reported to the General Executive Board, there in session, that the strike was ended. He did not there, then, or at any other time say that there was a string to the settlement of the strike. I was present, he made his report, verbally, to me as chairman of the General Executive Board in presence of the other members, promising to present a written report when he had more time. He then left for his home in East Saginaw, Michigan, and the stockyards strike of 1886 was at an end, with the men in the main back at ten hours without Powderly using voice or pen in the doing of it. Mr. Buchanan does not tell it that way, but I am stating facts from the record. Mr. Barry never, so far as I was able to learn, presented a written report.

Now listen to Mr. Barry and contrast what he says with Mr. Buchanan's statement. . . .

CHICAGO, ILL. OCTOBER 19, 1886

BROTHER POWDERLY:

The people here were fighting a losing fight. The packers set a trap for them and they fell into it. The City is in a state of siege. Eight hundred Pinkertons here. Four of them were beaten today. One of them was stripped of his clothes, and to put it mild, hell was knocked out of the four of them; they are all in the hospital. No arrests. This is the hardest body of people I ever tried to control. I have been working almost day and night since coming here. Will write you more fully tomorrow. It is now 1:00 o'clock A. M. I must stop, my eyes are going shut, with kind wishes to all.

As ever yours,
(*Signed*) T. B. BARRY

No charge against Powderly in that letter, nothing to indicate that I did anything out of the way.

On election day, November 2, 1886, having lost my right to vote in Scranton through moving from one election district to another, I spent the day in New York going from one polling booth to another with Henry George, then a candidate for mayor of New York and for whom I had been speaking for about a week. Next day I went to Philadelphia and found a telegram from Mr. Barry, which had been relayed from Scranton. It was dated November 2, sent from East Saginaw, Michigan, and said:

"Trouble in Chicago, they wire for me to come; shall I go?"

I had read in the evening papers that the packing house employees had struck again and that Barry was on his way to Chicago, so there was no need of my instructing him to go or stay.

Then began a fusillade of letters and telegrams from Chicago to the General Executive Board and General Master Workman asking for financial aid and stating that it was the Order's fight etc. By quoting one it will give an idea of all:

"All attempts at peaceful settlement ended. Packers show their hand and will fight the Order; you must issue an assessment for us at once and issue a boycott notice on beef and pork from Chicago. This is the Order's fight and must be won."[7]

Up to that time it was not a Knight of Labor fight, but by letting it run on it would become such.

On returning from Richmond I had a statement made out for me in our general office showing the number of enrolled Knights of Labor in the stockyards. That statement comprised all classes therein organized and totaled 1539, whether in good standing or not . . . and on that number only did they pay per-capita tax to an Order that they were on November 7 demanding financial assistance from. Mr. Buchanan is correct when he says: "not an appeal for assistance had been received by the managers of the strike," but he was referring to the strike Mr. Barry declared off, which was the second strike in the series of stockyard troubles.

[7] This was signed by William R. Degnan, of whom Powderly said: "Up to this time I had not heard of the interference of this man, and did not know whether he represented any portion of the Order." (*Ibid.,* p. 1481.) It was not a typical communication.

I am now telling you of the third strike. The Order had at that time upward of fifty strikes on hand; appeals for assistance had been sent out, for the General Executive Board had no authority to levy assessments at the time. We could not begin to help an eighth of those whose burdens we were forced to carry, and, worse than all, I was being censured for not supplying funds to those who were in need of them, censured by those who were asked to contribute, and damned by the public press for my action in calling for funds.

I never gave out an interview on that trouble during its existence, and when I refused to be interviewed, reporters made up and published interviews with me.

On the morning of November 9, I received this letter from Mr. Barry:

CHICAGO, NOVEMBER 7, 1886

BROTHER POWDERLY AND MEMBERS OF THE GENERAL EXECUTIVE BOARD Brothers:—

When I came here from Richmond I found about twelve thousand men on strike, resisting a return to the ten-hours work day. The town of Lake was in a state of siege with Pinkerton men in the employ of the packing firms. I labored with the packing companies for arbitration; this they refused, saying there was nothing to arbitrate. They had determined on ten hours per day in the stock yards and would accept no other terms. Mr. S. A. Kent, of the Chicago Packing Company, and Mr. R. D. Fowler, of the firm of Fowler Brothers, expressed a desire for a settlement and wanted an opportunity to break loose from the packers' organization; if given that opportunity they would establish the eight-hour day working at a reduction of one hour's pay between the 5th and 10th of this month in their packing houses. That was the terms offered the men some time before but refused by them, they insisting on ten hours' pay for eight hours' work. After looking the ground over here fully, I seen, [sic] or thought I did, that our people were fighting a losing fight, *so I ordered the strike off.*[8] The men for a time rebelled against my order, but after an exchange of opinion with them they obeyed the order and went to work. This was Kent and Fowler's chance to cut loose from the packers' organization and keep their word with me; this they have not done. The packers still refuse arbitration, and the men are firm for eight hours. Both sides are unwilling to yield. The packers met yesterday and voted to keep closed for thirty days, but I think they can't hold out that long unless they suffer a loss of hundreds of thou-

[8] Powderly's italics.

sands of dollars, as there are thousands of cattle and hogs that must be killed or they will eat their heads off, and meat in the houses that must be cared for or it will spoil. The men here are a determined, headstrong set, that hate a rat with the poison of their life. They will have to be allowed to continue this strike to a conclusion, but I don't think it would be safe to leave them to themselves without some one of the Board here to keep them in the channel of peace. They have all promised to shun saloons and abstain from drink while this strike lasts. There are five hundred Pinkertons here, and the first and second regiments are under orders at the Armory. There is no trouble here, and there is no sign of trouble. After the resumption of work P. D. Armour wanted his men to sign an ironclad renouncing the Order and all labor organizations. This the men refused to sign, with some few exceptions. Send instructions what I shall do.

Fraternally yours,

(*Signed*) T. B. BARRY

P. S.—There are twenty-five thousand men on strike here. T. B. B.

On the evening of the ninth I received this telegram from Mr. Barry: "Peace negotiations ended; packers declare they will not employ Knights of Labor. Want men to sign ironclad."

Considering all that had happened from the beginning of the trouble and the mass of letters and telegrams from Chicago, I made up my mind that if the men were "fighting a losing fight" when Mr. Barry first went to Chicago, they were fighting a lost fight in being sent back to work with a secret understanding between Mr. Barry and some others that they were to strike again on or after election day. The General Executive Board decided to send A. A. Carlton, one of its members, to Chicago to assist Barry, although the latter stated that he did not need any assistance. My first impulse was to go to Chicago, and I have always regretted that I did not do so. The situation was growing desperate. The peace which Mr. Barry said was prevalent was being interrupted occasionally by some man having his skull cracked. I consulted with the other members of the General Executive Board and with a committee which was then in session to revise the constitution of the Order, and, with the light we then had, we decided that more would be saved for the men of the stockyards by ending the strike then, than by letting it run into riot and possibly murder, with losses to the men due to a more embittered feeling than there existed. I believed the men could not win. I know of no one

conversant with the situation who did think so. I prepared, read
to the other members of the General Executive Board and Constitutional Committee, received unanimous approval, and sent this
telegram:

PHILADELPHIA, PA., NOV. 10, 1886

T. B. BARRY
    CHICAGO, ILL.

In a circular issued March 13, 1886, I stated the policy of the Knights
of Labor on the eight-hour question. That circular was read to and approved by the General Executive Board before it went out. It was afterward approved by the entire Order. In opposition to that circular men at the
stockyards struck for eight hours. The Order of Knights of Labor was not
brought into controversy, hence no action necessary during session of General Assembly. Men at stockyards struck again. You were sent to try to
settle, but in case of failure the Order was not be be involved or asked for
assistance. You settled by ordering men back at old hours. They have in
violation of law and without notifying us again struck for eight hours. The
Board instructs you and Carlton, who will be with you today, to settle by
putting men back at old hours until the Order of Knights of Labor takes
definite action on eight-hour plan. If men refuse, take their charters. We
must have obedience and discipline.

By order of General Executive Board:

CHAIRMAN GENERAL EXECUTIVE BOARD
T. V. POWDERLY

Mr. Buchanan says that a future [?] telegram was "sent open
instead of in cipher." So was the one just quoted and it was the
only one I sent or have knowledge of bearing on the subject of ordering the strike off. If the case is as stated by Mr. Buchanan that
Mr. Barry held the telegram for two days, he was frustrating one
of the purposes in sending it, for its main object was to get the
men back to work speedily. All rumors that the newspapers or
packers knew the contents of my telegram before it was communicated to the men were based on surmise, for no evidence has
ever been adduced to show that such was the case. Other letters
and telegrams passed between Mr. Barry and me for a few days
but it is for that one message I have been criticized and condemned. From neither Barry [n]or Carlton did I hear a word to
indicate that any one knew of its existence except the man to whom

it was sent. I did not give it out, but beneath every rumor that it had been given out lurked the intimation that I had done so.[9]

True, I counseled with the General Executive Board before sending that telegram, and it went not as the order of the General Master Workman but as the expression and command of the General Executive Board. When I wrote it, I read and reread it several times before laying it before the Board. When I read it to that body, I explained my reasons for writing it. One of my listeners said "that is a most unpopular thing for you to do." To that I replied: "It is not a question with me as to its effect on my popularity; is it, under the circumstances, right to do this?" There was not a dissenting voice and it became the action of the entire Board, or all of them then present in Philadelphia. I did not ask others to approve of it to evade or shirk any responsibility. I would have sent it just as willingly had there been no one to advise with.

It was my duty to know the real situation in Chicago and I did know it.

If there were twenty-five thousand men on strike in the stockyards of Chicago, 23,461 of them were not members of our Order, and, therefore, not in any way bound to obey either the General Master Workman or General Executive Board. Don't lose sight of that fact. I knew that with two regiments of the National Guard of Illinois resting on their arms in the vicinity of the stockyards awaiting trouble, it was only a question of time and a very short time when a breach of the peace would be precipitated, a riot would follow, and the military would surround and take charge of the packing houses. I had had enough experience to believe that if the men did remain absolutely quiet and sober, some agent of the packers or Pinkerton's could be depended on to start trouble. Once in the hands of the military arm of the state, the strike would be broken and the men would become demoralized.

Letting a strike, which under the way this one was managed, run on to its logical ending meant the discharge of thousands, the driving of men, women, and children from their homes, and the

[9] Compare with *ibid.*, p. 1483.

ultimate loss of their homes. I knew that they were expecting financial aid, and also that orators, political and otherwise, had been busy haranguing the strikers and always holding before them the great Order of the Knights of Labor, millions strong, standing back of them ready with the cash to sustain them. I realized that the strikers had been deceived into going out on the third strike, and it looked suspicious to me that men should be put back to work during the second strike, kept to work until election day, and then called out when the chance of a change in the number of votes cast would be in favor of the United Labor party.

I was criticized and condemned, of course, but not by the men whose places and homes my action secured. I do not recall the name of any man at work in the stockyards who condemned me for my action. I do recall that pot-house politicians, anxious to curry favor with workingmen, but who labored only with their jaws, condemned me. Anarchists and anarchist sympathizers all over the country condemned me, but when the volume of slander and vilification died down the men, the real actors in that unhappy drama, realized that under the circumstances my action was the best for the greatest number.

During the storm I remained silent rather than tell the truth to the world concerning our weakness—as an organization—in the stockyards and our total inability to sustain the men and their families financially. Some of the men who condemned me for my action in that strike were misled, as I believe Mr. Buchanan was, into believing that it was the first instead of the third strike that I ordered off.

Perhaps I was wrong in acting as I did. It may be that I was deserving of all the censure I received. I am not wise enough to know, but as I look back . . . I feel that I did the best thing for the men who had to earn wages at hard labor in the stockyards. It was easy for the man who never labored with his hands to go before these men and in encouraging them to "stand out till the death," as one man did, to say that his "heart bled" for the men. It cost him nothing to say that, but if he had to bleed pigs and cattle in order to keep a roof over his head he might talk differently. . . . The honest man is restrained by conscience. Nothing restrains the demagogue. He is not deterred by conscience, scruple, or fear of injuring his neighbor from inventing new stories, advancing new theories to bolster up the hopes of the masses who suffer. I always tried to put myself in the place of the man I acted for. I did what I believed to be the right thing in ordering the last stockyard strike off. I know it was the honest thing but at the same time the most unpopular thing I could have done.

In one of his communications from Chicago Mr. Barry said:

The officers of this District Assembly are to blame largely for this condition of affairs. The District here is, or was, subordinate to the Locals. The officers or Executive Board would take no action until they got their orders from the rank and file of the District.

There was a reason for that. The ambition to secure political position at the hands of the electorate had weakened or partially paralyzed the hand of the executive, and rather than decide questions through which he might make himself unpopular and thereby run the risk of losing votes, he remained silent. . . .

In stating my case I am an interested witness, but I could summon a great many others who, without departing from the path of truth, could give damaging evidence against those who had charge of the various strikes in the stockyards. Listen to just one. At the Richmond session from which Mr. Barry went as "an angel of peace" there was a representative from District Assembly No. 136 who resided in Chicago and who, except in sympathy, was not allied to the two District Assemblies, Nos. 24 and 57, to which some of the strikers belonged. Richard Powers, the leader of the lake seaman's organization, it was who called the attention of the General Assembly to the situation at Chicago. Mr. Powers had for years been a Knight of Labor and in addition was a warm personal friend of mine. In a personal letter to me after the termination of the last strike, Mr. Powers wrote me on the subject. On October 13, 1915, twenty-nine years after the happenings herein set down, I wrote to Richard Powers asking permission to publish his letter. I made and sent him a copy of it to refresh his memory, and on October 19,1915, received a reply from him in which he granted my request. Here is what an impartial man . . . who was not unfriendly to the strikers or those who managed their affairs, wrote to me without solicitation of mine five weeks after I declared the last strike off in the Chicago stockyards:

CHICAGO, ILL.
NOVEMBER 21, 1886

Dear Friend Powderly:

Your order calling off the stock yards strike was the best thing that could happen. The men were bound to lose. Whether Barry went home to look after politics or not it is certain he left the men in the lurch here. Only a few on the inside know that the strike was called off temporarily. You are getting all kinds of abuse from the hot heads but the great majority of the 20,000 men who were affected will bless you yet for saving them and their families. Don't pay any attention to the rumor that your telegram was given out on the stock exchange before it was given to Barry. Ketchum, the operator, would not do such a thing, he is too good a Knight of Labor. He told me he gave your message to Barry and that he swore like a trooper and called you everything but a decent man when he read it. Then he asked Ketchum not to tell a soul about it and put it away. They circulated that lie to clear their own skirts. Butler was not elected even with the strike settled and if Barry was running for an office he didn't get there either. If there was selling out, and I don't believe there was, for money anyway, Barry comes nearest to being the seller by tricking the men into believing he had full power from the G. A., that he had assurance of support, that the whole Order was back of him and them, and worse than all by giving it out that the strike was settled for good. He told me the men couldn't win and why didn't he warn the men not to go out again before they or the Order made preparation for it? What I hold most against him was allowing the men to remain in the dark after he came from Richmond as to his powers and authority. That was very wrong in Barry and now he is trying to shift the blame to your shoulders and is hand and glove with the anarchists who would poison you.

I find the feeling bitter against you but it is because they were lied to. Bide your time and it will come out all right.

Fraternally yours,
(*Signed*) R. POWERS

. . . Penned by a hand not unfriendly to Mr. Barry, it tells its own story and part of mine. I submit its reference to Ketchum and his treatment of my telegram to you for comparison with

Mr. Buchanan's statement that "it turned out that the bosses knew of Powderly's order before Barry had read the message." . . .

When the General Assembly met in Minneapolis in October, 1887, I made a full and complete report to that body of my action in the stockyards strike of the year before. I held back nothing that would screen me from criticism or censure, supplementing my written report with an oral statement. My report was referred to the Committee on State of the Order for action and report. As General Master Workman I had the appointing of committees and purposely placed a man on that committee who was so embittered against me that he would not speak to me. I appeared before that committee and answered every question put to me. I assumed full responsibility for what had been done. The unanimous report of that committee was in this language: "Your committee is of the opinion that our General Officers did the best they could to settle the complications and therefore recommend that their action be endorsed."

When that committee reported, George Schilling[10] of Chicago offered as an amendment the following:

WHEREAS, The men in the Union Stock Yards never asked the Order for assistance, and it was so understood; and

WHEREAS, It was never understood that because the General Assembly sent Brother Barry to Chicago that the Local and District Assemblies had relinquished their control; and

WHEREAS, We consider it an act of bad faith on the part of the General Executive Board to detail Brother Carlton to Chicago to aid Brother Barry in securing a settlement, then to order the strike off before Brother Carlton could reach the scene of action; and

WHEREAS, The General Executive Board was guilty of an act of heartless cruelty, as well as incompetency, in ordering twenty-five thousand men and women to return to work, under threat of taking their charters if not obeyed, at a time when the packers' pool demanded by resolution that no one could return to work unless they renounced their allegiance to the Order and similar organizations, thus placing the members in the painful dilemma of

[10] George A. Schilling, one of the leading figures in the Chicago labor movement during this period, was an infant when his family migrated to the United States from Germany. Always active in the labor movement, he was also a socialist and single-taxer. He was an intimate friend of John Peter Altgeld. Almost ninety years old (1939), he still lives in Chicago.

choosing between renouncing their membership in the Order for the sake of obtaining work on the one hand, or, if they refused to do this, threatened with expulsion by the order of the General Executive Board; therefore be it *Resolved,* That the General Assembly do not concur in the action of the General Executive Board in the matter of the strike at the Union Stock Yards in Chicago, Ill.

Respectfully submitted,

CHAS. F. SEIB   JOHN J. DELANEY
GEO. A. SCHILLING   FRANK F. KNOX
JOHN M. FOLEY   Representatives from D. A. 57
ROBERT NELSON
Representatives from D. A. 24

Motion and amendment were freely debated, after which a vote was taken; the amendment was rejected and the report of the Committee on State of the Order was adopted. A verification of the vote was demanded. The roll was called, and 117 voted to sustain the General Executive Board, forty-nine voted against sustaining it, with two, Barry and Powderly, not voting. . . . When the vote was announced I moved that the action taken be not given out by the press committee, and, since my reasons as stated on the floor do not appear in the record which I have quoted, let me say that I had, before the body, related the real facts concerning the numerical weakness of Knights of Labor among the men in the packing houses and the activities of anarchist sympathizers to keep the men in trouble in Chicago in the hope of securing action in behalf of the men who had taken part in the Haymarket riot of May 4, 1886.[11]

[11] On the night of May 4, 1886, a dynamite bomb was hurled at a column of police who were about to disperse a meeting, called to protest police brutality, held just off the old Haymarket Square in Chicago. It was immediately charged that the bomb, which was finally responsible for the death of seven officers, was the work of Chicago social-revolutionaries, commonly called "anarchists." Eight "anarchists" stood trial for the deed. On August 20, 1886, August Spies, Albert R. Parsons, Michael Schwab, Samuel Fielden, Adolph Fischer, George Engel, Oscar Neebe, and Louis Lingg were found guilty as accessories of an unknown bomb-thrower whose identity still remains a mystery. The verdict was the product of public hysteria, a prejudiced judge, perjured evidence, and a strange theory of conspiracy. The verdict was upheld by the State Supreme Court, and the United States Supreme Court found no grounds for review. Spies, Fischer, Engel, and Parsons were hanged November 11, 1887. The death sentences of Fielden and Schwab were commuted to life imprisonment, Neebe

By a great many I was pictured as an enemy of the eight-hour movement, and that was assigned as a reason why I ordered the strike off. Do not lose sight of the fact that it was not the strike for eight hours, or the second strike I ordered off. I was and am an advocate of the eight-hour work-day.

At the session of the General Assembly which met in Hamilton, Ontario, in October, 1885, I referred to the action of the Federation of [Organized] Trades [and Labor Unions] in declaring for a strike on the first of May, 1886, and asked that the General Assembly take action on the matter. John M. Foley, the same Foley whose name appears on the Schilling amendment, was a delegate to the Hamilton session. He introduced this resolution:

"That we assist the Federation of Trades in carrying out the object of making eight hours a legal day's work on and after the first of May, 1886."

That resolution together with my suggestion on the same subject went to the Committee on State of the Order and here is what they did:

"We recommend that the General Executive Board be instructed to do all they lawfully may to establish practical cooperation between the Knights of Labor and other organizations with like objects in view."

That was all that was done to prepare for the coming struggle. Frank K. Foster[12] characterized the action of the committee in making that recommendation, and the General Assembly in adopting it, as an evasion of a momentous question, likening the action taken to the making of soup by hanging a chicken in the sun so that its shadow would fall on a pot full of water hung over a fire. He ended by saying: "When you bring the shadow to a boil you'll have shadow soup but there won't be any nourishment in it."

---

had originally received a prison sentence, and Lingg committed suicide while awaiting execution.

Powderly steadfastly opposed any expression of support or aid to the eight "anarchists" on the part of the K. of L. (See David, *The History of the Haymarket Affair*, pp. 211, 325, 407-18, *passim*), and condemned their deed and beliefs publicly.

[12] Frank K. Foster (1854-1909) was active in the International Typographical Union, the K. of L., the Federation of Organized Trades and Labor Unions of the United States and Canada, and owned and published the Haverhill, Mass., *Daily Laborer* and *Weekly Laborer*.

To take action would bespeak preparation and collection of funds to do the work. What a convention refused to do I was, in some miraculous manner, expected to accomplish. The labor movement has had its heroes and its scapegoats. I have been both but never wanted to be either. A day will come when the present wage system shall be known no more. When that day dawns, strikes shall be known no more. When that day comes, that which I foresaw and worked for will be known and appreciated everywhere. Workers, students, everybody, will ask: why didn't we adopt this plan years ago and save the time and treasure wasted in strikes?

.   .   .   .

Since I am indebted to Joseph R. Buchanan for the text on which to base this chapter let me say a few words about him. He was a member of the General Executive Board from the Philadelphia session of the General Assembly in 1884 until the session held in Hamilton, Ontario, in October, 1885. He did not seek reëlection, and T. B. Barry was elected in his place. During our association of a year I learned to respect and admire Buchanan. He was earnest and able, of a winning personality and courageous. His courage plus enthusiasm made it necessary for him to keep his hand on the brake that he might not strike a too rapid gait on the rather rough and uneven road we had to travel. He was considered radically progressive then; now he would be classed among the conservatives. . . .

Full of genial good humor, witty and generous, he made friends rapidly. He and I had a misunderstanding and we parted. Before I resigned in 1893 we became friends again and have remained so ever since. I never entertained any but feelings of the kindest regard for Buchanan, but had I felt otherwise he furnished an opportunity to get even with him. He was nominated for Congress and invited me to speak to the electorate of his district in his behalf.[13] . . . Joseph R. Buchanan in Congress . . . would be

[13] He ran in 1894 in the Sixth New Jersey (Newark) district, and was badly defeated, polling less than one thousand votes in an overwhelmingly working-class district.

a gain for the workingman of the United States, and. . . . I
spoke for him. . . .

We are good friends now; there is no man for whom I entertain a higher regard than Joe Buchanan. Labor has had many
champions, it never had a more loyal or earnest one than Joseph
R. Buchanan. . . .

Chapter Thirteen

THE NEW YORK CENTRAL STRIKE

HUNDREDS OF STRIKES were begun and ended during the time I was General Master Workman of the Knights of Labor, and while I had something to do with all of them, I do not recall any criticism of me because of their beginning, ending, or management.[1] As a matter of fact I had nothing to do with any of them except the strikes I have referred to and that on the New York Central Railroad in 1890. The strike on the Philadelphia and Reading in the winter of 1887 and 1888 was conducted from start to finish while I was so sick that I was not permitted to read the papers containing accounts of it.

Before telling you about the part I took in the strike on the New York Central Railroad, I shall ask you to note that in that day all labor organizations were not on terms of good will toward each other. The Brotherhood of Locomotive Engineers, under the leadership of P. M. Arthur,[2] occupied a position in the labor world that could not truthfully be classed as enthusiastically friendly to other organizations of labor. The Knights of Labor told each member, the hour of his initiation, that it was his duty: "as opportunity offers to extend a helping hand to all branches of honorable toil." That admonition held good whether the branches of honorable toil were organized or not. The true Knight of Labor believed it to be his duty to "help and assist those who,

---

[1] See above, Chap. IX.

[2] Peter M. Arthur (1831-1903) came to America from Scotland in 1842. Associated with the Brotherhood of Locomotive Engineers from its inception (1863), he was elected Grand Chief of the Brotherhood in 1874, holding that office until his death. He represents the most conservative wing of the labor movement of the period. Opposed to strikes in general, maintaining the complete independence of the Brotherhood, unwilling to coöperate with other railroad unions, he, nevertheless, was instrumental in turning the Brotherhood into an effective collective bargaining agency.

with hand or brain, did anything honorable or useful to earn bread."

Perhaps it will shed some light on the subject if I tell what passed between Mr. Arthur and me. We were walking up Sixth Avenue in New York one afternoon; the matter under discussion was the right of ordinary or—as he called it—unskilled labor, to become associated with skilled labor in an organization of any kind. He took the ground that a workman receiving a dollar and a half or two dollars a day should not be admitted to an organization on terms of equality with the three, four, or five dollar a day man. Further than that he expressed himself as opposed to aiding, encouraging, or in any way fraternizing with what he called the "lower grades of labor." Plainly stated, his belief was that the members of the Brotherhood of Locomotive Engineers should not lend a helping hand of any kind to workingmen in other callings. A man with a broom, shovel, and wheelbarrow was at work in the street along side of the curb. Pointing to him I asked Mr. Arthur how he would classify that workman. His answer was: "Have nothing to do with him, he is now doing what he is fitted for, and to allow him to become a member of an organization with high-grade workmen in it wouldn't help him and would be detrimental to the welfare of the others. Let him stay where he is; he is occupying the place that in all probability he is best fitted for."

"Don't you think Mr. Arthur that we should exert ourselves in his behalf either to insure fair treatment for him or to aid him in his aspirations to better things if he entertains such?"

"I don't believe in meddling with him at all. Every man should occupy the place his Maker fitted him for and we should not interfere," . . . Mr. Arthur said in reply.

I then expressed myself something like this: "I do not believe that man's Maker intended that he should be or remain a scavenger any more than He ordained that you or I should occupy the positions we now fill. If that theory, and it is only a theory, held good you would be just what you started out to be and I'd be a machinist yet. If it is in that scavenger to become a lawyer, a doctor, a clergyman, or even a locomotive engineer we should do what we can to afford him the opportunity to give his talents full play. Anyway, I hold that one scavenger doing his work faithfully and well is worth more to society than all the drones in the world, and even though he aspires to become nothing more than a scavenger it is our duty to help him where he is."

That ended our discussion for the time being, but I learned that in a struggle between a railroad company and the Knights of Labor little sympathy would be shown the Knights by the Brotherhood of Locomotive Engineers, at least so far as their then Grand Chief was concerned. The meeting and conversation I refer to took place during the summer of 1885.

In December, 1887, the employees of the Philadelphia and Reading Railroad went on strike. A week or so before the strike was ordered, I, while on a Fall River Line boat, became very seasick. It resulted in a hemorrhage of the stomach, and for three months I was not well enough to leave my home. Before my sickness I had personally advised the officials of the Knights of Labor on the Reading system to exercise prudence, caution, and patience. They were well organized, they knew it, and were in a position to secure many concessions from the company if they pursued a conciliatory course in dealing with their employers. They struck for what they could have won without a strike. While their strike was in progress members of the Brotherhood of Locomotive Engineers from other systems applied for and obtained positions in the places made vacant by the striking Knights of Labor on the Philadelphia and Reading Railroad. The strike on the Reading system was a failure. I had nothing whatever to do with it and did not know of it until it ended, for I was not permitted to read letters or papers during my long illness.

Following close on the heels of the Reading strike came the strike of the engineers on the Chicago, Burlington, and Quincy Railroad. This was in the early part of 1888, I had not fully recovered from my illness, was still confined to my home when a delegation of members of the Brotherhood of Locomotive Engineers bearing credentials signed by P. M. Arthur, Grand Chief of that organization, called on me for the purpose of asking me to prevent victimized members of the Knights of Labor (whose places had been taken during the Reading strike by members of the Brotherhood of Locomotive Engineers) from taking the places of the striking Brotherhood men on the C. B. & Q.

I at once dictated a letter to be read in every local assembly of the Knights of Labor, and published in our Journal, advising our members not to take the places of the striking Brotherhood men on the C. B. & Q. In the name of united labor I urged them not to take their brothers' jobs, and in large measure my words were heeded. If criticism came to me for my action in that strike, it came because I opposed retaliation on the part of the Knights of Labor for the taking of their places during the strike on the Reading system a short time before. Many influential Knights of Labor in and around Chicago answered my appeal by voluntarily addressing meetings of former Reading employees with a view to preventing them from taking the places of the striking members of the Brotherhood of Locomotive Engineers. Some of these Knights were personally opposed to me, or what was at that time known as the "administration," but they generously responded to my appeal to stand by the Brotherhood of Locomotive Engineers.

I am not aware that I was ever censured for what I did during the New York Central strike. I advised against it and did every honorable thing to prevent, or at least postpone it. It came at a time when Chauncey M. Depew, president of the New York Central Railroad, was on vacation in Europe. Mr. Depew loomed large in the political eye at that time as a presidential possibility. When he went to Europe he placed on the shoulders of H. Walter Webb the responsibility of conducting the affairs of his office during his absence. My connection with the affair began on February 3, 1890. I had observed a tendency on the part of the New York press to lecture the Knights of Labor on the Central because of their agitation of the wage question. The signs were unmistakable, even ominous, and on the date named I opened up a correspondence with Edward J. Lee, Master Workman of District Assembly 246 of the Knights of Labor on the New York Central system. That correspondence is given in full in the proceedings of the General Assembly of the Knights of Labor held that year in

Denver, Colorado. Bear in mind no part of this correspondence was given to the public by Mr. Lee or me until the strike ended. I was with the men all the time during the strike and when Roger A. Pryor[3] of New York, counsel for the men, after hearing all we had to say and offer, advised the District Master Workman to declare the strike at an end, he did so and did the best thing possible for the men in doing it.

During the strike my headquarters were in the old St. Cloud Hotel, corner of Broadway and 42d Street, New York City. I had many conferences with Mr. Webb, who was the first vice-president of the road. I noticed that on each occasion I was given a seat in exactly the same place at Mr. Webb's desk and to his right. A door to his left seemed to open a little when I took my seat but I paid no particular attention to it. I recall that at the time I thought that a stenographer might be sitting on the other side of the door taking down what I had to say. Years after, an Irishman named Longan, who had the reputation of always hitting what he aimed at, told me that he, at Mr. Webb's order, sat in the next room during my interviews with that gentleman and had his instructions to shoot me at the first evidence of hostility on my part, or on a sign from Mr. Webb. As I recall it now I wonder why I was not shot, for Mr. Webb was one of the most nervous men I ever had anything to do with. He had heard and read so many bad things about me that he felt his life was in jeopardy every time I called on him. Perhaps it was in my favor that at the time I was totally deaf in my right ear and as a consequence had to turn my face away from Mr. Webb when listening to what he had to say. This gave Mr. Longan and Mr. Webb, too, perhaps, the impression that I had no desire to harm the latter. On one occasion Mr. Webb became so excited and angry that the perspiration started out on his forehead and he mopped his face vigorously. It was a good thing for me that Mr. Webb did sweating enough for both of us, for if I indulged in it and put my hand in

[3] Roger Atkinson Pryor (1828-1919), Southern secessionist, served in the Confederate army, and came to New York City in 1865 where he became a successful lawyer. He was appointed judge of the court of common pleas in 1890, and six years later became a justice of the New York State Supreme Court. He appeared as counsel for the Haymarket "anarchists" before the United States Supreme Court.

my pocket to take out a handkerchief Mr. Longan might deem it his duty to terminate the interview in manner and form prescribed by Mr. Webb.

.   .   .   .

I shall omit all of the correspondence except the last letter to Mr. Lee, and that, with my words to the General Assembly on the subject, will be sufficient to acquaint you of my participation in the great strike on the New York Central and Hudson River Railroad in 1890.

I would like to be able to truthfully say that during that strike the Brotherhood of Locomotive Engineers was in sympathy with the men engaged in the struggle. Having in mind my response to the appeal of Mr. Arthur during the Reading strike, I wrote to him, as I did to the chiefs of the other railroad brotherhoods, asking for a conference that we might coöperate in securing some measure of justice for the striking Knights of Labor. All of the others responded and through their chief officers met with the General Executive Board of the Knights of Labor.

Mr. Arthur never acknowledged receipt of my letter. Members of the Brotherhood of Locomotive Engineers openly sided with the Railroad Company and in many instances let go of the throttle to take hold of link pin, brake wheel, and switch to help the company win in a contest with their brothers who were forced into the struggle at a time when it seemed to be for the best interests of the company to have them strike. Whether they did this with the full knowledge and consent of Mr. Arthur I do not know. I do know that at the height of the contest he publicly declared that our troubles were of no concern to the members of the B. of L. E.

I did not order that strike and did everything in my power to prevent it. Knights of Labor who took active part in organizing assemblies were discharged for no other reason than that they were Knights of Labor. When the strike was on, and before I took a hand in it, I asked Mr. Webb to arbitrate all matters of dispute. He said in one interview that men could belong to any church, party, or society they pleased. I then asked him to tell me what the men had done to merit dismissal, and from his written reply I quote these words: "The future prosperity of the road demands that it shall give no reason for discharging any of its employees." . . . In my acknowledgement of Mr. Webb's letter . . . I said:

Perhaps you are honestly sincere in saying that, but it seems to me that it is because you have the power to will it that way that you say it. A day will come when you shall yield the power you now misuse in view of the common good and in obedience to the command of the people as voiced by their representatives. When that day comes the "future prosperity" of the New York Central will demand that a reason why it shall not be operated in the interest of the people through their government, will have to be more forceful than your puny edict in order to prevent a government of all the people from controlling and operating a great public highway that you now imagine to be your private property.

Here follows my letter to Mr. Lee, heretofore referred to:

SCRANTON, PA., AUGUST 6, 1890

E. J. LEE, ESQ., MASTER WORKMAN D.A. 246
ALBANY, NEW YORK

Dear Sir and Brother:—I fear very much that history is about to repeat itself and that the disaster of the Reading Railroad is to be repeated. During the past two weeks agents of the New York Central and Hudson River Railroad have been along the line of the Delaware, Lackawanna and Western, the Jersey Central, the Reading, and the Erie and other Eastern roads engaging men to come on there in a short time. You see that it is the desire and intention of the managers of the New York Central to have the men strike, and unfortunately they are getting ready to fall into the trap. Some of your men have been discharged, and the rest are about to throw themselves out of work and lose their situations for want of a proper exercise of patience. You will acknowledge that this is the best time—for the company—to have the men strike. You will acknowledge that there are not ten men along the whole line—organized—who can maintain themselves for two months without assistance. You must acknowledge, if experience is worth anything, that the strike that is not won in ten days is lost. You will acknowledge that the chances are ninety-nine against one in favor of the company should a strike take place, and in spite of all these things the strike seems to be the only thing the men can think of. No generalship will amount to anything with them, no diplomacy, no skill in meeting a difficult question. They will now take the bit in their teeth and go the whole length. After they are out a few days they will be cursing the Order for not supporting them, will lose sight of every advantage they gained through the Order, and will lose sight of the fact that their condition will in future be as slaves compared with what it was through the efforts of the Order. Chauncey M. Depew knows human nature; his subordinates know it; but our people will not study it or take lessons from the past. Bear in mind that every railway in this country will stand behind the New York Central in this fight, secretly of course, and they will supply men and money to win for them the fight. Labor is and has always been the underdog in the fight, and never will have the patience to put up with indignities that are purposely placed in order to goad them on to hasty action. I do not say that a strike should not be entered upon, but I know that now is not the time for your men to take such action. Think for one moment, and you will know that whenever a concession has been wrung from capital, it does not act upon the spur of the moment and attempt to win it back again. It waits; it lays its plans and goes about it cautiously; it takes advantage of the proper time and discharges men, imposes restrictions or does some other thing to drive the men to a strike at a time when public opinion will be against them; and then when the men fall into the trap it calls out the militia, or else controls the public press and by means of it moulds public opinion in its favor. Sections 123 and 124 of the Constitution give the power to the District, and the District Executive Board and I have no voice or say in the matter. As a consequence the whole fate of the Order rests on the shoulders of the officers of D. A. 246. All over the country the signs of the times show an awakening that, if not meddled with, will give to the laboring men of the nation the power in a year or two. And here we find a Presidential candidate, fearing that power, going to Europe, after leaving instructions behind to goad the employes of his road on to a strike during his absence, so that the attention of the working people will be taken away from vital issues and directed where, in all probability, nothing but defeat and failure will result. It is a pity that the labor movement cannot be allowed to move ahead for two years, the critical period, without having some such thing as this take place to shatter the hopes of the toilers. I am not finding fault with your men, for they have acted nobly so far. They have borne with indignities that have stamped them as true men. They are true men, but they lack the power to make a strike a success in the closing days of a century in which brain power has made it possible for money to be pitted against the hungry stomachs of men on strike. Brother Lee, it is madness for the men of the New York Central to think of striking; they cannot win, and you know it as well as I do. Only the enthusiast who never counts the cost will say that a strike on a system of railways can succeed in these days. The New York Central management knows that if organization can be kept up among the men until the World's Fair they will not be able to refuse the men any just concession. They desire to break your power before you have succeeded in organizing other roads, and with a defeat now they know that the chances for a reorganization before 1893 is an impossibility, and that the men will always be at their mercy. 1892 will be Presidential year, 1893 the World's

Fair, but the patience of the workingmen will not hold out to remain organized quietly, while doing their part to organize other parts so that they will be as one man when these years come. It is but right that you should be officially notified of the condition of the Order so that you will take no step in the dark. We cannot assist you in the coming struggle, for the workmen of this age will not respond to assessments to support a strike, no matter how just it is, and for that reason we can only look on and watch the battle between the men of millions and the men whose hard lot has rendered it impossible for them to lay up enough to maintain themselves in a strike. I am hourly awaiting a notice to attend a meeting to settle up a strike that was hastily entered into. I must go and beg of a corporation to let men back again when they want to go. Had they acted coolly they could in one year have made it impossible for that corporation to discriminate against them. The company knew it, goaded them and they struck—not at the proper time, but at the very moment when the company desired it. I hope that Brother Holland will be able to ward off the blow, but your letter leaves me no hope for that, and before this reaches you I expect that it will be too late to do anything except look on. My sympathy you do not want; it will do no good anyway. The handful of organized men in this country will aid and sympathize with you; but the country is full of idle, unorganized workmen, who are only awaiting such an opening as will be presented to them, and over these I have no power, no authority, no jurisdiction, that will prevent them from taking the places of your men. If a strike is inevitable, let it be entered upon by the men of the New York Central with their eyes open. Let them know what is behind and before them. They know what to expect from organized labor, but do not know what to expect from that vast unknown quantity—the tramps, who have been made such by the almost unlimited power of the very men against whom your men direct the blow. I can say no more; in fact, I do not know what to say; and I can only hope that the good sense of the men will prevail and the strike be averted. It will do no good for me to write to the New York Locals. My letters would not have any effect. Only your presence can do any good there.

Hoping for the best, I remain sincerely and fraternally yours,

T. V. POWDERLY
GENERAL MASTER WORKMAN

Following the reading of the correspondence I commented [in the address to the G.A.] on the conditions which then prevailed. . . .

Overlooking the good points, if there are any, in my letter of August 6, many malicious persons and papers have presumed to interpret my language as being in favor of a conspiracy to get up a strike either during the Presidential year or when the World's Fair will be in progress. Those who can impartially read the English language will see that no such interpretation can be placed on my words. In writing that letter I did not tell Brother Lee that my informant of April 16 told me that the question of breaking the power of the Knights of Labor before 1893 had been discussed by officials of the New York Central Road. What I said was that if organization could be kept up until the World's Fair the New York Central would not be able to refuse any just concession. Those who saw conspiracy in that sentence would, if they were just, say that no just concession should be refused in any year. I am opposed to strikes. . . . If we must have strikes, then we should prepare for them, and not allow every subordinate to rush the Order into them at a moment's notice or without any preparation. If 1893 should be the best year to gain what is just and right and proper for labor, and a flat refusal should be given, why that would be the best year to strike and not at a time when no preparation had been made. My experience tells me this: The time to strike, according to editors and statesmen, is—NEVER. . . . I get tons of advice as to how to manage men and keep them from striking, but if the philanthropists who load me down with their counsel would go before those who have the power to do what would keep men from striking, and cause them to do justice by their employes, they would accomplish something. The grind of every day experience which the man of large family and small means must pass through can never be known by the good people who calmly tell us to be patient and not strike. So long as labor quietly submits to every indignity she will have no hand but her own raised in her defense. When driven to desperation she strikes, then thousands fly to arms to offer advice—nothing more. The man with the well-filled stomach can never see through the same glasses as the man who has to bring up a family of law-abiding, well-dressed, well-educated, refined, polite, and well-fed Americans on a salary of one dollar a day.

One paper in speaking of the allusion to the World's Fair, styled my language as diabolical, and asserted that the man who would attempt to get up a strike at a time when we would be "celebrating with glad shouts the anniversary of the landing of Columbus, who made it possible for us to have a country so blessed and free, should be hanged." If Columbus had no higher aspirations in view when he discovered this land than to have men working from dawn until dark for ninety cents and a dollar, his memory would not be deserving of many "glad shouts" from the workingmen of this nation. . . . We who now occupy the earth are of the present and live for the future, and should not be obliged to obey the commands of dead men, no matter how much we may respect their memories, if these commands are not in harmony with the aspirations of the best of humanity who live the life that moves the world NOW.

During the Central strike we had an opportunity to learn who our friends were among the newspapers, and found that they were exceedingly few. We were given quantities of counsel, warning and censure. . . . Take a glance over the columns of the papers that gave so much advice during that strike, and scarcely a word of advice or kindly counsel will now be discovered. So long as labor patiently plods along, accepting reductions in wages, restrictions of rights, and tyrannical impositions, just so long will the great papers of this land now on the side of monopoly ignore the labor question. The advocates of either free trade or high tariff will attempt to show that labor, with a big L, is the sole and only thought in the minds of the editors who would gather votes for favorites instead of scatter[ing] dollars among the needy who earned them. Workingmen cannot buy many newspapers—capitalists can afford to be more liberal. Workingmen have nothing to advertise—employers advertise extensively. Workingmen can give no passes on railroads—managers of corporations can and do give them. Workingmen are never seen above the level of the earth in which they dig—capitalists are always near the editor's chair, and never go beneath the surface of earth but once, and then they stay there. The doors that close behind the wealthy never open to workingmen. A combination of capitalists may organize to steal millions, and the greater part of the press of America is either blind to the fact or else attempts to show that it will be a great gain to the nation. . . . A combination of starving workingmen, with no advantages of education, society, experience, or dealings with men of business, attempts to secure a few cents more per day in order to maintain their families and contribute to the wealth of the nation (instead of spending it in Europe), and no word of kindly encouragement is written in these great papers. Let that combination of workingmen strike, whether foolishly or wisely, to gain as many cents as their employers have stolen millions, and that same venal press will bristle all over with warnings of direful results if they do not at once submit and go back to work. During strikes we are always told by the press that there is a better remedy than the strike, and so far none of them have pointed it out. The end is gained when the strike ends, and when meek submission again marks the conduct of the weary slave these great papers forget to tell us what the remedy is. Some of them say it lies through politics, but let labor attempt to stand the equal of capital in politics and the same papers shriek out their warnings to the "labor leaders to keep out of politics." The plain, unwelcome truth is that the majority of papers are fed, owned and managed by agents of those who control our railroads and banks. So far as our case being put before the world through the medium of that part of the daily press is concerned, it will never be done, and the volcano must continue to smolder until its lava burns its way into ears that would not otherwise open to the voice of justice.

That which I hinted at in my last letter to H. Walter Webb is becoming a reality. We now have a "United States Administration" of Railroads[4] . . . free from politics and the manipulation

[4] This statement was penned during the World War. In December, 1917, President Wilson in accordance with his war power took possession of the railways of the

of politicians; there appears to be no reason why fair, just treatment should not be accorded the people. While the Knights of Labor in our declaration of principles, asked that the government should take possession of the railroads, under the right of eminent domain, I was not quite convinced that full and complete possession of the railroads by the government would be best for the workmen who operated the roads. I could not rid my mind of the thought that ownership of the railroads might mean ownership of the men who worked for wages on the roads. . . . Take a mental journey back to that time and fix your mind on election day. . . . Then the corporation boss, the saloon boss, the political boss, and the church boss exerted an influence with the voter inside and outside of the polling booth. There was no secret ballot; paid emissaries of political parties stood outside each voting place peddling tickets from cigar boxes. The name of each candidate and the office he stood for appeared on a separate ticket, folded in such a way as to enable the officers of the election board to ascertain who the elector voted for. Each party printed its own tickets for its own candidates and invariably selected different type and a different quality of paper to be used in getting out the tickets. It was utterly impossible for a man to cast a secret ballot. Fancy a man who had a family depending on him for support daring to accept a ticket from the man who peddled tickets for a party that the boss of mine or workshop did not favor. . . . It was that condition of affairs, more than anything else, that brought me into politics in 1876 and from that day until it became an accomplished fact I fought for the adoption by law of a secret ballot. . . .

The New York Central will not discharge a man now for belonging to a labor organization, and I regret that I cannot congratulate H. Walter Webb on the fact that the future prosperity of the road will never again demand that an American freeman shall be discharged for associating with others in order to improve his condition.

---

entire country and placed them under control of a newly established Railroad Administration headed by Secretary of the Treasury, William Gibbs McAdoo. Eleven months later the roads were returned to private ownership and operation.

Chapter Fourteen

IN IRELAND'S CAUSE

WHEN THE War between the States ended in 1865, a number
of men of Irish birth and blood who had been discharged from
the armies of the North and South became members of the Irish
Revolutionary Brotherhood,[1] more popularly known as the Fenian Brotherhood. . . . The aim of the Fenian was to free
Ireland that she, as a republic, might "take her place among the
nations of the earth." Conventions were held, plans discussed
and ways and means considered by which an army of well
equipped Fenians could be landed in Ireland. The practicability
of transporting a large body of armed men across the Atlantic
did not appeal to a majority, and it was decided to raise an army,
equip it and invade Canada. The first attempt was made on June
1, 1866, and failed, as did a second one some three years later.
But that is all a part of the history of that day; with it I had
nothing to do, and I mention it here merely as an introduction to
what follows. One evening in October, 1866, in passing a public
hall in Carbondale where a meeting was being held, I, impelled
by curiosity perhaps, entered the hall to learn that it was an Irish
gathering and was being addressed by General John O'Neill[2] who
had led the ill-starred expedition to Canada some five months before. An appeal was made to those present to invest their money
in bonds of the Irish Republic. . . . The tale of Ireland's wrongs
was told in song and story that night, and I, becoming enthused,
left the meeting, hurried home, a distance of a mile and a half,

[1] Powderly apparently meant the Irish Republican Brotherhood founded in Dublin
by James Stephens in 1858.

[2] John O'Neill (1834-78) came to the United States from Ireland in his youth, and
served for three years with Union armies in the Civil War. In 1866 he was elected
inspector-general of the Fenian forces in the United States and he also commanded
the fruitless Fenian invasion of Canada in 1870.

took five dollars' worth of five, ten, and twenty-five cent bills from a box in which I kept my savings, and got back to the meeting before it adjourned.

There was no silver or gold in circulation then; we called the bills which represented our fractional currency "shinplasters." On every pay day I handed all my earnings to my mother, and, when she gave me twenty-five or fifty cents, I accepted it thankfully and without thought of asking for more. I had stored away in a tin box some fifteen or twenty dollars with which I intended to buy a watch. From my accumulated savings I took the price of a five-dollar bond of the Irish Republic—that was to come into being when the Fenians became strong enough. . . .

In 1867 Captain Edward O'Meagher Condon,[3] who had served with distinction in the Union Army during the Civil War, went to England as a representative of the Fenian Brotherhood. An attempt was made in Manchester, by the Fenians, to rescue two Irish prisoners as they were being conveyed through the streets in a prison van. In the scrimmage that ensued a policeman was accidentally killed and Condon with three others were tried, found guilty, and sentenced to death. The fact that Condon was an American citizen was given consideration, and that, together with the additional fact that he had nothing to do with the killing of the police officer, secured a commutation of his sentence to imprisonment for life.

In 1875 an attempt was made to obtain a pardon for Condon. The matter was referred to in a meeting of a debating club of which I was a member. A committee was appointed to secure signatures to a petition to Congress in Condon's behalf; I was appointed as one of a committee of three, with M. J. Lovern and P. M. Barrett as the other two, to circulate the petition. We obtained the signatures of 21,000 citizens of the county. To me was assigned the duty of forwarding the petition to [the] Hon. Hendrick B. Wright,[4] our representative in Congress. He presented

[3] Edward O'Meagher Condon (1835-1915) was born in Cork, Ireland. After he was released from prison he returned to the United States.

[4] Hendrick B. Wright (1808-81) was elected to the Pennsylvania State legislature (1841-43), was a member of the Democratic National Conventions (1840-60), and served in the House of Representatives in 1853-55, 1861-63, and 1877-81. Powderly is in error in implying that Wright was a member of Congress in 1876.

the petition as requested during the early part of 1876. Captain Condon was released in 1878.

Except to read of Irish affairs, I took no further part in them until after I became mayor of Scranton in 1878. On Monday, April 1, of that year I was sworn in before a joint session of the city councils, and quite a gathering of citizens who were curious to know what the new mayor looked like. The following day, April 2, 1878, Earl Leitrim was murdered on his estate in Ireland and his body thrown into a ditch by some of the tenants he had evicted some time before.

On the morning of the 3d of April the papers contained press dispatches with details of the assassination of Earl Leitrim. That evening I attended a meeting of an assembly of the Knights of Labor and was introduced, while there, to a young man named William Synott who told me that his father, mother, and sisters had been evicted, and their cabin in Leitrim torn down by Earl Leitrim some months before. Mr. Synott was present when I was sworn in as mayor, liked the tone of my inaugural address, and took a fancy to me. He was a Protestant and told me that Earl Leitrim played no favorites when he wished to evict a tenant; Catholic and Protestant were treated with cruelty unparalleled when their little holdings were wanted as fields on which to raise and graze cattle to add to the revenues of Earl Leitrim. I had many meetings with Mr. Synott after that and from his lips got a most graphic and interesting story of the sufferings and trials of the tenant farmers of Ireland. It was from William Synott I gained my first knowledge and impressions of Michael Davitt. . . .

I had business in Boston in December, 1878, and so timed my going as to be there on the evening that Michael Davitt addressed a large meeting on the Irish question. It was at that meeting . . . that I first met Davitt and John Boyle O'Reilly.[5] . . .

From that time on through 1879 I closely followed every shifting scene on the stage of Irish affairs, and when it was proposed to invite Charles Stewart Parnell to visit the United States, I was one of the committee having the matter in hand.

[5] John Boyle O'Reilly (1844-90), an active Fenian, came to the United States in 1869, and participated in the Fenian raid into Canada the following year. He was a lecturer and writer, and became editor of the Boston *Pilot*.

The Irish National Land League was formally organized in Dublin, October 21, 1879.[6] Parnell, then a member of Parliament was elected president, and Davitt elected as one of the secretaries. It was in that same month that Davitt made his famous speech at Michaelstown in which he advised the tenantry of Ireland to hold back the rent until the rights of the renters had been recognized. Michael Davitt was the founder of the Land League. He ignited the fires of opposition to rack-renting landlordism and had them burning briskly when the Dublin meeting was held on October 21. . . .

Parnell accepted the invitation to visit the United States,[7] and on January 2, 1880, landed in New York. The invitation of the people of Scranton to visit that city was accepted, and on February 10, 1880, he addressed a monster meeting in the Armory in Scranton. Accompanying him were his sister Fanny Parnell, John Murdock of Inverness, Scotland, and John Dillon.[8] I, as mayor of Scranton, presided over the meeting, introduced the three speakers, Parnell, Dillon, and Murdock, and on calling for subscriptions, at the request of Mr. Parnell, some three thousand, five hundred dollars were handed in. That meeting was held in the interest of Irish land reform but it was far from being an Irish meeting. Americans, English, Scotch, Germans, Welsh, and Irish made up the meeting, but the greater part of the money collected was given by the American citizens of Scranton.

The committee that arranged for the meeting continued to act as a collecting agency for Mr. Parnell until August, 1880. On the 4th of that month Scranton Branch No. 1 of the "Irish National Land League" was organized. I was elected president and continued in that office during the existence of the Land League. . . .

Through the efforts of Father Lawrence Walsh of Waterbury, Connecticut, a National Convention of the Land League was

[6] The League sought to bring about the reduction of rack rents and to develop peasant proprietorship in Ireland.

[7] Parnell was requested by a resolution of the Land League to visit America "for the purpose of obtaining assistance from our exiled fellow countrymen."

[8] When Parnell hurriedly returned home, John Dillon (1851-1927) completed the organization of the Land League in the United States. In 1890 he made another journey to the United States. He ranks with Parnell and Davitt in importance in Irish history during the years 1878-1918.

called to meet in Buffalo on January 12, 1881. Elected to represent the Scranton branch, I attended the convention. The officers elected were . . . Patrick A. Collins,[9] Boston, Massachusetts, president; [the] Rev. Patrick Cronin,[10] first vice-president; T. V. Powderly, second vice-president; and [the] Rev. Lawrence Walsh . . . treasurer.

From that time until the Land League merged into the National League, my work became national in its character. The Knights of Labor were then working secretly, and, as many members were Irish or sympathizers with the struggle of the Irish people for land reform, they invited me to visit cities and towns throughout the country for the purpose of speaking at Land League meetings. I accepted as many invitations as I could and when the public, or Land League, meeting would be over a secret meeting of Knights of Labor would follow. In this way I was of use to both organizations, although it frequently taxed my powers of endurance to the utmost.

It may be of interest to quote from an address to the American people, issued by President Collins shortly after the adjournment of the Buffalo convention. I do this to give you an idea of what the Irish National Land League aimed at:

The Land League in Ireland continues its existence for the purpose of removing the cause of famine—landlord robbery of the people; for the purpose of compelling such changes in the law as will make every Irish peasant the owner of the soil he cultivates.

.   .   .   .

If the Irish people had the power to rid themselves at once of Crown and the landlords, they would use it, and the moral sense of mankind would justify and applaud it.

But in the Land League programme there is no suggestion of resort to armed force. Irish discontent and agitation are to run their course within the limits of British law and Constitution.

To lift the people of the Island up from misery, to educate them into a full realization of their condition, rights and power, to organize them in

[9] Patrick Andrew Collins (1844-1905) came to the United States from Ireland when he was four years old. A lawyer and active Democrat, he served in Congress for three terms, and was United States consul general in London 1893-97.

[10] Patrick Cronin (1835-1905) was born in Ireland.

solid mass against the authors of their wrongs, to force by lawful means such changes in the land laws as will make the people the owners of the soil they till—this is the mission of the Land League of Ireland.

The Land League in the United States is an organization auxiliary to that in Ireland. It has no part in shaping the policy of the Irish body. Its functions are to make the case of Ireland fully understood in America, so that the public opinion of this republic shall be intelligently and forcibly expressed on the side of justice and liberty in Ireland; and to aid, by our sympathy and means, the splendid march of the Irish people on to justice, prosperity, and self government. . . .

Through the efforts of President Collins and Patrick Ford,[11] editor of the *Irish World*, a convention of the "Irish Race" was held in Chicago on November 30, and December 1 and 2, 1881. It was a magnificent representative gathering, not of the Irish race alone but of others who sympathized with the Irish cause. As the delegate of Branch No. 1, of the Scranton League, I attended the convention, was one of its secretaries, and represented Pennsylvania on the committee on resolutions. On Saturday night November 25, 1881, I presided over a large meeting in the Academy of Music in Scranton. The meeting was addressed by [the] Hon. T. P. O'Connor,[12] member of Parliament, and in company with him I went to Chicago to attend the convention. It was held in McCormack's Hall and continued in session three days. In the committee on resolutions I first met Father Thomas Conaty,[13] then of Worcester, Massachusetts, afterwards rector of the Catholic University, Washington, D. C., and later on, until his death in 1915, Bishop of Los Angeles, California. T. P. O'Connor and T. M. Healy,[14] who represented Irish constituencies in the British Parliament, were present during the entire convention.

[11] Patrick Ford (1835-1913), born in Galway, Ireland, came to the United States in 1842, and founded the *Irish World* in New York City in 1870. For the remainder of his life he was a very active champion of the cause of Ireland, seeking complete independence.

[12] Thomas Power O'Connor (1848-1929), the extremely popular journalist and Member of Parliament, was made a member of the Privy Council by the first Labor Government in 1924.

[13] Thomas James Conaty (1847-1915), born in Ireland, came to America in 1850, and became the fifth Bishop of Monterey and Los Angeles in 1903. Joining the Irish nationalist movement after Parnell's visit to America in 1879, he became treasurer of the Parnell fund.

[14] Timothy Michael Healy (1855-1931) sat as a member of Parliament from 1880-1918, and served as Governor-General of the Irish Free State, 1922-28.

They attended an all-night session of the committee on resolutions but took no other than a listening part in the deliberations. On the return journey from Chicago, Father Conaty and I addressed Land League meetings in Cleveland, Ohio, and Buffalo, Rochester, and Albany, New York. During 1881-82 and 1883 I made tours through New York, Ohio, Indiana, Illinois, West Virginia, and Maryland in company with Father Conaty, [the] Hon. William E. [*sic*] Redmond,[15] James Redpath,[16] and Henry George; of course these men were not with me on all occasions, but I spoke from the same platform with one or the other of them on several occasions.

In Binghamton, New York, after the meeting was over and the reception committee had vanished, Father Conaty asked me if I had been reimbursed for my time and effort in the Land League cause. When I said: "Sometimes they pay my hotel bills," he laughed as he said, "That's what they do for me, but I am glad to be of service in so good a cause."

From meetings that I addressed in Pennsylvania some $87,000 were forwarded through Robert M. McWade, then city editor of the *Ledger*, Philadelphia, to the Parnell Committee in Ireland. Mr. McWade was treasurer for Pennsylvania, and through his hands there passed three quarters of a million dollars to the Parliamentary Committee. When the auditing committee went over his accounts they found that he had sent to Ireland some fifty dollars more than had been forwarded to him by the contributing branches of the Land League. When the committee called Mr. McWade's attention to the matter and asked for an explanation he said: "I cannot tell you how it happened. I suppose that in some way I got some of my own money mixed up with league funds and not being positive as to whether I had made a mistake I gave Ireland the benefit of the doubt and sent it all over to the treasurer in Dublin."

When the committee assured Mr. McWade that the receipts

---

[15] Powderly probably meant William Hoey Kearney Redmond (1861-1917), John Redmond's brother, who visited the United States in 1883 and 1884.

[16] James Redpath (1833-91) was of Scotch birth and came to Michigan in 1850. An energetic reformer during the bulk of his life, he was an editor, journalist, and lecture promoter. His interest in Ireland began in 1879.

from the local branches and vouchers all proved that he was entitled to a refund he refused to entertain the proposition.

. . . .

Early in 1883 a Coercion Act was passed by the British parliament and the Land League was suppressed.[17] The leading spirits of that movement brought into existence a new and more powerful organization known as the Irish National League. It recognized as members the common laborers of Ireland, and under the masterful direction of Michael Davitt these men joined the League in great numbers.

On April 23, 1883, the American Land League met for the last time in national convention at Philadelphia. A committee on conference was appointed to meet with a like committee from the new organization. This joint committee agreed on the union of both organizations, and, on motion of Father Patrick Cronin, the old Irish National Land League of America passed out of existence by being merged into the Irish National League. . . .

On the morning of April 26, 1883, a meeting of delegates from all over the United States and Canada met in Horticultural Hall, Philadelphia, ratified the amalgamation of the two bodies, and proceeded to hold the first convention in America of the new organization—the Irish National League. I was a delegate and the choice of Pennsylvania as member of the committee on resolutions.

After the adjournment of the 1883 convention I never again held office in the League. The Knights of Labor had thrown off the garb of secrecy, began to expand, and claimed every hour of my time. I frequently addressed meetings of the Irish National League but was not officially identified with it after 1883.

One day when Michael Davitt was in Scranton I, "by the power in me vested as G. M. W.," initiated him into the Knights of Labor. I gave him a letter "to the Order wherever found," to recognize him as a member. I do not know what local assembly

---

[17] Powderly must have had in mind the Protection of Person and Property Act of March 2, 1881, which with other legislation paved the way for the suppression of the Land League. The League, however, reappeared as the Irish National League in October, 1882.

Davitt affiliated with, but that he did great service in organizing throughout Great Britain I have ample evidence.

On Tuesday evening, May 8, 1888, District Assembly No. 208 of the Knights of Labor of England held their first public meeting in Smethwick. . . . The past District Master Workman and orator of the occasion was Michael Davitt. His speech was published in English papers of May 9. During his lecture Mr. Davitt related his experiences at the General Assembly held the previous year in Minneapolis, Minnesota. From the published report of his speech I quote this extract:

> The Knights of Labor is not an American society, or an Irish society or an English society. It is a society of all of these and more. It tells us that an injury to one man is the concern of all men. By its aid here in England we are enabled to meet on common ground for the first time and to each of us is given the great privilege of taking a member by the hand and calling him brother regardless of his country, creed, or condition in life.

The English papers . . . gave prominence to that part of Mr. Davitt's speech, some of them commented on it as the "dawn of a new era among the industrial people of the British Isles."

One day in the early part of February, 1889, on my way from the South I saw in a Richmond paper a London dispatch stating that a man named Henry Le Caron had testified against Charles Stewart Parnell in his suit against the London *Times*.[18] Le Caron claimed to have lived in the United States and to have acted as a spy on the Fenians, Clan na Gael,[19] and other Irish societies. The name appeared familiar. I searched my files on reaching home and found a letter received by me from one Henry Le Caron during the great Gould strike in the Southwest. It was dated April 3, 1886, was written on the letter head of the Southern Hotel, St. Louis, and received by me a couple of days after. As a

---

[18] Actually, Parnell refused to bring a libel action against *The Times* for its series of articles "Parnellism and Crime," on the ground that justice could not be obtained from a London jury. *The Times* published letters supposedly written by Parnell, who finally accepted the offer of a special commission of three judges to investigate. This court sat for more than a year, and discovered that at least some of the letters were forgeries. *The Times* settled out of court, agreeing to pay £5,000 damages.

[19] Fenianism was represented in America by the Clan-na-Gael, which sought to bring about a forcible separation of Ireland from England by means of a conflict between England and the United States.

specimen of the kind of advice I was the recipient of in those days
I give it here in full:

At such a time as this a few words of advice and encouragement may be
of service to you, and may possibly serve to solve the very difficult problem
so suddenly thrust before you. A peaceful, law-abiding strike will never
conquer such a power as you have to deal with. Moral suasion, so good in
trivial cases, becomes of no use when applied to such a "gold"-hearted fiend
as Jay Gould. Entreaty, argument, and sympathy appeal to him in vain, and
though they plead with him in thunder tones, the sound falls on leaden ears.
You must touch his pocket and meet force with force. You must not be
expected to publicly countenance any but peaceful measures. You will not
even know that any other has been resorted to. All that you need do will
be to give me the names of a few of your lieutenants along the Missouri
Pacific road, and I will attend to the rest. Name only those in whom you
can place implicit confidence, and I will place in their hands the material
that will, if properly handled, *destroy every bridge and culvert* on the road.
I have made a study of explosives, and can give you an unfailing remedy
for the wrongs of which your members complain. All that you need to do
will be to write the names I have asked for on the blank space in this sheet,
return it to me without [your] name even, and I will manage the rest.
Whatever is to be done must be done quickly. I know you by reputation
for years, and can trust you. All I ask is your confidence, and in return I
promise the most gratifying results.

(*Signed*) HENRY LE CARON

When I received that letter I at once communicated with Martin Irons . . . , and warned him against having anything to do
with Le Caron. I suspected that he was a spy in the employ of
the railroad company. I then filed the letter away and was fortunate enough to remember it three years later. . . .

The following day I went to Philadelphia to attend a meeting
of our General Executive Board. I had the Le Caron letter pho-
tographed, sent a copy to Parnell, another to Davitt and one to
each of several persons, whom I knew to be friendly to Parnell,
in London; the original I mailed to William E. Gladstone with
[the] request that he hand it to Parnell. In my letters transmit-
ting the copies I said nothing about sending the original to Gladstone. My reason for sending it to him was that I thought his mail
would not be tampered with; that of the others might be, and

[I] took no chances by mentioning in any of my letters to the others that I had mailed the original to Gladstone.

Immediately on receiving my missive, Parnell cabled me to send him the original Le Caron letter, but, before my answering cablegram reached him, Gladstone had placed it in Parnell's hands.

That letter was very damaging to Le Caron. Its publication in London had the effect of discrediting him, and was of assistance to Mr. Parnell. About the time it reached London, I gave it to the press for publication in the United States, and as a consequence much of it was cabled to England.

Three years later, in 1892, Le Caron brought out in London a book entitled: *Twenty-five Years in the Secret Service; the Recollections of a Spy*. On page 201 of that book, Le Caron deals with the proceedings of an Irish meeting in Chicago at which I was present. He mentions several names but does not attempt to quote anyone but me. He puts these words in my mouth:

The killing of English robbers and tyrants in Ireland, and the destruction by any and all means of their capital and resources, which enables them to carry on their robberies and tyrannies, is not a needless act. Hence I am in favor of the torch for their cities and the knife for their tyrants till they agree to let Ireland severely alone. London, Liverpool, Manchester, and Bristol in ashes may bring them to view it in another light.

Michael Davitt sent a copy of Le Caron's book to me and at the same time informed me that it was the intention to publish it in America. He gave me the name of the New York publishing house that was to reproduce the volume in the United States. I at once notified the publishing house that when the book appeared I would begin an action for libel. That book has never been published in the United States.

In November, 1892, Mr. Davitt in the London *Speaker*, writing of Le Caron's assault on me, said:

. . . There was not a word of this monstrous accusation given by Le Caron in his evidence. . . . The spy's motive in concocting this villainous speech is one of revenge for the publication by Mr. Powderly of a letter in the American press during the *Times'* Commission in which he recalled the fact that a person signing himself Le Caron had once written to him offering to blow up portions of the Missouri Pacific Railway during a strike, if the head of the Knights of Labor would consent to such a policy. Enough is known of Mr. T. V. Powderly, even on this side of the Atlantic, to make it unnecessary on my part to defend him from Le Caron's malignant and baseless imputations.

I was present at the Chicago meeting but made no speech there, and, had I done so, would not have given the lie to my every profession and act in the American labor movement by advocating violence or the destruction of property. Davitt gave a partial reason for Le Caron's reporting of a speech that was never made. He might have said that Le Caron's failure to entrap me during the strike in 1886 furnished an additional reason for his making for me the kind of a speech he would be pleased to have me make.

Property is the product of labor, I honor and revere labor and at no time, in no place, on no occasion have I ever advocated the destruction of that which labor creates. To my knowledge I have never killed any useful thing that God endowed with life. How could I advocate the use of the knife either here or in England? I have helped to win some victories for humanity during my life; not one of them bears the stain of a drop of blood of man or beast.

On several occasions I presided over large meetings in Scranton in behalf of the people of Ireland. As I look back at my work in that cause I feel that I should not be censured for saying that [never], except in one instance were my expenses paid by those for whom I gave my effort. I say this with pride and firmly believe that if the many lips now sealed with the stamp of death of those who worked for Ireland could voice their experiences of those faraway days, they would say of their labors what I have said of mine. Unselfishness characterized their every effort, to be of use was their ambition, and love of right their impelling motive.

.   .   .   .

I came near forgetting to say that I made preparations some years ago, when I was much younger and knew more than I do now, to establish a republican form of government in Ireland. To accomplish that purpose and be prepared for opposition on the part of some unreasonable person or force, I bought a Remington rifle, bayonet, accoutrements, and fifty rounds of ammunition. Of course I didn't think I would need that much but deemed it best to be fully supplied.

I was sanguine of success, for a number of other young men of Scranton were united with me in the project and were to accompany me to Ireland where . . . I intended to persuade the representatives of the British Government to retire, peaceably of course, so that the good cause would be promoted without delay. Something occurred, however, to prevent me from freeing Ireland, and the matter was indefinitely postponed.

One day a neighbor of mine who was also a work mate, was fatally injured in the shop and after a few days of lingering agony died. He was English, a Staffordshire man, and in every way a splendid fellow. He had had a great deal of sickness in his family, which consisted of a wife and four children. My wife informed me the day of his death that the family was practically penniless and something had to be done. We decided that inasmuch as it didn't appear to be a good time to go to Ireland, I should raffle off my rifle and devote the proceeds to the relief of the family of John Singleton. John T. Howe, who was a neighbor and a printer, agreed to furnish the tickets. He did, and the rifle and bayonet were raffled off for something like one hundred and twenty-two dollars.

The proceeds of the raffle of my Irish rifle were devoted to the relief of the family of an Englishman, and while I didn't free Ireland with my rifle, I helped to bury an Englishman with it. Show me the Irishman who has done any better than that for Ireland.

In what is herein set down with regard to my connection with Irish affairs, I make no attempt to do more than intimate that I tried to do something for the land my mother and father were born in, of which they cherished the fondest recollections and for which they entertained the deepest veneration.

.   .   .   .

Chapter Fifteen

A VISIT TO HELL

CROSSING FROM Jersey City to New York on the ferry one day, I met Father Thomas Ducey[1] then in the public eye a great deal because of his defense of Dr. McGlynn.[2] While [I was] walking up Cortlandt Street a man asked me for enough money to get something to eat. I had a fifty-cent piece in my pocket and quietly slipped it into the man's hand. That Father Ducey saw it was not my fault, for the man looked at it so suspiciously that I expected to see him bite it to test its soundness, he not expecting to get more than a nickel or dime perhaps.

As we parted from the man, who by the way I directed to a nearby restaurant, Father Ducey said: "You must have money plenty; how do you know that man won't drink it?" I said: "That man is hungry; he won't drink it. Let us go back and see what he does with it." We followed the man into the restaurant, took seats back of him, and noted how he tried to get the most for his money. After a while I leaned over to him and whispered: "Oh,

[1] Thomas James Ducey came to the United States from Ireland at the age of five in 1848. Twenty years later he was ordained, and soon made a name for himself as a reformer. His sermons irritated members of the Tweed Ring, and they vainly tried to silence him. He also fought municipal corruption in New York City in the eighties and engaged in social reform activities.

[2] Edward McGlynn (1837-1900) was the central figure of a controversy which rocked Catholic, reformist, and labor circles in the eighties. McGlynn became a Single-Taxer and supported Henry George in the latter's 1886 campaign. Earlier he had been directed to retract his views on the land question. In September, 1886, Archbishop Corrigan forbade him to speak at a Henry George meeting. When McGlynn did not obey, Archbishop Corrigan suspended him from the exercise of his priestly functions. McGlynn's conflict with the hierarchy continued; he was removed from his pastorate, summoned to Rome, and was finally excommunicated in July, 1887. He continued to be an active advocate of the Single-Tax, and was president of the Anti-Poverty Society. Assurances that his Single-Tax views were not contrary to Catholic teaching made it possible for him to be restored to the ministry at the close of 1892.

order a good meal, there's enough here to pay for it." He did, and gave ample evidence of having a good working appetite with him. When he finished he turned to thank me, and I asked him if he wouldn't like to have a drink to top off with. I ask my prohibition friends who may read this to note his answer: "No, thank you, not now. If you asked me to have a drink before eating I would have done so, but while I do drink occasionally I never think of it when I'm not hungry."

That night Father Ducey and I discussed the temperance question and the particular incident of the morning. . . . He did not understand "how so inveterate an enemy of liquor could ask a man to have a drink," and desired that I explain to him all about it.

I told him that I was not an enemy to liquor; that, although a total abstainer, I had no hatred of it. All during my childhood my father kept a decanter of whiskey or wine on a sideboard in full view of everyone; I never touched either, and not one of my brothers ever meddled with them. Once in a while when a friend from a distance called, would my father take down the decanter and glasses to treat the visitor. Except in that way I never saw my father drink. I never saw him under its influence. My mother never touched it. I was never told that I should not drink but there was no temptation in it for me. I was not brought up to either hate or like liquor. My opposition to it grew out of the way my fellow workers abused it by drinking too much of it. I had carefully investigated the drink habit . . . by discussing the question with drinkers in their homes, and had learned that with good pay and steady employment workingmen were more inclined to seek their homes than saloons when the day's work was done. It shocked Father Ducey when I told him that employers of labor who ranted loudest against liquor drinking were secretly engaged in debauching, not only full grown men, but boys by selling them liquor labeled "sundries" from their company stores. The plain truth at that time was that many employers would rather employ a man who drank than one who did not, for the reason that the slave to drink became the slave of his employer and could be depended on to work cheap. . . .

Many prominent prohibitionists of that day sought my influence to bolster up their cause but I was not long in finding out that a more detestable set of hypocrites did not exist. They made no pretense of keeping liquor from a man in order to stir an ambition in his breast that would cause him to reach out for better pay, better working conditions, and better home surroundings. No, their main argument with me was that workingmen could afford to work for smaller pay if they didn't spend so much money for drink. Of course all prohibitionists were not of that kind, but in the main they were faddists, reformed drunkards, or people who regarded us, the workers, as a class to be patronized because we were poor. Not only would they regulate our appetite for liquor but everything else. . . .

After discussing the temperance question for some time, I abruptly asked this question: "Father Ducey, were you ever in hell?"

My question . . . startled him . . . and . . . I continued: "Come to Scranton, spend a few days with me and I'll take you through hell. You preach that out of hell there's no redemption, but I assure you of redemption if you come." We arranged on a time, and during his stay in Scranton I piloted him through two or three coal mines. . . .

Dressed in a suit of waterproof clothing, I led Father Ducey to the "carriage," and as it fell into the mine it came near depriving him of breath. An experienced engineer could drop the carriage into the mine so swiftly that the uninitiated would imagine the rope had broken and expect to be dashed to pieces at the foot of the shaft. When we reached the sump, or bottom, of the shaft we got into a mine car and were driven about a half a mile to a gangway leading to a chamber where a miner and laborer were at work. I introduced Father Ducey and told the miner to allow him to help drill the hole in the breast; he did, and I confess I kept him at it longer than necessary. The process of drilling the hole, filling it with powder, adjusting the fuse, touching it off, and running out to shield ourselves from the blast by standing behind a pillar was all gone through with. The dull report of the shot rolled in and out of that chamber; it mingled with the echoes of other blasts going off in the mine; it died away to nothing and came back with a reinforced din that rendered the place even more unearthly than before. The smoke following the explosion made the foul air fouler. The appearing and disappearing lights that flickered here and there through the mine as mine workers passed and repassed so noiselessly as to give the impression that they were but ghosts . . . the constant drip, drip, drip of the water trickling from the roof, the distant hee haw of a mule, the rushing of a rat across our feet now and then and occasionally the sight of several pairs of eyes that shone like diamonds through the gloom, the almost overpowering odor of mine gas, . . . the yellow ooze and slime that lay ahead of every step in the main gangway, the goblin-shaped fungus growths that faced us at every turn in the old workings, dripping with what some miners call the death sweat, were all so new, so weird, uncanny, and so unlike anything he had seen before that Father Ducey asked if we could not hasten our departure from the mine. We walked from where he helped mine the coal to the foot of the shaft. I arranged this in order that he might know something of the perils and discomforts of foot passage in the mine. Mules drawing cars driven by boys who used language strong enough to fracture the roof tore along, the cars swaying from side to side. As they passed we had to step down off the track into the yellowish water on the side. Frequently a lump of coal would fall off one of the cars and narrowly miss us on its way to the ditch alongside of the track. As we drew near the foot of the shaft, noises that we did not notice on entering came to our ears with a distinctness and in such harmonious blending as to give the impression that they were produced by some vast instrument played upon by a wind from the spirit land. The voices of mine workers speaking to each other in the various chambers, thrown back from the solid walls of coal fronting them, found their echoes into [sic] the main gangway, and these, uniting with the sounds made by the miner at his work and the mournful moan of the "squeeze" where the roof was giving way in worked-out chambers, produced sounds such as can be heard nowhere else and which cannot be described by human agency. When we reached the surface and sunlight again, Father Ducey remained silent for a long time. It was fully half an hour after we reached home that he said to me: "That is hell, sure enough. I shall never complain of the price I pay for coal again."

I explained to him that the shaft we visited was only a vestibule to hell as compared to some mines in the neighborhood; that the expenses of the miner were so adjusted that he was being systematically robbed in overcharges for powder and other supplies, and charging more for coal in the hands of a middleman wouldn't help the miner any.

The following day I arranged to have Father Ducey visit the homes of three or four of my miner friends. He saw floors without carpets, walls devoid of ornament, diminutive bedrooms, but all as neat as wax and in perfect order. We stopped for supper at the home of Richard Evans, and Father Ducey had an opportunity to sample the fare of a coal miner. I had, of course, arranged previously with Mrs. Evans to bring Father Ducey with me, and to be sure and put nothing extra on the table. Notwithstanding my admonition, she did add a delicacy or two not on the regular bill of fare. I purposely selected a Welsh Protestant, rather than an Irish Catholic family, for I thought the latter would be sure to have something extra for the occasion, but Mrs. Evans wouldn't allow a priest to sit at her table and not get the best she could afford, particularly "when he came with Mayor Powderly."

During his visit to Scranton I initiated Father Ducey in the Knights of Labor far enough to let him know what we were aiming at.

Before parting . . . at the Scranton station he said: "I am leaving your city in wonder. You have little or no drunkenness here contrary to all the stories I've heard about you. I have been in hell, and it seems to me that if I had to work in such a place and live in such surroundings I would not only drink but stay drunk. I understand you now."

Father Ducey was quite well off in his own right; he had . . . entrée to the homes of a number of coal-mine owners in New

York, and no member of the Knights of Labor or United Mine Workers ever did better service for the coal miners of Pennsylvania than he, for he kept me busy supplying him with data to be used when crossing legs with coal operators under their mahoganies, whenever occasion presented itself.

Chapter Sixteen

JAMES McNEILL WHISTLER
AND OTHERS

ONE DAY in the beginning of 1881 I wrote my name on the register of the old Astor House, New York, for the first time. The Knights of Labor had attracted but little public notice up to that hour. Although chief of the organization, I was not recognized as one identified with it officially, so wherever I was known at all it was as mayor of Scranton. Labor mayors were scarce, and I was regarded as a curiosity. People would "stop, look, and listen" when I was pointed out. They would stare, some in awe, as it were, others in doubt, some in scorn, and all would turn away disappointed. I didn't have horns, my shoes didn't appear to conceal split hoofs; in fact I didn't differ much in appearance from other men of my size, build, and complexion. . . .

When the clerk at the Astor House, the courteous, gentlemanly W. Van Benscoten, read my name, he assigned me to as pleasant a room as they had in the hotel. . . . Thirty-two years after my first stop at that hotel, on May 24, 1913, the last Saturday it was open to receive guests, I wrote my name once again on its register, and the same clerk, in the same pleasant tone, said: "This is the last time we'll meet here, Mr. Powderly. Your old room, the one I put you in the first time you stopped here, is vacant, would you like to have it tonight?" I spent the last Saturday night and the last Sunday morning of its existence as a hotel in the Astor House and in the same room I occupied the first time I stopped there.

One autumn afternoon in passing through the corridor of the Astor House I almost collided with John Boyle O'Reilly as he came rushing out of the parlor. After our greetings had been duly exchanged and acknowledged, he, as if seized by a sudden inspiration, grabbed my arm and drew me into the parlor, whispering as he did so something about a Whistler. Two men stood chatting in the parlor. One was Allen Thorndike Rice,[1] the other James McNeill Whistler. I was presented to both by O'Reilly, who in doing so said something about a *rara avis*. I never could make out who he referred to, and before I could inquire Whistler lifted his glass—a monocle, I think—to his eye and deliberately sized me up. I had never heard of Whistler, wouldn't know him from a bunch of radishes, and thought, if I gave the incident a thought at all, that it was the proper thing to do since I was a curiosity anyway, and, while I didn't relish it, couldn't help being surveyed from all kinds of angles and viewpoints. When O'Reilly went on to say that I represented the "horny-handed sons of toil," Whistler lifted one shoulder a bit, and said in anything but an agreeable tone of voice: "A beastly lot, your iron workers and miners."

Turning to O'Reilly I asked: "Did you say this man is a painter?" O'Reilly nodded affirmatively, and was about to say something when I abruptly turned to Whistler and in my sweetest tone of voice, inquired: "House or sign painter?" Really I did not know he was a scenic or portrait painter, but I guessed at it. I did not think that his unkind remark about my constituents should be taken as a joke, and that was why I insulted him. I know I insulted him; he said so, and said it with such a flourish of fists, cane, and eyeglass that I expected to be the victim of an assault. He wound up his verbal succotash of abuse with a reference to brutes. I understood his classification to include me.

O'Reilly stood to my right; he knew that the proper thing for me to do was to knock the whistle out of Whistler. He was a friend, yes a kinsman of mine, distant, it is true, but near enough that day to restrain my good right arm from knocking Whistler through the window into Broadway. He didn't restrain it; I had to do the restraining myself. I changed my mind about killing Whistler when Rice said that Whistler was an artist, had spent

[1] Charles Allen Thorndike Rice (1851-89), a successful journalist, who purchased the *North American Review* in 1876, was an advocate of ballot reform. Appointed minister to Russia in 1889, he died suddenly when he was on the point of leaving for that country.

most of his time in an atmosphere where genius flourished, and didn't view the workingman from the same standpoint that I occupied. He said a lot of pretty things and ended by hoping we'd get well enough acquainted to like each other.

There was an oil painting on the parlor wall; I recall it as a Venetian scene. I said: "Excuse me gentlemen I want to see this picture," and walked as close as I could to the painting. When I rejoined the group, Whistler, in a pitying tone, reminded me that I should never view a painting at such close range if I desired to appreciate its good points. I made no explanation about being nearsighted; he gave me the opportunity, and I seized it. Squaring myself in front of him, I said: "I want you to listen to me awhile now. You call the men of labor a beastly lot and do it because you are as ignorant of them and their ways as I am of your wonderful art. When you wish to view your own work or that of another artist, you stand away from it to get the best impression of it. No matter whose product it may be, once it swings in view you dare not go close to it for fear of seeing its imperfections, its roughness, its beastly surface. Distance, in this case lends favor to the view. If you have ever given the worker consideration it must have been along the same line of thought you entertain when approaching the canvas for inspection. . . . Your work blossoms out after but a few years of training, steady copying, and hard labor, but labor it is whether you like to call it so or not, and your product, no matter how well done, is not perfect, for it is the work of human hands.

"The great artist of the universe, He whom we are taught to believe does all things well (though I doubt it when I see such fellows as you), created man as His masterpiece. We are told He fashioned him in His own image that he might approach nearest of all earthly things to perfection. Through all the centuries and ages that divine artist has been tracing His image on the canvas of time and eternity, yet you call His work beastly. You call it beastly because you treat the Godlike canvas, as you do the one you and your fellow artists use, by standing away from it whenever you subject it to inspection. To know laboring men you must not treat them as you do paintings, you must get close to them and when you do you'll see, if your God has endowed you with ordinary discernment, that no matter what the surroundings may be, no matter how rough they appear, no matter how beastly you imagined them—the human habitation of God's own art— you'll find in the honest man who faithfully does his work the greatest subject for an artist to transfer in oil and color to canvas.

"Come with me to Scranton, go down in the coal mines with me, meet the beastly coal miner of your imagination and when the scales of ignorance, prejudice, or caste have fallen away from be- fore your eyes you will not be offended by sight of anything rough or beastly, you'll see what you ought to be—a man."

Did he strike me with his cane as I expected when I was deliv- ering that tirade? No, indeed. He surprised me by throwing the cane on the floor, catching my right hand in his, and with the other giving me a whack on the shoulder as he said: "Damn me, but you're an artist yourself. I'll go to Scranton and see your burrowing workers."

O'Reilly and Rice clapped their hands in approval, and the Rev. Dr. George Hepworth,[2] who had entered the room some- time during my verbal onslaught on Whistler was introduced, and said some nice things about my views of art.

Whistler did not come to Scranton but asked Hepworth to do so, and he did, spending several days there with me. I took him through the mines, iron and steel mills, as well as the blast furnaces.

They were going to take dinner at some club and O'Reilly, as was his custom, asked if he could do any thing for me. I reflected awhile and said: "No, not now. I did think of asking you to add rough-on-rats or some equally as effective a flavor to this man's soup, but I've changed my mind. Maybe he'll turn out right yet."

I never met Whistler in the flesh again, but have heard from him often. Eccentric he was and hard to please, but he has lifted this old world into a clearer, purer atmosphere by having lived in it. . . .

[2] George Hughes Hepworth (1833-1902) was a colorful preacher and editor with humanitarian interests.

Chapter Seventeen

SOME VIEWS ON EDUCATION

BEFORE THE ECHOES OF THE STRIKE of the engineers on the Chicago, Burlington, and Quincy Railroad in 1888 had died away, I had a discussion with a prominent railroad official connected with that road on the subject of strikes. He took the ground that strikes should be prohibited by law. I told him that no law could prevent men from thinking, and, if they thought strike and were denied the right to do so by statute, they might do worse. I suggested that if the men who operated the railroads were permitted to work on a coöperative basis, hand in hand with the railroad management, there would be no occasion for strikes on railroads. Drain the water from the stock of the road, permit operatives of all callings to invest in and own the stock, give them seats at the directors' tables, and let them know every detail of railroad management with voice and vote in directing as well as operating, and strikes would soon be abandoned.

. . . I intimated that in every organization composed of railroad workers, there were bright, active, intelligent young men who could be educated to take charge of and manage a railroad. A time should be allotted to the discussion of railroad management in all its intricate detail. In this way, and in others that might be devised, the workers on, and owners of, railroads would ultimately include trackmen, car-repairers, brakemen, switchmen, engineers, firemen, conductors, foremen, clerks, shopmen, draughtsmen, mechanics of different grades, directors, superintendents, and presidents. They would all be workers on and for the railroad; there would be no shirkers or drones; there would be no necessity for a sprinkling pot to water the stock with. A dollar certificate of stock would represent a dollar's worth of property, and standing back of all this would be the government, exercising not ownership but a supervision that would prevent crowding, gouging, manipulation, and exploiting of railroad or worker.

He came to look somewhat with favor on my suggestion, but before anything came of the controversy he died. . . . When this man died he willed his wealth to an only son who thereby became a millionaire. One day in 1913, in going over some of his father's papers, he came across certain references to me. In a letter to a friend of his, and an acquaintance of mine, in Washington, he inquired concerning my whereabouts and intimated that he would like to have my views on some things concerning labor, and particularly organized labor. I was permitted to read the letter and on the suggestion of our mutual friend, I ventured to write a letter to Mr. Dolph. I shall call him Dolph, not because that was his name but because he resembled a man of that name. In his letter Mr. Dolph appeared to be interested in the kind of education the children of workingmen should have, and, referring to some things done during strikes, censured the strikers for "doing such horrible things." I came across a copy of my letter to Mr. Dolph last evening, March 13, 1919, and believe it may serve a useful purpose to reproduce it here. . . .

Why do you blame the workers for "doing such horrible things" when you have not taken interest enough in them to teach them how to do better. We have looked on and have seen youth driven to age under the lash of the most compelling of all masters—poverty. You have never raised your voice, except, perhaps, in condemnation of my advice to graft the common school on the college. . . . I do not believe any normal man or woman commits crime because of a love of crime. Necessity may be the mother of invention, but it is the parent of a great deal of the world's crime. . . . You don't know the workers from actual contact with them. Academically, you know them as you do pigs, goats, or some other animal you don't have to associate with. You know nothing of the good in labor or its aspirations. . . . There can be nothing nobler than honest labor faithfully done, but what is labor? Surely the hand-fashioned article cannot fully or fairly speak of or for the producer. The thought that goes before the hand's touch, the heart throb that goes with it, the hope for perfection that animates the worker, are not recorded on the cold, impassive surface of the thing that labor creates. . . .
And who shall speak, who can ever know of the latent talent possessed

by the worker, who can fathom the depths of genius or skill that could, perhaps, have wrought wonders for the world's good but which goes on in unending stream to oblivion. . . .

The world will never know, it never can know, what it has lost in the undeveloped spirituality or mentality of thousands who carried with them to death and silence a wealth that might have exceeded all we have ever known of progress in art or science.

. . . And you, who enjoy the blessings which a college education brings to its fortunate possessor, must not look upon the workingman as one uneducated or ignorant because he lacks what you enjoy. He may be unlettered but he is not ignorant, he is not uneducated because he may not have taken degrees within the walls of a university.

It is and always has been my belief that the capacity of every child should be inquired into and discovered. There are two ways of doing this; one is to prompt, urge, speed up, and spur the child on in his studies, and that is the wrong way. The other way is to place the material and instruments to work it before the child in loving kindness and if possible let him look upon it, dream over it, and try his hand on it by himself without causing him to feel that he is being spurred on and speeded up. . . .

Not all boys and girls are alike qualified to plan and execute, and if it is not in the child to do all things like other children, no cut and dried formula or course treatment will make him do it. . . .

To my mind every facility should be afforded every child to do the best that is in him; once a start has been made, the child, however modest or shy, will question when questioning becomes necessary. . . .

We graduate from our seats of learning men who become misfits in the professions and never rise above mediocrity as motormen or conductors on our street cars. Perhaps they would have made good house painters, wood carvers, carpenters, or engineers . . . and wouldn't they and the world be better off had they been started right in childhood in that preparatory school of labor I speak of? . . .

Come to Washington and I'll take you to the Civil Service Commission and introduce you to some of the brightest, brainiest, and most clever men and women who work untiringly to unravel the tangled web woven in school days around other men and women. Men and women apply every day to take examinations, in the hope of qualifying for positions they were not educated to fill. . . . The civil service examination at thirty-five or forty years of age should have been begun in the school at nine or ten. I know many anarchists; in my Knight of Labor days I knew many more. I never knew an anarchist who was a fool. . . . I have talked with anarchists and never met one who was not disappointed in the life work selected for him when he was young by parent or school teacher. Disappointed ambition, hope deferred, opportunity sidetracked or denied, have made anarchists of some of the most clever men I ever knew. They did not tell me the world was wrong for the reasons I detail to you. . . . From your standpoint and mine, anarchy is wrong but remember that the hungry calf looking through a fence at other calves fattening in rich pasture is not apt to consider why that fence was built to keep him away from what he is as deserving of as the other calves. Privilege builds fences today that could not exist had the right kind of education been given boys and girls in the right kind of schools. Again, there should be but one school for American children. If in after life they care to or can afford the time to go to other schools and study other languages, let them do so, but in our public schools let but one language be taught and that should be the English language. When a coming day finds us sensible enough to bring about the solidarity of childhood in one school, teaching one language under one flag, we may feel reasonably certain that the graduates from that school will feel a kinship for each other that the children of this day are strangers to. That kinship will emphasize and bring more clearly to view that independence the founders of this nation may have had in view when they based the declaration of independence on equality. Centuries of oppression, of cruelty, of subjugation handed down to the workers a fear of one higher up, a deference to one who might be an industrial, a political or a religious boss. The time is so far away as to 'seem more dream than real when I had to combat—almost alone—the old world terms: "Master and servant." . . . That old world command had been carried down through ages in which industrialists were trained in servility and taught to regard an employer as one selected by the Almighty to rule over and direct them. I took issue with that command and with those who pronounced it. They thundered in my ears the statement that "God ordained that there shall be hewers of wood and drawers of water and other men shall be born to rule them." . . . That "servant and master" idea was carried over the dam in the rising tide of education among American workers, and I thank the giver of all good for permitting me to take a not insignificant part in helping the tide to rise.

I am as severe in my condemnation of crimes committed by labor as you can be, but I condemn those who cause as well as those who effect. . . . You don't consider the effort or pain of the worker when you make a purchase, you buy the cheapest of its kind. You do not consider the difference between the employer who provides a well-ordered, well-ventilated workshop for the workers and an employer who provides no workshop and depends upon the sweatshop to enable him to keep up with the law of supply and demand in selling cheap. You would patronize the sweatshop product. . . . Maybe you don't know of the evils of . . . the sweatshop, of other evils in our industrial system, but the workers are being educated to know such practices as wrongs. God grant that they may temper reason and mercy with knowledge, else Longfellow's words may take on new significance with us:

"There is a poor blind Samson in this land,
    Shorn of his strength and bound in bonds of steel,
Who may, in some grim revel, raise his hand,
    And shake the pillars of this Commonwealth."

You have asked for Powderly's opinion and, at the risk of extending this letter to undue lengths, I give it to you. It is the same as when in 1888 I told your father that he was only clay as I was. He is dead and you are using the wealth he could not take with him. You will be powerless to take any of it with you, so do what you can to earn immortality by devoting some, yes much of it, to uprearing the school wherein all that is in the child of talent, of genius, of good may receive its just, and first, recognition and encouragement.

Mr. Dolph came to Washington, we discussed the subject matter, or matters, of my letter and it is gratifying to me to be able to say that his son is to take up the work begun by him, for his health failed during the early days of the war and he has passed to where I hope he may be permitted to look with approving eye on the fruition of his earthly hope for human betterment through the practical education of American youth.

.   .   .   .   .

Chapter Eighteen

HOW BLOODSHED PREVENTED
INCENDIARISM

THE STRIKE of locomotive engineers and other workmen engaged in operating trains on railroads centering in Pittsburgh, Pennsylvania, which occurred in July, 1877, spread to Scranton and involved machinists, blacksmiths, rolling-mill men, and mine workers of all kinds. A great many of these were members of the Knights of Labor, but, while members of the organization were thrown idle by the strike, the Knights of Labor as such took no part in it. Since I have dealt with that conflict in *Thirty Years of Labor*, I shall refer to one incident, quite personal to me in its effects, brought to mind by a perusal of the testimony taken in Scranton by a committee of the legislature of Pennsylvania during March, 1878.[1] . . . I reread this testimony, or part of it, on the 19th of March, 1919, and from the conclusions reached by the committee I quote as follows:

The causes which led to the riots are, in the opinion of your committee, as follows, to-wit: The riots grew out of the strike of the railroad men, and the strikes themselves were the protest of the laborer against the system by which his wages were arbitrarily fixed and lowered by his employer without consultation with him, and without his consent. There are many other causes that combined to bring about the strikes, but the cause mentioned underlies the whole question, and it is the foundation of all the trouble.

That statement of the committee, read by me shortly after I was sworn in as mayor of Scranton caused me, later on as General Master Workman of the Knights of Labor, to recommend that steps be taken to substitute coöperation for the "system by which

[1] Generally cited as *Report of Committee Appointed by the Pennsylvania General Assembly to Investigate the Railroad Riots in July, 1877*, Harrisburg, 1878.

wages were arbitrarily fixed and lowered without consultation with [the laborer] and without his consent."

I was corresponding secretary of District Assembly No. 16 of the Knights of Labor when the legislative committee held its sessions in Scranton. I attended all the hearings, but so little was known of the Order, of my connection with it, or of me for that matter, that my name was never mentioned during the hearings. Private members of the Knights of Labor gave testimony, and though I jogged their memories when they were in danger of slipping into inaccuracies, no member of the committee dreamed that I knew anything about the trouble. My purpose in attending these sessions was not to be seen or heard, but to see that the organization did not suffer through anything over-said or under-said about it.

Several local assemblies of the Knights of Labor met, on different nights of course, in a hall on Lackawanna Avenue. This fact became so well established that the hall was known as labor-union meeting place. One afternoon, during the time the strike was in progress, a man whom I knew by sight but not by name accosted me on the street and in an undertone told me a number of men were assembled in that hall and were "planning the burning down of a west side coal breaker." I immediately went to the hall and, eluding the sentinel at the outer door, gained entrance to the meeting room. I was at once detected as an intruder and questioned as to my right to interfere with their deliberations. I have never forgotten what happened that day. I said:

I was informed on the street, by a stranger, that you men were laying plans to burn down a coal breaker tonight; I don't know where you work but you have no right to do anything like that. If you were employed there you will not find your places waiting for you when this strike ends. If you don't work there, your act will prevent others from regaining their old places when work has been resumed elsewhere. But there is a reason far higher than that of securing employment which should prevent you from becoming incendiaries. The burning of that breaker would be a crime of such proportions as to earn for every man taking part in it a cell in the penitentiary. Surely you don't want to bring misery to your families and shame upon your children by such an uncalled for, fiendish crime. Again, if you will be influenced by no other consideration, reflect that that breaker is a living arsenal and your first step toward its destruction will result in bloodshed. Abandon this undertaking, go to your homes, and maintain your standing as peaceable, law-abiding men.

Instead of having the effect I intended, my words seemed to infuriate them. One man gained the floor and moved "that we adjourn now and go direct to the breaker and burn it down."

Whether his motion was put to the house or carried I never knew. A rush was made for the door, I placed my back against it and begged of the men to stop and consider the matter still farther. I knew no one in the room, but a number knew me; they gathered round me evidently to protect me, but there my memory lapsed for a time. Something struck me on the head, I lost consciousness, and when I regained my senses my face was covered with blood; my shirt front was anything but presentable. One of those who knew me said, "I want you to take the chair." I at first demurred, but he persisted and whispered that I could do good by so doing. Although I was weak and still suffering from the shock, I realized that I could possibly do some good by taking the chair and did so. This same man made a motion something like this: "That we rescind the motion to engage in this undertaking, that we adjourn sine die, go to our homes and never again meet for such a purpose."

I put the motion without waiting for anyone to second it; it was carried unanimously, and silently these men went their separate ways to their homes.

I did not then know the name of one of the men who attended that meeting and although I could not recall having met any of them before that day, it seemed that I could not turn a corner thereafter without encountering one of them, and they always spoke to me in the most friendly manner. From one of them I learned that it was in trying to pry the door open through the use of a long bench that I was injured. The bench slipped, they could not hold it, and it came down on my head. . . . That happened in August, 1877. It was in 1885, after I had served three terms as the labor mayor of Scranton, that I learned from one who was present at that meeting, that my warning, "Your first step toward its destruction will result in bloodshed," was regarded as prophetic when I, covered with blood, went down under the weight of that bench.

That incident furnished food for a great deal of conversation in labor circles for a long time. When reference was made to it in my presence, it was, as a rule, accompanied by some tribute to my courage in facing a crowd of angry men singlehanded and alone. Of course I always listened in silence and modestly accepted the compliments just as if I deserved them. The truth is it required no exercise of courage on my part to do what I did. Facing opposition was the most natural thing in the world to me; I was brought up to it. Anyway, there were less than forty men there that day. Since then I have many a time faced assemblages ranging from ten hundred to ten thousand, all or nearly all opposed to me, and if any one in attendance experienced a sense of fear, I was not the one.

The more thought I gave to the relations between capital and labor, or more properly speaking, between employer and employed, the more settled became my belief that if it is considered right for a man to work for another man, it cannot be wrong for him to unite with that other man and work with him to produce, harmoniously and efficiently, for a common end. I could not see any force in the oft-repeated statement: "the interests of labor and capital are identical." Since it never found its way into public print, I shall later on reproduce what I said on the subject of coöperation in my first address to the General Assembly of the Knights of Labor after I became the presiding officer of that organization.

Chapter Nineteen

"THE OWL"

ON THE SUPPOSITION that I, being a mayor "of communistic tendencies," might approve of a publication that would deal harshly with "the upper classes," an enterprising but not over-scrupulous young man who had been more or less trained to the newspaper business became editor, manager, and publisher of a new paper to educate and enlighten the people of Scranton. The paper was not printed in or issued from any newspaper office in the city, and inquiry elicited the information that Mount Joy, Pennsylvania, was the birthplace of progress and civilization. It was during my first term as mayor that this paper made its first and, probably, the last appearance.

One Saturday morning, on the arrival of the train from Harrisburg, a newsboy went through the streets of Scranton shouting: "*The Owl*, a new paper, all about how certain young ladies of this city entertain their gentlemen friends." Of course I was interested. I bought a copy and hastening to my office opened it up, at the same time bracing myself to endure the shock to my sense of decency and propriety. Except in one particular I was not disappointed; it exceeded my anticipations. It was a neatly gotten-up, four-page paper. The type was new, the composition perfect, but, with the exception of that part of the sheet untouched by ink, there was nothing clean in it. It was smut from end to end. . . .

Dark hints of darker doings threatened exposure of good women for supposed, undue familiarity with men who were not their husbands. Young girls, daughters of respectable parents, were pointed at so unmistakably that, though their names were not given, everyone in Scranton could guess and accurately guess, who they were. . . .

The circulation of *The Owl* gave rise to a great deal of conversation throughout the city. The "unco gude," while not approving of *The Owl's* exposés, smacked their lips in virtuous indignation as they intimated that people who lived in glass houses should at least pull down the blinds so as not to shock passers-by.

I made an effort during the following week to ascertain who the owner, or publisher, of *The Owl* was but did not succeed. When the train that carried the next installment of *The Owl* to Scranton arrived in the station, I had Chief of Police De Lacy on hand to act as a reception committee. His instructions were to not allow the newsboys to sell any papers until the mayor bought one. He assured the boys that the mayor wished to buy the first copy. I stood in front of the office; when the boys came up I bought a copy and then directed the little fellows to carry their papers into the office and deposit them on my desk. They did as I told them. Then I assured them that they would lose nothing by leaving the papers with me, and dismissed them. After waiting about an hour, a young lawyer made his appearance and in a blustering way demanded his papers. I asked him if they belonged to him; his answer was that they were the property of a client of his who was being injured by my action in preventing their circulation. I told him that his client need not wait one minute, all that I would require of him would be to come forward, prove his property, and take it. After threatening me awhile, he said he would have me arrested and punished for my high-handed outrage in interfering with the liberty of the press. Not wishing to waste the young man's time, I explained my position something like this: "The mayor is required by law to abate nuisances; the exact method of procedure not being prescribed by statute, he must use his own judgment in each particular case; he has abated this nuisance, and it shall remain abated. This paper is no more to be compared to a newspaper than a skunk is to be likened to a St. Bernard dog. It is the filthy production of an unclean mind, actuating a creature too cowardly to admit ownership. . . . Let the owner, proprietor, or publisher issue it under, or over, his own name and I shall not meddle with it, but until he displays manliness enough to do that *The Owl* shall not be sold, offered for sale or given away on the streets of Scranton while I am mayor."

"Do you dare to persist in suppressing a newspaper?" was his next question. I have a vivid recollection of my answer:

"Call it what you like, *The Owl* has made its last appearance on the streets of Scranton."

When the boys called on me to know if they could get their papers I paid them and told them not to sell any more issues of *The Owl.* I called a mass meeting of the regular newsboys—they all seemed to like me—and we decided not to allow *The Owl* to be sold in Scranton again. The policemen were devoted to me, so with the police and newsboys on my side I had no further trouble with *The Owl* and he blinked his eyes in Scranton no more.

I was not arrested for my autocratic, high-handed method of disposing of *The Owl.* A number of communications criticizing me for what I did appeared in the Scranton papers over the signatures of old friends of mine. Junius was quite noticeably shocked, Veritas expressed a feeling of disappointed sadness because I had slipped off the pedestal on which he had enthroned me. Argus, with his numerous eyes, saw faults where virtues ruled before, and Old Friend reluctantly raked me fore and aft for imperiling our free institutions by suppressing the press. Each one had something to say about the morals, or lack of them, of the victims of the new paper. I paid no attention to any of them. I had prevented a sewer filled to overflowing with filth, from defiling the streets of Scranton and did not, therefore, care a hoot what the friends of *The Owl* said to or of me.

It was fully a year before I ascertained who the editor of *The Owl* was and then only by accident. He fully explained to me that his enterprise had been financed by a man who had a grudge against one of the men whose daughter had been singled out for not too honorable mention in *The Owl.*

It also appeared that my sympathy, if not coöperation, had been counted on since I was supposed to hate anyone who betrayed evidence of prosperity and particularly the father of the girl in question, he being a bitter enemy of mine. His hatred of me did not influence me any, and I was not acquainted with his daughter. I did all my fighting in the open, with recognized weapons of warfare and was unaccustomed to the use of mud in waging my labor or political battles. I believed with Josh Billings, who sagely remarked: "The mud slinger usually misses everybody but himself."

I did not notice that anyone in Scranton missed any of his liberties because the mayor declined to license the limb on which *The Owl* perched and from which he hooted at decent folk.

Chapter Twenty

BOYCOTT COFFEE

IN ALL AGES and every clime certain individuals have, on occasion, made nuisances of themselves in their efforts to focus the public eye on abuses and wrongs that threatened the political or industrial safety of the masses. Years ago some discerning person discovered that, in the spelling at least, there is but little difference, only a trifle of space, between the masses and them asses; the same letters spell both words. Often the very people whose liberties were threatened by the shark and self-seeker poured the vials of their wrath out on the heads of their defenders. No wonder then that the observant . . . bystander . . . remarked that the masses must indeed be asses not to see that the way by which they were to be fleeced was being well paved by judicious advertising and editorializing in papers owned or controlled by those who, through skillful legal surgery, were bent on amputating their pocketbooks.

One day in 1888 I was invited to a seat in the New York Stock Exchange, in the gallery, however, and not on the floor where the trading was done. I may add that it was on my own invitation I went there. My going was prompted by reading the following in the Philadelphia *Call* of June 29th of that year:

NEW YORK, JUNE 29—The brokers in the coffee market were filled with consternation this morning by the springing of the sharpest corner ever marked in the Coffee Exchange. The bulls had effected a complete corner in spot coffee, and when the operators having June coffee to deliver attempted to buy it they found it was all held by S. Greener & Co. and Crossman Bros., who are the representatives of the bull cliques. In the first hour of business the price advanced 5¼¢ a pound, opening with a sale at 12¾¢ and advancing to 13¢ on the first call on a sale of 1,250 bags. After the call it rose 1¢ at a time until noon when 18¢ were bid and no coffee found for sale. The pool brokers intimated that the outstanding contracts will be settled at 20¢ per pound.

2 P. M.—The corner in June coffee was continued this afternoon, but a settling price was fixed on by brokers for the bull houses making transactions at 21 cents and 21.05 per pound, an advance of 8.05 points since the opening. The brokers claim that the short interest is very small.

On reading that, I went to New York on an evening train, and next morning found me seated in the gallery of the Exchange. A broker who recognized me came up from the floor, took a seat beside me, and in the conversation that ensued advised me to "buy coffee for it is sure to go to 28 or 30 cents." I questioned him closely. . . . I did find out that it was the intention to boost the price of coffee as high as they could. He said that on June 20th, the "June Option," a term used by brokers, was 13 cents a pound, and a search was begun for 1,500 bags of imaginary coffee for the purpose of effecting settlement with the bulls. It was discovered about this time that of 170,000 bags of coffee then in port, the sharpers had gained control of 120,000 bags, and the remaining 50,000 bags could not be obtained. When they were applied to for coffee, Messrs. Crossman and Greener disposed of that which they had never laid a finger on at 21 and 21½ cents a pound.

I devoted the next three days to . . . an investigation into the way the prices of necessaries were raised and how artificial scarcities were manufactured. I did this to make sure of my ground for I wanted to be founded on fact in what I resolved to do. On the evening of July 3, 1888, I took a train for my home in Scranton, reached there after midnight, and between that time and 9 A.M., July 4, had prepared a circular letter to the Knights of Labor, and whoever else it might concern, asking them to take action on the matter of increasing the price of coffee. From that circular I quote the following:

In the broad open light of the day, in the metropolis of the nation, in the advanced stage of civilization to which the nineteenth century has progressed, we find men who walk unwhipped of justice practicing a game that would win for lesser rogues, in some parts of this country, a halter, or a coat of tar and feathers at the least. If a man, hungry and sick, standing at the door of one of the restaurants in New York, should yield to the temptation forced upon him by poverty and steal a cup of coffee, a veritable cup of real coffee, he would be arrested and placed in a dungeon cell. On the morrow he would be tried in the police court and sent up to the island for his offence. Here are rogues who, under shadow of law, corner coffee by the hundred thousand bag fulls, and, by reason of opportunity and avarice, they rob millions of that which they are pleased to term their profits in a necessity of life.

Gambling in human flesh brought us face to face with a terrible war a quarter of a century ago. . . . A more refined method of skinning the poor is now in vogue. . . .

The grower of coffee and the consumer of that article have never met; they do not deal with each other at all. A vulture sits above the coffee field and notes the upward tendency of every coffee stalk, as it ripens he flies away to his home in the Coffee Exchange and there tells how much to expect, and before the grower and consumer can exchange words the Coffee Exchange shark, taking advantage of the necessities of the grower, fixes a price on the proceeds of his toil, because he can do so through the instrumentality of a trust. . . .

This is being written on July 4th, on the anniversary of our country's independence. On a day that, when it comes around each year, makes the American—a true American—heart swell with pride. . . . Could each man on the soil of the United States know of the iniquity of the coffee jugglers of Wall Street and the Coffee Exchange, of the system of extortion and legalized robbery which prevails there, he would . . . piously and . . . fervently pray that God might blot forever from the face of the earth the institutions which do more to make thieves, prostitutes, and murderers than all other causes combined.

The law is silent, its officers find no way to reach such thieves, and Christ will not favor us by coming to earth to rid the money-changing temples of New York of the gamblers in human souls. What will we do? Must we break the law in order to have it respected by others? No, we will respect the law and punish the law breakers by refraining from the use of coffee for thirty days, for sixty days, or for all time unless the men who have cornered coffee shall let go their hold.

BOYCOTT COFFEE. *Do not buy one ounce of it until this reign of plunder is at an end.* Go to your grocer and tell him not to invest in a pound of it, and ask him to watch for the turn of the tide in New York. To do as I suggest will work no injustice to the men from whom you buy your groceries. Do not buy coffee, but buy something else in its stead, and when you do invest in coffee again, have the article you invest in analyzed to see if it has been tampered with and adulterated. If it has, trace the adulteration until you find it, and you may be sure you can lay it to the action taken in the coffee exchange of New York.

Mechanics, laborers, miners, farmers, and Knights of Labor generally, practice a little self-denial for a time and break the corner in coffee by refusing to buy it. Let us test the law and see if we will be arrested for boycotting an article made too dear by rogues who boycott the best interests of the people.

. . . Under my instructions the leading papers of the country were on a given day supplied with copies of the circular. Every trade and labor paper, every farmer's organization, every trade-union, every banking, mercantile, mining, and manufacturing concern in the United States that I could get the address of, received a copy of the circular, and inside of ten days the price of coffee had fallen off eight cents a pound. . . .

Coffee, sugar, tea, and spices were the chief articles of food that could then be held off the market without deterioration. It did not injure coffee any to allow it to remain at a dock or in a store house for a short time. The cold storage plant, that agency which can be made a successful substitute for highway robbery in the hands of the unscrupulous, had not yet arrived to gather in the product of the farm and hold it away from the hand of the consumer until top-notch prices may be extorted. . . .

Of course I submitted with the circular a statement briefly detailing what I had learned during my three days' inquiry in New York. I knew that if it could be shown that I made a misstatement, or had exaggerated in the slightest degree, it would give those who profited by the action of the coffee manipulators an opportunity to prevent my effort from bearing fruit. I left nothing to chance and coffee did not climb to thirty cents a pound or remain at the price where I found it on June 30, 1888. Leading men and editors all over the country attacked me viciously through the columns of the press; they attributed every kind of a motive except a good one to what I had done. In their eyes I was, according to a scrapbook now before me, "a destroyer of confidence," "an enemy to the business interests of the country," "an unsafe leader for workingmen to follow," "one who would set law at defiance to win applause from the rabble," and a "dangerous character who without directly counseling violence did that which must inevitably result in action detrimental to the best interests of all classes." One of the foremost daily papers of the country, in a leading editorial said:

Mr. Powderly has not given careful thought or study to the live and let live proposition. Evidently he has yet to learn that there is a law of supply and demand which his insane command to boycott cannot repeal. He should be given to understand that his rash fulminations against reputable financial and commercial agencies do not find favor in the eyes of those who value the peace and welfare of society. . . .

No matter what they said, I succeeded, but the fact that I was successful did not give me any particular satisfaction. Success for self was not what I aimed at. Had personal gain or success been my object it is quite probable that I would have acted on the "tip" and bought myself rich through investment in "coffee."

As to the law of supply and demand: 170,000 bags of coffee were stored in a warehouse in New York, there was your supply. Out through the country were millions of people who needed coffee; there was your demand. Standing in front of that warehouse was a being who held in his possession, not the coffee, but the key to the warehouse, and he said: "that coffee shall not leave that warehouse, that coffee shall not supply the demand for it until it has doubled in price and I get the difference. I control the supply and shall not heed the demand." Who interfered with the law of supply and demand, who practically, for the time being, repealed the law of supply and demand? Was it Powderly or the man with the key?

One paper, a "journal of civilization," advised me in this way: "let market transactions alone and stick to the business of securing higher wages and better conditions for his constituents. He ought to know that the quotations on the stock exchange and the retail price of coffee may differ and coffee may be sold at a lower figure than stock brokers run it up to be."

Most assuredly I had a pretty fair idea that that could be true, but it was not true. Coffee was held off the market and for no other purpose than to raise the price. The cornering of coffee did advance the price, and consumers of that article throughout the country were expected to pay from ten to fifteen cents more per pound than before the stock gamblers began to juggle with the price.

As to securing "higher wages" for my constituents, I always differed from a great many of my constituents on the question of wages. I never knew it to fail that when the wages of any class of labor were increased, the prices of articles of household use went up in proportion and in many cases out of all proportion to the rate of wage increase. If only those who secured the raise in wages were required to pay a higher rate for necessaries it would not be so bad, but others who did not share in the wage increase were forced to yield tribute to those who had it in their power to control prices. Such a proceeding was to my mind like pumping water through a bung hole into a barrel while leaving a bung hole equally as large open on the other side of the barrel to allow the liquid to escape through. What a workman honestly and justly earned was what he should, in common fairness, receive, and his rate of compensation should not be subject to fluctuations in the stock market or the manipulation of those who had no hand or part in honest production. Could I succeed in securing a ten per cent increase in the wages of every member of the Knights of Labor, each one of them, and millions of others would at once be required to pay ten per cent or more for food, fuel, and clothing. All beyond the pale of organization and all salaried workers would in reality be made poorer by my successful effort for the Knights of Labor. The "Powderly Coffee Boycott," as it was called, stayed the hand that would have taken from the pocket of the consumer of coffee anywhere from eight to fifteen, or more, cents for every pound he bought. A careful statistician employed in a New York stock brokerage estimated that I caused a loss to stock traders of $10,000,000 during the month of July, 1888. If that was true then I was instrumental in practically increasing the wages, or incomes, of millions of coffee consumers to the extent of $10,000,000, and that without the loss of a cent to any man or woman engaged in honest labor or effort. . . .

The word "bolshevist" had not been imported to this country in 1888 to be used as a scarecrow to dangle before the eyes of timid people and masquerade as something really dangerous, or,

I suppose, I would have been called a bolshevist. . . . That my action may have been revolutionary is true, but I had before me some illustrious predecessors in revolutionary practice who after the lapse of years came to be regarded as quite conservative or, if not conservative, as demonstrators of American patriotism. Take, for instance, the men who rowed out to that ship in Boston harbor and prevented the collection of a tax on a quantity of tea by destroying it. . . .

We honor the memory of the participants in the Boston tea party now, and, while their action may be regarded as revolutionary, it was not incendiary. . . . I did not destroy any coffee, nor did I set fire to anything, not even the stock exchange, and yet my reward was as great and as gratifying as if I had done even that. I earned and received the execration of every profiteer of the year of our Lord 1888.

. . . . .

Until the masses cease to be them asses the high cost of living will prevail. Its standard will not be lowered until something else than medicating symptoms is attempted. Foods of every variety, fuel of all kinds, clothing of every description come from one source, they come from nature's storehouse—the earth. How idle the attempt to permanently reduce the cost of living when the land from which food and fuel are gathered or dug remains in cold storage, and in cold storage it will remain until that land is liberated from the grip of the speculator, until an equitable system of taxation through which the land itself instead of the labor expended on it shall meet the expenses of government.

Indignation community gatherings, municipal probing, and congressional investigations may throw light on certain causes of high prices, and, in some instances, effect reductions; but the principal cause of the advanced and advancing rise in the cost of necessities of life dates back to a time when electric lighting began to make the city street more attractive than it could be under the flickering glimmer of the gas lamp. Following the introduction of the electric street lamp came the electricity-driven streetcar, the telephone, the bicycle, and, finally, the automobile. After them came the moving picture theater, and then country life lost its charm for young men and women who were born and raised on the farm. By the thousand they flocked to the cities and large towns, leaving parents without that intelligent assistance so necessary to the efficient and economical operation and cultivation of the land. The city held out all inducements to the young; the farm offered none, for they, judging by their parents' pioneer experience in agriculture, regarded life on the farm as a sentence to solitary confinement and hard labor for life.

Chapter Twenty-One

A DAY WITH GROVER CLEVELAND

A DAY THERE WAS when the man who labored was driven to and chained in a dungeon cell when his many-hour task was done. He was worked as a beast, driven as a beast, and fed as a beast. Through slow-passing centuries he groped for and reached toward the light. Here and there he learned to read, and when liberation from mental bondage began, freedom of the physical became rapid.

When I walked along the Appian Way beyond the walls of ancient Rome and saw where the living bodies of six thousand followers of Spartacus were crucified, I realized that the laborer of my day has much to be thankful for. . . . I realized, too, that education, not of the book variety, is of slow growth; and an education in the value, not price, of land is absolutely essential today. Back to the land we must go or on to the poor house we shall go.

A new system of farm life must be inaugurated, a system that will make country surroundings more attractive must supersede the present order. . . . A man, agriculturally inclined today . . . should be, he can be, directed to a farm where he may find electric lighting, telephones, good roads, and neighbors—especially neighbors. Community centers, so much talked about in cities, can and will be established in farming communities. The homes of farmers in a given radius will be built in close proximity to each other, the automobile will carry farmer and his help to and from the field, the . . . improved machines . . . will abolish the "from sun up to sunset" plan of cultivating the land.

A few years ago I made a tour of upper New York State. I traveled by automobile and through country districts. A representative of the State Department of Agriculture accompanied me. On either side of the highway over which we passed lay "abandoned farms" that, in the aggregate, contained upwards of two hundred thousand acres. . . . Land that will grow clover is not of poor quality, and examination of several of these farms showed a luxuriant growth of clover. The land could then be bought at from ten to seventy-five dollars an acre. That was in 1909. A survey of several other states disclosed the fact that like conditions prevailed; idle, unlooked-after acres everywhere. In addition there are, in close proximity to every large city, uncultivated lands that in the aggregate run into millions of acres that are held for speculative purposes; their owners . . . are well enough off to live without work and [they] work other citizens who must pay high taxes on homes because these speculative landholders escape payment of a tax that would appear at all equitable when compared with the tax paid by a city property owner.

Then there are lands held by railroads and other large corporations. In most cases lands held by transcontinental railroads, or once held by them, were given to them by Congress, by that body that is frequently referred to as a servant of the people. Ask a Congressman to provide by law for restoration of these acres, or for purchase of land to be sold on long-time payments to private citizens for the purpose of cultivating it, and he will, in all probability, say that it would be paternalistic to do so. The paternalism was begun, so far as land was concerned, over fifty years ago. . . . Christian and Jew believe that God made man and the soil he treads; in the main they believe that soil was given to men to draw their sustenance from. No matter what men believe, what creed they profess, or whether they be Jew, Christian, or atheist, they know that the land is here, that man is here, must live on it, and that it should not be withheld from use. Nowhere, at no time can it, or could it, be shown by word of mouth or written instrument that the creator of land gave title to any man, or favored set of men to the earth or any part of it. . . . The very plan of man's entry to the world, his stay therein and his exit therefrom, negatives the proposition that that man can rightly hold absolute dominion over land. That men have and do hold land is true, that they hold it by title sanctioned by law is true, but it is also true that man, who did not make the land, made the law which vests title in him, and yet in defiance of that law, in utter indifference to its strictest provision, the many may take under claim of need, called right of eminent domain, the land held by one and use it for all. There is no such a thing as absolute title to land. To illustrate: I bought a lot of land from a speculator on which to erect a home. I paid $1,500 for it. The speculator paid taxes on it at one-third of its assessed valuation, which in the District of Columbia is at the rate of $1.50 per hundred dollars. When I bought the lot it was assessed for taxing purposes at $500. When I built a house on it, it was first assessed at $2,500 and on that lot and home I am still paying taxes at the rate of $1.50 per hundred dollars. The assessors of the District of Columbia, while they are prohibited by law from increasing that rate, can and do increase the valuation of my home so that it will bring a revenue in taxes to the District on many more thousands of dollars than it is worth. The house, like myself, is growing old but the assessor regards it as "ever fresh and green," and taxes it accordingly. I call that house mine; I have title to it, as good and binding a title as can be found anywhere; and yet that lot of land is not mine. The tax I pay is for streets, sidewalks, police protection, and the privilege of having neighbors. The municipality does nothing, expends nothing, to improve my property and it fines me—by increasing my taxes—if I improve it. If on May 31, of each year I have not paid the annual tax for thinking I own that land, I am penalized through an additional tax on June 1, and, after a stipulated length of time, that land that I think I own will be sold for non-payment of taxes if I am not able to pay the annual fine. So you see the people of Washington are financially interested in that land and in common have a claim on the property that prevents my exercising absolute dominion over it. Each year I have to keep on paying the municipality an assessment on land that a reading of my deed would tell you is mine in fee. The fee I have to pay each year is to prevent my eviction from land bought by me, not from the municipality, but from a speculator who was licensed to gamble in land that he did not, could not create. All over this country land is held and sold as it was and is sold in Washington. The plan of operation and method of levying taxes may differ, but the principle, or lack of it, of the speculator is the same. . . .

That it might be troublesome to inquire into the way title to some of the land in this country was obtained is true, but I doubt very much if such inquiry would be useless. In any event, the day is here for an overhauling of the way land is held from use. Our whole system of land tenure needs to be inquired into with a view to making the land serve the greatest number for the greatest good. Socialism, anarchy, bolshevism, and radicalism will be manufactured out of thin air to shout at the man who undertakes, in earnest, to readjust land-holding to the needs of the many. . . .

Thousands of acres of land have been seized by means that may be classified as theft, yet the thieves go unwhipped of justice and remain, apparently, secure in the possession of the stolen goods. An effort was made under the first administration of Grover Cleveland to secure the restoration to the government and individual of lands illegally taken by wealthy men and corporations, but . . . without good results.

Mr. Powderly goes out of his way to hunt up trouble for himself to no good purpose. He is now poking his inquisitive nose into the way land titles were acquired when he was in his infancy. It is intimated that he has presumed to direct the attention of no less a person than the President of the United States to the way the public domain has been parcelled out among alien land grabbers, American syndicates, and individuals.

So wrote Charles A. Dana[1] of the New York *Sun*, and Mr. Dana was, on that occasion within the bounds of truth, a position he rarely found himself in when discussing Mr. Powderly. A perusal of at least part of the correspondence relating to the subject will show that I not only presumed to direct the President's attention to the matter but he presumed to send for me and listen to what I had to say.

[1] Charles Anderson Dana (1819-97) began to lose his early radicalism during the period he was employed on the staff of the New York *Tribune*. He became editor of the *Sun* in 1868. His opposition to labor unions and strikes was one of the few positions he maintained consistently during an influential journalistic career marked by cynicism and inconsistency.

SCRANTON, PA., APRIL 12, 1887

GROVER CLEVELAND,
PRESIDENT OF THE UNITED STATES

Esteemed Sir:

Knowing how fully your time is occupied and feeling that even a moment of it cannot well be spared, I approach you as one who intrudes. The subject on which I write is of so important a character, its bearing on the future welfare of the people of the United States is so fraught with interest, that I feel that no apology is necessary. I shall at once proceed to explain the reason for writing this letter.

I, in common with many others who have had an opportunity to watch the tendency of the age in the acquisition of large holdings of land, view with alarm the encroachments of large syndicates, and alien landlords upon the public domain.

While I might as an individual experience a feeling of timidity in approaching you on this subject, as an officer of a society whose membership embraces hundreds of thousands of American citizens, I am bound by my obligation as a member and officer of that association, as well as my duty as an American, to present to you the views of the members of that organization regarding the manner in which the public lands have been disposed of in past years. First let me quote from the preamble of the Knights of Labor, the fourth declaration. "That the public lands, the heritage of the people, be reserved for actual settlers—not another acre for railroads or speculators, and that all lands now held for speculative purposes be taxed to their full value."

It is a notorious fact that millions of acres of the public domain have been fenced by cattle syndicates; proofs are not wanting to show that citizens who intended to effect bona fide settlement under the laws of the United States have been driven off the public lands at the muzzle of the rifle. Actual settlers have been compelled to vacate their homesteads at the bidding of powerful corporations, and they have been compelled to seek elsewhere for new homes; they have been dispossessed of their holdings without shadow or authority of law. Cases wherein the right of the American citizen to occupy a portion of the public land, has been trampled on are numerous.

The protection of settlers against the unlawful demands of unscrupulous corporations—of which the case of Guilford Miller is a conspicuous instance—is the first necessity.

It is claimed that from fifty to sixty millions of acres of the public domain are held by aliens, certain it is that upward of twenty millions of acres are thus held. An investigation of the methods by which these lands were acquired, and of the great quantities now held, unlawfully, by large syndicates, ought to be vigorously prosecuted.

One hundred millions of acres, of so-called indemnity lands, are now withdrawn from public settlement and use, without warrant of law and by the mere order of the Interior Department in past years. All of these unlawful withdrawals ought to be at once revoked, and all indemnity lands opened to settlers.

The unlawful and wholesale enclosure of public lands by cattle syndicates ought to be promptly and vigorously removed.

The one great question of the present day is the land question. The one great, crying evil of the present day is the absorption of large tracts of land by aliens, cattle syndicates, and powerful corporations. The necessity of the present age is prompt, vigorous, determined action on the part of the President and Congress of the United States against those who would defraud the government and people.

I feel that I do not address you in vain. I feel that in voicing the sentiment of the membership of the Knights of Labor I but ask that simple justice be done, not only to them but to the whole people of the United States. If petitions are wanting to convince you that the sentiments I express are the sentiments of the men and women who make up the membership of the Order of the Knights of Labor, they can be placed before you bearing the signatures of millions of citizens.

If in my humble capacity I can be of service to you in this great work I shall esteem it a pleasure to aid you to the extent of my ability.

I have the honor to be,

Very truly yours,

T. V. POWDERLY

G.M.W. K. OF L.

Following the receipt of that letter by the President came an invitation to call on him for the purpose of discussing "the subject matter" of the communication. I was not interviewed, gave nothing out for publication, but in some way an account of my call on the President was published. Up to that time Mr. Dana was friendly to me, not demonstratively so, but just friendly. He was not overly fond of Grover Cleveland and knowledge of the fact that I had "presumed" to accept an invitation to call at the White House and hobnob with the President alienated his affections, and he never forgave me. My interview with Grover Cleveland was simply a contributing cause for Mr. Dana's displeasure. A strike involving workmen employed in loading an Old Dominion steamship took place in New York. The strikers were not Knights of Labor, but members of District Assembly No. 49, K. of L. endeavored to effect settlement of the trouble. About the time they

tendered their services to patch up a truce, an explosion occurred
in the hold of an Old Dominion vessel and that incident was made
excuse, pretext, or reason for a personal editorial assault on me
in the columns of the New York *Sun*. From that time until the
day of his death, Mr. Dana missed few opportunities to editorially
intimate that my presence on earth was displeasing to him. With it
all, Charles A. Dana was one of my best friends. He never deceived me by an excess of adulation or flattery, and if at any time
the sweat band of my hat began to tighten round my head, a perusal of Dana's latest editorial on Powderly would always restore
my head to normal size.

There was another cause for his antagonism. The Rev. Dr.
George P. Hepworth was an editorial writer on the New York
Herald at that time. He took a deep interest in the question of
land restoration which I was then agitating, and in every way
possible, individually as well as editorially, he aided the movement. That may have had some influence on Mr. Dana. Many
years after while [I was] sitting chatting with Amos Cummings,[2]
who had been connected with the *Sun* and whose room was next to
mine at 1332 New York Avenue, Washington, D. C., he told me
of how Mr. Dana had been influenced to turn the editorial columns of the *Sun* against me. . . .

Perhaps as good a way as any to tell of my interview with
President Cleveland will be to add a copy of my letter to Dr.
Hepworth on the subject:

Scranton, Pa., April 25, 1887

My dear Dr. Hepworth:

I had an hour's talk with the President Saturday;
there was nothing accomplished except to arrive at an understanding on the
all important question of the illegal occupancy of the land. I am satisfied
that Mr. Cleveland is in earnest on this question and that he will go as far
as he can go under the law to restore the public domain to the care of the
people.

I am not violating any confidence by repeating an expression or two of
his; he said: "With a long pull a strong pull and a pull all together very
much can be done to remedy the present condition of this subject." He expresses himself as being sternly opposed to alien ownership of the soil, the

[2] Amos Jay Cummings (1841-1902), primarily a journalist, was also a Democratic
Congressman (1886-88, 1889-1902).

one thing that pleased me above all others was this: "I believe that all the laws relating to the settlement of the land should be repealed and one, simple effective law enacted which would cover the rights of the individual and the corporation, the simpler the law and the stricter it is enforced the better for the people. We are faced with a multitude of laws, many of them conflicting, all of them more directly in the interest of the corporation than the people and it seems to me that one plain, straightforward law should govern all." I agree with that sentiment, and I am confident that the President will do all that he can to bring it about. I assured him that the people were all with him in the restoration movement and would stand by him. He in a few words stated what I had already (thanks to your clippings), learned concerning the methods of the cattle thieves and other usurpers of the rights of the people.

I was in New York yesterday but you were not at the office and, not desiring to have a number of reporters harassing me, I came away on the first train.

After my return from the West I intend to have another interview with the President (at his request). I also intend to have a good, shrewd man go out West and go over the territory so that I may have, from the lips of my own representative, an account of the manner in which the lands have been fenced in and managed. What would you think of having a representative of the *Herald* accompany him?

Sincerely yours,
T. V. Powderly

I give in full the letters to the President and Dr. Hepworth so that nothing can be left to surmise or conjecture. . . . When Dr. Hepworth asked me how I came to place the President's language in quotation marks, I was glad to be able to say that I wrote down, read to him, and had Mr. Cleveland's consent to relate as spoken the words quoted in my letter to Dr. Hepworth.

When I next saw the President I submitted a concrete case of a syndicate that illegally seized land for grazing purposes and by way of contrast laid before him a clipping from a daily paper detailing the trial of a man for stealing a goose from a poultry dealer. Notwithstanding the effort of President Cleveland to cause the land thieves to make restitution, the case dragged on until his term expired. . . . In the case of the man who stole the goose from Washington market, New York, he was fined and sent to jail for a month.

The law condemns the man or woman
Who steals the goose from off the common,
But lets the greater felon loose
Who steals the common from the goose.

The rule of the land speculator must end, and the people must end it by law. The plan in vogue when I bought my lot had been worked out with a view to preventing poor people from owning homes. Where the owning of homes is discouraged the government that permits it is always in danger. The municipality that exercises such a careful supervision over the lot after the individual buys it should be equally as paternalistic in inquiring into and regulating the doings of the land speculator. A system of taxation to tax land for its full value for use should supersede the present one. Instead of fining a house-owner through taxation for building a house on land—fine the man, set of men, or syndicate who holds idle acres for speculative purposes. Make the land pay the tax instead of the labor expended on it. Compel every landholder to fix and name the price he places on his land and tax him accordingly. Tax him for holding and keeping land idle instead of taxing a man for home-building or working land.

The large landholding interests should be made to disgorge. I would not deprive them of the land without price unless they obtained it without price, by fraud or other shady transaction. In case they obtained the land by fraud perhaps it would be well to fine or jail them for their rascality. Oh, I know it will be called immoral to take land away from one who violates right in holding it, or, to speak more accurately, from one who misuses the public through unjust landholding. . . . If it is considered wrong to take land for a fair remuneration from one who does not work it and who expects to work someone in need of it by overcharging for it, what name shall we apply to the taking of the bodies and souls of men to cross thousands of miles of water to kill other men for the good of humanity? Men, not inanimate land, were called from their homes, they were called from their farms, their offices, from workshops and mines. They were obliged to sacrifice their positions, their prospects in life, and then offer their lives to make

the world safe, not for democracy, but for humanity. This was
done by our government without asking permission of anyone.
. . . If it was right and moral to take man from home and kin-
dred to fight for all of us, it cannot be immoral or wrong for all of
us—through our government—to take the land and use it for the
good of all of us. Land unlawfully held or even legally held may
be taken for the common good and in the long run this will have
to be done or the cost of living will always be high.

Yes, I know, I have heard it said before, that men would not
accept land as a gift and go on the land to work it; but men have
never been offered land as a gift, and every time our government
has thrown lands open to settlement, I have observed that men
by the thousand traveled hundreds and thousands of miles to
camp close by in order to make a rush for the land the morning
of its release to stake off a claim for a future home. I also know
that some rascals hired men to camp close to the land in order to
be first on the ground to select the choicest acres so . . . that
they might gamble in and sell them to real home seekers at fancy
prices later on. All this proves that men want land and men will
go on the land when we effect such changes in rural life as to dis-
tinguish existence on the farm from penal servitude.

. . . . .

I recently met an old acquaintance, a member of a labor organization of high-grade workmen, and in the course of our conversation he said his association intended making a demand for another
increase in wages. I asked him if he didn't think the butcher,
baker, and others would make a demand on everybody for higher
prices on meat, bread and other things right away and wouldn't
confine their high-class operations to members of his organization.
He admitted that they would, and when I followed up by saying
that increasing wages was like a kitten going around in a hurry
trying to catch her tail, he asked my views on the present condition of affairs. I gave them quite fully. He listened intently and
seemed impressed. All at once he said: "But how will freeing the
land, as you call it, help us who don't use it, how will it help the
poor washerwoman, the seamstress, the poor, crippled tailor or

cigar maker working in a tenement? These cannot go on the land and if they could they couldn't work it or use it."

Of course the poor washerwoman, seamstress, or crippled workman could not go on the land, but they don't have to, to use the land; it is brought to their doors every day, and their troubles come from lack of production and false distribution of land products. The owner of land cannot remove the acres from where their creator placed them at creation, he cannot take it with him when he dies. All he can get out of it is the use of it in what he digs from it and every being on earth whether he be tiller of the soil or delver in mine, home, or factory must live off the land. . . .

What I wrote into a ritual of the district assembly of the Knights of Labor in 1881 is true yet and more clearly discernible as a truth than when written:

> But ignorance and greed have established other standards in the world. While nature and industry may create in plenty, false distribution withholds and causes artificial scarcity and famine. Greed adulterates and idleness gambles in the products of toil and grows rich off the necessities of the producers, etc.

I was then representing the producers; were I gifted with a trifle more of prophetic vision in 1881, could that vision extend to 1919, I would add after "producers," the word "consumers."

Shortly after I was elected General Master Workman of the Knights of Labor in 1879 I was called on to address a public meeting in Pittsburgh. . . . During my speech I said:

> The fear so often expressed that if the number of hours of labor is reduced to eight per day, the time that men now work over eight hours will be spent in saloons and gambling dens, is groundless. There is a power now beginning to make itself felt which will in a short time render it possible for the toiler in the city to live in the country. A day will shortly dawn during which no horses or mules will be seen drawing our street cars, they will be propelled by an invisible force that shall revolutionize the streetcar transportation of all our cities and towns. Men will be enabled to have their homes away out in the country and by the aid of electricity get to and from their work in less time than they now use up in walking a few city blocks. Then instead of being subjected to the temptation of the saloon which he must pass, the workingman may take the electric car at the door of the workshop or mine and ride in it miles away to the door of his home. The

extra two hours that enemies of the eight hour system begrudged him will be devoted to the cultivation of a garden plot. There is plenty of land around Pittsburgh awaiting the attention of the home builder. He will be healthier, his wife and children will be healthier, and they will be happier than now. What the workman will yet take from the ground outside of Pittsburgh will be equivalent to an increase in wages. Don't give up the agitation for the shorter work day until this ally I tell you about is prepared to help you reduce the number of hours of toil.

Robert D. Layton, afterwards secretary of the Knights of Labor,[3] reported that speech and gave it to the press. He also furnished me with a copy, for I kept no notes of the meeting or my talk.

I have a distinct recollection of how men in that audience laughed at the idea of a streetcar climbing the hills surrounding Pittsburgh without horses or steam as aids to locomotion. . . .

The interviews with President Cleveland I have referred to were held in 1887, at a time when he could, and did, give thoughtful attention and consideration to them.

The following year Mr. Cleveland was a candidate for reëlection, and in September, when the campaign was at its height, he sent the following note to me: "If you can find it convenient to come to Washington during the next few days I shall appreciate it. I wish to discuss labor legislation with you."

I went, and, as the hour fixed for the interview was somewhere around one o'clock, I was invited by the President to lunch with him. At the table he told me he had resolved to appoint me United States Commissioner of Labor to succeed Carroll D. Wright,[4] whose term had expired.

I explained to Mr. Cleveland that to accept the appointment I would have to resign as General Master Workman, a thing I was unwilling to do. He asked if I could not do both, and I explained that the day was not long enough then by about thirty-six hours to do the work I was engaged in. I added:

There is another reason why you should not appoint me. During my

[3] Layton became secretary of the K. of L. in 1882.

[4] Carroll Davidson Wright (1840-1909) was the most influential, statistically minded social economist of his time. He did notable work as chief of the Massachusetts Bureau of Statistics of Labor, and was the first Commissioner of the United States Bureau of Labor (1885), which post he held for twenty years.

career I have made a number of very active, influential enemies. You can always rely on your enemy doing one thing well. While your friends will go to bed early and sleep the sleep of the just, you may depend on your enemy sitting up all night to get even with you. Every enemy I have will become your enemy the moment you appoint me. You are in the throes of a bitter campaign, and while I could not and would not attempt to turn one vote for you, these men might be able to do you harm. You can serve labor interests far better by recommending that the present labor bureau with the department name be changed to a real department of the Federal government with a secretary as its chief, sitting in your cabinet.

When [I was] parting from him that day, Mr. Cleveland thanked me for talking so unreservedly against myself and asked that I send him a memorandum embodying the suggestions I made concerning the scope of the proposed labor department. Following is the memorandum which I prepared and mailed to the President immediately after returning to Scranton.

It is difficult to briefly outline what I conceive to be the work of a labor department, for, as you know, I believe labor comes first in everything. I do not hold that only the hand, or manual, laborer is a worker. Every honest effort to speed humanity to better things is recognized by me as labor, whether it be of hand or brain.

First: A beginning should be made by tracing from date of its establishment in the United States the growth of every branch of industry that now exists, or has existed, so far as the facts may now be accessible.

Second: This inquiry should endeavor to ascertain the capital originally invested with all additions made thereto from time to time.

Third: The price paid for land per acre or foot at beginning of operations and price at time of inquiry. If the concern sells land to workmen, or others a comparison of original cost and selling price, or prices, should be made.

Fourth: A comparison of prices paid for land should be made with those sold by others in that neighborhood.

Fifth: A comparison of tax rate on homes of workmen with that on properties of like character in that neighborhood.

Sixth: Rents paid by workingmen for homes leased from such concern and terms of leases, securing copies of leases where obtainable.

Seventh: Condition of sanitation in workmen's homes. Ventilation, air space, size and number of rooms, number occupying them. Proximity to other buildings.

Eighth: Land worked as garden plots around homes of workingmen and probable revenue from same.

Ninth: Distances workmen have to travel to places of employment and cost of transportation.

Tenth: Reasons assigned for proposed reductions in wages by employers.

Eleventh: Reasons assigned by workingmen for resisting wage reductions.

Twelfth: Reasons assigned by workingmen for demanding increase in wages.

Thirteenth: Changes in cost of living and reasons assigned therefor.

Fourteenth: Women employed, number, wages as compared with men doing like work. Married women at work, and causes therefor. Conditions of workshop life should be fully gone into, treatment, sanitation, hours, toilet regulations, rest rules, light, whether complaints are permitted to reach head of concern, and if not, where they lodge on the way.

Fifteenth: Regulation of child labor. Need for same. Number, age, sex, physical condition. (One child may be in better physical condition at fourteen than another at seventeen.) Needs of parents for aid of children in providing a revenue for household. Educational advantages afforded children employed. Recreation afforded during work hours. Ailments of children employed and causes of same. Comparison of parents' certificate that children are of work age with municipal birth record where obtainable. Mortality of work children compared with those who do not labor, of like age, of course.

Sixteenth: Ascertain kind and amount of labor performed by women during pregnancy for purpose of studying effect on offspring.

Seventeenth: Necessity for workmen of certain grades in one center and oversupply of same class in another center and cause. In this connection the cooperation between State departments or bureaus of labor and the National Department of Labor, which we discussed the other day, would have to be established. It is possible, and should be made easy, to direct workmen from where they crowd each other idle to where they may help each other work. The Knights of Labor and trades-unions should not be expected to do this, but they can and will help to guard against sending a number of workers to where they are not needed for the purpose of enabling the unscrupulous employer to exploit them.

Eighteenth: Every corporation in need of workmen and every new concern beginning operations to file with the Department of Labor a statement of its need for workers, giving wage rates, hours, shop regulations, sanitary conditions, etc. This, of course, to follow details of class, or classes of work to be done.

Nineteenth: All government work to be under supervision of the Department of Labor.

Twentieth: We believe that land should be taxed for its full value for use and in this connection would expect the Department of Labor to ascertain what the various systems of taxation are throughout the United States. I am paying taxes by the foot on a lot 50 by 150 feet. Across the way is a farm of sixty acres, owned by a corporation. It is more favorably located than my lot, yet it is assessed by the acre and is taxed accordingly. I find on examination that on my lot I pay tax equal in amount to that paid on five acres of the corporation land. This system is iniquitous, but it prevails all over the United States and it will continue until but one kind of tax is paid on land by those who use it whether to live on or speculate it.

Twenty-first: Strikes, lockouts, blacklisting, and its legitimate offspring, the boycott, should all be studied, investigated and reported on. The causes leading to each and the means of effecting settlements should be examined into. The Department of Labor should be clothed with authority to step in and effect adjustment of difficulties through conciliation, mediation, or arbitration. I would give the employer the same right to invoke the good offices of the Department of Labor as the employee.

Twenty-second: Cost of living should be traced from cause to effect. From the time the earth yields its crudity to the touch of labor until it passes from the hand of the skilled workman as finished product; its cost at every stage should be inquired into and known. The same can be done with food supplies, the cost of everything entering the home and the reason why may be ascertained and should be ascertained.

Twenty-third: Electricity is destined to refute the argument that to reduce the hours of labor to eight per day will promote intemperance and shiftlessness. Suburban lines of transportation operated by electricity will supplant horse-power everywhere. It will then be possible for a shop or mine worker to reach his home in the suburbs by electric car in less time than he can now walk a few city blocks. He won't have to pass saloons on his way; he will reach home in time to devote part of daylight to working a garden plot. He will be inspired to own a home of his own. It should be cheaper out than inside a city and the Department of Labor should assist in shedding such light on prices and taxes as to check the land speculator.

Twenty-fourth: Full facts on the letting out of the labor of convicts to contractors should be secured. It is wrong to place a man in prison, feed him, and teach him a trade while punishing his body and society by starving wife and children, perhaps driving them to suicide or prostitution. Every convict should be made to work, but not for a contractor. He should work solely for the State and his wage should go to the support of his family or, in case of no family, be set aside to enable him to win his way among men again when liberated.

Twenty-fifth: The Department of Labor should afford common ground on which employer and employed may meet and know each other. If they do they will respect each other, and if they learn to know and respect each other they will in time learn that it is not to the interest of one to injure the other by hasty ill-considered action of any kind.

What I have suggested will be as texts to enlarge on. You lack the time to dwell on details.

Of course this will be a stupendous task and at best will take years to properly inaugurate. It will never be done, though, until a beginning has been made. The time to make the beginning is now.

I admit that this may, and with reason, be called paternalistic, but what of it? All good laws are, and we shouldn't fear names. It appears to me that if a government is "for the people" it must be paternalistic. Our government, having made a success of paternalism in some things, shouldn't turn aside from doing so in others.

True, the work I have indicated falls in large measure to the state bureaus and departments, but in time these will coöperate with and work through the Federal Department of Labor.

I know Mr. Cleveland read the memorandum, for, in addition to receiving his acknowledgment, Senator Turpie[5] told me afterward that the President discussed it with him, remarking at the time that: "Powderly didn't leave much for the rest of us to do."

．　　．　　．　　．

The first general labor conference ever held in the United States was called together in Louisville, Ky., August 14, 1865, shortly after the close of the Uncivil War.

The purpose of that conference was to restore to life and activity the trade-unions, North and South, that had slumbered or died during the war. . . .

In going over old papers [of that conference] I came across the following resolution as adopted on August 15, 1865:

Every department of the Federal government is now and has been officered by professional men, business men, or manufacturers. They are or have been employers of labor or counselors of employers of labor; naturally their sympathies are not with labor. There should be at Washington a Department of Labor to be officered by men who are of and with labor. The duty of that department to be the guarding of labor interests in every way now known or which hereafter may become known.

[5] David Turpie (1829-1909) served as judge and as a member of the Indiana legislature before being elected as a Democrat to the United States Senate in place of the expelled Senator Bright. In the spring of 1887 he was chosen Senator for the full term.

Chapter Twenty-Two

THE READING COMBINE

SOMETIME during the latter part of the year 1891, or beginning of 1892, the heads of three anthracite-carrying railroads operating in Pennsylvania—the Philadelphia and Reading, the Lehigh Valley and the Central Railroad of New Jersey—conceived a plan of controlling the transportation of coal to market so that one agency would direct and regulate the supply. The idea originated with the officials of the Philadelphia and Reading Company which, under the terms of the scheme, obtained control of the other two railroads. To each of these three roads was apportioned a certain tonnage. The organization thus established at first became known as the "Reading Deal," later on as the "Reading Combine."

During the month of January, 1892, certain newspapers published in New York, Philadelphia, and in towns along the three roads began a propaganda having for its object the education of the people in the belief, as one of them said, that "ruinous competition in the transporting of coal by so many railroad systems is productive of waste. By uniting these carrying companies under one head they will be enabled to more economically serve the interests of consumers of coal and bring about a reduction in prices paid by town and city dwellers."

Numerous articles favoring the plan appeared, over the signatures of men of standing, in leading journals throughout the anthracite field. A clergyman here and there loaned the weight of his influence to the scheme by expressing himself in its favor. The burden of all these tributes to the combine was that the price of anthracite would be lowered and the consumer would profit thereby.

When everything was ready the scheme was launched, and at

once editorials commending it appeared in many of the most influential newspapers.

Paid agents of the combine appeared in many towns in the hard-coal fields to talk for and work up sentiment in its favor.

I was a close observer of what was going on, and devoted some time to investigating the doings of those who favored this "new move in the interest of the coal-consuming public."

Passengers traveling to Philadelphia and points south over the Lehigh Valley and Central of New Jersey railroads are sent from Bethlehem, Pa., over the Philadelphia and Reading Railroad. One day on my way to Philadelphia I saw a clergyman exhibit a pass to the conductor. It was on a Central Railroad of New Jersey train. After changing cars at Bethlehem I managed to get a seat where I could see this clergyman when the P. & R. conductor appeared. This time he showed a pass over the Reading. When I could devote time to it, I visited a local assembly of the Knights of Labor in the town in which that clergyman officiated and learned from members of his own congregation that he was "strong for the combine."

I was well acquainted with another clergyman in that town, called on him, and, during our interview, learned that he did not look with favor on the Reading Combine. I also learned that when traveling he had to pay railroad fare and was not favored with a pass.

After studying the matter carefully I came to the conclusion that that combine was not a good thing for the people, and said so. I talked against it from the public platform and published articles against it in the public press. The only papers that would at first give me space in their columns were the Scranton *Truth* and the *Journal of the Knights of Labor*.

I traveled all through the anthracite region obtaining information and securing affidavits in opposition to the Reading Combine. My activities in that direction earned for me the ill-will of many of my best friends, and in Scranton I was characterized by some as "an enemy to the prosperity of the citizens of Lackawanna County." The Scranton *Tribune* in particular took marked exception to my effort to break the combine.

I was not actuated in what I did or said by hatred of corporations, by malice, spite, anger, or a love of the limelight. I spoke and wrote from an unbiased, unselfish, and impartial standpoint. I desired that the truth should prevail. In this I had an open field in the beginning, for outside of the Scranton *Truth*, edited by John E. Barrett,[1] who always defended the right, I had few competitors.

The ramifications of the Reading Combine extended from every anthracite-producing town in Pennsylvania to the principal cities in New York and New England, not forgetting Philadelphia. I visited most of these places, secured information, and obtained affidavits from those who could testify to the work done by, and the effect of, the combine.

Labor organizations were approached by emissaries of the Reading Combine and, before they gave careful thought or study to what they did, they passed resolutions and sent them to me protesting against my activities in "attempting to destroy an agency that is destined to prove a boon of great value to coal consumers in our large cities, many of whom are members of the Knights of Labor, and against whose interests the General Master Workman should not raise his hand."

In justice to these organizations let me . . . say that the action they took against me was in the early days of the combine, before its real significance and intent became apparent. Even then it was a small minority that voiced the opposition; the old practice of deferring action until nearly all members had left the meeting room was resorted to. Of course, the agent of the combine made himself very popular at fairs, bazaars, festivals, and other gatherings where workingmen assembled.

After pursuing my investigation far enough to become convinced that the subordination of the Lehigh Valley and Central of New Jersey railroads to the rule of the Philadelphia and Reading, which I shall hereafter call the Reading, was against the best interests of the people, I determined to make an effort to

---

[1] John Erigena Barrett, born in Ireland in 1849, came to the United States in 1871, and became one of the publishers of the Scranton *Truth* in 1884. He also wrote fiction with a labor content.

awaken the public conscience to the true inwardness of the proceeding. To my mind it was in direct violation of the constitution of the state of Pennsylvania; it was opposed to the future welfare of consumers of anthracite; it was a bold defiance of popular will; it was fundamentally wrong; in short, it was iniquitous. So, with all the strength I possessed, I began a campaign against the Reading Combine which continued until that organization, defeated and humiliated, retired from the field and relinquished its hold on the two competing lines I have named.

So far as I know, or ever did know, I was the only man connected with organized labor who fought the Reading Combine. Those who brought it into life did not forget me afterwards, but their remembrance of me was not calculated to add to my bank account or peace of mind. Outside of A. J. Cassatt[2] of the Pennsylvania Railroad Company, I do not recall another individual who became conspicuous in opposing the Reading Combine. I endeavored to enlist the aid of others in the battle against the combine, but failed. What I did was solely on my own initiative and responsibility.

Among the letters I published on the subject was one which appeared in the *Journal of the Knights of Labor* under date of February 18, 1892. Before that issue of the paper was intrusted to the mails, I sent a proof-sheet copy of my letter to Governor Pattison[3] at Harrisburg. From that letter I quote as follows:

Old-fogy journalists and many whose interests were closely intertwined with those of the great railroads of Pennsylvania advised the people to let well enough alone and not disturb vested rights by the adoption of a new Constitution. All that King George desired in 1775 was to be let alone— he objected to being disturbed in the divine right to rob the people of the colonies. Whenever a man or institution stands in opposition to the interests of the masses, the cry "let well enough alone" will be heard when justice for the many is demanded. The old Roman proverb says: "When a vice is useful it is a crime to be virtuous," and the ethics of legalized spoliation as

[2] Alexander J. Cassatt (1839-1906) entered the service of the Pennsylvania Railroad in 1861 as a rodman, and in 1883 was elected director of the railroad. Subsequently he became president of the Pennsylvania system.

[3] Robert Emory Pattison (1850-1904) first took office as governor of Pennsylvania in 1883, and held that office again 1891-95. He was specially interested in railroad questions.

practiced by the corporations of Pennsylvania would indicate that neither in word nor meaning should that sentiment be changed.

In the light of recent events it is well to turn to the pages of the Constitution of Pennsylvania and read a few selected passages therefrom, beginning as follows: "All railroads and canals shall be public highways, and all railroad and canal companies shall be common carriers."

On the public highway of the past—the turnpike—every man who had occasion to do so could drive his wagon or he could hire a wagon and team and carry his produce from point to point without let or hindrance from any other man. The road was his—no other man could lay a higher claim to it. Where stands the man so powerful as to transport a single pound of freight or produce on the "public highway" of 1892 if a board of directors decide that he shall be discriminated against? That part of the Constitution of Pennsylvania is as delusive as a concave mirror.

"All individuals, associations and corporations shall have equal right to have persons and property transported over railroads and canals, and no undue or unreasonable discrimination shall be made in charges for, or in facilities for, transportation of freight or passengers within this State, or coming from or going to any other State." All individuals are not privileged to exercise the right conferred by that section of the Constitution of the State. The individual has but to apply at the coal office of any of the great concerns operating railroads and mines in Pennsylvania and ask to have a single ton or a car of coal shipped from that point to either New York or Philadelphia to learn that there is a higher law than that written between the musty pages of our dead and buried Constitution. The rule of the corporation is that the consumer in either New York or Philadelphia must deal through the coal agent or middleman, and no single ton, or car of coal will be shipped. The law of the corporation is the higher law, for it is obeyed in preference to the Constitution of the State. That part of the Constitution of Pennsylvania is not operative; it never was operative and was not intended to be; it declares a falsehood.

Section 4, Article XVII reads: "No railroad, canal or other corporation, or the lessees, purchasers, or managers of any railroad or canal corporation, shall consolidate the stock, property, or franchises of such corporation with, or lease or purchase the works or franchises of, or in any way control any other railroad or canal corporation, owning or having under its control a parallel or competing line; nor shall any officer of such railroad or canal corporation act as an officer of any other railroad or canal corporation owning or having the control of a parallel or competing line; and the question whether railroads or canals are parallel or competing lines shall, when demanded by the party complainant be decided by a jury, as in other civil issues."

A short time ago the Philadelphia and Reading Railroad was in the hands of a receiver, whose duty it was to make proper adjustment of its affairs and receive payment for the stockholders. On its knees, plundered by thieving officials, it crouched, a beggar among corporations. With a load of debt crushing it down to where it became an easy prey, it is said to have passed beneath the rule of that combination known as the Vanderbilt System. Immediately we see the tentacles of the octopus stretching toward the upper coal fields and grasping parallel lines of railroad leading from the Reading to these fields. Two lines of railroad run parallel with each other from Easton to Wilkes-Barre, a distance of 100 miles. Every bend and turn of the Lehigh River from Easton to White Haven, a distance of 70 miles, is in view of the glistening rails of each of these two railroads as they turn and bend with the river. These certainly are parallel and competing lines within the full intent and meaning of the Constitution. No other two railroads in Pennsylvania can possibly approach nearer to each other in construction and similarity than the Lehigh Valley and Central Railroad of New Jersey, the two roads in question. Under the recent combination effected to freeze out competition, and consumers of coal as well, the Philadelphia and Reading Railroad Company has absorbed the Lehigh Valley and the Central Railroad of New Jersey, and so far as these corporations are concerned they are no longer competing lines. Every letter and line of Section 4 of Article XVII of the Constitution of Pennsylvania has been violated in the deal by which the Reading gained control of these two roads, and, from now until the interests of the law-protected robbers shall require that the combination be broken, the people will pay such tribute as may be levied by those who control the entire anthracite supply of Pennsylvania. It has been suggested that the Governor and the Attorney General of the State take action against the Reading for its audacious and open violation of the Constitution, but it is doubtful if that will give relief to the people of the State. Section 10 of that same article gives to the old corporations of Pennsylvania the privilege of overriding the entire Constitution in these words: "No railroad, canal or other transportation company, in existence at the time of the adoption of this article, shall have the benefit of any future legislation by general or special laws, except on condition of complete acceptance of all the provisions of this article."

In that section the power to accept or reject the Constitution was given to the canal and railroad companies in operation at the time of its adoption. That Constitution binds only the people in their individual capacity, and such railroad, canal and other corporations as were organized since 1873. All railroad and canal companies existing prior to that date are above and beyond the Constitution.

Emboldened by our defeat in failing to secure a majority in favor of a Constitutional Convention, the Reading Railroad has taken another step against the welfare of Pennsylvania. It has committed another theft, and it lays [sic] with us to bring the rogue to justice. In order that our position may not be misunderstood and that we may be strengthened in the stand we shall take, let each man of the 177,000 personally write the Governor to take official notice of the action of the Reading Company and call upon him to take the offenders before the highest tribunal of the State for a hearing and investigation. Demand of the Executive of the State that the fullest light shall be thrown upon this most outrageous of all encroachments on the rights of the people, not alone of Pennsylvania, but of the whole Eastern and Middle States. Act at once, get up petitions, write letters, interest others who are not members, send delegations to the Governor, and in every possible way strengthen his hands in the work of ridding Pennsylvania of the Jesse James wing of the corporations. If he will not act, secure his reasons, and, above all things, leave nothing undone to find out beyond the shadow of a doubt whether Article XVII is binding on the railroads and canals of the State. Let us ascertain whether we can legally redress our wrongs before resorting to ————.

T. V. POWDERLY

For four years beginning in 1887 and ending on election day 1891, I was "perniciously active" in working for the holding of a Constitutional Convention in Pennsylvania. The agitation for the Constitutional Convention began in the editorial office of the Scranton *Truth* and grew out of a conversation between John E. Barrett and T. V. Powderly on the subject of ballot reform. It was there decided that a Constitutional Convention ought to be held, and the columns of the *Truth* were opened for four years to a discussion of the question. Chauncey F. Black[4] of York, Pa., Mr. Barrett, and I left no stone unturned to secure the holding of the Constitutional Convention. The Legislature of Pennsylvania enacted a law which to the uninitiated seemed to favor the holding of the Constitutional Convention, and provision was made for the election of delegates to attend the Convention should it be called. The provision calling for the holding of the Convention was on a slip by itself, for the secret or blanket ballot was not in use at that time. The legislative and senatorial districts were authorized to vote for a certain number of delegates while the state at large was privileged to vote for a stated number.

Having taken such a prominent part in the agitation looking to the holding of the Convention, I was nominated for delegate by the Republican State Convention of 1891. I did not ask for or

---

[4] Chauncey Forward Black (d. 1904), son of Jeremiah S. Black, served as lieutenant-governor of Pennsylvania 1882-86, and ran for governor on the Democratic ticket in 1886.

in any way indicate that I desired that nomination, but when it was accorded to me I accepted it. When the votes were polled I had the empty honor of having received the highest number of votes cast for any candidate on either ticket throughout the state, but while I was elected, the proposal to hold the Convention was defeated. It was to the defeat of the Constitutional Convention that I referred in my letter of February 18.

On receipt of the proof sheet of my *Journal* letter, Governor Pattison gave out an interview in which he expressed a willingness to receive complaints against the Reading Combine. I read his interview in the morning papers of February 19, 1892, and on the same day I prepared and mailed the following letter to him:

SCRANTON, FEBRUARY 19, 1892

HON. ROBERT E. PATTISON
    GOVERNOR OF PENNSYLVANIA
Dear Sir:
            In the absence of any authorized form of making complaint I take this means of calling your attention to the attempted violation of the Constitution of this State by the Philadelphia and Reading Railroad Company. Within the last two weeks a combination has been effected by which the Central Railroad of New Jersey and the Lehigh Valley Railroad Companies have been absorbed by the Philadelphia and Reading; the two last mentioned railroads are parallel and competing lines, if such exist within the meaning of the Constitution; they operate in the same field and tap the same coal beds.

Section 4 of Article XVII of the Constitution of the State is positive in its declaration against such a consolidation of railway interests as will be effected if this gigantic trust is formed. As a citizen of Pennsylvania I herewith enter a complaint against the formation of the combination referred to.

Article XVII in every section and clause, is being violated and set aside by the actions of the Philadelphia and Reading Company. If there is in the Constitution of this State any authority for the action of the railroads above mentioned I, as one citizen of the Commonwealth, would esteem it a great favor if it be pointed out to me by the legal authority of the State itself. If there is no such warrant of authority in the Constitution of the State, then I demand, as required by Section 4 of Article XVII, that the complaint be decided by a jury.

I have the honor to be,
                    Very truly yours,
                        T. V. POWDERLY

It happened that Mr. A. J. Cassatt, vice-president of the Pennsylvania R.R. Co., wrote to Governor Pattison a protest against the Reading Combine. His letter bore the same date as mine and that circumstance was taken advantage of by my enemies, or perhaps I should say by the friends of the Combine, to indicate that I was acting with one corporation in fighting another. I knew nothing of Mr. Cassatt's intentions and I was not aware of what he intended doing. . . .

Governor Pattison acknowledged the receipt of my letter, and . . . informed me that he had referred my complaint to the attorney general of the state "to take such action as he may deem necessary to enforce the Constitution and protect every interest of the Commonwealth." Under date of February 23, 1892, W. U. Hensel, attorney general of Pennsylvania, wrote me as follows:

FEBRUARY 23, 1892

Mr. T. V. POWDERLY
    GENERAL MASTER WORKMAN, ORDER OF KNIGHTS OF LABOR
        SCRANTON, PENNSYLVANIA
Sir:
    The Governor of the Commonwealth has referred to me your letter of February 19 relating to the recent arrangement effected between the Lehigh Valley Railroad Company, the Central Railroad Company of New Jersey and the Philadelphia and Reading Railroad Company, whereby it is alleged the control of the first two named companies has been acquired by the last named in violation of the Constitution of the Commonwealth and to the prejudice of the interests of the community. I am instructed by the Governor to take such action as will enforce the Constitution and bring all who have violated it within its control.

    In a recently published statement I said that it was the usual practice of this office "to entertain any respectable complaint of the abuse, misuse, or non-use of corporate franchises, and upon due notice to give full hearing to complainant and complained against"; and "when it is made to appear that the public interest is affected and the circumstances render it proper and necessary that the Commonwealth intervene, resort is had to the Courts, wherein, by fit judicial process, inquiry is made and judgment is reached."

    In accordance with that practice, and referring to the subject matter of your letter, I beg to inform you that I have fixed Thursday, March 3, at 12 o'clock M., as the time when, and the Chamber of the Supreme Court at Harrisburg as the place where, I will hear the complaint you have already made or any further matter bearing upon the subject thereof which you may desire to present, either in person or by counsel; that I have notified the presidents of the Lehigh Valley Railroad Company, the Central Railroad Company of New Jersey and of the Philadelphia and Reading Railroad Company of this appointment, and that they will then and there be given a like opportunity to be heard in reply; and I have called upon them to furnish me then, or previous to that time, with copies of the leases or agreements under which they have made the arrangements complained of. I have also fixed the same time and place for the hearing of a like complaint made by Mr. A. J. Cassatt.

Very truly yours,
W. U. Hensel, Attorney General

Governor Pattison had given my letter and that of Mr. Cassatt to the Associated Press about the time they were mailed, and I read them in a Cincinnati paper while on my way to St. Louis. The letter from the attorney general awaited my return to Scranton on the 29th of February and I at once acknowledged its receipt. . . .

Scranton, Pa., February 29
To the Hon. W. U. Hensel, Attorney-General of the
    Commonwealth of Pennsylvania
Dear Sir:
        I have before me your letter of February 23, in which you say that you have fixed Thursday, March 3, as the time when, and the chamber of the Supreme Court at Harrisburg as the place where, you will hear the complaint I have already made or any further matter bearing on the subject thereof which I may desire to present, either in person or by counsel. While it will afford me the greatest pleasure to coöperate with you in securing such evidence as will prove that the Constitution of the Commonwealth has been violated in the formation of the combination by which the Philadelphia and Reading Company gains control of the Central Railroad of New Jersey and the Lehigh Valley Railroad Company, I cannot, from any actual knowledge of the facts in the case, make affidavit to the complaint I have already made or to anything in addition thereto. As stated in my letter to the Governor, I knew of no authorized form of making complaint. I was prompted to the act by a reported interview with the governor in which he was quoted as follows: "I have heard no complaint, and have no knowledge of the existence of such a combination, but will entertain any respectful complaint of the abuse or misuse of corporate franchises, etc., etc." On reading that interview, I determined that the governor would soon have cause for action, so that he could proceed against the parties who have formed the combina-

tion. I therefore made "respectful complaint" believing that, having called the attention of the Executive to the matter, my duty ended there.

It was a matter of no little surprise to me to find that, from a perusal of your letter, I would be required to proceed to Harrisburg to repeat the complaint I had "already made." If my memory serves me aright, there were no complaints made to either the Executive or legal authorities of this State in 1886, when Governor Pattison took cognizance of the existence of a combination to restrict the coal output of the anthracite region. In his reference of the matter to the Attorney-General, he said: "My attention has been directed to the fact that within the past fortnight certain corporations chartered by the Commonwealth of Pennsylvania, acting in concert, have ordered two advances in the price of anthracite coal, etc." It was my aim to direct the attention of the Governor to the fact that a combination was being formed which would have absolute control over the coal output, and which could, without let or hindrance, advance and double the price of coal.

In closing his presentment to the Attorney-General, the Governor said: "These facts, which have been reported to me and measurably authenticated, I deem of sufficient importance to refer to you for your consideration and for such action as the circumstances warrant." To my mind it was quite clear that the facts in the case now under consideration were measurably authenticated on the day I entered my complaint, and I furthermore felt that, if the facts in the former case were of sufficient importance to warrant the Governor in presenting them to the Attorney-General of the Commonwealth, the statements with which every paper in the land bristled for several days before I took steps in the matter were of even greater importance, since they comprehended a wider field of operations, a massing of a greater aggregation of capital, and, as a natural sequence, greater opportunities to advance the price of coal. I am, in common with the vast majority of the citizens of this state, powerless to produce such evidence as will prove a violation of the fundamental law of the Commonwealth unless the proper authority shall institute judicial proceedings and compel an obedience to the laws of the state.

Under your summons to me . . . I am not bound under penalty of any kind to repair to Harrisburg or anywhere else to give testimony. The fact that Mr. Cassatt has refused to appear would indicate that others would do the same.

In your letter to me you state that you have notified the presidents of the Lehigh Valley Railroad Company, the Central Railroad of New Jersey and the Philadelphia and Reading Railroad Company of this appointment, etc. You will pardon me for presuming to say to you that a mere notification to do a thing will not cause a guilty person to do it, and if there is vested in the authorities of this Commonwealth no stronger or greater power than that which is comprehended in a mere notification, then the investigation of next Thursday will not be prolific of good to the people of the Commonwealth.

I say this in all seriousness and earnestness, for I entered a complaint in the same spirit, and had reason to hope that it would enable the Governor to see his way clear to take the initial step against a combination that, to laymen like myself, at least, is in violation not only of the spirit but of the exact letter of the Constitution of Pennsylvania. I can swear to nothing, and yet am morally certain that this combination exists. Were I to ask the parties to the combination to allow me the privilege of examining their contracts, leases, papers, etc., it is probable that they would not grant my request; and without these or the evidence of witnesses I could not give you more than you have already learned from the daily papers. Private litigation is totally inadequate to protect the Commonwealth against wrong. . . . I expected and had a reasonable right to expect, that, as in the case of the attempted purchase of the South Penn Railroad by the Pennsylvania Railroad, the Governor would protect the interests of the Commonwealth and compel obedience to the Constitution. I am not prepared to believe that there is one law for the Pennsylvania and another for the Philadelphia and Reading Railroad. . . .

When writing to the Governor I had in mind more than the present combination, and when I said that "Article XVII, in every section and clause, is being violated and set aside by the actions of the Philadelphia and Reading Company," I had hoped that it would be possible to investigate the right of that concern to absorb the Philadelphia and Reading Coal and Iron Company and the Schuylkill Canal. Beginning on page 175 of the report of the Congressional Investigating Committee of 1888, you will find the testimony of Mr. A. A. McLeod,[5] then Vice-President of the Philadelphia and Reading Company, in which he admitted that the latter company had absorbed the two companies named above. . . . I . . . would suggest that it contains sufficient evidence from . . . those interested in this present combination to prove that the Constitution of the State has been broken repeatedly. The Philadelphia and Reading Coal and Iron Company controls by lease or otherwise 194,062 acres of coal, iron, and timber lands, and the $8,000,000 stock is owned by the Reading Railroad. Such a vast aggregation of capital operating within the limits of the Commonwealth is in itself a menace to the perpetuity of our institutions. . . .

I cannot, as you are aware, enter complaint other than as a citizen; the Order of the Knights of Labor has no corporate existence and cannot, therefore, be heard before the Courts. Were it otherwise, we would be represented by counsel, as you suggest. Since I acted in my individual capacity as a citizen in presenting the complaint, I should not be expected to

[5] Angus Archibald McLeod (1847-1902) became general manager of the Philadelphia and Reading Railroad in 1885, and was made vice-president in 1888 and president in 1890.

be represented by counsel to defend the Constitution of the State, since that duty falls upon the shoulders of the State authorities.

If you summon the employes of the Lehigh Valley Railroad Company and those of the Central Railroad of New Jersey, you will learn that an order has been issued from the office of the Philadelphia and Reading Company subordinating the officials and employes of the two first named companies to the management of the latter. Furthermore, it will be discovered that many employes of the Lehigh Valley Railroad Company have been discharged on the order of the management of the Reading combination. Investigation . . . will prove that a circular issued from the office of the Reading combine within the past two weeks notifies officials of the Central Railroad of New Jersey that in future it will be controlled by the Port Reading Company. The Port Reading Company, it is well known, is but an insignificant concern, and is the property of the Philadelphia and Reading Company. Why is the name of a branch road made use of instead of that of the company which owns it if the transaction is honest and constitutional? In this region the officials of the Philadelphia and Reading are making contracts with coal operators along the line of the Lehigh Valley and Central Railroad of New Jersey for the delivery of coal. Will it be argued that the Reading Railroad runs through this region or that that corporation can receive that tonnage in any other way than over the tracks of the two companies it has absorbed?

From the office of Drexel, Morgan & Co. this statement has been given out: "An arrangement similar to a lease has been made by which the Philadelphia and Reading takes control of the two railroads in question."

And the following is given out as the contract: "The Reading will guarantee to the New Jersey Central stockholders 7 per cent on their stock, and any excessive earnings over this amount will be divided equally between the New Jersey Central and the Reading stockholders. The Reading guarantees to the Lehigh Valley stockholders 5 per cent to next July; then for a year the guarantee is 6 per cent; and thereafter, from July 1, 1893, the guarantee will be 7 per cent. Any excessive earnings, if any, over 7 per cent, will be divided equally between the Lehigh and Reading stockholders, until the Lehigh holders get 10 per cent, after which the Reading will take all." The Reading Company, as it is reported in the papers, without denial, had deposited with Drexel, Morgan & Co. of New York $3,000,000 in securities to secure the Lehigh Valley lease and $2,000,000 in securities to secure the lease of the Central Railroad of New Jersey. . . . These transactions . . . furnish presumptive evidence of the existence of a combination such as is positively forbidden in Article XVII of the Constitution of this Commonwealth. . . . Your oath of office . . . requires that the slightest attempt at violation of the Constitution of the State should be noted in an official way by you. . . .

From such invasions of popular rights as are contemplated in this combination, the people of the State should be defended. The Constitution in its denial of such privileges to corporations is positive or meaningless. If positive, then your duty is clear; if meaningless, we should know it from the highest legal authority of the Commonwealth, that we may amend, alter, or abolish it, as allowed by the Bill of Rights.

It may be that I have taken the wrong course in attempting to have legal proceedings entered against those whom I believe to be conspiring against the peace and welfare of this state. I am not a lawyer, and cannot, therefore, be held to be blameworthy for not being conversant at the time I entered the complaint with the fact that there is on the statutes of the State a law "to prohibit foreign corporations from doing business in Pennsylvania without having known places of business and authorized agents." If that combination comes under the head of corporations, then it should be required to comply with Section 2 of that law, which reads: "It shall not be lawful for any such corporation to do any business in this Commonwealth until it shall have filed in the office of the Secretary of the Commonwealth a statement, under the seal of said corporation and signed by the president or secretary thereof, showing the title and object of said corporation, the location of its office or offices, and the name or names of its authorized agent or agents therein, and the certificate of the filing of such statement shall be preserved for public inspection by each of said agents in each and every of said offices."

In framing that law in accord with the Constitution of the State, it was the evident intention to have a record of all foreign corporations doing business within the State. . . . If a mere corporation is denied the privilege of doing business until it places its application and charter open to the inspection of all citizens, can it be less so for so vast an aggregation of capital, or, in other words, so vast a combination of corporations, as make up what is known as the "Reading Deal"?

In what degree is the importance of a corporation lessened in the eyes of the Commonwealth when it combines with other corporations? This is a foreign institution to Pennsylvania. It was born or hatched in New York, and while it may be indigenous to New York, it certainly is not unknown to Pennsylvania as a weed of rank growth likely to choke other and more useful plants out of existence.

If the law above referred to does not in any way apply to this case, it may be that the remedy may be found in "An Act regulating the election of the Secretary of Internal Affairs, defining his duties and fixing his salary" . . . signed by Governor Hartranft on the eleventh day of May, 1874. Part of Section 4 of that act reads . . . : "It shall be his especial duty to exercise a watchful supervision over the railroad, banking, mining, manufacturing, and other business corporations of the State and to see that they confine themselves strictly within their corporate limits; and in case any citizen or citizens shall charge, under oath, any corporation with transcending its corporate functions or infringing upon the rights of individual citizens, said Secretary shall carefully investigate such charges, and may require from said corporations a special report, as enjoined in the Constitution of the State; and in case he believes that the charges are just and the matter complained of is beyond the ordinary province of individual redress, he shall certify his opinion to the Attorney-General of the State, whose duty it shall be, by an appropriate legal remedy, to redress the same by a proceeding in the Courts at the expense of the State."

If, in making my complaint direct to the Governor, as I felt that in courtesy I should do, I have erred, I will cheerfully proceed to produce the required affidavits and place them in the hands of the Secretary of Internal Affairs so that that official may act.

I will not have the time to procure the affidavits before the 3rd, and could not place before you an iota more of evidence than is contained in this statement for the length of which I beg to be excused. Were I to go to Harrisburg on Thursday I could not do more than repeat what I have already written; but if you believe that I should do so, I will hold myself in readiness to obey your summons. I have an important engagement for the evening of the 2nd, which must be canceled if I go to Harrisburg, and I, therefore, ask, as a special favor, that you kindly wire me on receipt of this whether it will be necessary to attend, so that I may give due notice to the parties concerned in my arrangements for the evening of the 2nd.

Very truly yours,

T. V. POWDERLY

The publication of my letter in the *Journal of the Knights of Labor* subjected me to some pretty severe criticism. I was called "impudent," "impertinent," "grossly insulting," "unmindful of the dignity attached to the high office of Governor and Attorney-General," but I believe I was right. . . . It was following the publication of that letter that I began taking testimony regarding the activities of the Reading Combine on my own responsibility.

I secured the affidavits of over two hundred workmen who had been discharged from the service of the Reading, the Lehigh Valley, and the Central R.R. of New Jersey. I secured affidavits in Ashley, Pittston, Forty Fort, Nanticoke, Wilkes-Barre, Scranton, White Haven, Mauch Chunk, Bethlehem, Easton, two or three other towns in Pennsylvania, including Philadelphia. I also obtained affidavits of discharged workmen at the terminals in Jersey City. In New York City, through the coöperation of District Assembly No. 49 of the Knights of Labor, I obtained affidavits from upward of fifty consumers of anthracite to the effect that coal had been increased in price upwards of $1.80 per ton. Working people living in tenements . . . have to carry their coal by the pailful up two, three, four, and as high as seven or eight flights of stairs. Anthracite sold at ten cents a pail when the Reading Combine was formed. Two increases in prices of twenty-five cents a ton were made between the time I wrote the governor and the following September. The price of a pail of coal advanced from ten to twelve cents and since it takes ninety pails of coal to make up a ton, it will be seen that the "Knights of Labor against whose interests the General Master Workmen should not raise his hand" were getting an object lesson in what the Reading Combine could do in the way of raising the price of coal.

I obtained the affidavits of five reputable citizens in Pittston, Wilkes-Barre, Ashley, White Haven, and Mauch Chunk to the effect that they "saw agents of the Reading Dealers standing outside of the schoolrooms securing the signatures of little boys and girls to a petition to Governor Pattison not to take action against the Reading Combine." The boys who signed these petitions were directed to sign their names in full, that is, to write their first names and initials, while the girls were requested to sign the initials of their Christian names and their last names in full. The petition thus obtained was forwarded to Governor Pattison, but before it reached him I had secured evidence which warranted me in publishing the facts in relation to the whole scandalous transaction, and so well authenticated was what I sent the governor that the effect of the "great petition for the continuance of the Reading Combine" fell flat.

I then took the liberty of writing to Mr. Alexander McLeod in relation to this petition and provided him with such details that he laid aside the petition weapon as not being of such service as was expected. The children did not know whether they were signing a petition to hang the governor or to secure a pardon for their juvenile sins. . . .

I secured affidavits from storekeepers and small merchants in several of the towns who had been approached by agents of the combine and threatened with the boycott if they did not cease talking against it.

I secured the petitions of five clergymen who had been solicited to say a good word for the combine from their pulpits. I may add that I did not seek these latter affidavits; they were sent to me by the clergymen without solicitation.

I secured affidavits from the presidents or leading officials of several benevolent societies of Luzerne and Lackawanna Counties to the effect that the price of tickets for excursions that they intended running during the summer and fall of 1892 had been doubled as the result of the "Reading Deal."

When I had secured what I considered to be prima facie evidence that the Reading Combine was not intended to become a religious or benevolent organization, I took a satchel full of documents to Harrisburg, sought an interview with Governor Pattison, was received very cordially, and informed that I should retain them in my possession until I should receive notice from the attorney general to lay them before him. I am still awaiting that notification.

It seems that my letters were, by a number of editors, regarded as personal attacks on the governor of the state, and they proceeded to find just cause for complaint against me. One of them in his editorial said "a great labor man, professing lofty sentiments, has permitted himself to become an ally of the Pennsylvania R. R. Co., for it could not be a mere coincidence that caused him to write the governor on the same day and on the same subject as Mr. Cassatt."

In a letter of mine in the *Journal of the Knights of Labor* under date of March 17, 1892, I . . . said:

Quite a few of the Democratic papers of the State feel called upon to defend the Governor of the State from "assaults made upon him" by me. I have not uttered one word against the Governor or any other official since this controversy began, but, if calling the attention of the Executive to an attempted violation of the State Constitution is an assault upon the Democratic Governor, the quicker we arrive at a thorough understanding of the matter the better. If defense of the State Constitution is to be construed into an attack on a Democratic Governor, then the quicker those papers begin the study of democratic principles the better will it be for them, their Governor and their party.

.   .   .   .

On the whole, I do not know but that it is best to allow this deal to go on. It will grow bolder; it will grow more arrogant; it will raise the price of coal . . . it will become so insolent that it will cause all rightminded men to see the danger which faces them in allowing this octopus to grow and spread.

A coal operator, in taking me to task for opposing the deal, spoke as follows: "You are standing out in opposition to the interests of this city [meaning Scranton], for this deal will give work to our mines the year round. This will do away with the middlemen in the coal business and the profits will go to the workmen. A very slight increase, if it should be deemed necessary, in the price of coal will bring prosperity to all of us, and you are making a damn fool of yourself in opposing what will do us all good."

If those who now mine coal and own the railroads were desirous of doing so, the middleman would have to go out of business. The middleman, in the coal business, is the product of the present system of favoritism to relatives. He did not thrust himself on the coal companies by any means, and investigation will show many cases such as I stumbled over a few days ago. One of these middlemen is a nephew of the president of the company. He never . . . does . . . an hour's work a week, and, in fact, knows nothing about his business. His only qualification is that he stands in the same relation to the stockholders of that company that the last grandchild of Queen Victoria bears to the people of Great Britain—as a leech who draws without rendering an equivalent. This nephew of that president realized on his commissions, in 1891, just $117,893, a sum which should have been paid to the coal miners and workers. . . . What matters it to the working people who steals that $117,893 since they are robbed of it? They will realize no benefit from it. The great power is vested in this combine to shut down when it pleases and operate at will. Heretofore the fear that one company might kick over the traces and give the men a few more days in the month, or the people of the cities a few more tons of coal, caused the mines to work a portion of the time. With this combination in successful operation no such fear will be felt. "A very slight increase" in the price of coal will be deemed necessary, but it would be the height of folly to announce that increase now. In the first place, it might arouse the people against the combine, and, in the second place, the warm weather is so close at hand that to increase the price of coal would not materially increase the income of the combiners. Next fall, however, the price of coal will be increased. . . . With an increase of ten cents a ton in the price of coal, the retail dealers will increase the price of every pail of coal they sell. With the peck or bushel of coal selling for ten cents more than at present, the consumers of the large cities will buy as little as possible; they will burn everything that will take the place of coal. With consumption restricted, . . . there will be less labor done in the mines; and with the miners on shorter time than ever, there will be more bankrupt sales in the coal regions. When the present "very favorable" leases with which the Reading Company has bribed the individual operators of this region expire, there will be but one great railroad, one great common carrier, to take their coal, and that common carrier will say: "We will take your coal at our terms, we will make the contract to suit ourselves, and you have no say in the matter." When that day comes—and come it will if this deal is consummated— Powderly will not feel so lonesome as he does just now, for there will be others in this region who will realize that they have made of themselves just what the coal operator called me the other day. In the meantime it is no small satisfaction to know that those who protested last year that our Constitution was "good enough," "admirable," "wonderful," "all-sufficient," and that those who advocated a change were all wrong, are now either finding fault with the governor for not enforcing it, as they see it, or excusing him for not knowing what it means. . . .

Despairing of securing action at Harrisburg and having been effectually sat-down upon [by] the Democratic state officials, I called upon Governor Leon Abbett[6] of New Jersey, also a Democrat, for the purpose of enlisting his coöperation in the matter of dissolving the Reading Combine. I was by that official referred to Chancellor McGill, who at the time I called upon him had three or four committees in waiting and was a very busy man. Notwithstanding that fact, he accorded me a brief but very courteous interview. I hurriedly explained to him what I had done, what I hoped to do, and tendered him my services in placing evidence in his possession which would assist him in an effort to enjoin the combine from operating in the State of New Jersey. I found Chancellor McGill to be a straight-forward, energetic, thorough-going man. He was a man of few words, but I learned afterwards to know that he meant every word he said. While I was there he called in his secretary, introduced us and requested me to either hand or send him the evidence I had gathered, and later on I

---

[6] Leon Abbett (1836-94) was first elected governor of New Jersey on a Democratic ticket in 1883, and was reëlected in 1889. He was interested in ballot reform, improved some of the labor laws, and tried to change the tax laws in order to prevent the railroads from evading payment.

placed such data and affidavits as I possessed in the hands of Chancellor McGill's secretary. In the meantime I kept up my battle against the combine.

When Chancellor McGill had thoroughly digested the case he rendered a decision in opposition to the "Reading Coal Combine," and from that decision I take this excerpt:

Upon preliminary hearings here, we have great coal dealers complaining that they are not sufficiently paid for the product of their mines, combining so that already they control more than one-half of the coal fields upon which this State depends for fuel, and looking to the coöperation of the remaining anthracite coal producers to effect a change in the price of their output so that they may have more satisfactory returns from their investments. To say that these conditions do not tend to a disastrous monopoly in coal would be an insult to intelligence. It is possible that such a monopoly may be used as the defendants suggest—to introduce economies and cheapen coal—but it does violence to our knowledge of human nature to expect such a result. . . . If once a complete monopoly be established by the destruction of competition, whether that be through lease or coöperation, the promoters and sharers in it may have whatever price their cupidity suggests. The disaster which will follow cannot be measured. It will permeate the entire community—furnaces, forges, factories and homes—leaving in its trail murmurs of discontent with a government which will tolerate it, and all the other evil effects of oppression.

I had complained to the governor of Pennsylvania on February 19, 1892, and had done everything in my power to strengthen his hands in an honest effort to rid Pennsylvania of the infamous Reading Combine. The governor turned the matter over to the attorney general, who went through the farce of giving a hearing to complainants, and later on entering some sort of proceedings. Where the proceedings proceeded to is not known. . . .

Long after Pennsylvania was requested to act, the officials of New Jersey from Governor Abbett to Chancellor McGill took the matter in hand, and, as a result of their work, the Reading Deal was declared illegal. An injunction was granted against it, and the combination was not allowed to operate any longer in New Jersey.

Before Chancellor McGill handed down his decision and served the injunction on the promoters of the combination, Alexander McLeod, on behalf of the Reading Deal, expressed himself in these words: "The injunction will have no more effect than if it had been directed against the Sioux Indians."

. . . In commenting on Mr. McLeod's utterances in the *Journal of the Knights of Labor* I said:

If this is not anarchy, what is it? Judge McGill has given his decision. It is the law until reversed by some higher court or law. Where does McLeod get his authority to set it aside after the manner of a Sioux Indian? If he acts as an Indian, will he be dealt with as the Indian would? These are questions for all the people to examine into and act upon. Keep your eyes on McLeod and the Reading manipulators; see that they bow to the mandates of the court or go to prison as other criminals do. If it becomes necessary to engage counsel to prosecute McLeod for contempt, how many will subscribe to a fund to defray the cost of trial? . . .

How many will act in this matter, and how soon will you act? Make known your sentiments in short, pointed letters to the *Journal*, so that we will understand the true sentiment of the people.

When that letter appeared in the *Journal of the Knights of Labor* our members throughout Pennsylvania acted upon the suggestions contained therein, but it was no longer necessary to endeavor to exert influence on the authorities of Pennsylvania; they had slumbered on their rights, and since New Jersey officials had so energetically opposed the Reading Combine, I did not consider it necessary for me to do anything further in the matter.

Again I ask you to read part of a letter which appeared over my signature in the *Journal of the Knights of Labor* under date of March 9, 1893:

In the early part of February, 1892, the reading people of this country saw before them, in the papers one morning the startling announcement: "Gigantic Coal Combination—The Reading Leases the Central of New Jersey and the Lehigh Valley—The Entire Coal Supply of Pennsylvania to be Controlled by a Combination so Vast and so Powerful that All Opposition to it Must Prove Futile." Then came the daily recital of the spread of the Reading Combine, its march on the other coal companies; its wonderful resources and unlimited power were all portrayed in the highest style of the art. After waiting for a few weeks to see what steps would be taken by the authorities of Pennsylvania to throttle the unconstitutional monster that was spreading its feeders through the anthracite coal regions, one of the citizens of Pennsylvania, without consultation with any other person and acting in his private capacity as a citizen, entered complaint against the violation of the Constitution of the State, and requested that proceedings be begun against the combine. That letter of complaint was dated February 19, 1892. The 19th of February, 1893, fell upon Sunday, and, naturally, no stock gambling or manipulation could (publicly) be transacted on that day; but the day following, Monday the 20th, the complainant of a year ago heard the newsboys on the streets of New York shouting: "Collapse of the Reading Combine, the concern goes into bankruptcy, great alarm in the Stock Exchange, holders of Reading securities heavy losers, receivers asked for, etc."

From the day the combination was formed that citizen exerted every influence in his reach or power to cause the American people to look upon the scheme as one of piracy and the schemers as pirates. He tried to expose the tricks and plans to blindfold the authorities with fraudulent petitions, false affidavits and manufactured reports. It was with no small satisfaction that he heard the newsboys telling that his predictions had been verified. From the time the Combine was organized its promoters used every means in their power to mould public opinion in favor of their scheme of plunder, and many otherwise sensible people actually believed that the man who complained should be burned at the stake for attempting to stand in the way of the prosperity of the workingmen of the coal regions. In the office of the Reading Combine at Philadelphia sat a competent staff of writers who gathered up every item that could be turned to the advantage of the combine, enlarged upon it, had it reduced to cold type, then had it plated and sent out along the line of the Reading, the Lehigh Valley and Central of New Jersey to the daily and weekly papers for insertion as fresh, original news concerning the wonderful genius and financial wisdom of Alexander McLeod. If the files of the papers from Scranton, on the north end, to Philadelphia, on the south, are examined, many curious and startling lines will strike the eye. The following, for instance:

"The miners along the line of the Reading are loud in their praise of the combination by which they are assured steady work.

"There is a rumor, said to be well founded, that wages along the line of the Lehigh Valley and the Reading Roads will soon be advanced.

"The tonnage of the Reading is increasing so rapidly that additional tracks and cars must be built to accommodate the ever-increasing business. Already orders have been given for several thousand new cars, and it is expected that to duplicate the tracks of the system will give our rolling-mills full time for many months to come."

These and many other alluring and deceptive statements were written up in the Philadelphia office, set up by "rat" printers and scattered throughout the coal regions for publication in the press of the state. A length of this boiler-plate soothing syrup fell into my hands one day and I was privileged to see the note that accompanied it. It read something like this:

"My Dear ————:

No matter what else you may crowd out, see that this gets in the first issue of the ————— after it reaches you."

Unsophisticated, innocent persons who read the rosy announcements concerning the Reading each day swallowed these items of local news as though they were original and made at home. The attention of the people was turned away from the real issue, and legal proceedings were allowed to drag their weary way through—part way through—the courts. Abuse of the most vindictive character fell to the lot of the complainant, and on more than one occasion he was made to feel that it was not the most delightful thing in the world to interfere with a burglar or a highwayman in the pursuit of his calling.

That marked the end of my crusade against the Reading Combine, and it ended because the combine itself was ended.

Since I am writing about myself and what I did or tried to do in other days, I have not given time or space to a recital of what others did. I believe, however, that my principal service in that trying time was rendered when I helped to turn the search light of public scrutiny on the chief actors in the Reading Combine and focused attention on their attempt to defy the people, override the constitution, and control the entire output of anthracite of the United States. I did that even though I did not "at first succeed."

By turning to my *Journal* letter of February 18, 1892, you will see that it wound up with a ————. In explanation of that dash let me here reproduce a copy of a letter to Tom O'Reilly, the editor; it accompanied the article.

SCRANTON, PA., FEB. 14, 1892

My dear Tom:

Get the accompanying letter in the next Journal if you have to omit all I sent you the other day, it is very important.

You will note that I end the article with a dash and it may cause you some concern.

It is my purpose to get as large an audience as possible to consider this question. It is quite likely that papers unfriendly to me, or friendly to the Reading Deal, will not notice my article, but when they see that dash they will jump to the conclusion that I hint at dynamite, bomb throwing, or revolution and they will comment on it. In doing so they will have to reproduce the letter or part of it and in that way their readers will learn at least enough about the doings of the plotters to want to know more, that's the kind of a bomb I want to throw, that's the kind of dynamite, and if I can get the friends of the Reading Deal to use it, I shall regard it as all right. Yes, I know, my reputation may suffer but those who think ill of me won't speak well of me anyway; those who know me and think well of me will question whoever speaks ill of me. It will all come out in the washing. I am cutting this dash in a good cause, so let it go.

Hold on to this letter until we smash the combine.

Ever yours,

TERRY

The New York *World* and New York *Herald* sent able representatives to the anthracite fields to obtain material for their attacks on the Reading Combine. The *Herald* representative was Charles E. Russell. He carried a letter of introduction to me, and I put him in the way of securing first-hand information direct from coal miners and business men. The seven coal miners he speaks of in one of his articles to the *Herald* sat around him in my presence while narrating their experiences. I quote part of his letter to the *Herald* of May 5, 1892:

. . . It has made no difference whether the operator has made fifty per cent or five hundred per cent, whether coal sold in New York for $3 or $7, year after year the miner has gone downward. . . . But he has never in all his experience of floods, strikes and lockouts, suspensions and reductions, reached as low a level as that to which the Reading has brought him. The suggestion that the capitalists, who, to increase their fortunes, have put 60,000 miners in the anthracite region upon half wages and brought at least 150,000 in sight of actual want, will ever care a rap or repair their wrong is something the anthracite region cannot be induced to swallow. Seven of these coal miners from different collieries around Scranton sat down with me yesterday and told me their troubles.

I wish the clever gentlemen who were manipulating the deal could have seen them. It would be so inspiring to realize just exactly what their work has been. Six of the seven were Americans and the other was of English birth, but thirty years' residence in Pennsylvania. Their ages were between twenty-five and sixty. All were married, all had families dependent upon them, all were intelligent, straightforward, respectable men. They were practical miners, and that implies skill, courage, experience, and brains. Any observer would say that they were above the grade of ordinary workmen.

Yet since the Reading deal went into active effect in this region not one of these seven have averaged more than $7 a week.

Seven dollars a week, and some of them have eight mouths to feed! To buy daily food costs them more than that.

Four weeks now the Reading deal has been reducing the coal output in order to advance the price of fuel in New York. One of the men showed me the due bill he received today for his four weeks' work. It called for $19.99.

Five dollars a week for this man and he has six children!

The unskilled day laborer would reject such pay. Twenty dollars for a month of work in a place where a single unskillful thrust might bring down a thousand tons of rock and coal upon his head and where at all times he is exposed to cruel accidents. The money that is to pay those dividends must be precious stuff, as it comes out of the very lives of sixty thousand men.

The seven laughed sardonically when I told them of what President McLeod had given out about "improved labor conditions" in the anthracite region, and the oldest miner among them said: "I have worked in these mines twenty-two years, and I wish I had a dollar for every time I have heard guff like that. We don't care about such 'improved labor conditions.' If the Reading people will let us work all the time, that is all the 'Improvement' we will ask from them. It doesn't go down very well to be told that things are going to be better, when we can't earn enough to give our children bread.

"The output for May has been cut down to 2,700,000 tons. That means another month of half time. We don't see any signs of 'better conditions' in that. We don't want any charity or any of these men's money. Here are the people in New York and other places; they want coal. Here are we ready to get it out for them. . . ."

. . . The feeling in this part of the country is very strong against the deal, principally because of its disastrous effects on business. Mr. Powderly is called upon nearly every night to address a meeting against it.

That letter of Mr. Russell's gives an idea of how coal miners felt after three months' experience with the combine.

When Russell Sage[7] was asked on March 6, 1892, if he thought the "combination is absolute master of the coal trade," he said: "They think themselves so. They will raise the price as high as the public will stand. They are feeling the public pulse now."

Henry Clews,[8] the banker, whom I always regarded as a square, upright man, denounced the combine in a vigorous article in the New York *Recorder* of March 5, 1892. . . .

The York, Pennsylvania, *Gazette*, the organ of Chauncey F. Black, had this to say:

[7] Russell Sage (1816-1906), one of the shrewdest, conservative-minded financiers of his era, died worth some seventy millions of dollars.

[8] Henry Clews (1834-1923) was a successful Wall Street financier with an active interest in public questions.

The monopoly newspapers do not receive these palpable truths from Mr. Powderly with any degree of favor. They denounce them as extreme, and especially as "socialistic," the very reverse of which they are. It is Mr. Powderly's misfortune not to be in the pay of any monopoly, and the circumstance renders him an object of intense suspicion and of measureless denunciation on the part of those who are. He is only the head of a great labor organization, whose membership comprises the chosen victims of corporate aggression, and must, therefore, almost necessarily, be a rascal, a socialist, or a revolutionist of some kind. But as the only revolution proposed by him, at this time, is a peaceable return to government by the people, for the people—to the constitution, and the principles of the common law, in full force before the constitution—it is not impossible that after a few more lessons, as to the greed and perfidy of unrestrained monopoly, the public may begin to think it worth while to heed an honest representative of the abused masses, rather than the apologists of the common oppressor.

I never objected to criticism, and if it was fair did not care how severe it was. It would have been difficult for me to go very far wrong and not know it in those days, for my every move, good and bad, was given widest publicity. I might say in present day language "pitiless publicity." The most pitiless and unfair critic I had to deal with was the Scranton *Tribune*, a paper owned and controlled by coal operators residing in Scranton. They were men of standing, they were honorable men, but when it came to a question which affected their interests they "sided with themselves," as Josh Billings once remarked.

. . . .

While the fight on the Reading Combine was on, the steel workers, organized in the Amalgamated Association of Iron and Steel Workers, employed by the Carnegie Steel Company, at Homestead, Pa., struck against a reduction of wages. They were not a part of or allied to the Knights of Labor, but I entered the contest in their behalf. Before doing so I consulted William Weighe, the president of the Amalgamated, and then with his approval did all that lay in my power to aid the striking steel workers.

Out of the Homestead strike grew the investigation by Congress of the activities of the Pinkerton Detective Agency. I did everything possible to aid in the investigation and in the end found myself the principal opponent of the Pinkerton Agency. That is another story and I simply refer to it here to show that I had my hands full all the time. I may some day write the story of the Battle of Homestead and the illegal marching of armed men from one state to another. . . .

In the contest against the Reading Combine I paid my own expenses. No organization or individual assisted me to the value of one cent. I was not influenced in what I did by any one else. I was born in Pennsylvania, I love the state, I love its very name. I took an active part in the contest over the constitution in 1873 and tried to strengthen that document in the interest of the people in 1891. I regarded the act of the Reading Combine as the move of an assassin against the state; in my mind there was only one thing for me as a Pennsylvanian to do, and I did it.

When the curtain fell on the last act in that drama I wrote as follows:

SCRANTON, PA., MARCH 12, 1893

MR. ALEXANDER McLEOD
PHILADELPHIA, PA.

Dear Sir:

I write these few lines to say that if the success of corporate intrigue in defeating the constitutional convention in 1891 influenced you to organize the Reading Combine last year, you misjudged the people. If you were emboldened by the apparent indifference and apathy of the electorate in 1891 to act as you did in 1892, you now know that patriotism is not dead.

If in your defiant pronouncements you included the undersigned in your reference to the potency of a "Sioux Indian's whoop," let me assure you that while it was a pleasure as well as a duty to "whoop" against the Reading Combine, I shall, if occasion presents itself, be glad to "whoop" with you in any effort you may hereafter make for the welfare of the people of the Commonwealth of Pennsylvania.

Yours very truly,
T. V. POWDERLY

Eight months after I wrote that letter to Mr. McLeod, in November, 1893, the General Assembly of the Knights of Labor met in Philadelphia. I was run down in health and pocket. Four delegates, whose names I withhold for the sake of their families, had been instructed to "stand by Powderly." They came to me and personally assured me of their support; I did not seek it or have anything to offer or give in return. An able man and ardent socialist, Daniel De Leon,[9] was a delegate to that General Assembly. He was a bitter enemy of mine simply because I was not a socialist. I now use his own language to me at that General Assembly:

You are reactionary. The Labor movement is reactionary. The Knights of Labor under you stands in the way of progress. We have to get rid of you and supplant the order with a more radical form of organization. We may not be able to unhorse you but we will stay here all winter to defeat everything you propose or stand for.

The four men I referred to had intimated when they first approached me that they desired a hurrying forward of the work so that they could get away to their homes at an early date. After a few days they again sought me and assured me that though they would stand by me personally, they would "stay here all winter to defeat everything," I proposed or stood for.

I have referred to my resignation as General Master Workman elsewhere.[10] I did not have to resign, but felt it to be my duty to myself and family to relinquish a position in which bickering and contention would supplant united, harmonious effort.

One day in 1902, nine years after I resigned, I had occasion to call on the president of the Reading Company on a matter relating to his alleged opposition to an institution I was then interested in. He assured me that I had been misinformed, and, as we got better acquainted, he said:

We have not always been friendly to you and not without cause. Your unjust attack on what you were pleased to call the Reading Combine was not calculated to warm us up to you. Your own members did not approve of your course. When your annual conclave met in this city nine years ago we had the assurance of several of the delegates that they were not in harmony with you.

When I questioned that statement he had a messenger fetch a

[9] Daniel De Leon (1852-1915) joined the Socialist Labor party in 1890, and later dominated its thought and action for years. An able theoretician, he was an extremely doctrinaire Marxist. He was born in Dutch Curaçao, and came to the United States in 1872. After studying at the Columbia Law School, he lectured on diplomacy at the university. Failing to gain control of either the American Federation of Labor or the declining K. of L., he founded the Socialist Trade and Labor Alliance in 1895.

[10] See pp. 365-367.

file of papers which he, in my presence, examined. I recognized one of them as a printed list of the representatives to the Philadelphia General Assembly of 1893. Without uttering a word, Mr. Baer[11] laid the list before me and, in blue pencil, a number of names had been checked off; among them were the names of the four men whom I have heretofore referred to.

How he obtained that list, why those names were checked off, or what for, I did not then know and do not now know; I can only surmise that my work against the Reading Combine caused some one who favored that concern to influence weak, short-sighted men to yield to temptation, and, for love of promotion or hope of gain, perhaps, they turned against a man, who, whether right or wrong, wise or otherwise, conscientiously tried to stand between his fellow men and well financed robbery. . . .

. . . .

Here I am obliged to write finis just where a beginning has been made in telling the story of one of the most cold-blooded attempts to subordinate the people to the rule of greed. I regard my part in that work as a glorious achievement.

I came out of the battle a poor man—financially—but rich beyond anything money can buy in the consciousness of having done my duty with all the ability I possessed in opposition to one of the most powerful aggregations of wealth ever organized in America. I did not oppose it because it was an aggregation of wealth, but because it aimed at levying tribute on rich and poor in controlling a prime necessity, a bounty of nature that God intended for all. It is now 1919; under similar circumstances I would do the same today.

[11] This was the George M. Baer who, during the 1902 coal strike, won questionable fame with his letter in which he said, "The rights and interests of the laboring man will be protected and cared for, not by the labor agitators, but by the Christian men to whom God in His infinite wisdom, has given control of the property interests of the country."

Chapter Twenty-Three

COÖPERATION

PRELIMINARY to considering coöperation, let me ask you to take a retrospective view of the commercialism that has grown with the years since Jesus Christ said: "love your neighbor." When asked "Who is my neighbor," He answered in such a way as to cause all who pay heed to His words to believe He meant: "Mankind of every description."

Not only did Jesus Christ urge us to love our neighbors but our enemies as well. He vigorously opposed many of the practices of the commercialists of His day. . . .

When Jesus went into the temple of God and cast out all who were using it as a stock exchange in buying and selling there, when He overturned the tables of the financial ancestors of our modern stock gamblers, He was impelled by a virtuous indignation based on a conviction that they were engaged in a very selfish proceeding. . . . He did it because they were profiting through the needs of those who were obliged to use money; He did it because they were profiteers. The usury that was odious in His sight then has not been purified since then. What men should not do to wring undue profit from money in His day should not be done in this day with anything that money may buy.

Christianity, although based on the teachings of Jesus Christ, has recognized the kind of commercialism He condemned. Perhaps I should not say it has recognized it, but it has not frowned on it or opposed its practitioners as I believe He would do were He in our midst today.

Commercialists recognize competition up to a point where they are powerful enough, or securely enough intrenched, to control production; then they change from competitors to monopolists.

Once it was an axiom that "competition is the life of trade." Whether it gave life to trade or not, it has caused the ruin or financial death of many a trader.

Christianity has never attempted to abolish the kind of commercialism condemned by its Founder. He taught men to love their enemies. I have not been able to discover what particular kind of enemy He would have us love and am persuaded that, as with neighbors, He must have included enemies of all descriptions. Jesus Christ taught us to love our enemies; commercialism teaches us to hinder, to devour and kill them. Oh! yes it does, for love of enemy, or neighbor, cannot survive in an atmosphere where two enemies or two neighbors for that matter, strive to secure possession of the same dollar. Love of the dollar supplants love for neighbor as well as enemy. Have you not heard it said that "love of money is the root of all evil"? When I was young I frequently heard those words of Timothy quoted in all seriousness, and for a purpose. I do not hear them spoken or referred to so often, now. Too many ministers today regard their calling as a profession or a trade to make a living by and not as a mission from on high. They dig for the root of all evil as industriously as any member of the United Mine Workers Union. The member of the Union digs for it because his bread and butter depend on it and he makes no pretense of laboring for the dollar for any other purpose. The clergyman lays claim to a less selfish motive, but they [sic] dig for the same root and endeavor to secure as much of it "as the traffic will bear." . . .

During the greater part of nineteen hundred years, men were as neighbors and enemies engaged in commerce and trade. Finally nations as well as individuals began to buy from and sell to each other. International commercialists began to strive for as much of the "root of all evil" as they could honestly get or dishonestly gouge each other out of, and Churchianity, which largely supplanted Christianity and is often mistaken for it, has not stayed the grasping hand of an individual trader, a national commercialist, or an international murderer whose greed prompted him to reach out for the market of neighbor and enemy and gather in all that could be gained. . . . Striving for the world's trade, or the international "root of all evil," brought on a war that slaughtered men, violated women, starved children, and spread disease, want, and famine where God had blessed with sufficiency for every need. . . .

The great power that came to Christianity through the teachings of Jesus Christ has been largely frittered away through the practice of Churchianity. I am led to say this because I can find little or no evidence to prove that the ordained teacher and preacher of Christianity has attempted to walk directly in the footsteps of the crucified One in driving the waterer of stocks, the gambler in life's necessities, the despoiler of children, the exploiter of labor, or the grabber of profits from the temple wherein the products of industry are exchanged.

. . . .

One of the most successful commercialists the world has ever known got, as a result of his effort, three or four meals a day, his clothing, and a place to sleep. When called away he left his accumulations after him. Not one cent did he, or could he, take with him to the other world. You will say that the every day laborers had as much. Yes, but there was this difference: the commercialist was sure of his meals, sure of his clothing and his shelter, while before the laborer there stalked the never absent specter of the devil of fear; it was always before him, for a day's sickness, a misstep at his work, a disagreement with his boss might rob him of the opportunity to provide the meals, the clothing, or maintain the shelter. Where one man lives free from dread of future hunger and want, millions look toward the morrow with fear, and that eternal fear causes the laboring man to disregard the whisperings of his better nature as certainty on the part of the wealth-getter causes him to stifle the "still small voice" of conscience as he pursues the dollar to its lair. It must not be forgotten that a fear haunts the man of wealth too. His fear is that he may lose his wealth, be assassinated by a rival in business, some one he has despoiled of dollars, or by one of many he may have wronged. Of the two fears I would rather entertain that of the laborer, for his fear is or may be untainted by wrongdoing.

There is no necessity for either fear, and under coöperation both would disappear.

During recent years designing men, interested in perpetuating a decaying industrial system under which many work for the profit of few, have endeavored through cunning propaganda to identify the name coöperation with anarchy, socialism, communism, or bolshevism. They have pointed out the advocate of coöperation as unsafe, and I admit that they have good cause for so doing, since coöperation will render unsafe the system which enables one man to reap a profit from the proceeds of the labor of many men and at the same time lay claim to being a strictly honest man.

Coöperation is not anarchy, it is not socialism, communism, or bolshevism, but it would have to be all of these to work the chaos now manifesting itself in the world of industry. Coöperation is the antagonistic opposite of anarchy, socialism, communism, and bolshevism. Understand that I, in speaking of these isms, have in mind the popular conception of them now finding lodgment in the public mind. Coöperation is the essence of common sense not yet understood by the world's producers. . . .

The wage system, as I see it, has broken down all over the world. It has not made the laborer happy or contented, it has not caused him to feel secure in his trade or calling, it has not given him a reward for his toil commensurate with his dignity, his effort, his risks, or his needs, it has not proved a safeguard against an increased cost of living. . . . From its very nature it has caused employer and employed to regard each other with suspicion; it has not, as many assert, made the interests of employer and employed identical, and, finally, it has caused the loss of billions of dollars in strikes, lockouts, boycotts and blacklists. The businessman, standing between the striking or locked-out workmen and their employers, has, like the "innocent bystander" been the victim of the industrial warfare that has waged for ages between what has erroneously been called *capital and labor*.

Capital in the hands of the employer is the fruit of labor. Rarely is it all his own, often it is the contribution of the money of many men and women. Labor is always the capital of the workingman; frequently he has no other.

Before proceeding farther let me turn back just forty years to a day in 1880, when, in delivering my first annual address to the General Assembly of the Knights of Labor, I said:

ABOLISH THE WAGE SYSTEM

So long as the present order of things exist [*sic*], just so long will the attempt to effect lasting peace between the man who buys labor and the man who sells labor be fruitless.

So long as it is to the interest of one kind of men to purchase labor at the lowest possible figure, and so long as it is to the interest of another kind of men to sell labor to the highest possible bidder, just so long will there exist an antagonism between the two which all the speakers and writers on labor cannot remove.

So long as a pernicious system leaves one man at the mercy of another, so long will labor and capital be at war, and no strike can deliver a blow sufficiently hard to break the hold with which unproductive capital today grasps labor by the throat.

In what direction should we turn to see our way clear to a solution of the difficulty? Far be it from me to say that I can point out the way; would that I could with certainty do it! I can only offer a suggestion, which comes to me as the result of experience, and that suggestion is to abolish the

WAGE SYSTEM

This is the system which carries with it into the workshop, the mine, and factory a host of evils, which, if repeated, would exhaust the whole vocabulary of murmurings which fill the complaint-book of Labor.

This is the system which, serpentlike, pushes itself along wherever those bands of commercial iron and steel are laid, carrying discontent in its train.

This is the system which enables a half dozen men to sit at their tables in any of our large centers of trade, and, without thought of the welfare of the country, apart from their own interests, issue the mandates which direct the movements of the whole industrial population of the United States.

This is the system which makes every railroad superintendent, every factory or mine superintendent, an autocrat at whose nod or beck the poor, unrequited slave who labors must bow the head and bend the knee in humble suppliance.

To point out a way to utterly destroy this system would be a pleasure to me. I can only direct your attention to it and leave the rest to your wisdom; and I firmly believe that I have pointed out the most vicious of all evils which afflict labor today.

But are we prepared to lay siege to this bulwark of oppression? Remember that for centuries it has been slowly, yet steadily, creeping onward, making each year new and deeper inroads upon labor, until today it stands so well intrenched and powerful that even the staunchest heart in the ranks of labor's defenders shrinks at the thought of breaking down the barriers of fear, ignorance, and superstition, to which its existence has given birth.

The wage system, at its inception, was but an experiment, and for a time doubts were entertained as to its adoption; but the avaricious eye of the Shylock of labor saw in it a weapon with which he could control the toiler, and today that system has so firm a hold upon us that every attempt at shaking off the fetters, by resorting to a strike, only makes it easier for the master to say to his slave, *You must work for lower wages.*

We must teach our members, then, that the remedy for the redress of the wrongs we complain of does not lie in the suicidal strike; but in thorough, effective organization. Without organization we cannot accomplish anything; through it we hope to forever banish that curse of modern civilization—wage slavery.

But how? Surely not by forming an association and remaining a member; not by getting every other worthy man to become a member and remain one; not by paying the dues required of us as they fall due. These are all important factors in the method by which we hope to regain our independence, and are vitally important; they are the elements necessary to complete organization.

Organization once perfected, what must we do? I answer, study the best means of putting your organization to some practicable use by embarking in a system of

COÖPERATION

which will eventually make every man his own master—every man his own employer; a system which will give the laborer a fair proportion of the products of his toil. It is to coöperation, then, as the lever of labor's emancipation, that the eyes of the workingmen and women of the world should be directed, upon coöperation their hopes should be centered, and to it do I now direct your attention. I am deeply sensible of the importance, of the magnitude, of the undertaking in which I invite you to engage. I know that it is human nature to grow cold, apathetic, and finally indifferent when engaged in that which requires deep study and persistent effort, unattended by excitement; men are apt to believe that physical force is the better way of redressing grievances, being the shorter remedy; but even that requires patience and fortitude as well as strength. . . .

To the subject of coöperation, then, do I invite your attention, and I liken it unto the Revolutionary War. If you decide upon carrying it out at this convention, it will be the Bunker Hill of Industrial Independence; but you must also bear in mind, though the longest term allotted to man be yours to live, you will not see during that term the complete triumph of your hopes. The War for American Independence had its Bunker Hills and its Washingtons, but it also had its Valley Forges and its Benedict Arnolds. The enthusiasm of the hour will avail us nothing, and coöperation requires every Washington of labor to be up and doing. The laboring man needs education in this great social question, and the best minds of the Order must give their precious thought to this system. There is no good reason why labor cannot, through coöperation, own and operate mines, factories, and railroads. By coöperation alone can a system of

COLONIZATION

be established in which men may band together for the purpose of securing the greatest good to the greatest number, and place the man who is willing to toil upon his own homestead.

The Order of Knights of Labor was working in secret when those words were spoken. Mention of the name was forbidden beyond the walls of our meeting rooms. As a consequence but little attention was paid to that pronouncement when it appeared in print.

I believed in 1880 that what I said was true, I believe the same now. Read it again and note the words *"though the longest term allotted to man be yours to live you will not see during that term the complete triumph of your hopes."* By slow processes of evolution will coöperation come into being. . . . Only through the patient labor of peaceful, thoughtful, sincere women and men, who have educated themselves in the rudiments of coöperation and the need for it, can it be established.

When I delivered that address, the Order of Knights of Labor had, perhaps, twenty-five thousand members. Discussion of the advisability of establishing coöperative enterprises became general for a time but as the Order grew in numbers and influence, discussion of the best means of relieving present-day pressing necessities, occupied the attention of the larger part of the membership. Demands for leave to work fewer hours for others, rather than a study of how to work for themselves occupied the time and attention of a majority of our members. Demands for higher wages from another instead of distributing the proceeds of their toil among themselves caused most of our members to overlook the important question of coöperation.

When the first General Assembly of the Knights of Labor adopted in 1878 the "Preamble of Principles" of the old Industrial Brotherhood, it declared for "The establishment of coöperative institutions, productive and distributive." Air, light, heat, and water are the heritage of all men. They belong alike to all, and should not be monopolized by one man to the exclusion of other men. Air, space, the distribution of light, heat, and water should be subject only to the rule which places the needs of the many above the ambition, the avarice, or greed of the few. For millions of years great nature has been perfecting and storing in the treasury vaults of earth the coal and oil we now use for various purposes. No word or commission from on high conferred title to these bounties of nature upon any man or select set of men. They are of right the property of all and should be husbanded, guarded and utilized for all. . . . I defy any of the favored ones to show a valid title deed from Almighty God, or any human power directed by Him, to these deposits. The liberties of individuals are restricted, curbed, and, in some cases denied, by the people through their own organization, the State. Man cannot lawfully or morally withhold the bounties of nature from other men. What he fashions with his own hands from that which God gave in the original may be his, but God gave the same right to that original to all other men, and the State should protect that right and allow no interference with it.

As I write this, September, 1920, the labor cost of producing a ton of anthracite approximates $3.44; supplies, 91 cents; general expenses, $1.06; total f.o.b., $5.41. The freight charges per ton from Scranton, or Wilkes-Barre approximate $3.64, making a total of $9.05 as the entire cost of producing and transporting that ton from mine to tide water. Bear in mind that this includes wages of miner, laborer, mule driver, head man, slate picker or breaker boy, breaker boss, train crew, and rail workers from producing point to distributing point. The buyer by the pailful or bushel pays anywhere from $20 to $30 a ton for coal. Others pay from $14 to $18 a ton for it.

Between the arrival of a ton of coal at New York and its introduction to heating stove, cook stove, or furnace in the home, some one, not a laboring man or an employer of labor, gathers in from $9 to $12 a ton profit on it. In the case of the buyer by the bushel, from $15 to $25 a ton over cost of production is gathered in by industrious mortals who do not mine coal, who do not man freight trains or operate coal mines.

It would seem that municipal purchasing agents and municipal coal yards would help some in dislodging the profiteering middleman who secures a greater reward for his altruistic effort to pass coal from freight car to cellar, or possibly to a cliff-dwelling coal consumer in a tenement house, than coal miner or operator. In the frenzied discussion about coal prices, the storm rages round the operator of mines and the men who dig coal, while the real culprit, the non-producing middleman, laughs in his ample sleeve, and gathers in the dimes and dollars. Men who sneer at coöperation are themselves coöperating in helping the grafting middleman to levy unholy tribute on all the people because they have allowed this bounty of God to pass temporarily out of their hands. Here the people are the State, the State belongs to all the people, and no man can now, with safety, say: "I am the State." What the State gave it can take; it can do more, it can take man himself for the good or safety of the State, and it is veriest rot to say that it cannot restore to itself the coal and oil deposits so necessary to all and which it had no right to give away.

Examine the present ownership of our coal mines and ascertain if the alleged owners are the ones who dig the coal. You will find that the companies who own the mines are founded on shares of stock issued under charters from the State. A man who would not enter a coal mine to dig coal or who, perhaps, could not do so if he would, buys a share of coal company stock, he purchases it with the required amount of "the root of all evil." On it he draws a dividend. As he prospers, he buys more stock, and, perhaps, after a time owns enough of it to own the mine. The mineworker who does mine coal, on whose labor the community depends for fuel—for heat—gets his daily wage and no more. This is his reward, not alone for his labor, but for risking life, limb, and health every time he enters the mine. At the end of his life he owns no more of the mine than when he first entered it. During all this time his labor has been helping to make millionaires of a few other men. What kind of a fool shall I call the man who coöperates with many other men to make millionaires of a few men without giving thought to the study of a system of coöperation that will enable all to participate equitably in the proceeds of the labor of their hands and brains?

Chapter Twenty-Four

PROFIT-SHARING AND COÖPERATION

IT HAS ALWAYS BEEN a source of wonder to me that movements calculated to serve the many are so easily sidetracked by the few. I have sat unnoticed in meetings assembled to discuss some sane measure intended to benefit the majority and have heard perpetual-motion-tongued individuals rant about righting wrongs real or imaginary by physical force. Boastfully proclaiming themselves radical, they wearied and disgusted sober-minded men and prevented the taking of action that would be of service to the many.

I am confident that if a public meeting were called today to take action on the best means of establishing a coöperative enterprise, and some fifty men assembled, there would be four or five leather-lunged, feather-brained individuals present to keep their hair-trigger, swivel-mounted tongues busy in dilating on the beauties of bolshevism as practiced in far-away Russia. It would make no difference whether they knew anything of value about Russia or bolshevism. . . . They would roll their tongues around the wrongs of the proletariat as inflicted by the bourgeoisie. . . . When the meeting would adjourn it would do so no doubt without coöperation having received favorable mention. . . .

I have noticed that most of the spouters and mouthers of bolshevism could not be found guilty of having ever soiled their hands with honest labor. . . . Shunning labor with their hands, they expend their strength in exercising their tongues and lungs to the damage of a cause that decent, self-respecting men should study and promote.

I may appear to digress, but I do so for a purpose. I hope to call attention to these mountebanks whom I regard as paid emissaries of the enemies of industrial rehabilitation through the safe and sane process of evolution instead of revolution. Who pays them I do not know, how they obtain the means to enable them to "bob up serenely" at every public meeting of workingmen is a mystery. That they are conducting a propaganda of hate, of dissatisfaction, of unrest, is evident, and if workingmen would throw these propaganders out of their meetings, they would confer a lasting benefit on the whole industrial movement.

I must not be understood to say that there is not cause, just cause, for dissatisfaction and unrest, but frothy exasperations about the bolshevik ailments of Russia will not settle, or help settle, our domestic problems here in the United States.

The presence of the advocate of physical force at labor meetings is always reported in the daily papers. His utterances are given space under scare headlines, while the real remarks of sensible workingmen are rarely given publicity. This gives the enemies of labor the opportunity to brand all as radical, as socialistic, anarchistic, bolshevistic, or communistic. This practice has caused me to wonder if these creatures are not hirelings of the very system they denounce at labor meetings with forty-horse-power lungs. . . . Socialism, anarchism, bolshevism, and communism differ from each other, but in the public eye they are frequently looked at as one. Let me, in the interest of brevity, lump them under the one head and call it communism. Communism means everything in common, a division of earnings, possessions, responsibilities. Coöperation does not contemplate a dividing up of the earnings of industrious men among the many. It will guarantee to all men that which is rightfully theirs and no more. It will demand and exact from each according to his ability. Under coöperation there will be no I. W. W.ism and sabotage. . . . When coöperation comes into its own, he who commits sabotage will be destroying the capital of the man who works; he shall merit and receive the condemnation and execration of all workers.

The word *earnings* will take on its real meaning while the word *profits* will gradually fall into disuse.

Before real coöperation comes, the world of industry will pass through a series of profit-sharing experiences, each one falling short of reaching the goal. There will be future experiments in establishing coöperative institutions, productive and distributive, and by some they may be pronounced failures but they, while they may not be successful, will not be failures, for that which will render them apparently unsuccessful will point the way to doing better the next time, and the lesson will not be lost.

It was because a coöperative enterprise did not succeed thirty-five years ago that certain men asserted that the only remedy for industrial ills would come through the bullet instead of the ballot. I wrote a circular letter to the Order of Knights of Labor, and, commenting on the suggestion to use physical force, said: "The man who does not know enough to vote straight cannot be depended upon to shoot straight"; and, paraphrasing Bulwer-Lytton's *Richelieu*, added: " 'Tis said that in the hands of men 'entirely great the pen is mightier than the sword,' let me add to that by saying: in the hands of man entirely mouth, the gun is harmless as his word."

More men are preaching physical force today than when I wrote that, and they are just as far from being right as the advocate of physical force was then. Four years of international physical force has [*sic*] made the world worse than it was in 1914. War never settles anything permanently except the men and women who are the butchered victims of it. No war has ever been fought that men did not afterwards have to settle by doing that which could, and should, have been settled before the war started. The real victims of all wars were men and women who had no selfish or financial interest in them. They secured nothing for themselves save the task of bearing the heavy burden of debt caused by the war. No matter who gained, the man who toiled or tilled lost. It has always been so; it always will be so, unless and until men coöperate in producing and constructing instead of co-operating to destroy property and butcher each other.

. . . .

Profit-sharing is not coöperation, although it is by some mistaken for it. The principal argument against profit sharing is that it takes no heed of losses. "Are the workingmen who favor profit-sharing willing to share in the losses also?" is the first question asked by the opponent of profit-sharing. It does not occur to such that working people share in losses now, and always have shared in them. When men are laid off temporarily or discharged through industrial depression, when they are displaced to make room for younger men, when wages are reduced for want of orders to keep the industry going at old-time speed, they most assuredly share in the losses.

What is needed in profit-sharing in order to pave the way through it to coöperation is a share in management also.

Sharing in management as well as profit has received little consideration or thought on the part of employers or employed.

One employer, with whom I discussed the question of management-sharing, opposed it for the reason that workingmen were not competent to assist in managing an industrial plant, a mine, or a railroad. He was right, but it does not follow that working-men cannot, by applying themselves to a study of management-sharing, qualify as management sharers.

With the exception of sitting in at the directors' table, the millions of men who now successfully operate our railroads are managers. The millions who mine coal are managers. The men and women who keep our looms and lathes in productive activity are managers. Each one in his place does his part to manage the whole.

Factory life is in itself a coöperative life. Workmen who were widely separated and strangers to each other in the past were brought together, introduced to each other, and began a coöperative, even a communal life if you please, inside factory walls.

.   .   .   .

I grant that the operation of factories, mines, railroads, etc., has caused the public to lose sight of the individual in production; the single workman may appear insignificant, and that very thought has given birth to much of the indifference to his welfare that all men deplore.

Apparently men approximate to ciphers, yet it is the cipher properly placed that makes 100 out of 10.

.   .   .   .

Management-sharing should receive the careful study of workingmen. They should study management and put forward their brightest minds to qualify as directors as well as operators. It would be manifestly unjust to select as a manager one who had only a knowledge of the operating end of the concern.

With a clearer insight to management fewer misunderstandings will arise between those who operate and those who direct. Suppose we try management-sharing as well as profit-sharing and bonus-giving. Up to the present time the workingman has been rated by many employers as no higher than the mule he drives or the tools he uses at his daily task, and to that fact may be attributed much of the indifference some workmen exhibit when turning out the daily grind. "Get while the getting is good," has become the motto of a great many latter-day workmen. I have always contended that once a man enters upon the performance of a task under a contract expressed or implied, he is in duty bound to do the best that is in him to turn out the finished product as near perfect as he can.

When I was employed by the Dickson Manufacturing Company in the Cliff Locomotive Works at Scranton, Pa., I had charge of the guide crosshead and piston department. On December 19, 1875, the superintendent gave me directions to begin and finish the work on three locomotives, a small mine engine, a large freight engine, and a high-class passenger locomotive. In giving his instructions he said: "These locomotives will be placed on exhibition at the Centennial Exposition next year. I want you to do all the work on the passenger engine yourself. You will have from now until the first of June to do the work." When I asked why he assigned that duty to me, his answer was complimentary, and since you may guess at it there is no necessity for repeating it.

I completed the task as directed. Many a night when the line shaft would be in motion I went back to the shop and worked on that engine on my own time. I never thought of putting in a claim for overtime. I did it because I regarded that engine as mine. I polished the guides and rods with the cushion of my right hand. When it drew a prize at Philadelphia, I was as proud of it as the president of the company. True my name was not mentioned, I did not receive extra compensation, but that locomotive was a part of myself. I can say the same of every one of the engines I turned out while in the employ of that company. I never saw the wheels turn under an engine I built without experiencing a feeling of pride; it was my work, I had given the best I had to the performance of what I regarded as my duty. I worked for wages it is true, but I never thought of wages when the exhaust of one of my locomotives sounded in my ears. If anything went wrong with one of my locomotives in the test, I regarded it as a personal reflection on me. . . .

In addressing a meeting of machinists some time ago, I, among other things, said:

I shall say nothing about the shortcomings of your employers. You are familiar with them yourselves. My duty tonight is to hold the mirror up before you so that you may see yourselves as others see you, or as they think they see you.

During my Knight of Labor days I struggled for fewer hours of toil and larger pay for workmen. I think I was right in doing that. If I am correctly informed, you men think it is right to do as little in the short-hour day as possible while contending for still higher pay. I am told that workingmen think it right to "loaf on the job" now in order to curtail production. I have also been informed—and by workingmen too—that to slight the work, to turn out the inferior in order to have it wear out or give out quickly, is not regarded as reprehensible. I hope I have been misinformed, but if not let me say to you as earnestly and as emphatically as I know how that the workingman who resorts to such practices is as guilty of theft as if he put his hand in the pocket of his employer and took therefrom in money the equivalent of the time he steals. He is a double thief, for in turning out the inferior in workmanship he helps to rob the consuming public which embraces workingmen and women as well as others.

I am somewhat conversant with the history of labor and know that laboring men and women were treated as slaves, as beasts, for centuries and that many old-time employers were heartless oppressors. . . .

I have heard workingmen say: "Well they robbed us once, now it is our turn to rob them." No, men, it is not your turn to rob now or at any other time. It was wrong for the old-time employer to degrade, oppress, and rob your fathers, and it cannot be right for you to rob or oppress anyone.

Besides, you owe a duty to yourselves, you owe it to your children to let them look upon the face of an honest man when you enter your home, and you cannot do that if you purposely slight your work. The work you do is part of yourself, you should do it as well and as faithfully as you know how.

Bear in mind that the employer of today is the son of the father I had to contend against some years ago; he occupies a different view point and, perhaps, may look out on a broader horizon than his father did.

Again, many of this day's employers were the workingmen of yesterday. They know of your trials, your ambitions, your hopes, and you owe it to them, to yourselves and the public of which you are an important part to make friends of your employers in order to help pave the way to the co-operation of the future.

Do not make the mistake of supposing that I believe the employer of today who was an employee yesterday may be more just, more considerate, or more humane than a man who never worked for wages. Often such men are veritable tyrants but all the same they know every trick of the trade, every move of yours, and are better qualified to go before the world and lay bare everything you do that may not be just, reasonable and right.

I then devoted some time to a discussion of profit-sharing and coöperation.

Perhaps Leclaire,[1] the Parisian house decorator who originated or first directed public notice to profit-sharing in 1842, was the most successful of all employers who attempted to satisfy workingmen by sharing profits with them, but his plan did not meet with wide recognition, because sharing in management was not coupled with sharing of profits.

Workingmen have, for the most part, viewed profit-sharing with suspicion. They did not and do not now know where all the profits come from, how they were earned, or whether they were earned.

Juggling in stocks, taking advantage of competitors, bulling and bearing the market, may increase or reduce profits. Workingmen have no means of knowing what the legitimate profits of a concern may be unless they share in management as well as profits.

[1] Edmé Jean Leclaire (1801-72), the son of a village shoemaker, became an industrialist who was profoundly concerned with improving the condition of his workers. Rejecting Utopian socialist schemes as impractical, he introduced a system of profit-sharing in his establishment in 1842 which is described in his pamphlet *De la misère et des moyens à employer pour les faire cesser* (1850).

Sharing in management as well as profits will in great measure allay that fear I referred to. A change in management of a concern that shares profits may throw out all save the younger men, whether necessity for such a proceeding exists or not. With a share in management as well as profits, it will not be so easy to dispense with the services of a management sharer as to displace one who shares in profits only.

One of the greatest of all causes of unrest began when love for and interest in the American home began to decline and that decline began back there where workingmen were discharged and sent adrift by thousands to make room for other men. What is now called the turnover in the working force of shop and factory was in early days welcomed by employers, for new men were engaged at lower wage levels than the displaced workers occupied.

The prospect of securing and owning a home by the workingman began to fade soon after the ending of the Uncivil War. Men who labored for wages began to feel that it was far safer not to own homes than to tie themselves to town lots and run the risk of losing them at the whim or caprice of an employer who might feel like imposing unjust conditions on them. . . .

The man who owned no home took to the road in preference to accepting a reduction in compensation or other curtailment of his rights or privileges.

What is now called I. W. W.-ism had its origin among men who were made to feel that their employers had use for them only to reap a profit from their labor. I often heard workingmen say:

Nobody cares for me, why should I care for anybody? My employer don't own me, he don't have to look after or care for me I have to do that, and if he thinks I can live on poor pay he won't give me good pay. He don't care how I am knocked or battered about, why should I care to prevent damage to his tools, material or workshop?

Here was sown the seeds of that sabotage the world of industry knows today. Here began the study of socialism by the American workingman. Not all employers were cruel, but the wage system, as practiced, made them indifferent to the workers' welfare. . . . "Get while the getting is good" was the theory they worked on. That indifference drove men from homes and made them dwellers in tenements and apartment houses. New York City is not the only city in America where the tenement flourishes; it is simply preëminent as a hive of homeless house-dwellers. Go through New York from South Ferry to Harlem, and you will not find a laborer who owns the house he lives in. They hive like bees, and like the bees are deprived of the honey by the landlords.

Our city populations have been added to by men from Europe to whom we have extended no welcoming hand, no cheering sound or word of advice. They have been added to by young men who fled from the isolation of farm life as from a penal institution.

The source of our food supply has been drained of its workers. Silence reigns in the rural communities, and a babel of discord and muttered threats against our national life is heard in our cities. . . .

As Chief of the Division of Information in the U. S. Department of Labor, I had thousands of applications for farm help come to me between 1907 and 1914. Rarely did one of them contain an offer of wages that would tempt a strong, willing worker. . . . Most of the applications for farm help demanded high-class men morally and physically. One application contained this: "I want a man who don't swear, smoke, drink, play cards, run round nights, or have anything to do with women." That farmer wrote me several times to spur me up to send him a man of the model described in the specifications. At last I replied to him in this language: "I have caused diligent search to be made for a man who could fill the requirements set forth in your application. I couldn't locate him at first. I have found him, but he is not available. He is over in the cemetery and the marker above him says, 'Rest in Peace.' I'll not disturb him."[1] . . .

Before the [World] War the employing farmer wouldn't pay living wages. After the War he couldn't pay the wages demanded by men who would rather toil in the city than till in the country.

Diminished supply of food stuffs is followed by increased prices for everything we eat, drink or wear. Following this comes the demand for higher wages all round. Contentment cannot find a toe hold where dissatisfaction stands with both feet.

The relations between capital and labor, so called, are strained to the breaking point. Dishonest preachers of discontent are openly as well as secretly fomenting discord and preaching violation of law to correct the evils we all suffer from. Laws are disregarded by those who should enforce them. Even the time-honored law of supply and demand has fallen into disfavor.

Over all the hue and cry about adjustment of inequalities and differences is heard the voice of the soothsayer who offers his presto chango panacea for all our ills. . . . Our industrial ills cannot be cured by violence, by destruction of property, not even by good advice, nor in a hurry. In the meantime I expect to see idle men scratching hungry, empty stomachs all over this land inside of five years from now (September, 1920), unless workers turn toward and become intimately acquainted with the source of our supplies—Mother Earth.

From the time of the first lockout, when Adam and Eve were locked out of Eden for indulging too freely in the alcohol contained in that apple, down to the present time there has been a labor question. There always will be a labor question, and today it is more intricate, more complex and, apparently, less responsive to treatment than ever. That question will be more easily understood when men and women realize that patient endeavor alone can furnish the lamp to light our way to a solution of many of the ills in the presence of which we stand in awe and fear. First, there will have to come an understanding between employer and employed, such an understanding as will cause the worker to realize that his employer does not work him. The process of effecting this understanding will not come over night or by easy stages, for the road is long and the grades are steep, but it will come.

Here seems to be a good place to tell you what I said at the luncheon given by the National Chamber of Commerce to the U. S. Employment Service in May, 1918. I was not on the program for a talk, but many of the delegates knew me and called on me to speak. As near as I can recall it I said:

You are for the most part employers. You may have had disputes, controversies, or differences with men in your employ, and you may not entertain a good opinion of your help. It may be true, too, that you feel that you are better than the men who work for you. I rather think it's a good thing for every man to feel he is the best man on earth provided he strives in every way to be that best man. But do not run away with the idea that you are any better than your workmen, for you are not. They are as good as you and a change in our economic life may place you where they are now.

Heretofore workingmen and their employers have had contentions that did not help either and damaged the great employer of both—the public. Do not forget that you and your employees are a part of that public, and if you do not give heed to the welfare of the public you are injuring yourselves.

The war we are now going through has in many ways injected new difficulties into the industrial life of our country, and all of these must be met and settled. No outside interference will settle differences between employer and employed so well as they can settle them by getting together, by talking them over, and by waiving non-essentials.

When you go to your homes and workshops, meet your men, call them into conference, and talk it all over with them; you'll find them tame enough to eat bread out of your hand, you'll find them just as good as you are. Give and take with them, but don't expect them to do all the giving while you do all the taking. Lay aside your pride, its no use to you anyway and is often a hindrance. You'll find that your employees have hearts; let them know that you have hearts. Search for their hearts, find their hearts so that when this war ends you will all be ready to settle the complex problems of peace and help all of us in the United States to again travel toward prosperity. Yes, men, search for and find the hearts of your workmen so that they may not be reaching for your necks when the war ends and the day of readjustment comes.

I thought that was good advice to give, and they must have thought so too, for they applauded heartily.

My belief that coöperation shall one day take the place of the wage system remains unshaken. The fundamentals of coöperation will be taught in our schools yet.

We read and hear much about bonuses to employees of large and small manufacturing concerns. The paying of a bonus is profit-sharing under another name and will never settle the contentions between the employer and his help. Workmen have always looked with suspicion on the sharer of profits; they distrust the payer of bonuses. The real party to whom the bonus should be paid is the consuming public; that bonus can be paid in increased production, and increased production means cheaper food, cheaper clothing, cheaper rents, and fair wages. Underconsumption is being forced on the public through underproduction. Underproduction follows lack of interest in work, and high prices inevitably follow the trail of nonproduction.

Under coöperation each worker will share in the earnings, not the profits, of the concern of which he is a coöperator. The man or agency that strikes a blow at a manufacturing or mining concern running on a really coöperative basis will strike at the welfare of every one connected with the establishment. President and water boy will alike resent interference with the management and operation of a coöperative institution, productive or distributive.

Again let me say that coöperation cannot be forced. It shall come into successful operation when the people have studied it, experimented with it, and have learned that it is the nearest and sanest approach to a solution of our industrial problems.

In what is herein set down I have not attempted to lay down rules, or prescribe formulas on which to begin, or proceed, with coöperation. Each branch, or subdivision of industry must formulate its own rules with the understanding that coöperation, real coöperation shall result from its effort. . . .

Coöperation will not bring the millennium, but it will steer us clear of the pitfalls ahead and help us steer clear of the hell of despair so many thoughtful men and women now dread.

In the opening words of the chapter on coöperation, I quoted a saying of the Saviour, Jesus Christ. Let me in conclusion say that until men and women realize that He lived, worked, and died for all, regardless of country, clime, creed or color and that He meant just what He said when He told the men of His day to love their neighbors, they will continue to walk in the wrong path. He spoke not for that brief hour He spent on earth, but for all time and for the people of the eternity they live in. I firmly believe it is because we have not lived up to the advice He gave that we have traveled so far in the wrong direction. . . .

Love your neighbor means to treat him fairly, justly, honestly, squarely, and always be kind. It means to work with your neighbor and not against him. It means to assist and not hinder him when he is doing right, and if he is going wrong to point the right out to him. That is the right thing to do and one of the best proofs of that is to be found in the fact that we have religions of many denominations and societies of many kinds all tending toward that end. Surely out of all their marching and countermarching as a result of all their teaching and practice the right will prevail, and, when it does, we shall in every enterprise, every undertaking, be able to fulfill that command: "Love your neighbor" by *co-operating with him.*

Chapter Twenty-Five

I PRACTICE LAW, BECOME COM-
MISSIONER-GENERAL OF IMMIGRATION
AND MEET SOME OBSTACLES

LOOKING BACKWARD over the storm-beset pathway traveled by men who held positions of trust and responsibility in labor organizations during my official connection with that part of society called the labor movement, I recall the names and fate of many who, so far as I could observe, had performed faithful service for their fellow craftsmen, and, on severing official connection with their organizations, went into the saloon business as a means of gaining a livelihood. That there must have been a cause for this became evident to me, for they were not drunkards or given to drink; in fact, all of them that I knew were temperate men. They were men above the average in intelligence and education, they could adapt themselves to other callings in the field of industry, and why they selected and entered upon a business that must have been distasteful to them, was mystifying to me. When the hour struck for the severance of my official relationship with the Knights of Labor, I gained, through experience, a knowledge that helped me to a better understanding of the why and wherefore of other labor men embarking in the liquor-dispensing business.

Relieved of duty as General Master Workman of the Knights of Labor, I sought employment as a machinist in a shop where I had formerly worked at my trade. I had saved no money, was in debt, and the organization owed me, in salary and unpaid expenses over five thousand dollars. I had received a great deal of praise, adulation, commendation, and flattery for the part I played as chief of the Knights of Labor, but, while these might have been comforting to another man, I cared little or nothing for them. In any event, I could not realize anything on them in a financial way, and they provided nothing substantial in the matter of supporting my family. I cannot forget either that I had been the recipient of a much larger share of unstinted censure, condemnation, denunciation, and abuse from those I had worked for as well as from those I had opposed.

There were those who advised me to open a saloon; others believed I should "lecture for the good of humanity"; others frowned on my doing anything except sitting on a pedestal of some kind and basking in the reflected glory of past achievement.

From foremen of machine shops to master mechanics and from these to superintendents and general managers I patiently plodded my way. They received me kindly, treated me courteously, even genially, but did not employ me. The attacks made on me because of my activities as General Master Workman were still fresh in the minds of those I applied to for leave to earn my living . . . it became next to impossible for me to find an employer who had not been influenced in some measure by one or more of the many rumors circulated about me, or by charges recklessly made concerning some phase of my effort in the field of labor.

A statement made to me, or advice given me, rather, by one employer I applied to will serve for nearly all of them. . . .

It is too bad that you, after so many years of service in the cause of organized labor, should have to go back to your trade, you would not be content at it, and in any event you would be a disturbing element in our shops; the men would, in spite of you, select you as their spokesman in every controversy over wages, hours, or shop discipline, and we'd have to dismiss you finally. Try something else.

When I intimated that I had no capital on which to embark in a new business, that I knew no other trade than that of machinist, he ventured the suggestion that I could open a saloon, for that required little or no capital, and he knew a brewer who would equip me with stock and fixtures, etc.

I sought two men, then engaged in the retail liquor business, who had formerly held positions in organized labor and from them heard statements that assured me that the door to prosperity would be opened for me by others if I engaged in the saloon business. Each one had his saloon fitted out and stocked with all kinds of liquor on long-time and easy payments by brewers who simply required that he make a specialty of the kind of beer brewed by the firm or man who gave him his start in business.

Then I did some thinking. I who had always, and to my own material disadvantage, counseled laboring men to be temperate, had been advised to make drunkards of them for my own enrichment. Never for one moment did I consider the proposition, but just to see how it would look in print I penciled out an advertisement to insert in the papers and pinned it to the wall in my bed room. It remained there for years and when I finally parted from my Scranton home—and the mortgage appertaining thereto—packed that advertisement away among some papers and forgot it. On the morning of January 21, 1920, I came across it, and with your permission I lay it before you:

T. V. Powderly, ex-machinist, ex-president Machinists and Blacksmiths Union, ex-mayor of Scranton, ex-deputy president of the Industrial Brotherhood, ex-General Master Workman of the Knights of Labor, who always advised his fellow workers to be temperate and save their earnings, hereby announces that he has opened a saloon and solicits the patronage of those he formerly advised to lead sober lives. They will find his bar stocked with the choicest brands of whiskey, brandy, wine, gin, and other intoxicants, also a full line of ales, beers, and other soft drinks. He makes a specialty of the beer brewed by Guzzel, Hops, Water, & Company.

Give him a call and be convinced that he was a liar and a hypocrite during all the years he advised you to adhere to sobriety. You have saved money through his advice, call on him and help him enrich himself through your poverty. You have a bank account acquired by heeding his counsel, he now asks you to remember that one good turn deserves another, exchange your bank deposit for his liquor.

Don't take a shingle off his roof by passing his door, take one off your own and hustle for more.

. . . .

The Delaware, Lackawanna, and Western Railroad Company was at that time extending its lines west from Binghamton to Buffalo, New York. It occurred to me that I would make a good conductor, so I called on the general manager of the system, William F. Hallstead, a good man and a friend of mine. When I made known my mission he said: "You wouldn't be worth a damn to us as a conductor. You're too well known. Every bum, tramp, and hobo would travel over our line and they'd all expect you to carry them free or pay their fares. No, try something else."

I told you some time ago that I had studied law, was admitted to the bar and practiced before the courts of Lackawanna County, Pa. I have been admitted to the bar of the Supreme Court of Pennsylvania and the bar of the Supreme Court of the United States. There is no money in the practice of law for me. I did not know how to collect the fees I earned as other lawyers did. I believe that had I begun the practice of law early in life I might have made a success of it, but when practicing before the criminal court, I never could rid myself of the feeling that I was the prisoner at the bar instead of his counsel. I carried every case home with me. I ate it, I slept with it, I dreamed it, and did exactly as I did in my work as General Master Workman of the Knights of Labor. I did not know how to earn fees as other lawyers did. If John Doe was sued by James Roe and retained me to defend him, I managed to bring Doe and Roe together, had them stay proceedings, arrive at an understanding, shake hands, and forget their differences. The process of forgetting extended beyond their differences; Doe usually forgot to pay me a fee, and I, too, had to forget it. My former advocacy of the cause of the many became a handicap when I championed that of the individual before a jury. The cause of the many appealed to me, and in a measure I was successful when advocating it, but I never could plead for myself. When defending a chicken thief before a jury so heartily did I espouse his cause that I stood before that jury as a chicken thief, and since I never could talk for myself, I became almost tongue-tied when giving an imitation of a chicken thief before a jury of his peers.

I was more successful in practice before the civil courts and liked it better, but I had so long defended the underdog in the industrial field and was so well and intimately known that I was obliged to act as counsel for many poor men in the criminal courts. Many of them retained me when they had no money to fee another lawyer. When they could afford it they engaged other counsel—and paid for it. I had as large a clientele as any attorney in Scranton, but my clients regarded me as a sort of a legal free-lunch counter to come to when in trouble, with a more or less fervent "thank you" as a fee. Wasn't I the "poor man's lawyer"? I was, and as a consequence, I became a damn poor lawyer— financially, you understand.

. . . .

During the few years I was at the bar I learned a great deal more about law than you'll find in law books or gather from court proceedings. I learned to know that the Knights of Labor had a reason for adopting the sixth plank in our declaration of principles. That declaration calls for "The removal of unjust technicalities, delays, and discriminations in the administration of justice."

At the bar of every county there stands, representing the people and paid by all the people of the county, a public prosecutor known as a district attorney. A man charged with violating the law and indicted by the grand jury stands before that court guilty in the eyes of the district attorney. Rarely will the presumption of innocence weigh with him. He will labor zealously to convict the prisoner at the bar after he smells blood in the grand jury room to which only those giving evidence against the accused are admitted.

A poor man accused of a misdemeanor, standing in court before a petit jury with the weight of a grand jury indictment bearing heavily down upon him, but without funds to fee a lawyer, stands a poor chance of acquittal.

The court will assign counsel to defend that man, but such cases are usually entrusted to young, briefless lawyers who conduct the defense in perfunctory fashion and rarely ward off conviction from the luckless defendant.

In each court there should stand a public defender entrusted with the duty of defending every man brought before the bar accused of a crime. Yes, every man. The district attorney prosecutes every man brought into court under grand jury indictment. He does this in the name of the State, and is paid by the State or county. . . . So . . . every man before the bar of justice has paid a tax to fee the man who prosecutes him, and the State or county from the same general fund should fee his defender. The innocent man would not leave the courtroom with bitterness in his heart and a hatred of the commonwealth rankling in his mind if that commonwealth took as much interest in defending as in prosecuting him. If the prisoner at the bar could afford to retain private counsel, well and good, but rich and poor should stand as equals before the law. They cannot do so when the State prosecutes and does not defend its citizens. . . . We are organized in the State to "provide for the common defense," and defending a citizen is fully as much the duty of the State as is the prosecution of that citizen. The public defender should have access to the grand jury room as well as the public prosecutor. . . .

. . . . .

Some of the most high-toned, honorable men I ever knew practiced before the bar of Lackawanna County. The judges of that court were the equals in legal ability, integrity, and square dealing of those who sat on any bench in Pennsylvania. It is neither bench nor bar I criticize. The practice in our courts that had grown with the ages, that enabled a wealthy or influential lawbreaker to secure delays, favors, and sometimes immunity, is what I condemn. In the light of present day requirements that practice should be changed, and it will be changed. . . .

Let me tell you how and why I came to quit the bar. Despite the fact that I was no longer officially connected with the labor movement, reporters from everywhere would come to me for an expression of opinion on some phase or other of current disputes or happenings in the labor world. That I was practicing, or trying to practice, law made no difference to the enterprising newspaper reporter or the editor who sent him to me.

By editors of labor papers I was regarded as one who knew how to write on labor topics, and many of them besought me to display my wisdom in cold type through the columns of their journals.

During the time I was active as an officer in the Knights of Labor I wrote voluminously on the principles we advocated and on many that other men in the movement did not favor. I do not now recall that at that time any man of prominence in the ranks of organized labor openly favored my views on the drink habit, but that made no difference to me. . . . I was not then and am not now a prohibitionist. My work was directed to the end that workingmen would be educated to recognize the evils of drunkenness and avoid them for the sake of their families and to maintain positions of respectability in society. Prohibition will never make a man sober in his heart, it will never cure the craving for alcohol or destroy the means of getting it or making it, but educate a man to know that drunkenness places him beyond the pale of decent society, and he will change his habits.

Everything I wrote in those days appeared over my own signature. Of course this exposed me to all manner of attacks for I fought in the open. . . . Perhaps my stand was not always the right one but I thought it was. The editorials I wrote were penned since I ceased to be General Master Workman. I have furnished editorial matter, without price or hope of reward for several labor papers, always with the understanding that my name should not be disclosed. I now confess that many a time I have, with a sense of satisfaction, listened to men who were personally opposed to me speak approvingly of editorials I had written, they not knowing who the author was. I never wrote an editorial without feeling that it was not the right thing to do, for editorials are in reality anonymous. I do not think I am much of an egotist even though I do use the personal pronoun so often in this recital.

I am writing about myself and have to say "I" more often than if writing about another. I never favored or liked the editorial "we." The editor calls himself "we," but his readers know he is nothing of the kind. The first editor called himself "we" perhaps, because he wanted to talk like a crowd so that no one could fix responsibility for his brave or cowardly, sane or insane, wise or idiotic utterances. Let the editorialist drop the "we" and say

"I," adding his own name to his production, and those who know him best may be tempted to say: "Rot! Who cares what he says or thinks." Time was when great editors of great papers could call themselves "we" with a reasonable certainty that their readers knew who wrote the editorials. It is different now. It is no longer said that Horace Greeley or Charles A. Dana writes the editorials that appear in the *Tribune* or the *Sun.* . . . The personality of a great editor, well known to all men, has almost faded away, and in his place sits the chameleon-hued hireling who, because of his opportunity to hide behind "we," frequently plays assassin with the reputations of men and women he would not dare assail over his own signature, or personally to their faces.

The day is coming when every man and woman occupying an editorial chair will be known by their own writings and will be held personally responsible for the liberties taken by them with the names and reputations of others. . . . Public questions as well as public men and women will have to be dealt with fairly, for the name of the writer will appear at the top or bottom of every editorial. . . . Fair play, decency, honesty, justice, all demand that every editorial shall bear the name of its maker. . . .

I publicly and persistently advocated government supervision of public utilities during my incumbency of the office of General Master Workman. Railroads, telegraphs, and coal deposits controlled and supervised by the government were never omitted from any of my public speeches. From every platform I asked my hearers to study these questions, and in nearly every instance some writer securely hidden behind the editorial "we," sneeringly assailed—not the proposition, but the man who voiced it.

On one occasion I discovered the identity of a "we," who disposed of me in about three-quarters of a column of billingsgate in a daily paper. I called on him and invited him to discuss the subject matter of my talk—the ownership by the government of the anthracite fields of Pennsylvania—before an audience of his fellow townsmen and allow them to umpire the game as we played it. He declined and within a week attacked me personally in an editorial for something I never said or thought of saying. . . .

However, it's all over now, and I, of all men in America, have reason to be proud of the fact that what I proclaimed and advocated from over two thousand platforms, and for which I was unsparingly condemned as one for whom the hangman's noose or the guillotine would be most fitting, is now advocated by the foremost men of the twentieth century world. The knowledge that I had something to do with this great change in public sentiment is my sole reward for labor done. . . .

Of course many believed that I laid principle aside when in the presidential campaign of 1896, I took the stump for William McKinley. I feel that time has vindicated the position I took then and I may with propriety tell why I did it.

Many of the honorable men (?) who assailed me for the part I took in the McKinley-Bryan campaign of 1896 charged me with having deserted the position of General Master Workman of the Knights of Labor to become a Republican. Let me state the case as it stood at that time.

I resigned as General Master Workman on November 30, 1893. I became a member of the Central Republican Club of Scranton during the municipal campaign in January, 1894, and took a speaking part in behalf of the Republican ticket during that campaign.

During the State campaign of 1894, I spoke and wrote for General Daniel H. Hastings,[1] Republican candidate for governor of Pennsylvania. He didn't need my aid, but I was personally acquainted with him, liked him, and my services were freely given.

On September 13, 1895, I represented the Scranton Republican Club, as one of its delegates, at the annual convention of the State League of Republican Clubs held at York, Pennsylvania.

In 1891, while I was General Master Workman, I received the nomination from the Pennsylvania Republican State Convention for delegate-at-large to the constitutional convention to be voted for that fall. While the proposition to hold the constitutional convention failed, I was elected by a vote of 370,370, the largest vote given for any candidate.

One may be acquainted with a man and not know him; not only

[1] Daniel Hartman Hastings (1849-1903) served as governor of Pennsylvania 1895-99.

was I acquainted with McKinley but knew him well. Our acquaintanceship extended back to a day in 1881, when in company with Charles H. Litchman, Grand Secretary, and A. M. Owens, Grand Treasurer of the Knights of Labor, I called on him at his home in Ohio. Major McKinley, as he was then called, was at the time a member of Congress. Some years prior to our visit a strike had taken place among coal miners in Ohio. Trouble followed, a number of men were arrested for unlawful assembly and riot. When the case was called for trial, the accused men appeared without counsel, and when the judge asked why they did so, their spokesman said that they had no money to fee a lawyer. McKinley was present, heard what the man said, offered his services; they were accepted, and he undertook the defense of the accused miners. He secured a continuance until the next term of court, pleaded the cause and secured the acquittal of nine or ten of the indicted miners; one or two were fined or imprisoned for a short term, and there the case rested. An Ohio delegate broached the subject at the General Assembly of the Knights of Labor held in Chicago in September, 1879. A motion to recompense Major McKinley for his services could not be entertained for two reasons; one was that it would be unconstitutional to vote money out of the treasury for such a purpose; the other, and by far the stronger reason, was that there was no money in the treasury to appropriate for any purpose. It was agreed that the delegates should make personal canvass and secure voluntary subscriptions to a fund to pay McKinley for his services in defending our brothers. If my memory is not at fault, the sum of $983.00 was raised and forwarded to the Grand Treasurer. The three officers I have named had been appointed to collect the money and turn it over to McKinley. When we made known the object of our mission, McKinley said that he had not expected a fee when he took the case, and that his reward came to him in the feeling that he had been of service to poor, defenseless and deserving men. He inquired concerning the condition of the men he had defended and when told that they had been blacklisted and were in distress, he pushed the money across the table to Owens, saying as he did so: "They need it more than I do, take it and distribute it among them." Litchman who was the spokesman for the party said: "We cannot do that, the money was contributed for a specific purpose and we shall have to dispose of it as directed or be called to account for not doing so." McKinley then took the money, wrote out a receipt for it, passed the receipt over to Owens, and then said: "Now the money is mine and I can do as I please with it, won't you gentlemen take it and act for me in making it go as far as possible among the families of the men I defended." We did so, took receipts for the money, and made a printed report to each contributor to the fund.

I was there merely as one of the general officers and up to that time was not familiar with the details of the case. As I sat looking at McKinley that day, I realized that I was in the presence of a man who had a heart that felt for others' woes; he was unpretentious, unassuming and kind. The feeling manner in which he spoke of the men he defended, and the gentle, courteous way in which he greeted us gained my confidence and regard. That day began an acquaintance and friendship which still continues, for my friends do not part from me when that which men call death summons them to a realm beyond my range of earthly vision.

The money given to McKinley some time in the fall of 1881 was in process of collection over two years. From that day during all the years I was General Master Workman of the Knights of Labor, William McKinley was my friend. Frequently he consulted me with regard to matters of concern to labor. On several occasions he submitted to me, for criticism, manuscript of speeches he intended delivering at labor meetings. I spent many evenings with him at his Washington hotel during his Congressional career. I learned to know him intimately and well. I knew him as a man who was a friend to him who worked with his hands, and, when he was nominated for the presidency, I waited and watched the course of events until it appeared that he might be defeated.

One day in August, 1896, at the time when the tide in favor of Mr. Bryan had risen so high that it threatened to sweep him into the White House, I received a message from my friend John E.

Mulholland[2] of New York, summoning me to that city to meet the Republican candidate for the vice-presidency, Garret A. Hobart,[3] and the chairman of the National Republican Committee, Mark A. Hanna. It seems that he had submitted my name to them as one who might be able to help stem the tide and turn it in favor of McKinley.

With a full realization of what would come to me in the way of abuse, censure, and misunderstanding, I accepted the trust reposed in me, closed my law books, took the field for McKinley, and remained in it until I returned to Scranton on the morning of election day to cast my vote for McKinley and Hobart.

In the course of the campaign I spoke in Cleveland; it was on Saturday night. A labor convention of some kind was in progress there, the delegates, or most of them, attended my meeting and gave me a warm reception.

They distributed themselves in groups of threes and fours throughout the hall. At a given signal they would begin to groan, hoot, or hiss, and would keep it up interminably. The roar of opposition was deafening at times, but I stood my ground and, when a sense of fair play began to work among them, I had a triumphant wind-up and a cordial reception at the close. There were about five thousand present, and, as opposition always helped me, it seemed that about half of my audience could be numbered among the helpers at the start.

Cleveland was the home of Mr. Hanna. The day after my meeting I called on him at his invitation. He was quite worked up over the near riots that broke out wherever I spoke, and, among other things said: "You seem to kick up hell among workingmen wherever you go. Why man, you're taking your life in your hands." Here it is proper for me to say that I had written to McKinley asking that he use his influence to allow me to select, as places to speak, hot beds of Bryanism. I gave him a reason for making that request; it appealed to him, and I carried on my cam-

---

[2] John E. Mulholland (1860-1925) spent an active life engaged in varied reform movements. He fought for primary election reform, prison reform, Federal aid to education, the Saturday half-holiday, and a host of other comparable objectives.

[3] Garret Augustus Hobart (1844-99) achieved his one major distinction as vice-president.

paign along that line. I reminded Mr. Hanna of that arrangement, and then said:

> Kicking up hell in a good cause is my mission on earth.
>
> Where disturbances occur at my meetings I manage to secure the names and addresses of the disturbers. I also learn something about their standing in the community and file this information with the secretary of the National Committee so that he, or someone, may reach them. You'll have no trouble in towns I speak in if my advice is followed.
>
> Now as to taking my life in my hands. It's my life, not yours, so don't worry about it.
>
> If at any of these meetings they should kill me, nothing could then prevent the election of McKinley.

I need say nothing of the result of the election of 1896; its history is open to all.

Immediately after the inauguration of President McKinley in March, 1897, I wrote him making application for appointment to the office of Commissioner-General of Immigration. Mr. Mulholland and Vice-President Hobart strongly endorsed me. Mr. Hanna, though he had no objection to me, had pledged himself to an Ohio friend of his. At the request of the President he supported me.

No labor organization so far as I could learn opposed my appointment, but a number of influential labor officials made a protest against my confirmation, alleging that I was "an enemy to labor." Since my enmity to labor consisted of supporting McKinley for the presidency, that opposition did not weigh heavily with him.

Aside from sending in my application and requesting Senators Quay and Penrose to support me, I made no other effort to secure the appointment. Both Pennsylvania Senators cordially endorsed me, and on July 15, I received a message from the White House to come to Washington for a conference with the President. When I called at the White House the President never referred to my application. He simply talked for awhile about some incidents in our acquaintanceship, and all at once asked: "How do you spell your first name?" I told him and he said: "I think that will look well on a commission."

He then wrote my "name in full" on a card, handed it to Mr.

Cortelyou[4] with directions to send it to the Senate. Before parting from him [sic] that day he, with a twinkle in his eye, said: "I am taking a great risk in appointing such 'an enemy to labor' to this position but you'll have a chance to get acquainted with labor men by inviting them to your hearings on matters of concern to them. Don't forget, Powderly, that 'an injury to one is the concern of all.' "

The Senate having failed to confirm my nomination before adjournment owing to the fight made on me, the President gave me a recess appointment, and, on August 3, 1897, I was sworn in and entered upon the discharge of the duties of Commissioner-General of Immigration. My confirmation, after a spirited contest in the Senate, was effected on March 17, 1898.[5]

I shall pass over all but one of the many incidents in my career as Commissioner-General. I soon learned that all was not well at Ellis Island. Ill treatment of arriving aliens, impositions practiced on steamship companies, and discourtesy to those who called to meet their friends on landing were frequent. I appointed a commission consisting of one Democrat and one Republican to investigate conditions. They reported their findings in June, 1900, and as a result eleven employees were dismissed from the service of the government at Ellis Island for offenses such as overcharges for

[4] George Bruce Cortelyou (b. 1862) held many public service posts before he became President McKinley's assistant secretary in 1898. He was the first secretary of the Department of Commerce and Labor (1903), and up to 1909 he held two additional cabinet posts.

[5] From the *Congressional Record* and the *Executive Journal of the United States Senate*, as well as the contemporary newspapers, a somewhat different version emerges. The extent of the opposition to Powderly's appointment in the Senate is difficult to ascertain, because appointments were then discussed in secret executive session. The first nomination of Powderly was received by the Senate on July 17, 1897. On January 5, 1898, the nomination went in again, and, while he was serving under a temporary commission, the nomination was finally confirmed March 16, by a vote of 43 to 20. Several Democrats supported him, and Senator Chandler of New Hampshire was the only Republican to cast his vote against confirmation. Apparently, Powderly did not at first have the indorsement of Senators Quay and Penrose, who were pushing a Philadelphia candidate for the post, but they both declared to the press that they were satisfied with his nomination. Chandler spoke against confirmation on the ground that the Republican party could not afford to appoint someone so "distasteful" to labor as Powderly. There was sharp discussion over the question of whether the appointment was in exchange for a trade which Powderly made during the campaign. This was denied by Hanna, who also announced that he was not originally Powderly's supporter.

food, misleading immigrants as to destination, procuring admission of friends and relatives to see newly landed immigrants for a fee, overcharges in exchanging foreign for American money, downright cruelty to aliens, petty thievery, and false statements as to distances to be traveled.

It was charged against me that I was relentless in my pursuit of the offenders. That charge was well founded. My chief regret was that I could not send some of the culprits to the penitentiary.

I was called to the White House on complaint of political and religious friends of some of the offending officials. I stated my case to President McKinley and ended by saying:

I entertain no feeling against these men. I have not been influenced by consideration of their political or religious affiliations. The only thing I can say in their favor is that they are wholly impartial, they would as quickly rob a steamship company as an immigrant and are doing so right and left.

How can we expect a man whom we rob on his entrance to our country to respect us, our laws, our institutions, or our flag. I am trying to end that practice.

I know the Assistant Secretary, who has charge of Immigration, is not in hearty accord with my action, but the scandal is country wide and the right thing to do is to end it in the right way by driving the guilty ones out of the Government Service. The Secretary, Mr. Gage, is in accord with my views. Mr. Taylor is not, he takes the politician's view of it and fears it may injure your chances in this campaign. It cannot injure you if your appointees do their plain duty.

We were standing up when this conversation took place. Laying his right hand on my shoulder, and with those kindly eyes looking straight into mine, he said:

A great moral responsibility rests on you. Do your duty straight on to the end. I am persuaded that you are doing what is right. Go ahead, I'll back you in what you have done and in what remains to be done. God bless you and your work.

I may as well say here that while I was uncovering the rascalities at Ellis Island, the Assistant Secretary, Mr. H. A. Taylor . . . directed an attaché of the Secret Service Bureau to "Look Powderly up and *get him.*" That man did look me up. He went carefully and conscientiously over my record and from his report to the Treasury Department, through Mr. Taylor, I submit this excerpt: "I have been unable to find the slightest evidence on which to base a charge against Mr. Powderly. His course has been absolutely straight." When I add that the man who made that report has since then achieved distinction as one of the world's greatest, shrewdest detectives, you will realize that it was worth something to me to have William J. Burns make such a report concerning me.

. . . .

That clean-out at Ellis Island occasioned me no end of trouble. Every man who had been punished had friends, some of them quite influential, and they left nothing undone to blacken me in the eyes of President Roosevelt. He had assured me, when he became President, that I was to retain the office I then held. One day he asked for my resignation and I handed it in.[6] I then had an interview with him, and asked why he had dismissed me from the service. He assured me that he entertained no feeling against me, but that he had so many people complain of "friction in the Bureau of Immigration" that he determined to end it by removing everybody concerned in it. I took the liberty of saying that "Those who were detected in the commission of crime by a policeman always complained of his activities and that such activities always created friction. Mr. President you will find 2,800 pages of testimony concerning the Ellis Island transaction over in the Treasury Department. I have one favor to ask of you. Have some one in whom you repose confidence go over that report and tell you whether I did the right thing or not."

Mr. Roosevelt caused that report to be treated as I suggested, and, when the facts were laid before him, he sent for me and said that I had been completely exonerated, that I had not only done my duty, but had rendered a signal service to the cause of social

[6] Roosevelt's removal of Powderly from office on June 23, 1902, was based on the charge that the latter had politically coerced an Ellis Island employee. The specific cause of the President's action was a letter which Powderly had written to one McSweeney, which Powderly claimed he sent at the behest of McKinley. Powderly protested with justice that his behavior at Ellis Island was misunderstood, and that he had been consistent in his fight against graft there. Roosevelt apparently later became convinced that his dismissal of Powderly was an error.

justice, and he would not forget it. Before parting from him that day he, in this language, asked:

You have a bitter enemy in Archbishop Corrigan,[7] what has caused him to feel that way toward you? He came to me in vigorous protest against your doings at Ellis Island, and I couldn't at first believe he would knowingly or wrongfully attack any man as he did you. That report you referred me to gave me a key to his enmity to you, but I felt that there must be something more than that back of it.

I supplied another key to Archbishop Corrigan's enmity by relating what I have already set down in another place in this story.[8] I ended by saying: "I believed I was right then, I am sure of it now. God creates rocks and pebbles; sometimes we find pebbles masquerading as rocks."

In 1906 Mr. Roosevelt caused me to be sent to Europe to study the "Causes of Emigration to the United States."[9] On my return he invited me to discuss the subject matter of my report with him and after doing so he asked that I write him on the subject and dwell on the salient features of our talk. Following is a copy of that letter; it speaks for itself.

WASHINGTON, D. C.
DECEMBER 8, 1906

My dear Mr. President:

As requested by you at our last interview, I am presenting herewith, in substance, the suggestions made by me during our talk.

During the investigation of the "Causes of Emigration to the United States" made by me under your instructions last summer, I became convinced that at least three things are necessary to a proper regulation of immigration:

First: Selection of intended emigrants in their own countries some little time before date of departure for the United States

---

[7] Michael Augustine Corrigan (1839-1902), Powderly's unrelenting foe, had a notable clerical career. Ordained in 1863, he was consecrated Bishop of Newark ten years later, and was installed as Archbishop of New York in 1886. A patron of parochial schools, he was also a strict canonist and an unyielding conservative on social issues. Archbishop Corrigan's interpretation of the rule of the Church concerning secret societies would prevent Catholics from becoming members of the K. of L. as well as of a host of other organizations.

[8] See pp. 356-359.

[9] As a special representative of the Department of Commerce and Labor.

Second: The placing of representatives of the Immigration Service on
 ships carrying immigrants to the United States
Third: Proper distribution of immigrants who come to the United States
While no statute can be framed to make men better than God intended
them to be, we can go far toward causing aliens to fit into our American
life with less of disturbance to our economic conditions and more of safety
to our National institutions if we give heed to:
Selection abroad
Instruction on shipboard and at Immigrant Stations
Proper and beneficial distribution throughout the United States
As to selection abroad: In each of the countries from which emigrants
come to us there should be stationed, at suitable places, representatives of
the United States Immigration Service. Of course the consent of foreign
governments would have to be obtained before this could be done. The duty
of these representatives should be to pass upon the qualifications of those
intending to emigrate to the United States. Every such person should first
apply either in person, by proxy, or by mail to the United States immigration official having jurisdiction over the territory the intending emigrant
resides in.

The application should contain full information concerning the person
or persons it relates to. I need not enter into detail as to what this information should be. Suffice it to say here that every ascertainable fact in relation
to the intending emigrant should be fully set forth.

All applications should be made to the immigration official at least six
weeks before the time of departure from home of the intending emigrant;
this in order to afford time for investigation of the record, standing, health
and reputation of the applicant. I know of two persons who were admitted
at Ellis Island while I was Commissioner General who formed their resolution to come to the United States and actually started from home "between
two days," as we say. They were criminals of the worst type, who in order
to escape punishment fled from home immediately after the commission of a
crime.

Proper information and instruction should be imparted to the intending
emigrants before departure from home so that they would know just what
to face on landing in this country.

It is positively cruel to tell a man coming up from the steerage that he
must be deported "to the country whence he came" after he has severed home
ties, parted with all his European holdings and practically turned his back
forever to the land of his birth. I have witnessed so many heart-rending
scenes at our immigrant stations when poor, forlorn creatures were told
they must go back, that I felt like execrating the law which occasioned
such things.

And I would not entrust the duty of inspection abroad, or selection, to
consular agents. These officials are selected for a definite and far different

purpose. They deal with commercial matters in the main and pass upon the articles manufactured by human hands. They, in their zeal to carry out instructions from the State Department might be apt to class the hand or machine-made article as of more consequence than the creation of God Almighty, or else slight it in passing. Bars of pig iron, bales of cotton, bolts of silk, or crates of china ware might receive first consideration from them. No, leave the matter of passing upon humanity itself to men and women of ability, experience, and good judgment.

The work of making judicious selection of intending emigrants should be carefully done. It should not be entrusted to politicians, political favorites, creatures of corporate interests or those who oppose or favor immigration.

On board ship, literature printed in foreign languages by the United States Government should be placed in the hands of aliens destined to this country, by representatives of the Immigration Service. These representatives should be of both sexes and should be qualified to explain anything obscure or uncertain on the printed page. Above all things the difference between our form of government and that of their own land should be carefully dealt with. Our flag, our institutions and what they stand for should be carefully explained and the duty to uphold them should be fully impressed on the men, women, and the children of the steerage. It should not be left to the demagogue, the self-seeker or exploiter to misinform these people after landing when we can accurately inform them before they land. Having respect for governmental authority they will pay heed to what government officials tell them and will not be so apt to fall a prey to men and women having designs upon them.

Through proper selection abroad and instruction aboard ship the opportunities of the seller of steamship tickets to stimulate emigration from Europe and practically sell poor, unsophisticated people to employers in the way I told you about, would be kept down to the minimum and, as the new system became known abroad, abolished entirely.

The instruction aboard ship should be preliminary to that imparted at our Immigrant Stations and should consist of information concerning places the immigrant should not go as well as where to go. To illustrate: Galion, Ohio, may need workers of a certain kind, Cincinnati may have enough of that kind of labor. Cincinnati is on the map in Europe, but Galion is unknown there. This I find to be true of large and small towns in the United States. They know about our large cities, but are woefully ignorant about our small towns. Again let me illustrate: Budapest, Hungary, is about two hundred and fifty miles from Fiume, the only seaport in Hungary. That is considered a long trip to take over there. When considering traveling inland in America, they are apt to look on New York City and Saint Louis, Chicago, or Denver as being no farther apart than Budapest and Fiume. The minds of intending emigrants can be disabused of false impressions concerning distances and that is only one of many things foreign people need light on concerning this country. The hungry man is apt to eat too much and in doing so makes a mistake; a man who eats too much is a fool, whether he is hungry or not. As a nation, we may make mistakes and play fool with immigration. We are apt to do this to our detriment and that of the emigrant in allowing the stream of immigration to become a flood.

Through a governmental agency the exact industrial condition of every town in the United States should be and can be ascertained every week, or at most every two weeks. This will entail expense of course, but the "head tax" of the immigrant will pay it, while our present slipshod way of allowing the tide of immigration to flow where it lists is far more expensive and we pay the bill. In addition to that it is hurtful and in time may become dangerous. It should be easy to gather this information and impart it to newly landed immigrants as well as to our own people. Consider this; the Weather Bureau is prepared every morning to tell us what the weather is doing in every part of the United States; it is doing more than that, it is prepared to tell how the ocean is behaving along our seaboard. Ships are safely directed, commerce is protected and crops safe-guarded by our Weather Bureau; why not safe-guard humanity by promptly, properly, and accurately informing it where it may go with fair opportunity to do the best for itself and our country? You and I have to pay taxes to maintain the Weather Bureau, the immigrant would pay for his own protection and ours too.

Phonographs speaking all things necessary to inform immigrants in all languages; lantern slide lectures and verbal instructions on all pertinent subjects should greet the immigrant on being admitted at an immigrant station.

Of course these things will require time for preparation and formulation. I make no attempt at detail, for the coöperation of states, territories and municipalities will all be of use in this great and necessary work, and consultation with their chosen representatives should precede action.

I am mindful of your intimation to make this memorandum as long as I please, but notwithstanding that and your suggestion that you would "take a day off to read it," I feel that I have said enough to give a fair idea of what I was aiming at during our interview. As you know, I shall be glad to act on your advice to discuss this matter with the gentlemen you named.

As I told you there are those who look with suspicion on anything proposed by a labor man and since I am a labor man, I shall esteem it a favor if you will adopt my suggestions as your own, or else conceal the identity of the author.

Assuring you that I fully appreciate the confidence reposed in me, when you directed that I be assigned to duty in Europe, as well as for calling me into counsel on this matter, I am,

Very truly yours,

(*Signed*) T. V. POWDERLY

That letter was written over fourteen years ago. The things I suggested have not been done yet, but they will be done some day, and, when they are, the hysteria over immigration of the radical, the criminal, the mentally imperfect, the physically defective, the diseased and the degenerate will in large measure cease, perhaps it may die out altogether.

On July 1, 1907, I entered upon the duties of Chief of the Division of Information [of the Bureau of Immigration], under commission of [the] Hon. Oscar S. Straus,[10] Secretary of Commerce and Labor. That commission was ordered given to me by President Roosevelt. . . .

Now I shall return to William McKinley. In 1893 I was associated with A. W. Wright[11] of Toronto, Ontario, as one of the editors of the *Labor Day Annual*.[12] Mr. Wright was a member of the General Executive Board of the Knights of Labor. He wrote a sketch of McKinley, then governor of Ohio, and published it in the *Annual*. Such was our regard for Governor McKinley that he was never presented with a bill for the publication of the article. From that sketch let me quote:

To some the name suggests the thought of "monopolies" and a "robber tariff," while to others the name stands for a bold, yet wise statesmanship, a lofty patriotism, and the carrying out of a distinctively American as distin-

[10] Oscar Solomon Straus (1850-1926).

[11] Alexander Whyte Wright (1847-1919) was born in Ontario, Canada, and was the first Canadian member of the General Executive Board. He was editor of the K. of L. *Journal*, and of the Toronto *National Labour Reformer* among other papers, held several public offices in Canada, and also had a successful business career.

[12] The *Labor Day Annual*, undertaken by Powderly and Wright as a money making venture, was made up of articles, sketches, and advertisements, and seems to have produced more headaches than money. A Mr. Gray, at one time advertising agent of the *Journal of the Knights of Labor*, employed as business manager of the *Labor Day Annual*, solicited advertisements from business concerns by extreme misrepresentations and turned out to be a forger and a bigamist. The *Annual* appeared only in 1893. In the preface the editors wrote:

"It seems not unfitting that it (Labor Day) should be regarded as Labor's New Year's Day and that the Labor Day Annual which is intended to be Labor's Year Book should be published on that day. It is the hope of the publishers to make the Annual a feature of Labor Day. . . ."

guished from an European industrial policy. "High Winds," says the proverb, "blow on high hills," and on the position of preëminence upon which, by the spontaneous wish of his party and his own ability, Governor McKinley has been placed, he could hope neither to escape the blasts of the hostile criticism of enemies, nor the sometimes no less unwelcome praises of his friends.

> "The man his party deems a hero,
> His foes a Judas or a Nero—
> Patriot of superhuman worth
> Or vilest wretch that cumbers earth,
> Derives his bright or murky hues
> From distant or from party views."

It is doubtful if any great or even any prominent man can have justice done him by his contemporaries. . . . To form a true estimate of Governor McKinley it would be as unwise to accept unquestioningly the glowing panegyrics of his friends or the somber-colored criticisms of his enemies, or opponents rather—for even among his antagonists he has no enemies.

McKinley was a very approachable man; a hard-luck story seldom failed to enlist his sympathy. One evening I stood talking to him in front of the Ebbitt House when an old man besought his aid to get something to eat. Though shabbily dressed the man was clean, neat, and gave evidence of having seen better days. His lips trembled as he voiced his plea. McKinley beckoned to an attendant of the hotel, whispered something to him and then in a kind, sympathetic voice told "my friend," as he called him, to go with the attendant to the dining room and have his dinner. The man hesitated, looked down at his well-worn clothing and inquired if he would be presentable enough to sit at the hotel table. McKinley then bade me goodbye and accompanied the old man to the dining room, saying as he parted from me: "I don't think they'll object to our sitting together in there."

The kind, sincere geniality of McKinley reflected rather than attracted light. He was not of the tribe of limelight hunters. He employed no press agents and did no personal advertising of attributes to which he laid no claim.

I met Mark Hanna but once before the campaign of 1896, and I doubt if at that meeting I impressed him so vividly as to cause him to remember me. I was called to Ohio by Knight[s] of

Labor coal miners one day in 1881, and had occasion to call on Mr. Hanna in their interest. When I asked him if he would grant an audience to a committee of the men his answer came in the form of a question, "Can't the men talk, why did they send to Scranton for you?" I inquired if he would meet the committee. He answered in the affirmative and ended by saying that he was not handling such matters. Arrangements were made for a meeting. Next day I presented the committee to him and then said that my mission having been accomplished, I might as well retire. I shall never forget his answer, spoken in a tone of voice that was none too reassuring: "You may stay or go just as you please, there's no string to you." The men asked me to remain and I did. I do not recall that I was of any particular service that day. I interposed an objection to some rather heated language that passed between the committee and Mr. Hanna, and with no further evidence of a breach of the peace manifesting itself the meeting came to an end. It occupied about an hour of time during which I, as the innocent bystander, listened to an assortment of language robust enough to keep one from going to sleep. It appeared that Mr. Hanna was not the man they should have called on, but at parting he said something like this: "While I have little or nothing to do with these things, if you boys ever want to see me or have me do anything for you, come to me direct, don't send off to Scranton for Powderly; he don't know as much about these matters as we do. If I can't do anything for you myself I'll put you in touch with some one who can." I recall that the men were well pleased with Hanna, but I do not remember ever hearing his name again until, as McKinley's personal friend, Hanna became the manager of his campaign for the presidency. . . .

I do not and never did believe that Mr. Hanna wished to control President McKinley or dictate to him what he should or should not do as President. It is my sincere conviction that his desire was to lend his every effort to making McKinley's administration a successful one.

It is too soon to place a just estimate on McKinley. He left no story penned by his own hand to judge him by, and time, the great alchemist, has not yet transmuted the varied opinions of men and the effects of his labors into the enduring gold on which his fame shall be inscribed. When the yellow hues shall have faded from the picture painted of him by a hostile, sensational press, he will appear in luminous, unfading colors as one of our great Presidents. Less than two decades have passed since his labors among us came to an end. The love and reverence manifested by the people of all the states, when they bowed to the inevitable . . . was heartfelt and genuine. A nation's tribute of love and sympathy such as was given to McKinley would not have been given to a bad man. A weak man could not have won it; only a strong man could command it. He was a great man.

> Great men grow greater by the lapse of time,
> We know those least whom we have seen the latest,
> And they, 'mongst those whose names have grown sublime,
> Who worked for human liberty are greatest.

Chapter Twenty-Six

COLLECTIVE BARGAINING; THE OPEN AND CLOSED SHOP

COLLECTIVE BARGAINING, a term now generally understood to mean mutual arrangements, or agreements, between workingmen and employers, was not in use when I was officially active in organized labor. I do not know who originated or coined the expression, but my first acquaintance with it came through Andrew Roy of Ohio,[1] who, in 1874, took an active part in effecting an organization among the coal miners of that state. Mr. Roy wrote some articles for the *Workingman's Advocate* of Chicago, Illinois, in which he insisted on the "right of the miners to bargain collectively with their employers." I was a reader of and subscriber for the *Workingman's Advocate*, and for many years kept track of labor matters and labor defenders through its columns.

Without giving it a name, the aim of organized labor, from the beginning, was to be recognized as an equal in arranging schedules of pay, working hours and conditions generally in mine, mill, and factory. The employers of my day were nearly a unit in opposition to collective bargaining.

The march of industrial progress had not gained such impetus as to cause the employers to open their shops to union men. When I hear men talk of the open shop I am inclined to say that there is no such thing as a shop open to all men following the calling or trade carried on within its walls. The shop I knew was not an open one to the man the employer did not want whether he be-

---

[1] Andrew Roy was a leading figure in the post-Civil War labor movement and particularly in the organization of coal miners' unions. He was state inspector of mines in Ohio, and prominent in Greenback-Labor politics. He also wrote a *History of the Coal Miners of the United States.*

longed to a union or not. We were a somewhat benighted lot away back in the 'seventies and 'eighties of the last century.

Andrew Roy, in those days, never heard a telephone girl say: "Line's busy now"; never heard a phonograph pour its soul out through a neighbor's window on the fractured air at midnight. He often heard the hoarse hoot of the multitude, but never was inspired by the coarse toot of an automobile to make for the sidewalk in a sudden and undignified manner. He never side-stepped for a bicycle. A street car without horses or mules as motive power to persuade it through the streets, he never saw. Twisting a little thing like a key on a fiddle would have helped some, but he never used one to light up his room electrically. He never heard a bell punch or saw a cash register. Though he had often been touched for a drink, he never touched a push button in the wall to order one. If you intimated to him that you could talk on a wire to a man one hundred or one thousand miles away, he might humor you by listening to you until some friend would happen along and take you home. No, the unenlightened man was in utter ignorance of these things; so was I, but with their dawn there came a great change in the industrial world, yes, a complete revolution that men and women in middle life today are not conscious of although they grew up in the throes and pangs of its childbirth. Do not forget, my friend, that these things I speak so lightly about have had great influence and weight in changing the whole aspect of industrial affairs since Andrew Roy first spoke about collective bargaining in 1874.

Picture to yourself three or four men seated together in a small room making shoes. Time—1870, season—summer, with windows open and the free air circulating around free men. One is proprietor and manager of the shoe shop, the others work for him and in doing so work with him. At their work they discuss politics, religion, economics, science, everything they had read about in the morning or evening paper or had heard of in any way. Sometimes they quarreled, almost coming to blows, but after a short period of sullen silence they would take up discussion of some subject they could agree on.

The proprietor of that shoe shop was not only manager and

boss, but companion to the men he worked with and bossed. The men weren't watching the clock, anxious for the coming of quitting time; they didn't care whether they got their pay on Saturday night, for their credit was good and always endorsed by their employer. When that boss took orders for boots or shoes he knew to a certainty that he could depend on the skill, efficiency, fidelity, and haste of the men in completing his contracts. There was no need for collective bargaining in that shop, and it was typical of shoe shops, tailor shops, tin shops, and other shops throughout the country.[2]

．　　．　　．　　．

The employer today is, in many instances, a stock certificate or a bond with coupons on it. The shop may go to the devil and the men with it so long as dividends are paid. Heartbeats are seldom recorded, and conscience is often smothered or on vacation. . . .

Shares of stock are represented by foremen, superintendents, managers whose duty it is to drive, urge on, speed up, and turn out the finished product good or bad so long as it is done quickly.

Workmen of 1921 do not see the real employer, the real boss; he is a phantom. The stock certificates deal with the workmen whose labor creates dividends through committees called foremen, superintendents, or shop inspectors, but they do not come in contact with the real owners of shop, mine, or factory.

Workingmen should once for all realize that they are businessmen. It is their business to do their work intelligently, carefully, skillfully, and well. . . . They cannot, in their individual capacity, talk to the stock certificates. The foremen and superintendents, dressed in a "little brief authority," are frequently so impressed with a sense of their own importance that they misrepresent the real employer in misrepresenting the workmen to him.

I am within the bounds of truth in saying that fully one half of the disputes, troubles, and strikes of my day grew out of the desire of petty foremen, or bosses, to shine luminously, or make big fellows of themselves, in the eyes of a board of directors.

[2] This is, of course, a somewhat idealized picture of industry at the time.

Denying to workmen the right, not privilege, to organize and bargain collectively is as unjust to the real employer as to the real workingman.

A thousand or a hundred men working together naturally form a community of interest that cannot be entirely selfish. The interest of the employing concern should be as dear to them as to the owners of the stock certificates. A thousand or a hundred men cannot talk separately with either the stock certificates or those who represent them. They must of necessity speak in a collective capacity; in plain Anglo-Saxon, they must bargain collectively, or fail in the accomplishment of results that will be beneficial to employer and employed.

Employers for some reason do not want to bargain collectively. Perhaps it is because they do not care to recognize or deal with a union that they oppose collective bargaining. They may as well abandon that idea, for the labor organization is here to stay. If by any ill-fated move it could be abolished by the organization of capital it would be the worst thing that could happen to capital as well as labor.

I am not quite in harmony with other labor advocates on the duties and responsibilities of labor unions. I believe they should stand out unequivocally on the same plane of equality with organizations of capital in being incorporated under the same law that incorporates the mining, manufacturing, or railroad company. I have thought so since I joined, and became deputy-president of the Industrial Brotherhood in 1874.

The Industrial Brotherhood was made up of the representatives of the trade-unions of that day. I represented, in part, the Machinists and Blacksmiths Union in the Industrial Brotherhood. That organization adopted a preamble, or declaration of principles that in January, 1878, was adopted in its entirety by the Knights of Labor in their first General Assembly at Reading, Pennsylvania.

Turn to that preamble and you'll find that it demanded at the "hands of the law-making power of State and Nation". . . . "The recognition, by incorporation, of orders and other associations organized by the workers to improve their condition and protect their rights." No, they were not theorists, visionaries, or cranks who made that demand. They were hard-headed, clear-brained, thorough-paced trades-unionists who originated it and first promulgated it.

Up to the time I was first elected General Master Workman, and for the fourteen years I held that position, I advocated on every platform I spoke from the right of labor organizations to incorporate. Strange to relate the only ones to then protest were employers of labor who objected to "placing labor unions on the same plane of equality with incorporated bodies of employers."

Those who oppose collective bargaining say that they want the open shop. . . . What they mean is a shop open only to those they favor or approve of. Not labor unionists alone but others find the door of the open shop shut against them. The boss may not want Catholics, Jews, Protestants, atheists, Democrats, Republicans, or socialists in his shop. . . .

The supposed closed shop is not a closed shop either. What unionists ask for when they talk of the closed shop is the right to be recognized in the making of bargains through organized effort; that conceded they will not press the closed shop idea.

There is not, and never will be, an open shop open to everybody or a closed shop closed to anybody of ability or respectability.

No employer has the right to say what manner of man shall join a labor union. No labor union should, in justice to its own interests, compel an employer to select men for membership in it. The right to earn bread in the sweat of his own face can not be taken from any man.

I can imagine nothing worse happening to organized labor than to make membership in it a condition of employment. To promulgate such a decree and to enforce it through the strike would be suicidal. For a union to demand that the man entering the shop shall first apply for admission and then raise the initiation fee so high that he cannot afford to pay it is to resort to might and not right. The closed shop through coercion would not survive the storm of opposition it would encounter among workingmen themselves.

To force every man into the union through the closed shop would compel the lazy, shiftless, incompetent, and dishonest workman to enter the union. Such a policy would in time lead to rating the pay of the good workman on the ability or capacity of the inferior workman. If the employer is not justified in basing the wage paid the efficient and skilled man on that earned by the inefficient and shiftless man, the union has no right to demand that the poor workman shall get the same pay as the good workman. A dead level in a closed shop will never flourish in America. The partially closed shop, evolving from present conditions without compulsion, may come. The rigid rule of the closed shop will not come until the American workingman surrenders hope, ambition and becomes reconciled to the idea that there is no use in his attempting to excel in his calling. The individual should progress through good service; the union should do the same, but it cannot render good service with bad material or by driving the bad in, and on an equality with the good.

When it is admitted that the individual shall not be allowed to follow the calling of his choice except by joining a union or any other organization, we shall have to admit that the industry of which that union is a part shall flourish only as the union shall have become that which the unions I knew strenuously objected to—monopoly.

I have not changed my views on the closed or open shop since, as General Master Workman, I, in answer to a letter from a local assembly of the Knights of Labor, wrote as follows:

SCRANTON, PA.
DECEMBER 3, 1885

ALBERT A. CARLTON, ESQ.,
LYNN, MASS.

Dear Sir and Brother:

Receipt of yours of the 29th ultimo, is hereby acknowledged.

If I understand the purport of your letter, the Local Assembly would have me, as General Master Workman, render a decision which would in effect designate your employer as an organizer of and for the Knights of Labor. True, you do not recommend him as a "fitting and worthy" person to be an organizer but should I decide that "he shall employ only those who are Knights of Labor or from whom he shall exact a pledge to join the Order," I would to all intents appoint him an organizer.

Suppose that he conceived the idea of wrecking your Assembly. All that would be necessary, on his part, would be to select and hire a few men who would enter into a secret agreement with him to do everything possible to create friction, kick up a rumpus at every meeting, or do some other thing to create discord or bring disgrace upon you. With a slight addition to the wages of such men your employer could trust to their cupidity or innate deviltry to bring about the disruption of your Assembly.

You say your Assembly has passed the creeping point and you now feel strong enough to make this move. Be careful. Your present strength may lead to future weakness, don't ask me to help reduce your strength.

The thing for you to do is to go to your employer and frankly explain to him that it is your desire, and you feel that it will be to your interest, to see him prosper. Tell him there is that in the teachings of Knighthood to cause you to regard his success as an asset to you. Say to him that in employing Knights he will be engaging the services of efficient workers and responsible men and leave the matter of hiring men to him.

Then to build your Assembly up to greater strength and usefulness, have each member so conduct himself as to win the approval of good men of your craft. Draw such men to you, hold them, and so gain the esteem and good will of the best among workmen and that of your employer as well. Do that and you will not jeopardize your future well-being as an Assembly by causing your employer to act as an organizer for the Knights of Labor.

It is true that conditions have undergone a radical change since I wrote that letter, and the inventions I referred to had much to do in revolutionizing the processes of production; but I still think that there is a better way to bring about harmony between employer and employed than to resort to force.

Of course I still contend that coöperation is the true remedy for the ills of industry and hope to see those on both sides of the industrial fence take it up for more serious consideration and study than they have yet devoted to it.

In the meantime, it would be well for the Christian employer and workman to at least attempt to obey the command of the Jewish carpenter of Nazareth to do by each other as they would be done by, instead of doing each other as they have been for so many years. In no controversy about wages, hours, conditions, open shop, or closed shop have I heard the first expression in favor of applying the Golden Rule to the settlement of disputes between the workers we know as employers and employees.

Chapter Twenty-Seven

ECCLESIASTICAL OPPOSITION[1]

THE ATTITUDE of the Roman Catholic Church toward the labor organizations of the twentieth century is openly friendly, and a sympathetic toleration is manifested whenever any action is taken, or contemplated, on a matter of difference or dispute between the church and an organized body of workingmen. To be rightly understood, let me substitute clergymen for church, for the church as a whole never condemned the Knights of Labor in the United States. The attitude of many influential priests of the church was decidedly unfriendly, and in many places the Order was subjected to scathing criticism and condemnation. This continued until His Eminence Cardinal Gibbons[2] espoused the cause of the Knights of Labor in the latter part of 1886.

Much of the storm centered around me in those days, and since I, for the most part maintained silence in the face of attack, let me now briefly relate something of the part I took in it.

One Sunday morning shortly after I became a member of the

[1] See the Note at the end of this chapter.

[2] James Gibbons (1834-1921) was the youngest of the 1,200 bishops of the Catholic Church when he was consecrated Bishop of Adramyttum. After being appointed to more important bishoprics, he was made cardinal in 1885, taking office the following year. His seeming liberalism on the labor issue was matched by his political conservatism, for he opposed the initiative, referendum, recall and the popular election of Senators. While he was in Rome he worked actively to secure ecclesiastical support for the American labor movement. After the Canadian hierarchy opposed the K. of L. on the grounds of its secrecy, Cardinal Gibbons received from Powderly the assurance that secrecy, designed to protect the worker from attack by the employer, was imposed by a pledge and not by an oath, thus leaving Catholic Knights free to reveal everything in confessional. His plea against condemnation of the Order, addressed to the Prefect of the Propaganda, is regarded as one of his outstanding documents, and he received assurances in Rome that the K. of L. would not be condemned in the United States. His position on the labor movement was undoubtedly conditioned by his opposition to socialism. His viewpoint on the labor question is revealed in a letter to Powderly, dated September 21, 1887. It is quoted in *Proceedings of the Knights of Labor . . . 1887*, p. 1647. A note in the Cardinal's hand in Powderly's correspondence reveals that the latter requested the letter.

Machinists and Blacksmiths International Union in 1871, when I presented myself at the door of the Scranton Cathedral to attend eight o'clock mass, the usher in charge at the entrance laid his hand on my shoulder, turned me around, and shoved me toward the steps leading to the street. I knew the man quite well . . . and it occurred to me at first that he was joking. I attempted to walk around him when he again intercepted me, and said that if I did not go away peaceably he would use force to compel me to do so. Realizing that he was in earnest and not wishing to create a scene, I walked toward the door, he following close behind me. At the door I asked for an explanation, and received this answer: "I have my orders and you cannot come in here today or any other day until you quit the masons."

At that time I knew absolutely nothing about the masons and did not know to what the usher referred. I told him I was a machinist and not a mason, but he persisted in denying me admittance, and after an interchange of some language not suitable for church use I went away.

The cause of the trouble was pinned to the lapel of my coat in the emblem of the Machinists and Blacksmiths International Union. It represented the inside and outside callipers and anvil, and as I now know the emblem of blue lodge freemasonry it bore a striking resemblance to it. Some one reported to Father Richard Hennessy, then officiating at the Cathedral, that I was a mason and as proof pointed to the badge I wore. It seems that the usher was present when the priest was informed of my alleged membership in the masonic fraternity and heard Father Hennessy say that I should be excluded from the church. Taking the remark seriously, the usher interpreted it as a command, and acted as I have described.

Shortly after that I went one evening to confession to Father Hennessy, who, on recognizing me said, in a voice loud enough for a number of people who were in the church at the time to hear: "It's time you came to me, kneel down you blackguard." My preparation for confession was jarred some by that remark, and, hoping he would conduct further conversation in a lower tone, I knelt down. This done, he, in a voice louder than before, said:

"You are damn'd; your soul will roast in hell unless you quit that society."

Up to that time I was in ignorance of the existence of a society of masons. If I had ever heard the name, I must have looked on the organization as one composed of men working as stone-masons. The most natural thing in the world for me to do was to inquire what society he referred to. When I made the inquiry, Father Hennessy became very angry and threatened to horsewhip me if I didn't promise him to resign from the masons. He said a number of other things, none of them complimentary, all of them so loud that every person in the church could hear him. I was not known as one who would accept insult without question, yet I was not hasty in speech. Had it been a shopmate who used violent language toward me I might not have acted as I did, but here was a man from whom I expected better things. Remember, that as a Catholic about to make preparation to approach the sacrament, I tried to believe that priest represented God, and that my confession would be made to God rather than the priest. When he ended his tirade I arose, stepped out of the confessional, and, instead of leaving the church, as, perhaps, I should have done, said in a tone loud enough for listeners to hear,—yes I wanted them to hear it: "I didn't come here to make my confession to all these people and you have no right to talk that way to me. I can't give you what you deserve here, but if you come outside of this church, I'll give you the damnedest thrashing you ever got." . . . He said no more, and I left the church.

I investigated, obtained all the facts in relation to the matter, or thought I did, and wrote to Father Hennessy explaining that I knew nothing about the order of masons; that I was a member of the Machinists and Blacksmiths International Union; that the emblem I wore was that of the last named order and that I had been unjustly treated by the usher and himself. I never received acknowledgment. . . .

Just one step from 1871 to 1876. Edward O'Meagher Condon was then in an English prison. I did what I could to effect his release. I circulated a petition for his liberation and secured some 23,000 names to it in Luzerne County, for presentation to Congress. With three others I called on Bishop O'Hara[3] to secure his signature to this petition. He refused to sign it because, as he said, it was political in character, and he explained to us that he never meddled in any way in politics. We endeavored to show that this was not a political matter such as would embarrass him, and he summarily dismissed us, remarking to me as he did so that I was mixing up a little too much in matters that did not concern me.

In May, 1878, I was a delegate to a state convention of the Greenback Labor party in Philadelphia. I reached my home in Scranton at one o'clock Sunday, May 19. That afternoon two Knight[s] of Labor friends of mine, James White and John Rhinehart, called at my home and told me that [the] Right Reverend William O'Hara, Bishop of Scranton, wished to see me at the bishop's residence that evening. I met my friends by appointment and accompanied them to the episcopal residence.

On the way to call on the bishop I asked if they knew why he wanted to see me, but they did not explain. I did not know until after the interview terminated that the bishop had called me out from the altar that morning and had, in effect, excommunicated me by warning the people of the congregation to have nothing to do with me in [the] future.[4]

I warn you against these pernicious secret societies; they are devised by designing men to dupe the unwary and draw them into their toils for the purpose of using them as tools for their own personal advancement. We have one instance of it in this city in a man who has hoodwinked the workingman into electing him mayor. He is a busybody and a slanderer. He has circulated the rumor that I have approved of one of these secret societies; I have not even considered it. He is a fraud, an impostor, and I warn you against his scheming. Beware of being misled by such a character. Have nothing to do with him!

That's what the Associated Press carried out of Scranton that evening. Reporters weren't so busy or alert then, or I suppose I would have heard all about it, with variations, before White and Rhinehart called on me.

We were admitted to the bishop's reception room where we

---

[3] William O'Hara (1817-99), born in Ireland, became the first Bishop of Scranton in 1868.

[4] In spite of what Powderly says, he was not excommunicated, either technically or "in effect."

remained for about a quarter of an hour before he entered the room. After exchanging greetings with the others, the bishop turned to me to make known his reasons for sending for me. I am not trusting entirely to memory, and while this is being rewritten in 1917, it was originally, though more in detail, written within ten days after the occurrence. The bishop asked if my name was Powderly, if I was not the mayor, and, on my answering in the affirmative, said: "You are a bad man, a scoundrel; you lied about me and must beg my pardon, get down on your knees, sir."

I was not expecting such a salutation. For a moment I was so confused that I could not think of a word to say. When I at last found my tongue, I said: "I am not a scoundrel, I did not lie about you, and I shall not beg your pardon."

At that the bishop became very angry; he poured on me a torrent of invective and abuse such as I never listened to before. I am not, and was not then, of angelic temper; never pretended to be. That I spoke warmly in my defense is true, but I mastered my inclination to answer the bishop in kind, and said: "You sent for me and I came, is it to treat me in this manner you summoned me; if so, we may as well end this meeting now, for I shall not take any more of your abuse."

Ignoring my remarks—indeed he was so angry that I do not think he understood me—he pointed to the floor and said in a most violent manner: "Kneel down, sir, and beg my pardon for what you have done."

I refused to do so, and asked him to tell me what I had done to merit such treatment. His answer was: "You wrote a letter to West Virginia about me; you lied about me, you slandered me, you scoundrel."

To that I said: "I remember writing to a man in West Virginia concerning you, but wrote nothing disrespectful of you."

His reply to that was not calculated to place us on a peace footing: "Yes you did, you slandered me, you lied about me in that letter, you scoundrel, and must beg my pardon. Kneel down, sir."

By that time I was very angry, and said: "I wrote to West Virginia about you, I did lie about you in that letter for I said you were a kind, just man, and that was a lie, for no man ever used such language to me before. I will not beg your pardon."

He then stood up, taking the crucifix which hung at his girdle in his left hand, he raised his right on a level with his forehead and was about to speak when I took a step or two toward him and said: "Wait, don't do that, you are going to curse me, and I am innocent of any intentional wrong. Do not invoke the image of Him you represent in a wrong. Let me bring you a copy of what I wrote and then after you read it, if you must curse me, do so. Remember that curses, like chickens, are said to come home to roost. I believe I am right, you can't be sure I am wrong. Don't curse me, but let me show you just what I wrote about you."

He lowered the crucifix, and, pointing to the door said: "Leave my house, sir."

Had he been another man, I would have struck him no matter what consequence might follow. Two valued friends and co-religionists of mine stood by and heard what had transpired. I was humiliated beyond expression, for though I had but recently gone through a political campaign and had been the recipient of unstinted abuse, I had not grown so callous as to receive such treatment and bear it patiently. I answered Bishop O'Hara in this language, and now after the lapse of thirty-nine years can see no word or syllable I would omit:

"No, I shall not leave your house, I cannot; it is not your house. My father and mother came to this valley in 1829, and ever since then, they and their children have been paying into the church. In the cathedral across the lot there is money of mine, part of my earnings are in that convent across the street and money of mine is invested in this house. There's not one cent of yours in it; it is not your house; you, sir, are but a tenant here. You weren't known here when this building was erected; you are here as a servant of God. Even though you had a million dollars in it, I'll not stir a foot from it until you retract the abuse you have heaped on my head tonight. Were it a dog I had invited beneath my roof I would know enough to treat him considerately; you are the most vindictive, unreasoning man I ever met. I'll not leave your house."

He turned from me and left the room.

On the way out Mr. White told me what the bishop had said of me from the altar that morning. Both White and Rhinehart openly afterward denied a rumor circulated to the effect that I threatened to strike the bishop. I didn't offer or threaten to strike him. Our interview was substantially as I give it, except that I leave out much of the bitter, insulting language of Bishop O'Hara.

Next morning the Rev. Dr. Dunn, secretary to the bishop, came to the mayor's office and said that the bishop wished to see me immediately.

I handed Father Dunn a card bearing this inscription:

T. V. POWDERLY
Mayor
Office hours 9 to 12
and
2 to 5

I said as I handed the card to Father Dunn: "Give this card to the bishop and tell him if the hours are not agreeable to him, he may name any other hour in the twenty-four to come here or to my house, and I'll meet him; but I shall not run the risk of receiving such treatment as he gave me last night by going to his house to see him again."

Father Dunn, who was one of the best of men and a good friend of mine, said that if I didn't go, the bishop would read me out on the following Sunday and in worse terms than the day before. I made this answer:

"Tell Bishop O'Hara that if he denounces me next Sunday from the altar he will answer for it next Monday in the courts. I do not intend to be trampled on at the instigation of a lot of pothouse politicians, for I now know where the animus for the attack came from. Had I known last night that he attacked me on the altar yesterday morning, I don't know just what I might have said or done to him. I'll be in my seat next Sunday, and, if he uses such language as he did yesterday, I'll proceed against him in the courts."

I gave Father Dunn a copy of the letter which caused the trouble. That afternoon I consulted several attorneys with a view to taking action in the courts against the bishop. Catholic lawyers wouldn't take the case, and the only Protestant attorney who would be likely to do so, while an able lawyer, was a bigot whose hatred of the Catholic Church, rather than the justice of my cause, would be the impelling motive in representing me in the courts; I would have nothing to do with him.

Father Dunn, so he informed me, placed my letter in the hands of the bishop who, in the priest's presence, compared it with the document on which he denounced me and said: "This man has been misrepresented."

Note those five words, they are the only ones ever uttered by the bishop in recalling his unjust charges against me from the altar.

At the General Assembly held in January, 1878, at Reading, Pa., there was a delegate in attendance from Lewiston, Kanawha Co., West Virginia, named William L. Van Horn. While at Reading he learned that I was a Catholic, and on returning to his home mentioned that fact in the presence of some workingmen who were members of the Knights of Labor and who were also Catholics. A question arose in the locality as to whether a Catholic could be a member of a secret, oath-bound society, such as the Order of the Knights of Labor was at that time. At the request of the Catholic members, a letter was sent to me making inquiries concerning the attitude of the Roman Catholic Church toward the Knights of Labor. Following is a copy of that letter:

CLARKSBURGH, WEST VA., MARCH 21, 1878

MR. T. V. POWDERLY
   LOCK BOX 445, SCRANTON
      LUZERNE CO., PA.
Dear Sir and Brother:

              I trust you will not deem me impertinent in thus addressing you, and at the outset I beg to state that it is not of my own accord that I do so. The delegate from this section to the General Assembly which met at Reading, has stated that you are a Catholic. Owing to the extreme secrecy of the Order and the opposition of the Catholic Church to secret societies, a question has arisen in this locality, which if not settled quickly will work injury to our cause. Can a Catholic be a member of the ***** and remain in good standing in his church? It has been rumored that the bishop of Scranton has approved of the ***** and to learn the truth is why I am writing to you.

Please give this your early attention and let me know what stand the bishop takes, or if any of the priests in your neighborhood have approved of the Order please let me know and oblige,

Yours in S.O.&M.A.

(Signed) A. M. OWENS

This is a copy of my answer to that letter:

SCRANTON, PA., APRIL 3, 1878

A. M. OWENS, ESQ.,
CLARKESBURGH, W. VA.

Dear Sir and Brother:

I take it for granted that you are a member of the ***** although you do not say so in yours of March 21st and shall answer you accordingly.

Bishop O'Hara, the bishop of this diocese has not approved of the ***** so far as I know. A committee representing the locals of this city waited on the bishop and laid the matter before him. It was stated in L. A. 217 that he had learned of the existence of the ***** and was about to denounce us. This gave rise to a great deal of uneasiness here, for the greater part of our membership belong to the Catholic religion.

The committee that met the bishop were not all Catholics, but he received them cordially and went over the question with them at some length. On making their report the discussion died away and of late I have heard nothing about it. From the record of 217 I take this extract; it is from the committee's report:

"Your committee waited on Bishop O'Hara and was given a patient hearing. . . . He then informed us that he saw nothing in what we presented to him that was objectionable but he could not approve of the organization. He said that when a building association was established if the members should come to him to ask his blessing, or get him to approve of it, he could not do so because it was not a part of his duty and while he could not approve of it there was no reason why it should not be established and act. He furthermore told us that he would look into the matter and in the event of his discovering anything wrong or objectionable in the ***** he would let us know. We therefore recommend that until the Bishop takes official action against us we continue to organize and we furthermore recommend that all discussion of the subject cease from this time forward."

The above is all that has taken place on [the] matter and I do not believe we will have any trouble, for Bishop O'Hara is a kind and reasonable man, and if he does take notice of our Order I feel that he will deal justly by us.

I do not know that any of the priests of this city, or diocese, have ever taken any action regarding the Order, if so I have never heard of it and I have been secretary of this D. A. since it was first established.

Hoping the above will be satisfactory to you and that it will be the means of settling the rumor you refer to, I am,

Fraternally yours,

(*Signed*) T. V. POWDERLY

D.C.S. D. A. 16

When Dr. Dunn read these letters he remarked that the bishop had been grossly deceived by the party in West Virginia who had made a copy of my letter. It seems that when Mr. Owens received my letter he turned it over to a Catholic member of the organization, and he, or some other person, in order to cause the priest of the locality to look favorably on the organization, copied the letter and in doing so, inserted some things that made it appear that I had personally received from Bishop O'Hara an indorsement of the Knights of Labor. . . .

On submitting these copies to Dr. Dunn, and after he had read them, he asked me where my connection with the "International" came in. He was informed that there was no connection with the "International," and inquiry brought to light the fact that I had been under suspicion for a long time of being a member of the International.[5] Now it becomes necessary to retrace my steps some six years.

When I joined the Machinists and Blacksmiths International Union I was for some months the only Catholic in the Scranton branch. Early in 1872 two other Catholics were admitted to membership and at once one of them made his membership a matter of confession, and, in attempting to explain what the objects of the organization were, he dwelt at some length on the fact that it was "International." I was elected president of the Scranton union about that time and was called on by the bishop for an explanation of my membership. I stated the case just as it existed, and, while the bishop found no fault with the purposes of the association, he seemed to take exceptions to the word "International." Notwithstanding the fact that as used in the name of the

[5] The International Workingmen's Association, the First International, of which Karl Marx assumed leadership after it was founded in London in 1864, probably had thirty sections and only about 5,000 members in the United States in 1872.

union it simply meant the establishment of an organization in North America, and, [by] admitting members in Canada, Mexico and the United States, it became international in character, the word served as an excuse on the part of some person to charge affiliation with the "International" of Europe, at that time active in the Old World. My explanation appeared to be satisfactory to Dr. Dunn, and, on pressing him for his reason for asking me why he so particularly inquired about the "International," he stated that two prominent residents of Scranton had informed the bishop on the very evening that I had my interview with him, that I was not only a member of the Knights of Labor but of the "International" as well. I pursued my inquiry far enough with Dr. Dunn to learn that these two men had been with the bishop when Messrs. White, Rhinehart, and I called at his residence, and that they left the house just as the bishop came into the reception room where we awaited him. From where I sat while waiting for the bishop I had an unobstructed view of the veranda and the walk leading from the front door to the street. I saw two men leaving the house just before the bishop came into the room; I recognized them as two old party politicians . . . who had done everything they could do to encompass my defeat when I ran for mayor of the city. . . . I did not need the aid of a detective to ascertain why the bishop was so angry with me when he entered the room that night.

I had, up to that time, the greatest respect for Bishop O'Hara, who claimed to be Christ's representative on earth. Then, when I was forced to believe that he could do an injustice, I asked myself these questions: Is this man really the representative of Christ, of the living God? Does he stand in the relation of Our Father who art in Heaven? Is he, by Divine right, authorized to act for God in earthly things as well as spiritual? If so, would Christ treat me with such rank injustice? Would God, were He in person taking me to task, use the language the bishop used? If this man stands as Christ, as God, if he represents a Divine institution, how does it happen that he can be deceived? How is it that two political ward heelers can pull the wool over the eyes of Almighty God?

And if they attempt to do so, why does he permit it to the injury of a man who has not knowingly wronged any man?

My connection with the Machinists and Blacksmiths International Union, my interest in securing the freedom of a brother man from what I regarded as unjust imprisonment, my activity in the Knights of Labor, my defeating the combined opposition of the Democratic and Republican parties and winning the election of mayor of Scranton on the labor ticket, the alarm with which conservative men looked on my election, and the influence which politicians brought to bear on the bishop ran back over a track that, for me, had many obstructions. I was an agitator and as such must be watched, frustrated, and submerged, and the bishop of Scranton . . . was made the instrument of injustice in the hands of politicians. . . . I saw Bishop O'Hara as a man, a man with some of the faults and also the vices of a weak man. Then came the question: If this man is not the Vice Gerent of God, if he does not fairly represent God—as he claims to do by divine authority—is the institution he represents divine? I did not find the answer. I carefully scrutinized the doings, the conduct, and the practices of the priesthood. I came to this conclusion: they are merely men, ordinary men, men with passions, men with weaknesses, men with failings, and men whose daily lives are no better, and, in some instances, not so good as that of the ordinary workingman's.

On June 6, 1878, the General Assembly of the Knights of Labor was called together in special session by Grand Master Workman U. S. Stephens, who, in his letter calling the body together, announced that:

The business is to consider the expediency of making the name of the Order public, for the purpose of defending it from the fierce assaults and defamation made upon it by press, clergy, and corporate capital, and to take such further action as shall effectually meet the grave emergency.

A majority of the representatives attending the General Assembly voted in favor of a resolution which provided that the Grand Master Workman and Grand Secretary should have power to give to district and local assemblies permission to make the name of the Order public in their jurisdiction.[6] Since that would necessitate a change in the constitution of the Order, and since all amendments to the constitution required a two-thirds vote, a motion to adopt the resolution failed of passage for want of the required number of votes.

Before adjournment I introduced a resolution as follows:

That all District and Local Assemblies under the jurisdiction of the G. A. take into consideration and discuss the propriety of the following propositions:

1st: Making the name of the Order public

2d: Expunging from the A.K. all scriptural passages and quotations

3d: Making such modifications in the initiatory exercises as will tend to remove the opposition coming from the church.[7]

That resolution was carried by a two-third vote, and a plan adopted whereby the general secretary should be notified of the action taken on these propositions prior to the convening of the next General Assembly.

. . . . .

When the General Assembly met in St. Louis in January, 1879, it was found that no action had been taken by the subordinate bodies. On page 75 of the proceedings will be found a resolution introduced by me and unanimously adopted by the body allowing a district assembly or a local assembly attached directly to the General Assembly, to make the name of the Order public in their own jurisdictions whenever they deemed it for their best interests to do so.

When that was promulgated, District Assembly No. 20, composed of miners, mine laborers, and others working in and around the mines in Schuylkill County, Pennsylvania, took action, and by a two-third vote decided to make public the name of the Order in that jurisdiction.

The agents of the Philadelphia and Reading Coal and Iron Company had busied themselves in circulating rumors that the new Order, meeting so mysteriously at various places, was but a

6 When the request was made by a two-thirds vote.

7 There was a fourth proposition: To dispense with the founding ceremony for districts and locals.

revival of the Molly McGuires [Maguires]. To give the public an idea of the aims and objects of the organization, a public demonstration was arranged for July 23, 1879, at Shenandoah, Pennsylvania. Uriah S. Stephens (then G.M.W.), Charles H. Litchman, general secretary of the Order, Samuel Cary[8] of Ohio, Charles N. Brumm of Schuylkill County, Pennsylvania, and I, were the speakers. The meeting was held in Columbia Park, and was largely attended by workingmen from all over Schuylkill County.

When my turn came to speak, and after I had occupied the platform some five minutes, a man standing in front of me handed up a pamphlet with request that I read it. I had made very few public speeches at the time, was easily flustered, and instead of reading the document laid it on the table and continued my talk. Mine was not a written speech; I did not use notes, and, so far as I know, a newspaper man named Thomas Fielder was the only one who reported the meeting fully. He was connected with the Shenandoah *Herald* of which T. J. Foster, now of Scranton, was editor and proprietor. When I did not read the pamphlet, several men in the audience asked me to do so. I then picked it up, and as I began to read it to myself a man shouted: "Read it out loud!" Turning to the chairman, I asked him if he knew what it was, and he said that it was all right and I should read it.

It turned out to be the constitution and by-laws of the Catholic Workingmen's Society of Girardville, Pa. I read the document and that you may form your own impression, I quote as far as Article five.

CONSTITUTION

AND

BY-LAWS

of the

CATHOLIC WORKINGMEN'S SOCIETY

of

ST. JOSEPH'S PARISH

Girardville, Penn'a.

---

[8] Samuel Fenton Cary (1814-1900) was an active temperance worker in the United States, Canada, and Great Britain, and served as an independent representative from Cincinnati in the Fortieth Congress.

PREAMBLE

WHEREAS, We are firmly attached to the Holy Roman Catholic Church, the Spotless Spouse of Our Lord and Saviour Jesus Christ, and are the obedient Spiritual children of his infallible Vicar on earth, consequently we cannot without violence to our conscience enter into secret oath-bound societies, so often condemned by the Sovereign Pontiff and the Pastors of the Church. Whilst the objects our fellow workmen propose to accomplish by these unchristian and dangerous societies are honest and beneficial to our class, we cannot approve the means they have adopted. We consider that the same lawful objects may be reached by lawful and honest means in the broad light of day. Since, then, these unlawful societies are closed to us by the dictates of the conscience, we desire to be so united that we may not be led into foolish movements for want of organization, and that if any question interesting to our class shall come up for discussion, we may deliberate on it and act together, and not merely follow the decisions of others, whose wisdom we may in vain dispute as individuals.

WHEREAS, We also believe that the interests of employers and workmen are correlative and that these interests have never been served by strikes or other violent procedures. A strike is a declaration of war, and should never be made when the good relations of the employers and workingmen are to be preserved.

WHEREAS, We know, too, from experience that such violent measures as strikes have always caused a breach in the good relations that ought ever to exist between employers and workmen, and that they have invariably resulted in injury to the latter.

WHEREAS, We have confidence in the justice of our employers that they will pay us for our labor as high a price as the market will enable them to pay, and we assert that any attempt to dictate to them the method of conducting their own business, would be a ridiculous presumption on our part.

WHEREAS, That strikes are immoral, is proved by the injury to property which so often follows from them, and the dishonesty into which they force those who take part in them without adequate means of support, or reasonable prospect of paying the debts incurred during the period of idleness.

We, therefore, resolve to form a Workingmen's Society under the teaching and guidance of the Catholic Church, the only authority on earth that can guide us safely and peaceably in the order which God has established on earth.

CONSTITUTION

ARTICLE I

The name of this Society shall be "The Catholic Workingmen's Society of St. Joseph's Parish, Girardville, Penna."

ARTICLE II.—Object

To unite Catholic workingmen whom the dictates of their conscience and the Catholic Church forbid to join Secret Societies, so that they may act in concert and after deliberation on all questions relating to their labor; to condemn strikes as wrong in principle and evil in their effects, and to place before the workingmen of the Coal Region, the necessity of resorting to peaceful arbitration, in all cases of dispute between employers and workingmen.

ARTICLE III.—Membership

This Society shall be composed of Miners, Laborers, and Mechanics employed by the Philadelphia & Reading Coal and Iron Company in this Parish, and shall be governed by a Board of Directors, composed of two Directors chosen from each Colliery in the Parish, under the Presidency of the Pastor of St. Joseph's Church.

ARTICLE IV.—Branches

Each Branch shall be composed of inside and outside men of each Colliery. The officers of each Branch shall be a President, Vice-President, Treasurer, Trustees, and Directors.

ARTICLE V.—Board of Directors

Sec. 1. The Board of Directors shall consist of two members elected from each Colliery.

Sec. 2. Its officers shall be a President, Vice-President, Secretary, Treasurer, and Marshal.

The President of the Board shall be the pastor of St. Joseph's Church, for the time being.

No member under thirty years of age can be elected Director.

.   .   .   .

When I concluded reading I turned to Article five, reread it, and asked this question: "Which of the collieries in Girardville does the pastor of St. Joseph's Church now work in?"

You notice the first section says the board of directors shall consist of two members elected from each colliery, and in the second section it says the pastor of St. Joseph's Church was to be president of the board of directors for the time being. Not hearing an answer to that question, I laid the pamphlet on the table and said this:

I know nothing about this, never saw it before and did not know there was such an organization in existence. To me it looks like an invention of the enemy to divide us, and my advice is to have nothing to do with it. Your employers do not engage your services because you are Catholics and they employ non-Catholics to work with you. It is my opinion that the corporation which owns these collieries has had something to do with the formation of this society. If tomorrow they should decide to reduce wages they would act very impartially about it and reduce Catholic as well as Protestant. You have an organization which discriminates against no man and which favors no man because of his religion. I am an officer of it and should know something about it. Its aim is to help all men to improve their condition and there exists no reason why a sectarian organization should be formed in this country where men of all religions must work side by side. I am also a Catholic and have no hesitation in advising you to have nothing whatever to do with the Catholic Workingmen's Society.

A voice from the audience called out: "But the Pope advised the organizing of this society."

My comment on that was:

Well what of it? The Pope is too far away and does not understand our condition as well as we do. If the inevitable consequences of the growth of this society manifest themselves in hatreds, suspicions, and quarrels between men of different faiths, and the corporations take advantage of your differences and reduce your wages or otherwise oppress you, the Pope will not and cannot restore your wages or in any way lighten your burden. Stick by the Knights of Labor and you'll stand a far better chance of improving your lot than by dividing on religious lines.

That's . . . all I said on that platform or anywhere else on that subject that day. My question concerning the colliery the priest worked in was inspired by the wording of the article, and, in reality, was simply facetious and was so taken by my audience. I was not lamb enough to believe that society had been organized by direction of the Pope, or that Catholic workingmen of their own initiative established such an organization.

From Thomas Fielder I afterward obtained a copy of my speech and what I quote is my only reference to Pope, priest, church, or the Catholic Workingmen's Society of Girardville. Had I known as much about its origin then as I learned afterwards, I would have denounced it and its founders with all the strength of my being. . . .

The following day, the Philadelphia *Times* contained an account of the demonstration. You will find it just as I give it:

MINERS AT A PICNIC
Yesterday's Demonstration of the Knights of Labor
A Quiet Time

Special Dispatch to the Times

Shenandoah, July 23

There was a large demonstration of the Knights of Labor here today. General Cary of Ohio; U. S. Stephens, national president of the order, of Philadelphia; and C. H. Litchman, national secretary, of Massachusetts, were present and made speeches, which were all of greenback tendency. They denounced the money and corporation power. The idea that the gathering meant the consideration of a general suspension of mining in the region was exploded when a large body of workmen congregated in Columbia Park and entered into the enjoyments of the day. There was considerable money spent. The speeches of Cary, Brumm, and others were calculated to inflame the men, but the liberal treatment of Mr. Gowen and the company has rendered that work impossible at this time. Talks with the men reveal perfect satisfaction with their condition. They have no complaints to make, and they came here today, so they said, to enjoy themselves and not to conspire to strike. Mayor Powderly, of Scranton, national vice president of the order, in his speech denounced the Catholic Workingmen's Society of St. Joseph's parish, of Girardville, as organized by the Church, with the pastor of St. Joseph's Church at the head, to wean off the Irish element of the Knights. As a Catholic, he said, he respected his Church, but defied its power to break up an order organized to secure the workingmen their rights. There was no disturbance during the day, and the multitude dispersed quietly before dark.

Note the tone of that dispatch. It evidenced a sense of relief that the miners conducted themselves peaceably. . . . To get the proper viewpoint of the situation, it may be well to tell you that that part of Pennsylvania had for years been terrorized by the Molly McGuires [Maguires]. During the existence of that society everything that could be done through corporate funds and influence had been done to connect the miners' unions with the reign of terror inaugurated and continued by the "Mollies." The press of Schuylkill County was largely influenced by the then president of the Philadelphia and Reading Company, Franklin B. Gowen, and had been requested to publish everything detrimental to the Knights of Labor that could be gathered up.

On reading the report in the Philadelphia *Times*, I realized that its purpose was to create the impression that I had defied priests and church indiscriminately. Accordingly, I sent this to the *Times*:

SCRANTON, PA., JULY 24, 1879

To the Editor of the Philadelphia *Times*:

Your Shenandoah correspondent reports me as saying that I "defied the power of the church to break up an order organized to secure the workingmen their rights," etc. When the constitution of the Girardville Association was handed to me and my opinion asked, I said that I, too, was a Catholic and defied any person to say that I would not do as much for my religion as any ordinary man. So long as the Knights of Labor were organized I could see no necessity for any more labor societies; that in my opinion this would act as a wedge between Catholic and Protestant workingmen and create dissension rather than unity. If you will be kind enough to allow this correction space in your columns you will oblige me very much, for I feel that it was not the intention of your correspondent to misrepresent me. In reference to my being national vice-president of the Knights of Labor, I take pride in acknowledging that I am, and when in a short time our aims and objects are made known to the world and the garb of secrecy thrown off, you will agree with me in saying that the three cardinal principles of the Order—education, arbitration, and conciliation—are such as no honest man need be ashamed to study and practice.

Very respectfully yours,

T. V. POWDERLY

A day or two after my letter appeared in the *Times* Father O'Connor of Girardville, Pa., over his signature, published the following in the same paper:

To the Editor of the Philadelphia *Times*:

In the *Times* of July 26, appeared a letter from Mayor Powderly, of Scranton, concerning your report of his speech made at the Knights of Labor picnic held in Shenandoah on the 24th inst. The Miners' Journal and Evening Chronicle of Pottsville report Mr. Powderly as having uttered the same sentiment of defiance at the Catholic Church, and, in addition, as having denounced Catholic priests and a Catholic Workingmen's Society which was organized in Girardville last February by the approval of Archbishop Wood and in accordance with the instruction of the encyclical letter of Pope Leo XIII. It is the impression of those who were at the meeting, as it is also the boast of the Knights of Labor, that Mayor Powderly made a fierce attack on the Catholic Church and the priests of this country. He said he was a Roman Catholic, and I need not say that no one was dumb enough to believe him. He might have been once a Roman Catholic, but since his speech at Shenandoah he will not surely have the affrontery to call himself a loyal son of that church whose Divine authority he defied.

His letter in the *Times* is neither an explanation nor a denial of his reported speech; it is a mere evasion. It does not deny that he defied the Church, but it gives what purports to be what he said when shown the constitution of the Catholic Society of Girardville. In fact there is no reason why the vice-president of the Knights of Labor should explain how he can call himself a Catholic and in the same breath defy the Catholic Church and malign her priests. If he spoke otherwise his words might need an explanation, such as the Scripture gives of the renegade Prophet Balaam on a memorable occasion. It is sufficient explanation of his conduct that he stood side by side with notorious Socialists and contested with them for the foremost place in their atheistic teaching. It sufficiently explains his hatred of the Church and her priests that he is a sworn member and high officer of a society whose ritual prescribes for the meeting room "a square altar," "a closed Bible" and teaches that Christianity is a failure inasmuch as "it leaves to the Knights to develop in their prayers the highest type of devotion or admiration possible by the race of humanity" and addressed God as the "soul of Archangel and the Bu." Certainly no man who swears to uphold such a doctrine can love the Church of Christ; the high priest of that square altar of Saint Simonianism cannot but hate the priest who stands before the altar of God. Mr. Powderly is reported to have said that he came from Scranton expressly to make this attack on the Catholic Church, or, as he put it, "to take the bull by the horns." It was his part of the programme and he filled it. Mr. Brumm was perfectly safe in attacking Mr. Gowen, but, no matter how dear it may be to his heart, he would scarcely think it polite to attack the Church from this standpoint; but the managers found a man in Scranton who was not ashamed to say "I am a Catholic and I defy the Catholic Church and denounce the teaching of the Pope as expressed in the Catholic Workingmen's Society." I must say, however, that his Protestant hearers understood him to speak in a Pickwickian sense; his Catholic hearers were simply shocked.

Perhaps Mayor Powderly had in his mind the 19th of May, 1878. According to the *Times* of May 20, 1878, the venerable Bishop of Scranton had to denounce from his altar the Knights of Labor for circulating the false rumor that he looked with favor on them, and many seemed to think at the time that Mr. Powderly had something to do with circulating the rumor. The Bishop also deplored the prevalence of secret societies and said they were "devised by designing men to dupe the unwary for the purpose of using them as tools for their personal political advancement." The venerable and far-seeing pastor knew what he was saying—his words are being proved.

The Catholic Workingmen's Society of Girardville has been organized to keep the workingmen under the safe guidance of the Church and to save them from being led astray by the unscrupulous leaders of Socialism. The society makes no question of Catholic or Protestant. We are perfectly aware there is no Protestantism in the constitution of the Knights of Labor, but there is what the first paragraph of the syllabus calls "Absolute Pantheism." It is the desire of the workingmen of Schuylkill County to place themselves more closely under the guardianship of the Church which has made labor honorable, has elevated poverty to the dignity of a virtue, and has given us the heavenly precepts of humility and obedience. When it is a question of being led by the wandering emissaries of Pantheism, Catholics do not hesitate to follow her whose infallible voice, as Pope Leo XIII, says "can alone on earth render workingmen and their associates contented with their lot and patient of toil and induce them to lead a quiet and tranquil life." I will conclude this long letter by the wish that Mr. Powderly is now thoroughly ashamed of the wicked part he was led to play at Shenandoah; that he regrets his foolish and Quixotic onslaught on the Catholic Church and the priests of Schuylkill County; that he is extremely sorry for allowing his admiration of the spy McNulty go so far as to lead him to express sorrow that the good McNulty had not robbed all the national banks of the country. I thank Mr. Powderly for having brought the teachings of the encyclical of Pope Leo XIII so strongly to the minds of the Catholic workingmen of the coal regions. "Because the followers of Socialism are chiefly sought among workmen," the Holy Father says, "it seems fit to encourage societies of artisans and workmen, under the guardianship of religion." I hope that through Mr. Powderly's efforts Catholic workingmen's societies will be established in every parish in the coal region during the coming year, and that the mild teaching of the Church will also influence for good the hardworking men outside her pale, who have no one to guide them amidst the darkness and errors of this sinful world.

DANIEL O'CONNOR.

ST. JOSEPH'S CHURCH, GIRARDVILLE, JULY 29

The correspondent of the Philadelphia *Times* was the same man who reported the meeting for the papers Father O'Connor names—the *Miner's Journal* and *Evening Chronicle*. Not one of the papers said that I denounced priest or church or hurled defiance at any one. . . . Mr. Fielder had not given me a copy of my speech when I wrote the *Times*, or I would have sent that part of it relating to the Girardville society in for publication. I have never replied to Father O'Connor's unmerited attack. I did not organize any branches of the Catholic Workingmen's Society and did not grieve any when the one at Girardville ceased to exist in September, 1879, just two months after I paid my respects to it at Shenandoah.

It had happened that shortly before that time a man named McNulty had been charged with robbing a national bank. This same man was then in the employ of the Reading Company as a spy on the Knights of Labor. While I was speaking a voice in the crowd asked, "What about the McNulty gang?" I did not at the time understand the force of the question and was not aware that McNulty was operating as a spy in that locality. His alleged robbery of a national bank occurred elsewhere. I ignored the question and from several quarters came suggestions that I say something about McNulty. Here is what I said, all I said, and exactly as I said it:

I don't know anything about McNulty now. I knew him when he was a boy, we went to school together; he was a nice fellow then, and while I have heard bad things about him, I know absolutely nothing of him. It has been charged against him that he broke into a national bank, but I suppose we will have to forgive him for that for we are opposed to national banks—but in a far different way. Breaking up a system and breaking into a bank are two different propositions. I know nothing about McNulty. You who do know him are better qualified to talk about him than I.

I am indebted to Mr. Fielder for this also.

Now let me look over what Father O'Connor wrote against me. He refers to the *Miner's Journal* and *Evening Chronicle* of Pottsville reporting me as saying certain things. The dispatch that appeared in both papers, so I was informed, was written by the same man. That man got his account of what I said from those who were at the meeting (for he was not present) and then placed his own construction on it. The report in both papers, however, did not differ materially from that which appeared in the Philadelphia *Times* and which I quote above. In neither paper was I made to express one word of hostility to either the church or the priests, and whatever Father O'Connor's motives may have been, his effort was calculated to befog the issue and cause the workingmen to believe that I had attacked the church itself. . . .

. . . . .

He charged me with uttering defiance of the Catholic Church.

He charged me with making a fierce attack on the Catholic Church and the priests of Schuylkill County. He charged me with standing side by side with "notorious Socialists." He charged me with "contesting with them [the socialists] for the foremost place in their atheistic teachings." He charged me with belonging to a society that "teaches that Christianity is a failure in as much as it leaves to the Knights to develop in their prayers the highest type of devotion or admiration possible by the race of humanity" and addresses God as "the soul of Archangel and the Bu." He charges that "Mr. Powderly is reported to have said that he came from Scranton expressly to make this attack on the Catholic Church."

Nowhere, in any paper, at no time or place was I so charged. It was, on the contrary, stated in the reports of the meeting to which Father O'Connor referred that the constitution was handed to me while I was speaking. I had never seen it before, had never heard of it before; I knew absolutely nothing about the object of the pamphlet. I did not know that such a society as the Catholic Workingmen's Society of St. Joseph's Parish of Girardville had been organized . . .

I will give Father O'Connor credit with having, in his zeal as a priest, forgotten his duty as a man, in that he first assailed me and, then, possibly took time to consider the effect of his words. He must have known that such a letter as he wrote, circulating among Catholics, would have the effect of doing me injury—as it did— and it was his duty as a man to first acquaint himself with the facts, to first give me a fair hearing, to first question me and this he did not do; this Bishop O'Hara did not do. . . . It was their plain duty to have given me a hearing before condemning me, and, above all else, before bearing false witness against me.

Men and women whom I knew and who knew and respected me in the city of Scranton, who formerly received me with a welcoming smile and hand shake, when they met me, turned away from me on the street and refused to speak to me. Men and women who were Catholics, on meeting me, crossed their foreheads and turned quickly aside so that they would not have to meet or speak to me.

Only the man in whom regard for his neighbor's friendship is dead could endure what I endured in my home and not feel it.

In the city of Carbondale, the city of my birth, the priest on the altar, Father John McGrath, turned to his congregation one Sunday and, with my wife as a listener, said: "I warn you against this society that that fraud of Scranton is duping you into for his own purposes. The bishop has denounced him, and he'll soon be silenced."

.   .   .   .

I gave careful study to the preamble of the Catholic Workingmen's Society of Girardville, instituted inquiry as to where it had been printed, and who had drawn it up. I did not learn where it was printed, but I did ascertain that it was drawn up at the instigation of no workingman, and that, before it was promulgated, it received the endorsement of Franklin B. Gowen, then president of the Philadelphia & Reading Railroad. On this latter point there can be no doubt for my informant was Mr. Gowen himself. . . . Father O'Connor may not have known that Mr. Gowen approved of that constitution, but if he did not he was ignorant of his subject when abusing me; if ignorant of the origin of that document, he was not warranted in attributing it to "her whose infallible voice" he asked me to have such regard for. That episode proved to me that it was absolutely necessary to carefully inquire into every act of such a man as Father O'Connor. And when, following his assault, priest after priest stood in the pulpit to denounce me, I cannot be blamed for doubting such infallibility.

.   .   .   .

"Her whose infallible voice," as Pope Leo XIII says, "can alone on earth render workingmen and their associates contented with their lot and patient of toil and induce them to lead a quiet and tranquil life," is what Father O'Connor asks workingmen to listen to. Of course, a voice that speaks behind the mask of papal infallibility from the office of a corporation would be most likely to counsel workingmen to be "contented with their lot and patient of toil." I did not read that encyclical, I am not competent to criticize it in the absence of knowledge of its contents, but I do not hesitate to say that the workingmen of America know what is best for them, and the Pope cannot know how to apply the remedy for the wrongs they suffer so well as they can. So long as working-men remained passive, accepted low wages, ill treatment and degrading conditions, spokesmen of the church did not, as such, raise their voices in vigorous protest. . . . It was only when work-ingmen revolted against ill-treatment that priests of the church openly opposed the cause of labor. The Knights of Labor and their then General [sic] Master Workman received censure and denunciation from a great many priests . . . for defending the right of workingmen to organize for their own protection. Here and there a priest was brave enough and man enough to protest against such treatment, but it was because he was a man that he did so. The battle was fought and the victory that labor enjoys today was won in opposition to the hostility of many of the lead-ing men of the church, and history will not, if accurately written, demonstrate the contrary. Even now a prominent churchman will stand on the altar or public platform and assert that some men are born to be "Hewers of wood and drawers of water,"—that some must toil and others be their employers. . . . I do not be-lieve that Divine Providence intended that unequal conditions should exist in society, or that the church teaches such a doctrine, and, if she does, she should not expect independent, self-respecting workingmen to follow her when she counsels men to be "contented with their lot and patient of toil." Only one of God's creatures, so far as I know, is contented with its lot—the hog—all men have aspirations to improve their lot, to rise in the scale, and to reach for the best that they may aspire to. Had I, as the official head of organized labor in the United States at that time, accepted the insults of the priests who assailed me as being deserved, as was suggested to me to do, had I voiced no protest against such treatment as was accorded to those I represented, the church would not have spoken for outraged labor. It had to do it itself. All along the centuries it has had to do so, and in the end, when workingmen have won a victory by adhering to principle, then the church is never slow to accept all the honors, or rather to appropriate them and assert that it was "her infallible voice" that did it.

In those days I never heard a prominent churchman defend organized labor until organized labor had won recognition in another way. On the other hand, they have counseled submission, on the part of workingmen, to their "masters." They have advised obedience to the established order. And always have they rung the changes on that saying: "The poor ye shall always have with you." All my life have I been impressed with the unnecessity for having the poor always with us. I do not believe in that doctrine, no matter who said it. I believe it is the duty of man to so treat his fellow man that he will be enabled to bring his family up in decency—that the children of this year's poor may be educated to ward off next year's poverty; that instead of taking it for granted that we will always be poor, we should make the effort to secure a just share of that which our labor creates so that we will not remain poor. They tell me this is Christ's law. I do not believe it. I do not believe He intended, as a result of his teaching, that ambition should be smothered in the breast of the workingman, that man should remain the slave of poverty if he can honorably rise above it, and I also believe the system that makes men poor and keeps them poor should be, and can be, changed. But it must be changed by the poor becoming educated, by their discarding differences of religion and politics and acting in unison. What I say every thinking workingman in the church will say if he speaks his honest sentiments.

When I hear a clergyman preach a doctrine of submission to a superior, of humility, of contentment with one's lot, and use that saying: "The poor ye shall always have with you," I cannot be blamed for contrasting his conduct with his profession. . . . When . . . I hear that same man, Sunday after Sunday, calling for money to build a sumptuously appointed house in which to live, I ask myself why does he not live at least a little closer to that poverty which he holds up as a virtue. . . .

I know towns in which costly, elaborate churches have been built and the tenor of Sunday urging is to pay in the assessments for the glory of God, that God's house may be built in a manner and style befitting our regard for His Holy Name. In their own residence they will not live the life they hold up as being the correct one, as being the one most pleasing to God, as being the one they urge their parishioners to be content with. In the House of God they are not satisfied to officiate unless it is as rich and expensive as they can urge the people to pay for. Once in a great while a priest will be found who deplores such practices as I refer to, but he has no standing with his superiors. . . . Yes, the poor ye shall always have with you when you take everything and give nothing but platitudes in return.

I will be told—yes, I have been told by clergymen—that it is because of their improvidence and intemperance, that people are poor. If such are the causes of poverty, if poverty is a holy state, and we are, according to God's word, always to have poverty, why then improvidence and intemperance—two agents which work these results—must be regarded by God with favor; they must meet with his approval. I am led to think so, since but few priests do anything, or say anything, to banish either from their parishes. In support of this let me go back to Schuylkill, Carbon, Northumberland, Columbia, and Luzerne counties in Pennsylvania during the years just preceding the establishment of the Knights of Labor in the coal regions.

The Molly McGuires [Maguires] were all Irish, they were all Roman Catholics, they were misguided men, and they left a trail of murder, arson, and mayhem behind them.[9] Archbishop Wood[10] of Philadelphia anathematized them, priests of the coal regions denounced then, scolded them and cursed them. Bishop O'Hara of Scranton denounced them and upbraided them. The Ancient Order of Hibernians, a good charitable society, was denounced by the Roman Catholic priesthood, and its members cut off from communion with the faithful at the altar rail because the Molly McGuires [Maguires] made use of certain branches of the

[9] Powderly's remarks on the Molly Maguires should be compared with the data in J. Walter Coleman, *The Molly Maguire Riots:Industrial Conflict in the Pennsylvania Coal Region*, Richmond, 1936, a thorough, scholarly study by a Catholic.

[10] James F. Wood (1813-83), first archbishop of the metropolitan see of Philadelphia, abstained from politics and was a bitter foe of secret societies, excommunicating Catholics who belonged to the Molly Maguires.

A.O.H. in which to work their schemes of murder and arson. I listened to many a sermon against the Molly McGuires [Maguires], but never heard the parent of the criminal association denounced.

Trials were held, men were arraigned and convicted. Judgment was passed on them, and they were hanged. I went to the prison cell of one of them. I asked him how he became mixed up in this awful work and he said:

Personally I had no ill will or grudge against ———. I could not for I did not know him, never even heard of him, and do not know now what he looked like. I was drunk that night, was invited to go with these men, and so far as I know had no hand, act, or part in killing ———. I was with those who did it though and must suffer for it. *The cause of my being here is strong drink.*

Every man who lived in Pennsylvania at that time knows that it was the rum hole, the low groggery, that worked the harm or most of it. They know that in these places the schemes of murder were hatched, and they know that prominent Mollies, body masters and officials, were saloonkeepers. I venture the assertion that if the priests of the coal regions had begun, and continued, an unrelenting war on the saloons of their parishes they would have broken up the Molly McGuires [Maguires], and would have spared their people and the state of Pennsylvania, the shame of their awful work. . . . What has all this to do with my case?

When I stood on the platform on the 23rd of July, 1879, in Shenandoah I said this, among other things:

Workingmen, shun strong drink as you would a scorpion. It debases, it weakens, it ruins you. There is not a crime in the calendar that cannot be charged against it. The saloonkeeper may be your personal friend, even your relative, but he is your worst foe if you patronize him. I draw no line between drinkers; they are all in danger. If saloons had not flourished in this region, and if the men who work had not patronized them, had not frequented them, not one man would have been hanged as a Molly McGuire [Maguire]. In any event, no matter what has been done, no matter what the consequences may be to me, I shall never stand on a platform while I hold office in a labor organization without warning my hearers against strong drink, without asking them to shun the saloon, and so far as my influence will go no man who sells liquor shall ever darken the door of a local assembly of this Order.

Neither Father O'Connor or any other priest in Schuylkill County repeated my words on liquor, and they must have been told about them. A young priest in Luzerne County, on reading what I said, endorsed my sentiments and urged workingmen to act on my advice. He was the son of a saloonkeeper, too, and said he knew that what I said was best for the men. . . .

Owing to the fact that no intoxicants were sold at the picnic, a saloonkeeper of Shenandoah set up a beer stand on the roadside a short distance from Columbia Park. I was informed of this fact after the speaking was over and advised the men to pass by on the other side when going home. Most of them did. Some resented the idea of setting up a temporary saloon to catch their dimes and dollars, and used an assortment of stone-quarry language in discussing the matter with the spirituous director of the beer stand. My name, without my knowledge or consent, was used in the debate. Seven years after, in 1886, a man named James Horgan introduced himself to me in the Bingham House in Philadelphia, and in our conversation told me that he had charge of the beer stand at Shenandoah the day the picnic was held. He said that one of his patrons asserted in presence of a number of men gathered round the stand that "Powderly raked hell out of the church, the clergy, the saloons and beer drinkers" at the picnic. Mr. Horgan informed me that his employer requested him to tell Father O'Connor of Girardville of all he had heard of my talk, and that he complied with the request. Whether Father O'Connor was influenced in his assault on me by that story I do not know; you may judge for yourself.

In 1884 I delivered a course of lectures on the labor question in Maine. On reaching Portland, on my way home, I received a summons from Bishop Healy[11] of the Portland diocese to call upon him. It was on Saturday. I reached the city at one o'clock, received his message on my arrival at the hotel, and without waiting for dinner went to the bishop's residence. I sent up my name, and, with it, the information that I was very tired (the truth is I was not only tired but sick) and that if he could see me soon it would be agreeable. I sat in his reception room an hour and three-

---

[11] James Augustine Healy (1830-1900) was consecrated bishop of Portland in 1875.

quarters before he came in and then he told me he had been resting. He received me very coldly and his first question was:

"Are you a Catholic?"

I answered in the affirmative, and he continued:

"Then what right have you to speak in my state without my permission?"

Thinking that I might have misunderstood him I asked him what he meant by "his state," and received this reply:

"I mean my state, the state of Maine. You are, so I am informed, lecturing in it, and I want to know why you do so without first obtaining by permission."

I replied that I did not understand why I should obtain his permission.

"Aren't you a Catholic?" he asked.

"Yes, I am a Catholic but what has that to do with it?" I answered.

"It has everything to do with it. You are in duty bound to consult your superiors in such matters. The talks you are giving have a bearing on faith and morals, and I first want to know what you intend speaking on before granting permission to allow you to traipse through this diocese."

I arose and taking my hat said:

"I speak only on the labor question, I do not meddle with religion, I do not interfere with the faith or morals of any man, I am a freeborn American, and do not acknowledge your right, or the right of any other man no matter what his religion or position in society may be, to question me for doing that which I have a right to do under the laws of my country. If that is what you wanted me for and you have nothing else to say to me I shall retire."

As I walked toward the door he raised his hand and said:

"Stop, I have a word or two to say to you. You have done wrong as a Catholic. You should have counseled with me before speaking in this state, and I shall bring the matter to the attention of your bishop. Do not speak in my state again until I give consent."

Up to that time I listened to him patiently but, when he repeated his use of the term "my state," I became indignant, lost my temper, and told him that there were a few people in the state of Maine who did not belong to him, that human slavery had been abolished, and that it was a piece of presumption on his part to assume that Maine was all his. Perhaps I should not have said that, it did not better the matter any, but I feel that the provocation was sufficient to call out what I said, and have no apology to offer for it. I continued my lecture tour through Maine.

In the early part of the year 1886 the Knights of Labor began to grow rapidly. . . . Out of this sudden growth grew a number of misunderstandings concerning the status of the Order. Strikes, lockouts, boycotts, and other disturbances in the world of labor followed each other in rapid succession, and, while the Knights of Labor was not, as an organization, concerned in one-fourth of these troubles, the name was used in all of them. Men in an effort to redress wrongs they had endured for years reached out for a sustaining hand to the Knights of Labor, and invariably gave out the impression that the Order stood back of them. The newspapers made no effort to set the public right; in fact, the press was largely instrumental in causing the public to believe we were at the top, bottom, and middle of all the trouble.

Cardinal Gibbons had his attention called to the state of affairs then existing, and for the purpose of getting at the truth invited me to call upon him at his residence at Baltimore. Accompanied by John W. Hayes[12] and Tom O'Reilly[13] I called on the cardinal

[12] John W. Hayes was one of Powderly's closest friends until they broke completely in 1893, following some earlier differences between them. In that year Hayes played a leading role in the coalition which forced Powderly out of the Knights. Born in Philadelphia late in 1854, Hayes is still alive and active in his real estate business. After losing an arm as a railroad worker in 1878, he became a telegrapher. On the failure of the telegraphers' strike of 1883, Hayes went into business and did well. His membership in the Knights began in 1874, and he was probably connected with the Order as a prominent official longer than any other individual, serving on the *Journal of the Knights of Labor*, the General Executive Board, as Secretary-Treasurer, and, finally, as G.M.W. from 1902 until the central office of the Knights was given up in 1916.

[13] Thomas O'Reilly, who edited the *Journal of the Knights of Labor* for some time, was one of Powderly's closest associates during the closing years of the latter's term as G.M.W. In 1893 he and A. W. Wright were apparently Powderly's two most trusted confederates in the general office. During Governor Hastings' term in office, O'Reilly was associate librarian of Pennsylvania. Later he was associate editor of the *Carpenter and Joiner*, and in 1901 he became Powderly's confidential clerk in the Bureau of Immigration. He played an extremely important role as intermediary in the negotiations between Powderly and Cardinal Gibbons.

on October 28, 1886 and had a lengthly interview with him. During that interview every phase of the labor situation was taken up and discussed. The cardinal questioned me about certain parts of our constitution but never once referred to the secret work or ritual. The story circulated so industriously that I presented the cardinal with a copy of the "A. K.," or ritual, was without foundation of any kind. The cardinal did not concern himself with our rules of order or methods of conducting business. His evident purpose was to familiarize himself with our economic aims and methods of carrying them forward.

In this connection the various trade and labor organizations of that day were discussed. From press reports the cardinal, naturally enough, gained the impression that all of these organizations were part and parcel of the Knights of Labor. As best I could I explained the aims and objects of the various unions, and, in doing so, told His Eminence that I was not authorized to speak for any of them. I at the same time gave him the addresses of the officers of these organizations so that he might, if he desired, correspond with them.

Just before our interview came to a close, the cardinal said that he intended going to Rome in a short time and that he would take pleasure in placing the Knights of Labor and the American labor movement in a favorable—and proper—light before the Sacred College. During that interview I among other things explained to him that Catholic workingmen had, by the church, been prohibited from joining societies such as the Masons, Odd Fellows, Knights of Pythias, etc., and were in consequence denied the right to come in contact through these agencies with men who could be of material service to them in the field of industry; and, inasmuch as the church had hitherto closed the door to all fraternal societies except such as were religious in character, or under the spiritual direction of priests of the church, workingmen were becoming restive, and any further step in the direction of forbidding entrance to, or membership in, the Knights of Labor would be regarded by them as a blow aimed at their material well-being.

How well Cardinal Gibbons fulfilled his promise is set forth in a report made to the General Assembly at its session in Minneapolis, Minnesota.

That report, though presented in my name to the General Assembly, was written by Tom O'Reilly and published in the proceedings of that session before I had time to revise it.

Credit is due the cardinal for making an earnest defense of the Knights of Labor and of the right of workingmen to organize. I feel that at least the concluding words of his plea in our behalf should occupy a place here. . . .

The workingman has the right to organize for his own protection, and it is the duty of the public at large to aid him in finding a remedy against the dangers with which civilization and social order are menaced by avarice, oppression, and corruption. It seems to me plain that the Holy See cannot entertain the proposal to condemn the Order of the Knights of Labor.

1st. Because such a condemnation does not appear to be justified either by the letter or by the spirit of its Constitution, of its laws or by the declaration of its heads.

2d. That such a condemnation does not appear necessary in view of the transient form of the organization and of the social condition of the United States.

3d. That it would not be prudent, on account of the reality of the wrongs of the workingmen, and the fact that the existence of such is admitted by the American public.

4th. That it would be dangerous to the reputation of the Church in our democratic country.

5th. That it would be powerless to compel the obedience of our Catholic workingmen, who would regard it as false and iniquitous.

6th. That it would be destructive instead of beneficial in its effects, forcing the sons of the Church to rebel against their mother, and to range themselves with condemned societies, which they had hitherto avoided.

7th. That it would turn into doubt and hostility the marked devotion of our people toward the Holy See.

8th. That it would be regarded as a cruel blow to the authority of the bishops of the United States, who, it is well known, protest against such a condemnation.

In the winter of 1886, I was called, in my official capacity, to Quebec. On my way I stopped off at Montreal at the request of the Knights of Labor in that city, and, while there went, also at the request of local Knights, to the Bishop of Montreal[14] to ex-

---

[14] Bishop Fabre, who became archbishop in 1886.

plain the workings of the organization to him. He had several priests in attendance, and on my appearance drew a copy of the constitution of the Knights of Labor from a drawer in the table fronting him, and turning to the part in which the decisions of the General Master Workman appeared, said:

"You are the grand president of this Knights of Labor. You are a Roman Catholic; you make decisions. Is that not so?"

I answered in the affirmative. He then laid the book open before me, and, placing his finger on a decision, asked:

"Is that your work, did you make that decision?"

Again I answered in the affirmative, and he said, severely:

"You are no Catholic. You must know that the church frowns on divorce, it demands that its children shall not only not be divorced but that it shall be discouraged. What have you to say in extenuation of your offense?"

The decision to which he referred read in this way: "The member whose wife sells liquor must obtain a divorce either from his wife or this Order; the latter can be obtained in the shape of a withdrawal card."

I explained to him that it was not, with me, a question of divorce in the sense in which the term was understood by the Church; that on my assuming the office of General Master Workman I found saloonkeepers had gained admittance to the Order; that I made a decision which demanded their withdrawal; that on their withdrawing they had relatives take up the business, and some of them placed their saloons in their wives' names; and then I made the decision . . . hoping that its effect would be to drive the liquor selling element from the Order. I also told him that the decision had been endorsed by the General Assembly, composed largely of Catholics, and that not one of them imagined that he was favoring divorce of husband and wife when he voted in the affirmative on it. Then he said that it was so much the worse, since the whole body had practically endorsed the separation of husband and wife. I assured him that I would bring the matter before our next General Assembly, and recommend that a change be made in the wording of that decision. He grudgingly said that he would regard that with favor, and the interview ended. I said to him, however, that in eliminating that objectionable phrase I would have something as strong and effective take its place, so that no agent of the liquor trade could become or remain a member of the Knights of Labor.

I then proceeded to Quebec, attended to the business which called me there, and left that city without appearing on the public platform. Keep that in mind. While I was in Quebec a committee of Knights of Labor took me for a drive around the city and out to the Falls of Montmorency. In passing the spot where General Montgomery attempted to scale the heights and fell, they pointed out the place where an avalanche of rocks came down some time before and crushed the lives out of a number of workingmen and women who lived at the base of the hill. I was told by the committee that the sun did not shine on that spot after three o'clock in the afternoon.

Then they drove up on the plateau and through the city. Here I saw a high board fence around some land. Upon inquiring who owned the land, they told me it belonged to the church. They were all Catholics, and I had no reason for doubting them. When passing a church they pointed to a statue on the top of it and said it was covered with pure gold—"a sheet of pure gold" was the term used to describe it. When we had passed down to the lower level we reached a point where I could see the golden statue on the top of the church. Something in my face caused one of those with me to ask what I was thinking of. I maintained silence until pressed for an answer. I said:

You tell me that valuable, nicely located land is the property of the church and that the saint's statue is covered with pure gold. I don't know whether such is the case but you ought to know. I have seen the miserable place in which your workingmen live at the base of that rock pile, where their lives may be crushed out at any time by another avalanche, and where the sun does not shine after three o'clock in the afternoon. I was thinking it would be a good thing to take the golden coat off that statue, the saint don't need it, melt the gold into dollars, take down that fence from around that church property, erect houses there and call these poor people up into the sunlight of God where they may not be exposed to such terrible dangers. Somehow I feel that if Christ were in this carriage with us He would speak to you somewhat as I do. That is all I was thinking about.

Before they had gone to bed that night they reported to Cardinal Taschereau[15] that I said the above, and in addition urged that the chalice and altar ornaments be melted into coin as well as the gold on the statue. He, without seeking further information publicly, charged me with making that declaration in a public speech. I said it just as I tell it here; that is all I did say. I was in earnest, and believed that I more nearly voiced Christ's sentiments in saying it, than Cardinal Taschereau did when he denounced me, saying that I used that language in a public speech. . . .

All through Canada a wave of denunciation from Catholic priests swept against me because of that statement. It did good though, for many who felt that way and lacked the courage to speak out before became bolder and expressed themselves in favor of my sentiments. . . .

When priests of the church no longer denounced the Knights of Labor openly, some of them did far more effective work against the Order in another way. Shortly after Cardinal Gibbons made public the result of his visit to Rome, a lockout took place in a shoe manufactory in Philadelphia. A committee of shoe-workers called on Archbishop Ryan[16] for the purpose of asking him to have a priest of Philadelphia retract some unkind things he had said about the Knights of Labor admitting "hens to membership." The hens referred to were the women who worked at the shoe trade and were members of the Knights of Labor.

This committee was composed of men and women. The archbishop was not at home, and they held their audience with Father Horstmann,[17] then attached to the archbishop's residence but later a bishop in a western city. Before they had an opportunity to reach the matter which called for their presence there, he asked them a number of questions and he then told them to be on the

[15] Elzear Alexander Taschereau (1820-98) was appointed Archbishop of Quebec in 1871, and became the first Canadian cardinal fifteen years later. He condemned the Knights in 1885 in a circular letter and forbade religious Catholics to join or remain as members in the Order.

[16] Patrick John Ryan (1831-1911) won fame and great popularity as a preacher and orator, and was called the "Chrysostom of the West." Consecrated Bishop of St. Louis in 1872, he was transferred twelve years later to the metropolitan see of Philadelphia. He later had contact with labor in 1896 as the arbitrator of a streetcar strike.

[17] Ignatius F. Horstmann was later Bishop of Cleveland, 1892-1909.

lookout for me; I shall not attempt to quote him, for I made no note of what the committee told me but in substance it was: Have a care of that man, he is a politician, and politicians are selfish. They will use you for their own purposes. This man Powderly has his eye on the presidential chair; he wants to be president of the United States, so be careful how you act on his advice.

That committee reported to me within twenty-four hours after that interview. They did not have an oportunity to discuss the "hen" question with Father Horstmann, for all of the committee were friendly to me, the chairman especially, and, when he heard me discussed in such a manner, he abruptly terminated the interview.

That statement went the rounds of Philadelphia. I had enemies in the Knights of Labor as well as out of it, and the effect of the priest's words was to cause those who should have had confidence in me to regard me with suspicion. That harmony which should exist was disturbed, and dissension in the ranks of labor means power for those who believe that workingmen should be content with their lot in order "that the poor ye shall always have with you."

The Knights of Labor were powerful then and growing more so each day. I had indiscreet friends who would insist on naming me in connection with the presidency. I do not deny that I had faults, that I made mistakes, that I should have done better than I did. I was called many hard names, but I do not remember that I was ever called a fool. I would have earned that title had I for one moment, while at the head of the Knights of Labor, allowed the thought to enter my head that I could be elected president of the United States. I did everything in my power to head off such rumors, and never with my consent was my name associated with a scramble for any political office.

For one moment let me admit that I would have accepted a nomination for, and election to the presidency. Why should a priest of the Roman Catholic Church regard my elevation to that office with dread? Was I not as good as any other man? It was not that he feared that I would become president that he said that. I am warranted in the belief that it was his design to instill distrust of me in the minds of his hearers, and whether he intended it or not, that is just what he succeeded in doing. He said many other things of me to the committee before he reached that, things that they knew to be false . . . It is true that since then he changed his mind about me. I have heard that he later on expressed admiration for me, but it was at a time when his words could do me no good and a contrary course on his part would work no harm to the cause of organized labor. Personally I never sought or coveted praise or encomium. My aim was to strengthen the organization, make it a power for good, use that power in the interest of the lowest of the low, educate the masses to know their rights and duties, and prevent disagreements between employers and employed to the end that strikes would become unnecessary. I will add one other thing, I wanted workingmen to be sober, to shun liquor, to shun saloons and save their money. . . .

In 1887 I received another summons from Cardinal Gibbons to call upon him. I went to Baltimore and had an interview with him. It was in relation to the work done by the past session of the General Assembly of the Knights of Labor. He wished to know what had been done in the way of making changes in the constitution. Here a word in explanation of a matter that has not been published is necessary.

When I had my first interview with the cardinal he suggested that certain changes would be advisable in the preamble of the Order. I promised him to bring the matter before the next session and leave it to that body. This interview took place within three weeks after the General Assembly of the Order had met at Richmond, Virginia. At that session a committee was appointed to revise the constitution, codify the laws of the Order, and, when that had been done in accordance with the directions of the general body, to publish the constitution. The constitution was, in accordance with that plan, printed early in 1887. When it appeared, the newspapers commented on it . . . the cardinal, thinking a new convention had met and having a copy of the constitution before him . . . not finding the changes suggested therein, sent for me. I explained to him that I had no power to change what had been ordered done by the General Assembly, that my position was unchanged, that I would present the matter to the next session as I had promised. After some discussion of the cause of labor in general we parted. Before leaving, the cardinal asked me not to say anything about my visit to him, that it would not be necessary to make it a matter of publication, and, if it met with my approval, it would be best not to mention the fact that I had seen him. I told him I would not speak to any one about it, and with that understanding we parted. There was no other person present at that meeting. I did not speak to a newspaper reporter or anyone else about it, but three days afterward, the New York *Sun* published an account of my visit to the cardinal, and in doing so gave a garbled statement of what had taken place. It made me say that I promised the cardinal to change the constitution in accordance with his suggestion. There could be only one result of such a publication. I was deluged with correspondence from all parts of the Order. Some wanted to know why I took it on myself to promise what I could not do; others charged me with selling out to Rome; others said I had betrayed the interests of the Protestant members in order to win the favor of the pope, and a dozen other motives were attributed to me. Had I not been silenced by passing my word to the cardinal not to speak, I could have given the public the truth and no harm would have followed. That publication inaugurated a warfare on me that continued until I resigned the office of General Master Workman in 1893. I went to New York and saw Amos Cummings, then connected with the *Sun*. He told me that the item which appeared in the *Sun* was prepared in the residence of Archbishop Corrigan and sent down with the Archbishop's approval to be published in the *Sun*. . . .

There was no witness to the meeting between the cardinal and me. I spoke to no one about the meeting, I wrote to no one, and gave no hint to anyone concerning it. I have never spoken to Cardinal Gibbons about the occurrence, but have always believed that, if he did not authorize that publication, the confidence reposed by him in Archbishop Corrigan had not been respected.

A strike took place in New York about the time of my meeting with the cardinal. While it was not a Knights of Labor strike, members of the Order were involved in it, and officers of District

Assembly No. 49 of New York were active in the work of making the strike a success. All at once dynamite was used by some miscreant. The papers denounced—not the perpetrators—but the Knights of Labor. I was called to New York, and, while there, Archbishop Corrigan sent for me. I, in company with George Murray and Thomas B. McGuire,[18] responded to his invitation. He severely arraigned the Order of the Knights of Labor in general and the New York members in particular. He did not forget to say some unpleasant things of me. Then this followed:

ARCHBISHOP CORRIGAN. Why do you allow such men in your Order? They are reprobates, disturbers, and they are responsible for this outrage.

POWDERLY. The Order of the Knights of Labor is not responsible for this strike; the men whose names you mention are active in the work of counseling the strikers and doing what they can to effect a settlement; they are not representing the Order while so doing. There is nothing before us to show, or even suggest, that these men had anything to do with this explosion. Anyway we must take men as we find them, and when we find them we take no contract to make them better than their God made them.

ARCHBISHOP CORRIGAN. These are bad men; you must cut them off from your society or I shall take measures to put an end to their nefarious work.

POWDERLY. I do not believe they are bad men. I cannot cut them off from the Order. That is not in my power and if it were, I would not do it without a fair trial.

ARCHBISHOP CORRIGAN. You are the head of this society; you have that power; the papers credit you with autocratic power in its administration.

POWDERLY. Yes, I know they do, but their stories are without foundation. I have no such power and the papers have no ground whatever on which to base the statements you have read. You have no more right to believe these same papers when they assert that certain men are guilty of crime than you have to believe that I have autocratic powers because they say I have. There is a way to test these matters before judging.

ARCHBISHOP CORRIGAN. Your word is law with that Order, nevertheless, and, whatever the machinery of the society may be, you must put it in motion and punish the guilty, make an example of them.

POWDERLY. I have not even the power to prefer charges against these men. I can only present the newspaper accounts which have appeared against

[18] Thomas B. McGuire was born in New York City at the close of 1849, and served in the Union army when he was fourteen. Active in the labor movement from 1874 on, he was Master Workman of D.A. 49, a general lecturer of the Order in 1889, and was serving his second term as a member of the General Executive Board when Powderly was forced out in 1893.

them to their Local Assemblies and ask for an investigation. In any event, even though these men be guilty, and proved guilty, the Order of Knights of Labor should not be held responsible for what a few members do.

ARCHBISHOP CORRIGAN. You are wrong, quite wrong. Your society is responsible for the conduct of its members. You undertake to correct the evils of society in bulk [this with a sneer], and you cannot evade responsibility for what members of your society do.

POWDERLY. Am I to understand that because a few bad men belong to a society and their names appear in the newspapers as doing, or favoring, certain things, that the society as a whole should be held responsible for them?

ARCHBISHOP CORRIGAN. Most assuredly so, unless it promptly repudiates them and purges itself of the odium attaching to it from their being members. You must get rid of them.

POWDERLY. Does that rule hold good with all societies?

ARCHBISHOP CORRIGAN. It does. Were it otherwise society at large would be in danger from men, in societies, urging others to crimes they themselves dare not commit, and, these crimes once committed, the society could escape condemnation on saying individual members were to blame and not the society as a whole.

POWDERLY. That is the first time I ever heard such a doctrine and I have no doubt you believe in it. Now let me see if I understand it right. These men [here I named the five men then under discussion] are all members of the Knights of Labor. The one longest in membership joined the Order in 1880, and is but seven years a Knight. He is about forty years of age and was about thirty-three years of age when he joined us. The others are about the same age, but most of them have not been Knights of Labor more than two or three years. These men are all Irish, they are all Roman Catholics; they were born Irish and have been brought up in the Catholic Church and are Catholics now. In accordance with your theory these men must be expelled from the church, or the church will be held responsible for the crimes they are supposed to have committed. Will that be done, will you demand of the pastors of the churches where these men attend that they drive them from the church?

ARCHBISHOP CORRIGAN. Sir, this is not a matter with which you have anything to do, and your suggestion is purely gratuitous; it is insulting to a priest of the church to be so questioned and in such a manner.

POWDERLY. And furthermore, these men at best have been in the Knights of Labor but a few years, seven at the most. The Knights of Labor, from top to bottom, teaches the exact reverse of what these men are charged with. It does not counsel violence or even strikes, and so they must have acted, if they acted in this matter at all, in direct violation of the teachings of the Order of the Knights of Labor. Now, with that knowledge before you, and if it is not before you it is your own fault, for our laws, our rules and teachings are open to you, and can be examined at any time. I know the church does not teach violence, that it does not encourage its members to indulge in such practices as are under discussion, but if this Order must be held responsible for what members do, who have been with us but a few years, what shall be said of the church that has had their allegiance all their lives; how can it evade responsibility? You say that I have undertaken to "correct the evils of society," and I have no doubt you are in earnest. But give us time. The church has been in existence for centuries, its teachings are well known; these men are members of it, they have been members since old enough to reason, and surely, if the church could not make good, pure, correct living men of them in thirty-three years, you ought not expect the Knights of Labor to make angels of them in seven years.

ARCHBISHOP CORRIGAN. It is none of your business what the church is doing or has done. These men are reprobates; their example is bad; they are dangerous to the community, and must not receive the encouragement or protection of your society, or I will ——

POWDERLY. Stop right there. These men will not be expelled from the Knights of Labor, they will not be suspended even. They have not been charged with this crime by anyone except you, so far as I know, and to me it seems that it comes with a bad grace from an archbishop of the church to condemn men unheard, without trial and on mere rumor. I shall not, now, even present this matter to the locals they belong to, and, if they are attacked further, shall urge them to institute civil suits for damages in the courts.

That terminated the interview. Of course there were other things said, some of them quite personal to me and none of them complimentary. I did not name anyone, as was stated from the archbishop's house afterwards, as being likely to be sued for libel, neither did I defy the archbishop as was also stated from his residence, by whom I do not know. I only know that so far as the attack on these five men was concerned, it ended right there. I have a suspicion, however, that the stand I took had its effect on the archbishop no matter how much he may have desired to proceed against the men who were involved, or how much he would have liked to denounce them from the altar. I may also say that Archbishop Corrigan asked me at that interview if I was not the man whom Bishop O'Hara had to denounce for misrepresentation some years ago. To this I simply made answer: "You have the address of Bishop O'Hara and if you desire to know who he denounced, or what for, you can readily get the facts first hand, for I do not suppose you would believe me anyway."

.   .   .   .   .

I believe I was right that day. My conscience has never upbraided me with having been in the wrong in that controversy,
and, if I was right, Archbishop Corrigan must have been wrong.
He may have been a good archbishop, but he was not a forgiving
man. I had ample proof of his hostility up to the hour of his death.
He never forgave me for taking a stand in defense of a fellow
mortal. I did not, therefore, have to look far for a motive for the
publication, shortly after that interview, in the *Sun*, of my meeting
with His Eminence Cardinal Gibbons, and which he requested
me not to publish.

The hard work of the year 1887 taxed my powers to the utmost. I was worn out, weary, and weak when on December 11, of
that year I came from Boston to New York on the Fall River
Line. Rounding Point Judith I was taken violently ill. There was
a storm at sea, it was particularly rough at that point, every one
on board was affected, but I seemed to suffer most of all. The
vomiting brought on a hemorrhage of the stomach, and for three
months I was not able to leave my home.

The Anti-Poverty[19] agitation was then at its height in New
York. Father McGlynn was undergoing his ordeal for the stand
he had taken on single tax, and other questions.[20] Henry George
had launched a paper called the *Standard*.[21] I was well acquainted
with him and, preceding his candidacy for the mayoralty of New
York in the fall of 1886, I was on the stump in his interest. On
election day Henry George, Dr. McGlynn, and I drove round to
the various polling places for a while, and then another gentleman
named Croasdale[22] took his, Mr. George's, place in the carriage.

When the *Standard* was established, Mr. George came to
Philadelphia for the purpose of obtaining the mailing list of the
Journal of the Knights of Labor, so that he might mail his paper
to the subscribers of the *Journal*. I could not give him the mailing

---

[19] Powderly refers here to the meetings and agitation of the Anti-Poverty Society
founded March 26, 1887. It was strongly single tax in viewpoint, and its social and
economic views were colored by religious sentiment. Father McGlynn was its
president.

[20] See footnote 2, p. 188.

[21] The first issue of the *Standard*, which contained a sharp attack on the Catholic
hierarchy, appeared in New York City, January 8, 1887.

[22] William Thomas Croasdale (1844-1891) was a journalist of reformist sentiments who became managing editor of the *Standard* in 1891.

list, and told him so very frankly. The constitution of the Knights of Labor was positive in its declaration against allowing even the General Master Workman to have a copy of that mailing list. To my regret and sorrow Henry George took offense because of my refusal. He talked the matter over with Dr. McGlynn, who asked me to make an exception in the case of Mr. George. I was obliged to refuse. It is best to use the exact language:

The constitution prohibits the giving out of the mailing list. I have no right to give it out, I have no right to a copy myself. I have never seen a copy of it, and the only safe way for me is to refuse to allow it to go out. You will see from the constitution, a copy of which is inclosed, that it is not in my charge; the General Secretary alone has control of it. It seems to me that if Mr. George should send his edition over to Philadelphia and have it mailed from our office, on our mailing list, it would help him. I want to help him, but cannot do it in the way you suggest. I am under oath to administer the laws of this Order as I find them, not as I would have them, and you will, I know, pardon me for refusing to do this for Mr. George.

That refusal angered Dr. McGlynn. In addition to that, I refused to ally myself with the Anti-Poverty agitation and in no way interfered in the quarrel between Dr. McGlynn and the church.

One Sunday night, while I was sick, Dr. McGlynn, standing on the platform in Cooper Union, charged me with squandering the funds of the Knights of Labor in sending an emissary to Rome to gain the sanction of the pope for the Knights of Labor. That was at the time Cardinal Gibbons was exerting his influence to cause the pope to look with favor on the Knights of Labor. The press of the country took the matter up, and that, together with the publication in the *Sun* of Archbishop Corrigan, did a great deal of harm to the cause of labor.

When I was able to look over the papers, I saw this unjust accusation of Dr. McGlynn, and at once wrote him asking that he retract his statement. I had sent no emissary anywhere, it was not in my power to expend, or order the expenditure of, one cent of the funds of the Knights of Labor. I so informed Dr. McGlynn who, at the next public meeting of the Anti-Poverty society, again attacked me, and said he knew that I had sent an agent to the pope. I learned long afterwards that a friend of mine in New

York, Tom O'Reilly, said in the presence of Dr. McGlynn and
Mr. George one day that he had gone to Rome on an errand for
me. It was pure bluff, not one word of truth in it, and in reality
intended to enhance the speaker in the estimation of both George
and McGlynn. It was not done to injure me, but Dr. McGlynn,
smarting under my refusal to give him our mailing list, felt justified in attacking me, particularly since he was having war with the
pope on his own account at the time.

The A. P. A.,[23] then beginning to blossom out, took the matter
up and, following the publication in the *Sun*, waged an aggressive
campaign against me. Then, at a time above all others, when they
should have observed silence, a number of priests took up the
cudgel in my behalf. They invariably started out by stating that
I was a most devout Catholic, that I was a faithful child of the
church, that I had the blessing of the pope, that I was doing what
I could to mold the work of the Knights of Labor into Catholic
channels, that I had divulged all secrets of the Knights of Labor
to Rome. Each time they spoke they made enemies for me that
they were powerless to check or oppose. I spoke to and wrote
some of them to drop the matter, but it made no difference; the
battle went on, and the war grew fiercer against me. Had they
kept silent, had Dr. McGlynn not given circulation to that falsehood, had Archbishop Corrigan not published that interview, I
would not have had an easy road to walk, but it would have been
smoother than I found it. Left to myself I would have attended
to the A. P. A., but when they had such allies I found my work
very difficult.[24]

In 1891, the General Assembly of the Knights of Labor met
in Toledo, Ohio. Prior to the convention, an agitation had sprung
up in Toledo on the public school question. The morning I arrived
in Toledo a reporter called to see me to ascertain what my views
were on the public school question. I told him that I had no time
to be interviewed on such a subject, for our convention was then

[23] The American Protective Association, founded in 1887 in the Middle West, was
a typical American expression of anti-Catholicism and intolerance, similar to the
earlier Know-Nothing movement and the Ku Klux Klan of the 1920's.
[24] The charges against Powderly made by several Protestant ministers were
preposterous. See Ware, *The Labor Movement in the United States, 1860-1895*, pp.
100-101, and below, pp. 396 ff.

awaiting me. That evening a public meeting was held in a large hall in Toledo. I was to respond to an address of welcome. During my talk a man stood up in the audience and asked me what my views were on the public school question. During the morning, however, one of the priests of Toledo sent to the hotel where I stopped and asked me to call on him at once. I was not present, did not personally receive the message, and do not know who did. Word was sent to the priest that I was too busy at that time to go. That was the fact, even though I did not see the messenger. I was told next day that the priest was angry with me for "snubbing him." No thought of snubbing him entered my head; had I received his message, I would have answered it, and suggested a meeting at another time. In any event, I did not then, and do not now, see any reason why I should drop my work among a number of men and respond to any invitation at so busy a time for me.

When this man asked for my opinion on the public school question I said this:

The Order of the Knights of Labor has taken no stand on that question as yet, but I shall answer your question. Bear in mind that what I shall now say will be my individual opinion; it must not be taken as the opinion of the Order of the Knights of Labor.

I am in favor of the public schools, God bless them. I regard them as the bulwark of our national safety; in them lies the perpetuation of our republican institutions. I have not had the benefit of a good education, but what little I did get came to me through the common school, the Little Red School House, and rather than see harm come to our common school system, I would allow this right arm of mine, [I raised it over my head as I spoke] to be torn from its socket.

That is what I said, all I said, and the way I said it. . . . That did not please the priest who sent for me, and I was informed that he attributed my failure to call upon him to my hatred of the parochial schools. . . .

Again a deluge of letters came to me. A. P. A. bigots wrote me to say they found some good in me. Bigots with Roman collars on them wrote me to say there was no good in me. . . .

On learning what the priest said of me I did not, as I intended doing, call upon him.

The assaults made on me right along by the rabid socialist and

anarchist elements kept me fairly well employed in defending the
Order from their attacks. Here let me say that I refer to the
socialist element that laid its plans for reform over the top of a
beer glass, and blew their work away in the froth. The anarchist
element I speak of is that which resorted to violence in seeking
reforms. For the socialist who would make society better by
making better laws than we now have, I have respect. For the
anarchist who believes that man should be good enough to live
without the restraints of law and does his best to teach his neighbor how to be so good without blowing his head off by dynamite,
I have respect. It is not of these men I speak when I refer to
socialists and anarchists. I have respect for the belief of every
man, no matter what it is, if he is honest in it and does not counsel
evil in order to effect good.

A number of men had been tried for taking part in the Haymarket bomb explosions in Chicago. Seven [*sic*] were convicted.
Their friends wished to have the Order of the Knights of Labor
take their case up and, as a body, pass resolutions asking the
governor of Illinois to commute their sentence to imprisonment
for life. As General Master Workman I refused to entertain a
motion to pass such resolutions. I did not hate the condemned
men, I did not oppose every man doing what he could to cause
the governor to deal leniently with them, and I did not desire
their execution as has been said. What I opposed was committing
the Order of the Knights of Labor to the teachings of anarchy.
That was all that I did do, and that would I do again. In all the
years I was at the head of the Knights of Labor I did my level
best to steer that bark clear of everything but the direct line laid
down for its guidance. It is true that I recommended changes in
the laws, that I recommended advanced steps in preamble and
declaration of principles, and, if my suggestions were not endorsed, I did not advocate them. But once they were endorsed, I
did everything in my power to place them before the public. At
times I would be urged to favor some doctrine which the Republican party favored; at other times the Democrats would urge that
I take up some question favorable to that party; then the Prohibi-

tionists would solicit my effort in behalf of some of their measures. I steered clear of all of them.

Then Democrat, Prohibitionist, and Republican would at times claim me if I said, or did, something that tended their way. I never veered to right or left while General Master Workman. I was an American and a Knight of Labor, and that was sufficient for me. I did what I regarded as my duty, and was not concerned whether it pleased partisans, churchmen, or infidels. I worked for all regardless of their politics, or lack of politics, regardless of their religion, or lack of it. What I aimed at was to elevate the man who worked, to inspire him with a respect for himself and his calling, to place duty before right with him and to cause him to see the cause of others while viewing his own. . . .

Let me say that while I was General Master Workman I not only did not drink, but would not enter a saloon for fear of encouraging members to do so. I tried to teach by example as well as precept. Until I was forty-five years old I never touched a drop of liquor and then only on the advice of a doctor. I drink whisky now whenever I think it will do me good, and if I want a drink I will go into a saloon to get it and go in the front door. . . . I believed, and believe now, that the worst [enemy] to the working-man is the saloon. It has worked more ruin than any other cause. It has brought desolation to more homes than any other agency. It has starved more children—physically and spiritually—than anything else I ever knew. It has caused the murder of wives, and has driven women to prostitution . . . I did what I could to cause Knights of Labor and workingmen generally to keep away from the saloon. Once in a while I would get a word of commendation from some clergyman, but coupled with it would be some quotation about what St. Paul said. . . . I was not talking against what was good for men's stomachs, but that which I believed was bad for their brains, and it did not matter to me what St. Paul had said. . . .

Frequently it has been said to me: "The priest is only a man; he is liable to err as other men do; he has his passions, his habits, his vices as well as his virtues just the same as other men, and too much should not be expected of him." If that is true, then he has no right to be a priest. If donning the robes of priestly office does not bring a greater dignity than other men wear, if it does not ennoble, if it does not sanctify and remove the man from contact with the same passions, appetites, and sins that beset other men, then such a man is entitled to no more respect than other men. If he does not so regard his sacred calling as to at least appear better than other men, there must be something wrong with the man or his calling. One who becomes a priest swears to follow Christ. I do not know what the oath is, but it must be one which commands the person who takes it to lead a pure, godlike life. The Roman Catholic Church, it is claimed for it, is based on the teachings of the Saviour, Jesus Christ. To the letter then, a priest of the Church should obey those teachings, follow them, and give everyone to know that he is following them. There is not, there cannot be, middle ground for him. He cannot serve Christ in the morning, himself in the afternoon and the devil at night. No. He must serve God all day long. . . . How can a priest treat his fellow man unjustly if he believes in Him who was crucified? How can a priest bear malice when he stands on God's altar representing divine humility, godlike mercy, unbounded charity? How can a man blessed by God with the miraculous power the priest lays claim to be guilty of wronging his neighbor?

On November 30, 1893, I resigned as General Master Workman of the Knights of Labor. I had held the position for over fourteen years, and if ever a man gave unselfish hours to his work, I did. I do not care what censure or eulogy others may pronounce on my work. I know it was sincerely performed, that I was in earnest in it, and that I did the best I knew how within my limitations. At the convention where I resigned, a combination was formed to elect men to serve with me on the General Executive Board in violation of the constitution. Under the law, the General Master Workman had the right to nominate eight candidates, and from that number four would be elected. This combination insisted on voting for those who were not named by the General Master Workman. They did this without attempting to amend the constitution. I had no objection to their electing whom they chose, but I did object to a plain violation of the fundamental law of the Order, and I also objected to serving with men so elected. Since I was to be held responsible for the acts of these men, I could not honorably remain in that position while not being able to direct their actions. These men were believers in anarchy or socialism or both, at least they so stated. I did not question their right to hold such opinions, but did question their right to foist these views on the Knights of Labor and cause men who did not hold such views to become responsible for them. I tendered my resignation. It was refused. I tendered it again and insisted on its being accepted; it was then accepted, and I stepped out of office.[25]

[25] Ware, *The Labor Movement in the United States, 1860-1895*, p. 369 says that Powderly was removed from office, after charges had been made against him by Secretary John W. Hayes, when New York socialists, led by Daniel De Leon and T. B. McGuire, and political-minded Western agrarians, led by James R. Sovereign of Iowa, joined forces against him. Sovereign became G.M.W.

Powderly, long before this, had spoken of resigning from the office of G.M.W. in confidential letters, and he had attempted to resign before 1893. On February 19, 1892, Powderly wrote to Hayes requesting him to present his resignation to the General Executive Board. "I have not hastily resolved upon this course," he declared, "and do not take the step without having given it the most serious consideration. My reasons are numerous, many of them I do not care to even refer to, they are of such a nature that they appeal to me in behalf of my self respect to relinquish the claim I have upon the office of General Master Workman." His communication to the General Executive Board, dated February 20, 1892, reads:

"When the G.S.T. presents to you my resignation I ask that you give it careful consideration and accept it. I have always entertained the warmest friendship for brother Hayes and believe that he reciprocates that feeling but I believe that we cannot much longer remain friends. For some reason he has endeavored to alienate from me every friend I have. There is not one, with whom I am any way intimate, that he has not either quarrelled with or endeavored to have me estranged from. I do not think he is actuated by malice and yet his recital of entertaining a spite against me from 1885 until 1891, as confessed by him during the Plate Printers difficulty, almost shatters that belief.

"Of late he seems to be possessed of the idea of acquiring riches and his mind constantly travels in that channel. When we are alone for a few moments his conversation turns to great schemes and plans for organizing land companies, manufacturing companies, or some other kind of a move toward getting rich. I have listened to him up to this time but of late it has appeared to me that the matter will eventually assume a serious aspect. Officers of a labor organization should not be mixed up in anything like speculative affairs of any kind but to my oft repeated objections to such moves he says: 'Oh it will only be a nine days wonder anyway and we may as well make the most of it.' If I speak to him as I sometimes feel he may do, as so many have done and assail me for other reasons and I don't want to have any more fights with officers, members, or others in a labor organization. I prefer to get out quietly and allow matters to run on as I feel they will without me. To speak frankly, when I have to humor a man for whom I have done all that I could it is time for us to part company. I do not care to say this in his presence for he will treat it as lightly as he does my objections to his schemes. I do not wish to sacrifice his friendship and ask that you accept the resignation."

The combination that effected that purpose was made up of Roman Catholics and members of the A. P. A. and members of the A. O. H. acting in unison. It is true that other Catholics stood by me, equally true that no A. P. A. stood by me, and I mention the complexion of this combination merely to show how men can set aside their religious bigotries when some selfish end is in view.

After I left the office I heard it said, I read it in the papers, that it was the A. P. A. that caused my resignation. I heard it said, but never saw it in the papers, that the masonic order had a hand in the transaction. I was told that in a certain masonic lodge the plan had been laid to encompass my overthrow as General Master Workman.

I went to my home in Scranton on the night of November 30, 1893. On December 1 I took up the study of law. I had registered as a student when first elected mayor of Scranton. On September 24, 1894, I was admitted to the bar after ten months of persistent study. I had done in ten months, at the age of forty-five, what even a younger man should have taken three years to do. It told on my health, but I recovered. While building up a law practice I had to do other work, for I sacrificed over five thousand dollars on resigning the office of General Master Workman. In order that other officials, clerks, etc., might receive their salaries, I allowed mine to remain in the treasury, and there it remained. I endeavored to get it afterwards but could not.

I did some lecturing here and there. I received many offers to lecture from Chautauqua and accepted such as I could fill. I was never asked to speak at a Catholic gathering, and . . . the report so industriously circulated at the time that I would not talk at the Catholic Chautauqua was without foundation. Those in charge of the institution know that I was not invited and could not, therefore, accept or refuse. But for accepting invitations to talk at these other gatherings, and for attending, I was severely criticized by a certain priest, Father O'Reilly of Scranton. One day I lectured in Prohibition Park in Staten Island, N. Y. While I was talking a man handed me a clipping from a paper which gave an account of the homecoming of a bishop. He asked me to comment on it. All I did was to read the clipping, which told of the beautiful white horses, four in number, that drew the bishop's coach, of the gold-mounted harness, of the carpet laid from the coach to the bishop's door, and of the presentation to the bishop of a sum of money. It was a Protestant bishop of some denomination, but I do not remember which. All I said by way of comment was:

That bishop did not appear to be walking in the footsteps of Him who came to this earth through a manger to teach humility. He had no horses with gold-mounted harness to draw Him; He rode on an ass and while there may have been asses engaged in this proceeding, they were not in front of, or drawing that coach. I don't think that bishop fairly represented Christ on that ride.

That is what I said; that was all I said, and neither in that speech or any other one did I mention the name of the bishop . . . it was contained in the clipping I read from.

A newspaperman in Scranton saw [a] reference to the matter in the press, and in a lengthy article he commented on it, intimating that I referred to Bishop O'Hara of Scranton. I was severely handled in that article, and I wrote a letter explanatory of what transpired at the meeting; it did not make matters any better so I let it drop. I did not refer to Bishop O'Hara; he was not in my mind. What I said was entirely without feeling and based entirely on the clipping I quoted.

A client came to me about that time and after some shifting around he said he would settle with me and take the case to another lawyer. I questioned him, and after some hesitation he told me that Father O'Reilly of the Cathedral Parish advised him to get a more experienced attorney than I was. [The] Right Reverend William O'Hara who denounced me in 1878 was still bishop of Scranton and the immediate superior of Father O'Reilly.

Soon after a young man, connected with me in the labor and temperance movements, called and said that in a conversation with this same priest he [Father O'Reilly] assailed me bitterly and warned the young man to have no dealings with me because I was a mason and, as a consequence, was not a Catholic. I asked permission to repeat to Father O'Reilly what he had told me; he refused to do so for fear of incurring the priest's displeasure. I let the matter drop.

I had a client named Swift, a Catholic, one whom I admired as a man, apart from any business contact with him. I was conducting his case to his satisfaction, in fact had been successful in his interest, when he came to me and confidentially informed me that a friend of his had advised him to get a more experienced lawyer. On questioning him he said it was Father O'Reilly. He then asked me if I was a mason. I questioned him as to whether Father O'Reilly had told him I was a mason, but elicited no information. I had heard a story about guessing eggs when you see shells. I thought I saw shells. Notwithstanding the fact that Mr. Swift's matter had been conducted to a successful termination, he left me. Perhaps Father O'Reilly told him not to pay my fee.

I knew Father O'Reilly to see him, but was not acquainted with him. I called at his residence one day to ask why he made such statements concerning me. As I approached the house Father O'Reilly entered it, and must have seen me. I was told at the door that he was not at home.

In several ways I was made aware of his enmity, and up to this hour I have not been able to ascertain the cause of it. That was in 1895. In 1897, I left Scranton to become Commissioner-General of Immigration by appointment of President McKinley. On one of my visits to Scranton a friend asked me what I had done to Father O'Reilly and followed with a statement to the effect that the priest had used bitter, even vitriolic language in referring to me. Among the things he said was: "Mr. Powderly had the backing of the masons or he'd never get that appointment. He has had that society back of him for years or he would never have gotten along as he did. He'll come to the end of his rope before long though."

That was a few days after Christmas, 1897, and though the end of my rope has not been reached yet and it is now 1917, Father O'Reilly, Father Hennessey, Bishop O'Hara, Father O'Connor, Cardinal Taschereau, and Bishop Horstmann have all reached the end of theirs. . . .[26]

[26] On March 18, 1920, Father John McGrath, who denounced me in Carbondale, Pa., in 1878, died in Denver, Colorado. [Powderly's note.]

One day in the year 1900, a committee of three, representing the Knights of Columbus, called at my office in the Treasury Department, Washington, D. C., and invited me to become a member of that order. . . . They very fully explained the aims and objects of the order, and, in the conversation that followed, one of them said something about the secrecy of the society. Here I asked if it was really a secret society and received this answer: "Yes, it is secret except to the church. In a word it may be said, indeed it has been said, that the Knights of Columbus are the Catholic free-masons." That committee, composed of courteous gentlemen, left the application with me, and, when they retired, my thoughts traveled back to 1871 and then down the years to the moment that committee left me.

I recalled every incident connected with my work in the Machinists and Blacksmiths International Union, the Industrial Brotherhood, and the Knights of Labor wherein the question of church authority had been raised, and this came to my mind. While I was General Master Workman of the Knights of Labor, I made it a practice to get to the scene of dispute as quietly as possible. My aim was to reach there before trouble started, before either side, employer or employed, got a chip on the shoulder, for I realized that there was, and I think always will be, a knocker for every chip. I managed, whenever I could, to get to town before the time set so that I could look the field over without the aid of committee or brass band. On walking about, I usually selected some man wearing a masonic emblem as a person to make inquiry of. That day, holding the petition of the Knights of Columbus in my hand, I recalled the fact that never once was I misled or misinformed as to local conditions by a man who wore the masonic emblem. If that man was not a party to either side of the contention or dispute, he invariably gave me a candid, truthful account of the trouble. Often I had said to myself: "That organization must be based on sound principles to attract such men to it." I never filled out the application of the Knights of Columbus.

Shortly after, I obtained a blank petition for the degrees in a masonic lodge, and on October 2, 1901, was initiated as an entered apprentice in Osiris Lodge No. 26 of Washington, D. C.

I have since then taken all the degrees in the York and Scottish rites of freemasonry except the 33d, and at every step have expectantly looked forward to the next to ascertain why the church is opposed to freemasonry. I have not yet found a good and sufficient reason for that opposition.

It was reported to me by a man who claimed that he had it on good authority that the plan to embarrass me and drive me from the head of the Knights of Labor was laid in a masonic lodge. The number and location of the lodge were named. Some two years after I became a mason I visited the lodge in question and made inquiry in such a way as to elicit full information.

I was given permission to examine the records of the period when the alleged plot against me had been formulated. I was privileged to meet and question the men who held office in the lodge at the time. The same man who was secretary in 1893 was secretary of that lodge in 1903; he assured me that no such action had ever been taken, and, to his knowledge, my name had never been mentioned in the lodge.

.   .   .   .

I need hardly tell you that I was taught to believe that the Catholic Church was of divine origin and the events I have related caused me to question that teaching. I have come to the conclusion that while the Catholic Church is a marvelous and wonderful institution, the practices of many of its spokesmen are neither godlike nor divine. Divine or not, it is the most admirably arranged and skillfully managed of all worldly institutions. Made by men away back in the dim-lit centuries, it has been managed and continued by men up to this hour. Able men, educated men, good men, bad men, and indifferent men, but men they were who have guided its wonderful march through the years. Some of the best men I ever knew were Catholic priests, but I have known just as good men who were Jews, Protestants, agnostics, or infidels. They were good because they were men, and not because they were priests. Some of the most vindictive, revengeful, arrogant, and intolerant men I ever met were Catholic priests and bishops, but they were vindictive, revengeful, arrogant, and intolerant because they were men and not because they were clerics. Becoming priests did not make better men of them. . . .

Many a priest of the Roman Catholic Church in the day I am speaking of was a tyrant by nature, and his elevation to the priesthood gave him the opportunity to exercise, in a limited way, his tyrannous will. Perched upon a lordly summit from which he looked down on the poor as something to drive, to coerce, to brow-beat and berate, he seldom exercised toleration, moderation, or charity in dealing with the poor of his charge. When driving, coercing, and berating failed, this ecclesiastical autocrat would not hesitate to "launch the curse of Rome" at the head of the offending one. Up to this self-exalted figure of overbearing arrogance, poor men looked in awe, before it they bowed in abject subserviency, and to it they yielded an unquestioned obedience. They had been taught, as I was, to regard the person of the priest as sacred, to look upon priest and church as one, and as a consequence to talk back to a priest, or contradict him in any particular, was something then unheard of. Such a priest was never slow to point to any misfortune befalling one who refused to yield to his wish, will, or whim as the vengeance of God for disobeying the priest. To invoke God's wrath for some act of disobedience or disrespect shown such a priest as I describe was not unusual in those days. The idea of visiting the erring one and reasoning with him in kindly spirit did not appeal to the priest who assumed to direct the hand of God in a vengeful instead of a forgiving way. Unfortunately, it was the priest of this type that I frequently had to meet and deal with in the stormy days when I was active in trying to change the old order to the new.

. . . . .

My idea of a priest is not that of a person following an iron rule in governing from above, but of one who governs himself wisely in temper, speech, and conduct, and who unfolds the teachings of religion in wisdom, charity, and kindness.

While the treatment I was subjected to—and I have not told a tenth of it—shook my belief in the Catholic Church, my faith in the goodness of God was never disturbed. On the contrary, the more I reflected on the conduct of churchmen, the more convinced did I become that such as these could not fairly, honestly, truthfully, or lovingly represent God. A man who could not deal patiently with a fellow man, who could not or would not give one kind word to that fellow man, could not, cannot represent Him who gave His life for that man. . . . My belief in the existence and goodness of God gave flat denial to the claim of mortal to stand in His place or act for Him on earth.

The existence of God cannot be hidden from reasoning man. He speaks to all men in all languages. He walks with all men on all their journeys through life and in all lands. He is alien to no man or clime. . . . He speaks to man in every zephyr, every wind that blows and through every rustling leaf. . . . Infinitely wise, He knows all things. Infinitely just, He can do no injustice. Infinitely merciful, He cannot be cruel. Infinitely loving, He cannot hate. Infinitely perfect, He cannot harbor anger, envy, malice, jealousy or revenge. He talks to all men and always at all times, in all places He may cause His hearers to understand Him. He does not need the aid of earthly tribunal to interpret His message to man. . . . So brilliant, so luminous, so clear is the light He holds before the feet of men that no one need go wrong. The natural instinct in every human heart is to be honest, truthful, kind, and just. "Live honestly, injure nobody, and give to every man his due" is God's law.

Believing in God, I can place no man before Him. To no man does He give orders or commands through the lips of another man. He has never commissioned any man anywhere at any time to tell me to obey my fellow man unless I am party to making the law which that man may be authorized by common consent to administer. Every soul stands equal before God's law. He has no favorites. In His eyes I stand the equal of every other man; if I am the equal of every other man, then I shall "call no man master" at the behest or command of another man. This I would have to do were I to follow the guidance of such men as Father O'Connor of Girardville, Pa., as pointed out in his letter of July 29, 1879.

That letter was written thirty-nine years ago, it is now

1917. . . . Thirty-nine years ago the church, or more properly speaking many of the men who represented it, frowned on every effort of workingmen to improve their condition through organization. I have listened to priests condemn men from the altar who were on strike. I have inquired and ascertained beyond question that in certain mining towns corporation funds had been donated to the building of churches in which workingmen were denounced for striking against the donating corporation. I do not say that Father O'Connor accepted money from the Philadelphia and Reading Company, for I do not know what he did. If I knew it, I would say it. But I ask you to read again his letter against me to the Philadelphia *Times*, . . .

. . . Franklin B. Gowen, president of the Philadelphia and Reading Coal and Iron Company . . . is dead, but before he died he told me that he went over, approved, and even made changes in the constitution and by-laws of the Catholic Workingmen's Society of Girardville, Pennsylvania. During our conversation Mr. Gowen said: "I had no dread of socialism or socialists. My fear was that the Molly McGuires [Maguires] would be galvanized into life again."

It could not be socialism that Father O'Connor dreaded. Uriah S. Stephens, Charles H. Litchman, and General Cary are all dead, but no word or act of either at any time or place on earth could give any man cause to brand either one a socialist. On the contrary Stephens and Litchman were avowed enemies of socialism. I don't know what Charles N. Brumm's attitude toward socialism was or is. I do know that not one sentiment in favor of socialism was uttered that day at Shenandoah.

I am not a prophet but I venture this prediction. A day will come when what is best in socialism will prevail, and when that hour dawns the movers on the world's stage will witness the representatives of the Roman Catholic Church occupying front seats on the band wagon, holding the lines, claiming full credit for inaugurating the new era and for being the real authors of socialism. The church never changes, they say. You who read these lines may not live in the time when what I say shall come to pass, and men who shall live in that day cannot of their own knowledge deny or affirm that the church opposed socialism in the closing years of the nineteenth, or the opening days of the twentieth century. . . .

I am well aware that it may be said the priest who condemned the Knights of Labor did so on his own responsibility, and the church should not be held responsible for what he said or did. I agree with that, but the church is made up of its people; it is not the inanimate stone or marble of which the building is composed that constitutes the church. Representative men, duly ordained to administer the affairs of that great organization, are the church. When they speak, the church speaks, and that such men are fallible and can err, every thinking man now knows. As a whole the church never condemned the Knights of Labor or me, but representatives of the church did, and that was sufficient for me.

.   .   .   .

A few more words and this story of where my work crossed currents with the church—or its spokesmen—shall end. As an individual atom I would never, perhaps, have incurred the censure or merited the approbation of a solitary churchman. My beliefs, or disbeliefs, would no doubt have escaped public notice had they not prompted me to give practical effect to them. I believed that He who said, "The laborer is worthy of his hire," spoke the truth, and my aim was to win for the laborer a full, just reward for his toil. Perhaps I did not always do the wise thing, but, so far as intent was concerned, what I did was honestly done. Never was I inspired by a wholly selfish motive or actuated by a desire to further the ends of personal ambition. A desire to serve others in the labor movement was my purpose. In doing that, I was not inspired by hatred of the employer. I never believed that he was wholly wrong or that the workingman was wholly right. I believe I was, in a measure, successful in causing workingmen and women to regard their labor as honorable, to become more self-reliant and independent and to realize the value, to themselves and to the community, of their labor. Instilling in the minds of the workers a desire to be free from boss rule, particularly industrial boss rule, was the gravamen of my offense. I am persuaded, therefore, that attacks on me or my cause for the alleged reason that I was a member of, or represented, a secret society were mere pretexts to cloak the real motive back of them.

If it was wrong for the Order of Knights of Labor to be a secret society in 1879, it cannot be right for the Knights of Columbus to be a secret society in 1917. It may be urged in this connection that the Knights of Labor was oath bound, and members of the Knights of Columbus are pledged to secrecy by a word of honor. That argument has no weight whatever, for the honorable man who passes his word to keep a secret is as solemnly bound to observe secrecy as he who takes an oath to do so. I never favored an oath to bind Knights of Labor to secrecy, and, when the oath was finally abolished, it did not diminish the virulence of the opposition to us. In fact, it was after the abolition of the oath that the Order of Knights of Labor was condemned by the church in Canada.

Read and read carefully the preamble of the Catholic Workingmen's Society of Girardville, Pennsylvania, where it says that Catholics cannot "as obedient children of His infallible vicar on earth enter into secret oath-bound societies so often condemned by the Sovereign Pontiff and the pastors of the church." The oath was abolished in the Knights of Labor in 1881, yet Catholic members of the Order were in many places throughout the United States denied the sacraments of the church until Cardinal Gibbons took the matter to Rome in 1887. Even then, priests in some localities manifested hostility to the Knights of Labor.

One day in conversation with Father Thomas Ducey of New York, who was always friendly to us, I asked him why the church opposed the Knights of Labor since we were no longer oath bound, and he said that it was due to the fact that we were pledged to secrecy; that our maintaining secrecy gave the public cause to believe that we contemplated, or were doing, something inimical to the interests of society; that if our objects were good there existed no reason for secrecy.

Again I ask you to read the preamble of the Catholic Workingmen's Society of Girardville, Pa., particularly that part of it which says "we consider the same lawful objects may be reached by lawful and honest means in the broad light of day without secrecy," and then ask yourself why the church now favors the Knights of Columbus, secret as that order is, when it cannot allege as a reason for secrecy that its members would be discharged or victimized by corporation or private employer because of membership in it. Ask yourself still another question: has not the church changed its attitude since 1879?

.   .   .   .

I write these lines without feeling. I am deeply conscious of the importance of what I utter and desire that the truth, which can injure no one except possibly the one who tells it, should be told. I feel that time has vindicated me and the work I did, or tried to do, in other days. I feel that God must have looked with approving eye on that work, or it could not now have the support of so many good men and women of all shades of religious and political belief. I am satisfied that in the main I was right, and am prepared to face my Creator in the firm belief that to Him alone shall I answer for "every word spoken, act done or object intended" during the time I held the commission with which Knights of Labor honored me as their General Master Workman.

.   .   .   .

To be a sincere, practical, and devout Roman Catholic, one should believe in all that the church teaches. If his conscience prompts him to rebel against edict, command, or dogma of the church, he, while he may give no outward sign, either strains or severs his relation to the church fully as much as though he openly avowed his disbelief. If he ignores the voice of conscience, and continues to remain outwardly a professed member of the church while inwardly rejecting her tenets, he becomes a hypocrite, and if the church is that divine institution its spokesmen proclaim it to be, then such a man is lost. I say lost, for while he may deceive his fellow men, while he may conceal his real self from his confessor, he cannot conceal anything from God, and, as he must know his own heart, he must also know that outward semblance of devotion or piety will avail him nothing with God.

Frequently, when at my desk, during my Knights of Labor

service, I raised my eyes to a picture of the Crucified Christ on the wall confronting me. Always I wondered why men who spoke in His name did not walk in His footsteps. Were they His representatives or merely mouthpieces, and was their service but lip service? I often asked myself this question: If Christian teachers had always followed Christ in word and deed would we need such an organization as the Knights of Labor? I have read the life of Christ, have pondered over His teachings, His effort, and have asked whether I could take a vow to follow Him and then refuse, or fail to travel the road He walked.

It is a solemn thing to pledge oneself to be a follower of Christ. A weighty responsibility rests upon such a man, a responsibility that should not be shifted, evaded or lightly laid aside. Expediency, self interest, love of place or power, envy, anger, hatred, and ill-will must all be laid on the altar of service to God through serving man when a promise is given to follow in the footsteps of Jesus Christ.

Am I not justified in saying that all who profess do not practice? Christ practiced what He professed.

Christ taught humility.

He taught that no favoritism should be shown.

He loved the poor.

He daily walked among the poor.

He denounced the unjust rich.

He took the side of the laborer in the unequal struggle of life.

Christ preached absolute, undeviating justice.

Christ was merciful to the sinner.

He despised riches for himself.

He had not whereon to lay His head.

He not only gave to the poor but commanded others to do so.

He sternly forbade man to bear false witness.

I have enumerated some of the things Christ professed and practiced. Now carefully, with unbiased and impartial eye scan the record made by those who have taken vows to follow Him, and you may agree with me in saying that all of them do not practice what Christ taught.

They do not practice humility.

They play favorites.

They do not love the poor.

They do not walk among the poor.

They do not denounce the rich.

They do not take the side of the laborer in the struggle of life.

They do not preach, teach, or practice absolute, undeviating justice.

They are not merciful.

They do not despise riches.

They live in palaces, when they can, instead of not having whereon to lay their heads.

They do not give to the poor.

They bear false witness.

This indictment, bear in mind, is based upon the practices among many Roman Catholic churchmen . . . from 1871 to the time when the laboring men of America caused the world to change its attitude toward the man who earned bread in the sweat of his own face. I had something to do with that change in the attitude of society.

During all the time I was under fire I maintained silence. No sound of opposition to, or criticism of church or churchman passed my lips. No word of mine can be quoted as against either.

I have named a few of the Catholic clergymen who were not friendly to the Knights of Labor or to me, and it is but just to say that I never believed they fairly represented or exemplified the Christian spirit of the church in their conduct. After Cardinal Gibbons returned from Rome in 1887, Archbishop Ireland, Bishop Keane, Father Francis Carew of Carbondale, Pennsylvania, [the] Rev. Edward Molloy, and [the] Rev. P. J. McManus of Scranton, Pennsylvania, [the] Rev. John Loughran of Minooka, Pennsylvania, [the] Rev. Father McKenna of Marlboro, Massachusetts . . . Father, later on Bishop, Thomas F. Conaty, and many other priests whose names do not occur to me, became openly friendly to the Knights of Labor.

During the great Southwest strike on the Gould system in March and April, 1886, [the] Rev. C. F. O'Leary of Missouri, rendered invaluable service to the striking Knights of Labor.

Advising and protesting against violence and violation of law, he fearlessly championed their cause. No man in or out of the organization did greater service to the men than Father O'Leary. So earnestly and zealously did he strive for a just recognition of the rights of labor in that great struggle that he incurred the enmity of a great many employers and businessmen along the traffic lines affected by the strike. They complained of his activities to his bishop, and he was subjected to ecclesiastical displeasure for a long time.

.   .   .   .

When I laid down the burden of official responsibility and care in Philadelphia on November 30, 1893, by resigning as General Master Workman of the Knights of Labor, open opposition to me on the part of over-zealous churchmen ceased so far as the world at large could observe.

I determined that should I again take a prominent part in labor matters I would not expect to find ecclesiastics any different from or any better than other men. . . .

I had seen enough and endured enough to become convinced that priests of the church, whether acting as priests or private citizens, were just as likely to err as other men. . . .

As one free from the responsibility of office in the Knights of Labor, I resolved that my life onward would be free from dictation from any other mortal, that I would render no account of my dealings with my fellow man, or my belief in God, to any other man on earth.

I have tried to so lead my life as to injure no man in word or deed, to pay my debts, to help others without ostentatious display whenever and wherever I could, and, in so doing, recognize no creed, clime, condition or color. I claim the right as an American, freeborn and under the tongue of good report, to serve God in my own way in dealing fairly and squarely by all of His children with whom I come in contact.

When the last day shall end for me, and I am summoned to answer for the good and bad I did on earth, I shall stand there all alone. No tribunal or institution or man of earth shall be potent to aid or injure me. I do not believe that God will ask what country I came from, or whether I professed a creed. I shall be judged there by the record I made here. I believe He will hold the scales level and with even hand as my virtues and vices are placed in the balance. By them shall I be judged. Knowing all things He may not question me, but should He do so He may ask: "How earnestly and honestly did you, Terence Vincent Powderly, strive to do unto your neighbor as you would have your neighbor do unto you?"

NOTE

Norman J. Ware, who is sharply critical of Powderly throughout his volume, says that "In no other relationship did Powderly show so great dignity and ability as in his handling of the problem of the Order and the Church." (*Op. cit.*, p. 102.) When Cardinal Gibbons appeared on the scene, the issue was an extremely critical one.

In the nineteenth century, the acceleration of the Industrial Revolution, the growth of trade-unionism, the spread of Marxian socialism, and other related developments had affected the relationship of the Church to the masses. The growing gulf between the two and the Church's fear of the expansion of radicalism lay behind the *Rerum Novarum* of Pope Leo XIII and the appearance of official Catholic labor organizations and a social program. In the United States, however, there has been no large-scale effort to create a distinct Catholic labor movement. An attempt in this direction after the encyclical of 1891 produced sharp objections on the part of American labor leaders. This may be ascribed, in part, to the position of the Catholic Church in this country and to the fact that so many of its members were the lowly Irish.

As Irish workers became union members, their point of view began to be somewhat reflected by the Church, which undertook the task of guiding union thought, policy, and action in the proper channels. David J. Saposs has remarked that in the period between the close of the Civil War and the Spanish-American War, the Church "busied itself in guarding its faithful against misbehavior which might bring scorn, condemnation, and discredit upon the Church. It was, however, more concerned that its faithful be not misled from the path of theological righteousness for fear that it might lose control over them. In other words, it was interested in seeing that the labor movement provide the proper moral and theological environment." ("The Catholic Church and the Labor Movement," *The Modern Monthly*, May, 1933.) The need for this was specially emphasized by the Molly Maguires, for those involved were Irish and apparently Church members.

The Church was traditionally hostile to secret societies, especially to those with rituals and vows which might conflict with the confessional. Opposition to labor organizations marked by secrecy, as so many then were, was, therefore, to be expected. The attitude of the priests in the Pennsylvania mining counties where the K. of L.—founded by Protestants—was gaining Catholic members was generally unsympathetic and thrust the question of the secrecy of the Order to the fore. The condemnation of the Knights by a priest in Schuylkill county affected its growth there, and was responsible for the special session of the General Assembly in Philadelphia (June 6, 1878), to consider making the name public. Powderly, of course, favored the move in this direction.

As the Knights grew in numbers—and in seeming strength—in the middle eighties, the hierarchy of the Church became concerned. In Canada, it took decisive action, and condemned the Order. Cardinal Gibbons was farseeing enough to recognize the danger of repeating in America the blunders which had alienated a significant segment of the industrial working class from the Church in Europe. When he, in conjunction with Powderly, saved the Knights from condemnation, he accomplished a task of major importance, and influenced the future development of the American labor movement. As a result of this, the strong position of the Irish and Catholics in that movement was made possible. This, in turn, it may be added, helps to explain the conservative character of American trade-unionism.

Chapter Twenty-Eight

EQUAL RIGHTS FOR BOTH SEXES

IT WAS WITH no small degree of satisfaction that I saw the Nineteenth Amendment to the Constitution of the United States give life and practical effect to the twentieth declaration of the Preamble of the Knights of Labor. When the first General Assembly met in Reading, Pennsylvania, in January, 1878, it adopted the Preamble referred to. . . .

The thirteenth . . . declaration of that Preamble was: "To secure for both sexes equal pay for equal work," and for many years it expressed the opinion of Knights of Labor on the equality of labor so far as compensation was concerned.

. . . I had grown up in the belief that the product of the human hand or brain, speaking for the producer, proclaimed that there should be no sex in industry, and that the worker should be awarded full and fair compensation as well as recognition for labor done, regardless of sex.

The economic pressure which forced women into stores, shops and factories was not so well understood by men workers at that time as to cause them to realize that the women were not interlopers intent on taking their jobs from them. When I questioned members of the General Assembly of the Knights of Labor as to their willingness to admit women to membership in the organization, I did not strike a very responsive chord.

One of my first moves in the direction of admitting women to membership was to prepare a resolution having that object in view, but, before it was introduced, Phillip Van Patten,[1] one of the delegates, presented the following: "*Resolved:* That working

[1] Phillip (also Philip) Van Patten, a native American, was an active member of the K. of L., and a leading figure in the American socialist movement in the years 1876-84. He served as national secretary of the Socialist Labor party.

women may become members of this Order and form Assemblies under the same conditions as men." That resolution was offered at the Chicago General Assembly on September 4, 1879, was voted on the following day, failed of passage for want of a two-thirds majority, and, on reconsideration, was laid on the table until the next session.

At the Pittsburgh session the matter came on for discussion. I had personally sounded every representative, and when the vote was taken it was unanimous. That was on September 9, 1880.

During my temporary absence from the General Assembly on that day, a committee consisting of the general officers was appointed to prepare a ritual for the government of assemblies of women. That committee was to meet at the call of the General [sic] Master Workman . . . before the assembling of the next General Assembly. I never issued a call for that committee to meet. When the Detroit session convened in September, 1881, I was asked why I failed to call the committee together. My answer was: "On September 9, 1880, the General Assembly voted to admit women on the same conditions as men. Under that resolution women are Knights of Labor on an equal footing with men. A separate ritual will bespeak inequality, lead to confusion, and is unnecessary." I made that statement before the committee on law on September 8, 1881. My views were sustained and a separate ritual for women was never prepared or asked for again. . . .

With a rapid and large increase in membership during the years 1885, 1886, and 1887, there were admitted a number of politicians, who, having failed to secure office or other recognition in the Democratic or Republican parties, attempted to turn the Knights of Labor into a political party. Having the ear of the press, or a part of it, they began a vigorous campaign to secure my support in the work of making a new party out of the Order of Knights of Labor.

Owing to the fact that much of our Preamble would require political action to give it practical effect, the run-down political hacks who had gained entrance to the Knights of Labor assumed a virtuous indignation in denouncing me for "standing in the way of progress by opposing a new party."

When the clamor for a new party to be composed of Knights of Labor grew insistent a few years after women were admitted, I opposed such a course. Then, when it was recalled that I had always advised our members to take political action by making their influence felt as citizens through the parties they were affiliated with, in the securing of remedial legislation, the old line politicians assailed me for not favoring a new party which they could juggle with, barter, or trade on to their personal advantage.

I then called for a referendum, "a solemn referendum," if you please, through which only those members who could exercise the right of suffrage as electors should register their opinion. The vote was decidedly against turning the Order into a party but the sly, crafty members who had hoped to gain recognition for themselves, gave vent to their disappointment in assailing me for not favoring a new party. They cunningly conveyed, through the public press, the impression that I had always favored a new party when advising our members to take political action. . . . They sought to arouse the opposition of women members of the Knights of Labor by declaring that I had denied to them the right to vote on the question of turning the Order into a political party. The women members were not influenced by such reasoning, for they were as anxious as I could be that the vote inside of the society should fairly represent the vote that could be polled as citizens on the outside.

One of the most persistent and bitter of my critics was a clergyman who wrote: "If Mr. Powderly is in favor of political action, as we have always been led to believe, he should not stand in the way of his Knights of Labor forming a party. Legislation favorable to his cause can best be obtained in that way."

From my answer to him, which by the way, he never published or acknowledged, I quote these lines.

Perhaps it might serve your ends to see the Knights of Labor go on the rocks through a fiasco at the polls, but I shall not be the one to advocate such a thing. If "legislation favorable" to the church can best be obtained by the church demonstrating its strength in a partisan way, why don't you advocate turning the church into a party?

Surely you do not expect me to be lamb enough to believe that the church never takes political action, and you know it is not done in a partisan way or by turning the church into a party.

Go carefully over the statutes and ordinances of states and municipalities exempting church property from taxation and you will not be able to trace such action to a partisan source, yet it is all political and has been done by politicians who paid heed to the voice of the church as expressed by its spokesmen.

You know that millions of dollars worth of church property escape payment of taxes, and you . . . know that this result was not brought about by asking the prayers of the faithful to influence legislation. You know it was done by careful planning, persistent effort, and wise manipulation of the law-making machinery of both old parties. You know the church was generous enough to permit both parties to share in this work and that it acted in a strictly nonpartisan way while doing so. Evidently you favored that way of doing things and yet you condemn me for advising Knights of Labor to secure legislation by working among, or on, members of the same old parties who were so generous to the church.

Honor bright now, don't you think the church way of securing legislation is better than to turn the church into a party. If you do not believe in that way of doing things, may be we can pool our issues and merge the church you represent and the organization I represent into a party and make an effort to "sweep the country" as you suggest. I fear neither of us could wield a broom sufficiently powerful to do so much sweeping and do it successfully as a party.

I am writing this in April, 1921, summoning to my aid scrapbooks and letter-copying books which bear witness to much that happened in the latter eighties of the last century.

The agitation of that day—we call it propaganda now—in the hope of making a new political party out of the Knights of Labor, continued until 1892, when the varied forces of reform met at Omaha, Nebraska, nominated General James B. Weaver for President on the People's party ticket and gave those who would make political capital for themselves an opportunity to "sweep the country."[2] How they swept it is history.

Additions to the Preamble of the Knights of Labor were being

[2] This is somewhat misleading. Powderly had opposed an independent labor party. From 1889 on, however, the K. of L. was closely linked with the farmers' organizations which led in the creation of the People's party two years later. In 1890 the K. of L. declared for an independent labor party, but it refused to sponsor the People's party when the latter was actually founded. The Knights, however, did give the party full unofficial support. Weaver's popular vote in 1892 ran over a million, and he received twenty-two electoral votes.

adopted right along, and, when the General Assembly met in Denver, Colorado, in 1890, the demand for "equal pay for equal work for both sexes" was the twentieth instead of the thirteenth clause.

I never liked the declaration favoring equal pay for equal work. It suggested equal drudgery as well as work. . . . I determined to effect a change in that declaration. Experience taught me that division on a vote often meant disunion. I kept sounding representatives to each General Assembly until 1890, and, when we convened in Denver, Colorado, that year, I felt that a unani-' mous vote would be polled in favor of the change I intended to recommend. Anything short of a unanimous vote would supply the opposition with a fulcrum on which to rest the lever for reconsideration or repeal. I determined that there would be no fulcrum.

Referring to the letter I had submitted to the membership, calling for the referendum on taking political action, let me here quote a little of what I said in my annual report to the Denver session:

It was not a mere matter of sentiment that caused me to send out that letter, although many well-disposed persons seem to think that every member should vote. That would leave us just where we were before, and the same cry would continue to go up that the Order should become a party. I felt morally certain that the vote would be against turning the Order into a party. If all [members] had voted, and the vote was in favor of a party, and but half of the number were voters, it would mislead the unthinking. That we have unthinking members is plainly manifest, or they would not clamor to vote on a question that they can vote on only in a sentimental way. We have had enough sentiment; let us be practical. Woman is obliged to work the same as man. She contracts debts and pays bills; she owns property and she is swindled out of it; she has to obey laws and she has to break them; she must look on and see rascals elected to office, but has no voice in their selection, although the evil results of their election will fall as heavily on her as any one else. We ask in our Preamble for equal pay for equal work, but will never get it until we have manhood enough to place the weapon in the woman's hand with which to punish the offenders against law, decency, order and good government. I recommend that we change the twentieth clause in the Preamble to read:

"To secure for both sexes equal rights." That will place all members on an equality and will enable all to assist in making the law. Add to that another clause reading as follows:

"All members are requested to qualify as electors as quickly as possible." When we do this there will be nothing lacking in our Preamble, but until then we have no right to ask the woman member of the Order to stultify herself by voting on a simple question on which she cannot have a voice at the polls. Let us be manly enough to demand for her the same rights that man enjoys.

The General Assembly acted unanimously in favor of my recommendation, and from that hour until the Nineteenth Amendment to the Constitution of the United States was adopted, every Knight of Labor endeavored to "secure equal rights of both sexes."

On all public occasions I advocated the measure and many a time was requested to explain just what I meant by "equal rights." I gave the same answer to all by saying that "Every right a man enjoys should be shared by woman."

On one occasion a man, evidently under the influence of liquor, interrupted me to demand that I enumerate all the rights that would follow the adoption by the state of a law granting equal rights to both sexes. Lacking the time to specify in detail just how many rights were to be enjoyed in common by both sexes, I said:

Man is entitled to no right that woman may not share. If you feel that you have a right to visit a saloon in the evening, after supper, and practice at the bar until midnight, your wife, if you have one, has a right equal to yours, to practice at the same bar for the same length of time.

As to woman voting, I do not believe that she can make a worse job of it than man has. The chances are all in favor of her purifying the atmosphere of the voting booth and I am quite willing to help her do it. . . .

In response to appeals from Miss Susan B. Anthony[3] and Mrs. Elizabeth Cady Stanton,[4] I frequently spoke from the same platform with them and in return for my effort in their behalf they openly favored the granting, by employers, of rights and privi-

---

[3] Susan Brownell Anthony (1820-1906), whose life was spent in the cause of reform, fought for abolition, negro suffrage, and woman's rights. She was a leader in the woman's suffrage movement.

[4] Elizabeth Cady Stanton (1815-1902), after working for abolition and temperance, expended all her energies to secure equal rights for women. She was among those who called the famous woman's rights convention at Seneca Falls in 1848.

leges in mill and factory to women employees that men only had enjoyed before.

I had enlisted in these two women and Miss Frances E. Willard[5] a moral force that was of great value to the cause in which the Knights of Labor were engaged.

One evening in the early eighties Miss Anthony was my guest at my home in Scranton, and, during her stay with me, I initiated her into the Knights of Labor. I initiated Miss Willard in the headquarters of the Knights of Labor in 1887.

It was during a meeting in Detroit, Michigan, at which Miss Anthony and I spoke from the same platform that she said: "Being opposed, as I am, to man suffrage I cannot consistently favor woman suffrage, therefore I am in favor of that which does not recognize sex at the ballot box—Equal Suffrage."

The working women and men of America, yes, and of the world, have reason to hold in grateful appreciation the memory of these heroic women who struggled for freedom of opportunity for all, and counted no sacrifice too great to lay on the altar of equal rights for all. They paid no heed to the clamor of opposition; they regarded the great wide ocean of humanity as one and sound to its greatest depth; firm in the belief that they were right, they were not daunted by the sibilant voice of the spray. . . .

To have shared in the labors that were crowned with success in 1920 was a proud privilege. To have seen the millions of enfranchised women wending their way in solemn, thoughtful procession to the polling booth was worth living for. That the Knights of Labor shared in the glory of that achievement is of great concern to me, for I am an American, and, I believe, a better one because I am a Knight of Labor.

[5] Frances Elizabeth Caroline Willard (1839-98) endeavored to secure equal rights and independence for women and was a leading figure in the temperance and prohibition movements.

Chapter Twenty-Nine

PART OF MY REWARD

CARELESSNESS, mendacity, calumny, dishonesty, and envy or petty jealousy, and, worse than all, stupidity, all played their separate parts in dealing with the officials of labor organizations in the past. The man who worked with his hands had not yet risen far enough above the miasma of that contempt for the toiler that had overshadowed him through centuries of serfdom and subjection to a master, to extend his vision beyond the limits of his own cramped environment. The dread of the master's lash, insult, or harshly spoken command was his by inheritance. That independence of act and word now known among the men of labor was just budding into blossom, and the tendency of church and society generally was to reprove rather than encourage the working man who displayed manliness enough to contend for what he regarded as his just due. As a boy beginning the climb of life's industrial incline, I wondered why strong, skilled, and apparently independent workingmen approached the man of prominence, the clergyman, and the petty foreman with an air of abject servility, hat in hand, with faltering voice, and, in many cases, trembling in every limb.

A press, almost wholly inspired by and subservient to corporate and political boss rule, upheld the tyranny of the foreman of shop, mine, and factory. Workingmen independent enough to demand fair play, square dealing, and considerate treatment, were singled out for dismissal from employment. They were frequently mentioned by name in terms of reproach if not of censure, from the pulpit, and many times they saw their names unfairly set down in the dishonorable mention column of the daily or weekly paper. . . .

Such was the field I entered when I began my work as General [*sic*] Master Workman of the Knights of Labor. For ten years I had been working among toilers in the Machinists and Blacksmiths International Union, the Industrial Brotherhood, and the Knights of Labor, when in September, 1879, I was called to the chieftainship of an organization the motto of which should be written deep in the heart of every man and woman in the world: "That is the most perfect government in which an injury to one is the concern of all."

On that march toward industrial emancipation my pathway was obstructed even more by envy and petty jealousy on the part of Knights of Labor than by the opposition of employers of labor, and all the time press and pulpit contributed their full share toward keeping a smoke screen of misrepresentation before the eyes of the people. I made mistakes, many of them. Every mistake was magnified in the press under large type headings. Every word I uttered that could be distorted or given a meaning different from that intended by me was picked up by many papers and served to the public in a way to cause members of the Knights of Labor and others to distrust me. Other papers went out of their way to praise me for things I never did and never thought of doing. They did this for a purpose, for you know it is easy to

> Damn with faint praise,
> Assent with civil leer
> And, without sneering
> Teach the rest to sneer.

Evidence of friendship, good will, or encouragement as gathered from the utterances of the adherents of one religion furnished cause for enmity, ill will, and discouragement from many who worshiped before a different or opposing shrine. I have no recollection of having either deservedly or otherwise been antagonized by a Jewish rabbi. Several of them spoke and wrote approvingly of my effort in behalf of the Knights of Labor. A few of them did criticize some of my acts or utterances, but in kindly spirit and either by mail, addressed to me personally, or verbally, but never through the medium of the public press.

Coupled with the criticism came a word of advice or caution that helped me in my work.

The action taken by Cardinal Gibbons in representing the cause of labor before the Vatican at Rome in 1887 became for more than the proverbial "nine days," a subject for discussion in press and pulpit. Much of the discussion was based, so far as I was concerned, on things I never did or said or thought of doing or saying. . . . Every act of mine was misinterpreted by some, every utterance was distorted by others. A number of Protestant clergymen, evidently inspired more by intolerance than by Christian charity, picked up and acrimoniously commented on garbled reports of what I had done following the return of Cardinal Gibbons from Rome. . . .

Before entering upon a recital of some of the things that occurred in the last year I held the post of General Master Workman, let me dwell a moment on a statement made by Cardinal Gibbons in his *Retrospect of Fifty Years*, published in 1916. In his admirable presentation of the case before the Sacred College at Rome, the cardinal among other things said:

Now, their president, when sending me a copy of their constitution, declared that he is a devoted Catholic; that he practices his religion faithfully, and receives the sacraments regularly; that he belongs to no masonic society or other association condemned by the church; that he knows nothing in the organization of the Knights of Labor contrary to the laws of the Church; that, with filial submission, he begs the pastors of the Church to examine their constitution and laws, and to point out anything they may find objectionable, promising to see to its correction. Assuredly there is in all this no hostility to the authority of the Church, but, on the contrary, a disposition in every way praiseworthy. After their convention held last year in Richmond, he and several of the principal members, devout Catholics, made similar declarations concerning the action of that convention. . . .

The last paragraph of that statement of the cardinal records the first meeting I had with him. During that interview, I noticed that he had on the table at which he sat a copy of the constitution of the Knights of Labor. I managed to get a close view of it and saw that it was the edition of 1884, and not the latest, or 1885, constitution. There were present at that meeting a number of priests, bishops and archbishops. Accompanying me were John

W. Hayes and Thomas O'Reilly, or Tom O'Reilly as he preferred to be called. On leaving the cardinal's residence, I remarked to the gentlemen who accompanied me that he, the cardinal, did not have before him a copy of our latest constitution, and Mr. O'Reilly said that he did not have a copy of the 1885 publication at hand when he wrote the cardinal sometime before. He was at that time the Master Workman of District Assembly No. 45, the telegrapher's district, of the Knights of Labor, a position which corresponded with president. Whether Mr. O'Reilly in writing the cardinal signed his own name as D.M.W. or president, or whether he signed my name as he was at times authorized to do, I do not know. It was understood that, owing to the uncertainty of my whereabouts, Mr. O'Reilly, to whom I had entrusted the duty of attending to matters relating to the church, could on special occasions use a rubber stamp facsimile of my signature with "per T.O.R." beneath. Whether Mr. O'Reilly did this or whether the cardinal mistook him for the G.M.W. or president, I do not know, but I do know that I never made the statement concerning my religious status as given in the foregoing extract from the cardinal's book. There existed no reason why I should do so, and had I done so it would have been untrue; it would have been misleading and unfair to the cardinal no less than to me, for it could very easily be ascertained that I was not the devout Catholic described in the lines I quote. Had I been so, however, it would have made no difference, and there would have been no cause for objection or complaint. There was no question raised as to the religion of any of us. Indeed, the question of religion was not discussed that day except in so far as I stated the position of Catholic workingmen on being denied, by the church, the right to join secret fraternal societies.

That to which I take exception in the cardinal's statement is embraced in these words: "and to point out anything they may find objectionable, promising to see to its correction." I did not and could not make such a promise. I candidly and unreservedly explained to the cardinal and those present at that interview that no power of correction lay with me; that the authority to correct, alter, or amend our laws was lodged in our General Assembly. I assured the cardinal however that I would be glad to receive suggestions of change from him and would place them before the General Assembly at its next session, and through Mr. O'Reilly that was done. That was all I did, it was all I had the right to do, and I heard no suggestion of anything to the contrary from Mr. O'Reilly either at that time or subsequently.

The statement in the New York *Sun* item, to which I have referred, was to the effect that I had promised Cardinal Gibbons to make such corrections in the constitution and declaration of principles of the Knights of Labor as the cardinal suggested, without referring them to our General Assembly.

That publication, as I have said, began a campaign of misrepresentation against me which continued for upward of five years. Until the last year of my incumbency of the office of General Master Workman I took no public or official notice of the matter. On December 26, 1892, I received a letter which . . . gives a fair idea of the tactics resorted to at that time to play cuttle-fish in public waters. . . .

EUREKA, CALIF., DEC. 14, 1892

T. V. POWDERLY, ESQ.
  GENERAL MASTER WORKMAN K. of L.
Dear Sir:
        I desire to ask you a question. A Reverend Gentleman of this city some time ago upon the request of the Orangemen preached a sermon in relation to the anniversary of the Gunpowder Plot and in the sermon he took occasion to say that "The Knights of Labor could not adopt a constitution and by-laws until it had been submitted to the Pope, when he struck out several sections and permitted them to adopt it." Meeting the gentleman today, I rated him somewhat on using such sensational slander to tickle a clique that had no business on American soil. He stoutly maintained that he had authentic proof. I told him I knew it was a slander on organized labor and was manufactured for the particular purpose of weakening the Knights of Labor. He said if I could prove to him that I was right he would retract and correct his expression in public print over his signature, as he wanted only the truth, and further that he was willing to accept your statement of the matter as full proof.

Please be kind enough to give me a clear statement of the matter.

Fraternally yours,
WM. AYRES

. . . The letter . . . inquired after a matter of great concern
to the Order, and I answered it as follows:

SCRANTON, PA. DEC. 26, 1892

WILLIAM AYRES, ESQ.
  EUREKA, CALIF.

Dear Sir:
        The Reverend gentleman of whom you write was imposed upon
by some unscrupulous person. The constitution of the Knights of Labor is
subject to change at every convention; we meet once a year. At our last
gathering in St. Louis there were as intelligent a set of men there as ever
sat down to deliberate upon public questions; the majority were Protestants,
they made radical changes in the constitution of the Order and never
thought of asking whether their action would please Pope or Bishop. The
constitution of the Knights of Labor has never been changed to suit the
views or fancy of any man outside of the General Assembly of the Order.
The Pope has never changed it by the crossing of a *t* or the dotting of an *i*
and all statements to the contrary are without foundation.
        The constitution of 1886 was submitted to the heads of the various Chris-
tian religions, the Pope included; it was not changed to suit any of them. At
that time the press of the land accused us of being anarchists, and in self-
defense we placed our constitution before whoever cared to examine it. We
have never consulted any one as to what changes we intended making. The
Order is an American institution, it was born in Philadelphia; its founder
was a Protestant, and long before I became General Master Workman,
even before I became acquainted with him, he submitted not only our constitution but the A. K., or ritual, to Bishop Wood of Philadelphia. Our
constitution is public property and whoever wishes to may see it but no one
can make changes in it except the General Assembly itself.
        I do not believe a man of God would knowingly bear false witness, and
therefore ask you to allow him to read this.
                                Fraternally yours,
                                T. V. POWDERLY

        That should have been sufficient in the absence of proof to the
contrary, to set the matter at rest, but it simply provided the introduction to a deluge of charges against me of "bartering away
the rights of American freemen for a mess of pottage from Rome"
which continued until the following March and subsided then only
to give way to a new onslaught from another quarter. It will tell
you a little about what came my way in those days, and give you

some idea of my state of mind while undergoing the ordeal of an operation that amputated me from official connection with the organized labor movement. It will disclose how those opposed to my work enlisted church, or more accurately speaking ministerial, influence to help draw the proverbial "red herring" across the path I walked in.

Early in March, 1893, a clergyman in attendance at a session of the Milwaukee Minister's Association made a statement damaging to me, wholly untrue and without the least semblance of foundation. I saw reference to the charge in the press despatches the day after it was made, and then a fusillade of letters of all kinds concerning it was directed at me from all over the country. Although out of order as to date, I shall first lay before you the copy of a letter addressed by me to the clergyman in question. My letter quotes the language used by him and I need not repeat it elsewhere:

Scranton, Pa. April 7, 1893

Rev. J. G. White
Stanford, Illinois

Dear Sir:

Some four weeks ago the press despatches carried throughout the country a statement which you were represented as having presented to a meeting of the Milwaukee Minister's Association. You are credited with saying:

"I have convincing proofs that Pope Leo, Cardinal Gibbons, sixty clergymen and bishops and ten archbishops are backing a man who is endeavoring to raise a revolution in this country."

You were asked to name that man and the following is published as your answer:

"That man is T. V. Powderly, who, under the pretext of aiding and assisting the laboring man, is plotting, with the aid of the Roman Catholic Church, to overthrow this country."

The same press despatches said that you would present to the Milwaukee Minister's Association, the proofs which you claim to have in your possession, and since then I have heard nothing of the matter so far as the alleged proofs are concerned. I write to you now for proofs, but in justice to you, it is proper that I ask whether you were quoted correctly in the papers. Did you make the statement as quoted above? Did you charge me with conspiracy with the Pope, Cardinal Gibbons, and others to overthrow this country?

Do me the favor to extend the courtesy of an answer to the questions which I now submit to you, and oblige,

Very truly yours,

T. V. POWDERLY

Now let me go back to March 16, 1893, and give you a copy of what I wrote to a brother member of the Knights of Labor who sent me a newspaper clipping giving an account of what Mr. White said:

SCRANTON, PA. MARCH 16, 1893

G. H. MANELL, ESQ.

NEW BUFFALO, MICHIGAN

Dear Sir and Brother:

Accept my thanks for your kind forethought in sending me the clipping about Rev. J. G. White. I have no knowledge of who Mr. White is, but I do know that his statement is a complete falsehood from beginning to end so far as it relates to me. I have not seen Cardinal Gibbons, except for a brief moment at a public meeting in this city, in years. I have not had one moment's discussion with either priest, bishop, archbishop, or cardinal concerning the affairs of this country or anything else relating to public matters, during the whole course of my life. All that I had to say to Cardinal Gibbons concerning the Knights of Labor has been published in the records of our Order, in the *Journal* of the same, and has been public property for years. Outside of that, I have never had any dealings with any of these gentlemen, and there is no truth in the statement that I am plotting with the aid of the Roman Catholic Church to overthrow this country. When he accuses me of "endeavoring to raise a revolution in this country" he is right, for I am doing that very thing and do not intend to cease for one moment because of the ravings of a madman or a liar. The revolution that I would bring about is one based on equity for all the people of our country; one that will restore natural opportunities to the children of men, one that will make our flag the emblem of all the people and have it stand for industrial worth, not wealth. I would revolutionize the country by educating its people to know that the ballot is the most powerful weapon that man can wield. This revolution will be effected through peace and in harmony with the Declaration of Independence which says:

"That whenever any form of Government becomes destructive of these ends, it is the right of the people to alter or abolish it, and to institute a new Government, laying its foundations on such principles, and organizing its powers in such form as to them will seem most likely to effect their safety and happiness."

Our present system of administering Government appears to be too partial to the monopolist, the money changer, and the purchaseable tools of monopoly. This system is an encroachment on our plan of Government "of the people, by the people and for the people," and is destructive of the best interests of all the people. It should give way for such a form of Government as will be in direct harmony with the Declaration of Independence of the United States, the Constitution of the same, and the needs of the people of the present day and generation. This is the revolution I am engaged in, this is the revolution that you, my brother, are engaged in and it is because I have, persistently and with what ability I possess, urged forward the ball of revolution on these lines, without advocating violence or bloodshed that clerical bigots and hired tools of monopoly have assailed me.

I am willing to place this matter in the hands of a number of Protestant clergymen for investigation and will abide by their decision, for I think it is high time that steps be taken to protect me from such unscrupulous slanderers as Mr. White.

With best wishes, I remain,

Sincerely and Fraternally yours,

T. V. POWDERLY

An ardent Knight of Labor and personal friend of mine, Mrs. Alzina P. Stevens, was then publishing a paper called the *Vanguard* in Chicago. She took up the cudgel in my behalf, and wrote a spirited editorial in my defense, or as she said "in defense of the Order which is being assailed through Mr. Powderly." She sent me a copy of the editorial and with it a letter of sympathy and encouragement. In acknowledgment I wrote her a long letter which, without permission from me, she reproduced in the *Vanguard*. Since that letter tells part of the story, I shall let you read a portion of it:

During fifteen years I have been active in the Knights of Labor as an officer, my friends lived and died as Protestants and Catholics without a thought of what their creeds might be ever entering my brain. Many who struck at me, many who endeavored to encompass my ruin and destroy my usefulness, were Catholics. No religious convictions or affiliations interfered with their hatreds, and all through the struggle my warmest friends were as numerous among Protestants as among Catholics. When approaching unknown thresholds, with darkness deepening at every step, I leaned as confidently upon Protestant encouragement as upon anything else. Those who were close to me never accused me of entertaining the slightest trace of religious bigotry. I could not be a bigot if I tried, for my early life was spent among many

Protestants, and even in those far-away days I felt that the invisible barriers of creed should not separate living men. Those who love their country are of one religion, no matter what church they may go to. Those who would enslave the masses would enslave those who kneel before the same altar with themselves. The love of creed will not restrain the gambler, the speculator, the monopolist, or the self-seeker. If the liberties of the American working people are endangered, if Catholics are engaged in attempting to enslave this country, will not Catholics themselves be slaves in the slavery of their Protestant brethren? How can a blow be struck at you without injuring me—how can I destroy your liberties without shattering my own? Is not self-interest itself strong enough within us to prevent us from jeopardizing institutions that we all love and would defend with our lives. Am I not as dear to Rev. Mr. White as though I were of his faith; did not the same Christ die for both of us? Did that Christ leave a record of partiality for a set of men or a certain class that would warrant any man or set of men in daring to assert that He died for them alone? Should not Mr. White hesitate about slandering one of his brothers and at least attempt to find out from that man if he could give even a semblance of an excuse for his treason to the Republic—that is what he charges me with. God's law was written for mankind and not for a certain set of men; it was not for one man or one class of men that Christ ascended the cross. To all men, Catholic, Protestant, Jew, pagan, atheist, and agnostic, God gave the earth, its gifts, its fruits and its flowers. To all men He gave equal rights to sunshine, life and happiness. To all men He gave the pure air of freedom, which nothing can enthrall and which stretches from the grass to the stars.

Christ died a merciful death as compared with the lingering torture which men feel today who struggle for the right and whose every act is misconstrued, even by those for whom they act. I can look back through the gloom of two thousand years, scan the faces of that group that stood beneath the cross and see the scoffing, sneering face of at least one among them who said: "It served him right for endeavoring to raise a revolution in this country."

My struggle—and my life has been one long struggle—has been for equity among men. Born within these hills, which now shut out the light of the setting sun, I could not help loving liberty, but I love it no less for the sake of others than myself. I want no liberty for Catholic which Protestant and pagan may not enjoy. My struggle has been for justice to mankind on earth and not beyond the grave; that struggle could consistently go on for all who toiled on earth without prejudice and in that spirit was it continued. Mr. White is a minister of God. If he believes in God he must feel that God is just, that He would not lie about even the humblest of earth. If Mr. White believes not in the Golden Rule he cannot represent God faithfully before his flock. If he bears false witness he does not fittingly fulfill the duties of his holy calling. If he does that which will injure any cause, any movement, without being able to show a good cause or reason, he cannot hope to enter upon that blessed immortality which he holds out to his flock as the reward for a just and truthful life among men. You say you are a Presbyterian; I never knew what church you belonged to before. You know what my sentiments are and do not need this letter to cause you to know that Catholic and Protestant stand on equal ground in my eyes. This is a serious charge and will work harm to the Order I represent, no matter what I may do. It may do more: it may provoke scenes of bloodshed before it has an end, for nothing arouses the fury of the beast in men so thoroughly as a difference of opinion concerning the spiritual flight of that part which the beast is supposed not to possess. I am heart-weary of the fruitless task that I have so vainly endeavored to perform and would lay down the burden for the good of this country. I want to do this, for the conviction has forced itself upon me that my days of usefulness for the people are ended, but I would make at least one effort to pass into private life with a denial of these cruel lies from other lips than mine.

I am willing to select Rev. Lyman Abbott, Rev. T. DeWitt Talmage, Rev. M. C. Lockwood, and any other minister of the church you may see fit to name, provided of course, that he is not a Catholic. The three gentlemen whom I have named are not Catholics, two of them I have never met, but their names stand for truth and honor, and I am willing to place every act of mine, every document I possess, and every particle of testimony before their eyes for investigation. Let Mr. White place his alleged proofs before them and I will cheerfully abide by the decision of these men.

You may think that I attach too much importance to the utterance of Rev. Mr. White; far from it. This is not the first time I have had to fight this lie, and since the beginning of this year it has been constantly before me. From Michigan, from California, from New England and the South, the same cry comes to me, and I am morally certain that if the opportunity is presented to me I will prove that the conspiracy is not one in which my personality or voice has ever intruded itself.

Fearing that I was becoming so discouraged that I would resign, Mrs. Stevens wrote me another letter, urging that I "continue the good work for humanity." I here give my answer in full:

SCRANTON, PA. APRIL 11, 1893

My dear Mrs. Stevens:

You may rest assured that my work will not cease with the end of my official career in the Knights of Labor. In any event, I must do something else in order to make a living, for you know that one cannot support even himself on air. All of the good things that have been said of me will not materialize into bread and butter, and I must do for myself and family what those I am laboring for have to do for theirs. If I engage in business of any kind with another, I am held responsible for his utterances and shortcomings. Things that would be endured without a murmur from an associate of another man, will call for censure in one associated with me. You see I have earned such a reputation that in order to live up to it, I am expected to mount a pedestal as a sort of a god. I must not be a lawyer, for a lawyer's occupation is regarded with suspicion, and as a consequence I must not even cast suspicion on the labor movement by earning a living in that way. I cannot be a saloonkeeper, for that would be in opposition to my past teachings; it would injure the movement, and I would not sell liquor anyway. I must not be a banker, for we are opposed to the practices of some bankers, and I must not, in that way, injure the movement—besides I lack the money to be a banker. I must not work for a corporation, for then I will be a tool of monopoly, and that will injure the movement; but there is no danger of that, for no corporation would engage my services. The Knights of Labor are nearly a year behind in payments on my salary and expenses and are no longer able to pay me even a single cent, but all the same I am expected to mount my pedestal and pose as a great, good man. You know I am not great, and I hope that there is still good in me.

I have held a most anomalous position before the public for the last twenty years. All of this time I have opposed strikes and boycotts. I have contended that the wage question was of secondary consideration; I have contended that the short-hour question was not the end but merely the means to an end; I have endeavored to direct the eyes of our members to the principal parts of the preamble of our Order—government ownership of land, of railroads or regulation of railroads, telegraphs, and money—but all of this time I have been fighting for a raise in wages, a reduction in the hours of labor, or some demand of the trade element in our Order to the exclusion of the very work that I have constantly advocated and which the General Assembly of the Order commanded me to advocate. Just think of it! Opposing strikes and always striking; battling for short hours for others, obliged to work long hours myself, lacking time to devote to anything else. Battling with my pen in the leading journals and magazines of the day for the great things we are educating the people on and fighting with might and main for the little things. Our Order has held me in my present position because of the reputation I have won in the nation at large by taking high ground on important national questions, yet the trade element in our Order has always kept me busy at the base of the breastworks throwing up earth which they trample down.

Again, no man in this country has so many domineering bosses as I have, for each member feels it to be his right to abuse me as he pleases or to order me around to do as he likes and not as I think. A general commanding an army, everyone of whom considers the general his servant, a leader endeavoring to lead and yet pulled by the coattails by several hundred thousand, more or less, who pulled me just because they dare not pull anyone else. On the other hand, my relations with my brother officers, or at least one of them, are not pleasant, and I wish to be free even though I use that freedom only to scratch dirt with the chickens. I, who have been preaching independence to others, have for twenty years been the slave of thousands and as my reward am as little understood by the people I work for as Sam Smithers or Dink Botts. In a word, I want to be free so that even though I do not speak so often, I can command attention when I do talk. My correspondence is greatest, in the inquiry line, on matters that I have fully written up in the columns of our *Journal*—a *Journal* which our members never take out of its wrapper. Read this week's *Journal* and you will see that in one place I say that I believe the majority of workingmen have earned jail sentences because of their utter indifference to their own well-being, and instead of seeing the point I aimed at, I will get resolutions by the dozen, from local assemblies, denouncing the man who would express such a sentiment. My sole aim has been to educate the man who works or rather to have him educate himself; I desire to reconstruct him, as it were, and cause him to *think*, as well as work. In doing that, I have no doubt gained the good will of the intelligent and educated to a great extent, and that is gratifying to me; I no doubt have the respect and esteem of fair-minded employers too.

To another man this would be very consoling, but I do not care a damn for it since the man at the bottom of the ladder for whom my effort was expended, neither understands or appreciates my work and in reality appears to know no more than when I stepped from his side in the workshop twenty years ago.

Mrs. Stevens, there is no labor question, there is no social question, there is no political question, and it is not for the workingman as such that I have striven—it was with me a labor of love for humanity and I fought for the uplifting of the poor man, whether he works, begs, or steals.

I have one regret now, I saw many an opportunity through which I could have made myself fairly well off without a sacrifice of principal [*sic*] or honor, but did not avail myself of it; had I done so, I would now be in a position of independence and would be free to talk, write, and act as I please. Had I acquired a competency even through opposition to labor's claim, the workers would pay more heed to me than they appear to now. As it is, I must soon "ask leave to toil" from some brother worm and no doubt shall have to smother my sentiments for a time.

When passing judgment on me, exercise a large share of your charity and good judgment, for I need both. The truth of the matter is, I am too poor to longer occupy an official position in the poor man's cause.

I never knew a time when I had to answer so many questions relating directly to the real meat of the movement, as now, and I have reason for encouragement in an awakening anxiety to learn more of our aims and purposes, but this awakening is among people who are not members or supporters of our Order and I grow sick at heart when I think that I must turn away from all this in a short time just because I cannot afford to continue in the work.

Expressing the hope that you will overlook the extreme length of this letter, I am,

Faithfully yours,
T. V. POWDERLY

In a measure, that letter describes conditions then existing. It gives an insight [in]to my financial status and my views on what I was obliged to do instead of what I felt that I should do.

Not hearing from Mr. White, I . . . [wrote a second letter] to him:

SCRANTON, PA. APRIL 21, 1893

REV. J. G. WHITE
STANFORD, ILLINOIS

Dear Sir:

On March 6, you charged me with conspiracy against the life of this country. That charge included the highest crime known to the laws of the United States—treason.

On April 7, I wrote you asking whether you were correctly reported. I registered the letter so that I might, if possible, ascertain whether you received it. On April 11, that letter reached Stanford. The receipt was signed by you, returned to me and I hold it with your autograph, certifying that you received and read my letter.

You, if correctly quoted, asserted that you had "convincing proofs" of my guilt. You should lose no time in vindicating the laws of the land by producing these proofs and I am doing all that I can to aid you in performing that duty.

I again ask if you used the words quoted in my letter and hope that you will do an act of justice by all concerned in answering me at once. It never serves the purpose of an honorable man to hesitate a moment about so grave a matter and for your own sake I hope that you were so situated as not to be able to answer immediately.

I want to know if you spoke the words quoted. I intend to find out. I will find out but would rather have the information over your signature. I have no desire to do you an injustice even in thought, I have no desire to hurry you, but you have had ample time in which to decide whether to answer me or not. Remember that continued silence about this cannot be considered either kind or courteous.

I remain,

Very truly yours,
T. V. POWDERLY

Except to send me a brief message inviting my attention to a long letter which appeared in a Columbus, Ohio, publication, Mr. White never answered my letters. His contribution to the Columbus paper could in no sense be taken as an explanation of his conduct. It was pure, unadulterated drivel, the output of a mind so small that the thousandth part of the germ of fair play, if there is such a germ, could find no abiding place on it without overshadowing it. Mr. White hated the pope, but that individual was four thousand miles away, a safe distance, so I was singled out to be brayed at by biped donkeys masquerading as mouthpieces of Almighty God. A few days after I wrote my last epistle to Mr. White, I traveled from Philadelphia, Pa., to Columbus, Ohio, on the same train with [the] Rev. Washington Gladden,[1] and in the course of our conversation the White episode was discussed at length. I intimated that I contemplated taking action against Mr. White in the courts and I recall Mr. Gladden's counsel not to do so. Among other things he said:

Every reading, thinking man and woman knows you, or about you; they do not know Mr. White, and you may only advertise him and lose valuable time doing so. His chief claim to attention lies in the fact that he is a clergyman, but you should attach no importance to that, for a clergyman has rare facilities, and more of them, to make a fool of himself than most men. Don't waste any time or money on him.

I acted on that advice. Among the letters of inquiry concerning Mr. White's verbal onslaught was one from a respected and honored member of the Knights of Labor who appeared to be much concerned about it. My answer will give a general idea of what was contained in Mr. Chamberlain's letter to me:

SCRANTON, PA. APRIL 23, 1893

I. D. CHAMBERLAIN, ESQ.
  STROMSBURG, NEB.
Brother Chamberlain:
                    I have yours of the 15th instant, with clipping containing Rev. Mr. White's charge that I am trying to "overturn this coun-

[1] Washington Gladden (1836-1918), Congregational pastor, active journalist, voluminous writer, and civic reformer, sought, as a Christian socialist, to have the social order christianized by the church through justice and the spirit of social service. He advocated the right of labor to organize and urged coöperation between labor and capital.

try" and note that you are worried about it. Calm yourself while I assure you that I shall not attempt to overturn one of the states, much less the whole United States. Mr. White flatters me; he, inferentially at least, attributes to me a power or a desire to exercise a power I do not possess. To overturn this country—its government I believe Mr. White must have in mind—I would need to enlist the active coöperation of the majority of all the people of the country. You speak truly when you say "the whole people would rise to squelch you" and since that is unquestionably true, why do you worry about the matter.

There is just one point of resemblance between Mr. White's charge and my work; he don't want to have the country overturned and I don't. So you see we are in accord on that score. In all else we are at variance. Mr. White I do not know, but if he ever had faith in the people, he must have lost it. I always had faith in and trusted the people; I shall continue to retain that faith and trust them no matter how they may be lied to and bedevilled by religious or political prostitutes.

It is quite true that the flatulency of such religious dyspeptics as Mr. White makes it difficult for me to do my work, for I must devote hours each day to answering letters of inquiry from people alarmed by Mr. White's attack. That's what hurts and it hurts because it eats up time that could be put to better use.

Calm yourself, Brother Chamberlain. I shall not attempt to overturn this country or any part of it, and nothing can harm our country or its government so long as the elect of the people have confidence in and respect the will of the people. So long as men selected by the people obey their expressed will and do their honest best to fairly represent all the people, our country will be safe and it cannot be overturned by any power on earth.

Let the people guard their own interests from the rule of wealth, from the interference of crafty scoundrels masquerading as ministers of God, from designing self-seekers of every description; do their own thinking on all questions and no power can injure our country or its institutions. The one and only agency that can ever injure the United States will be the people themselves when they forget that "eternal vigilance is the price of liberty" and lapse into a state of lethargy and indifference to their own welfare as free men.

Don't bother me with any more childish letters but do your best to educate your neighbors in the fundamentals of government by the people, by all the people mind you. Teach them what their rights are and do your best to so stiffen their backbones that they will "dare maintain" their rights against every power that may oppose them.

The country is not in danger from anything I am doing or shall do. As one of the "common herd," I am doing what I regard as my duty by that "herd." Those who would corral that "herd" and enslave it are the ones to fear, they are the ones who start and circulate falsehoods about me in order to stampede the people and render them helpless when insidious advances are made toward subjection of the people to the rule of wealth. Their object is to focus the public eye on something I did, or didn't do, so that their selfish schemes may be prosecuted in stealth and with little or no fear of detection.

Do your part, I'll do mine.

With good wishes, I remain,

Fraternally yours,

T. V. POWDERLY

. . . .

You will notice that between the time I wrote Mrs. Stevens and my reply to Mr. Chamberlain, my mental equilibrium had been restored and I was again in the fighting mood to which she had pointed in her letters. . . . That ends the greater part of the correspondence relating to Mr. White's ebullition. The matter of circulating voluminous misinformation on religious, or shall I say irreligious, topics continued. A rumor "from a well informed source" made a Knight of Labor of Cardinal Gibbons through my influence and personal ministration. The Cardinal in turn initiated Pope Leo. This story, so industriously circulated, I took no notice of, and, because of my silence, it was given out that I had used some means of overcoming the pope's opposition to secret societies by "changing the form of our obligation to please his holiness." The rumor reached Canada and a personal friend of mine wrote me for information on the subject. True, his letter antedates the others I have given or quoted, but it has such a direct bearing on the doings of that period, and fits in so well with what followed, that it should be made a part of this recital. It indicates my thought on the difference between battling for justice for the people of this world and a selfish scramble to feather a spiritual nest in the next. I submit the letter and my reply without further comment:

OTTAWA, Nov. 21, 1892

T. V. POWDERLY, ESQ.—G. M. W.

PHILADELPHIA, PENN.

Dear Sir and Brother:

You will excuse the liberty I take in asking your personal attention to the following questions, and in requesting that you kindly furnish the necessary proof to establish, beyond all reasonable doubt, that the approval of the Pope at Rome has been given to us, Roman Catholics, to become Knights of Labor. My questions are:

1st. Did not Cardinal Gibbons and yourself visit Rome and place before the Pope the A. K., etc., of our Order?

2nd. Did not the Pope sanction them and approve of the K. of L.?

3rd. Did not the Pope become a K. of L.?

In explanation I may say—There are, in this city, clergymen endeavoring to undo our work; causing members to fall back from their assembly; influencing those outside the ranks and keeping them from joining. They say the church does not approve nor disapprove, but that one cannot be a thorough good Catholic and a Knight of Labor. In fact, they say it is preferable that Roman Catholics should shun the K. of L. altogether. This kind of advice may seem ridiculous to you, and you may be astonished that any sensible man would pay attention to it, yet the fact is evident that large numbers are swayed away from our ranks.

If you could secure Cardinal Gibbons' opinion over his signature, on this matter, I am satisfied great good would result.

I have undertaken to prove that not only has the Pope approved of our Order, but that he himself was virtually initiated and is really a Knight of Labor. Am I right?

By giving this matter your earnest and immediate attention, you will confer not only a favor upon the undersigned, but you will assist us in building up our membership in this District.

I remain,

Yours fraternally,

J. GEO. KILT

M. W. 2806

Address—

477 CUMBERLAND STREET

OTTAWA, ONT.

SCRANTON, PA., DECEMBER 1, 1892

J. GEO. KILT, ESQ., M. W. L. A. 2806

477 CUMBERLAND STREET

OTTAWA, ONT.

Dear Sir and Bro:

All of this fuss and worry about our Order and the Church appears to me to be very unnecessary. If we were about to start a building association, a stock company, a railroad corporation, or any other concern to make money and issue watered stock, we would not inquire whether the Church or the Pope sanctioned it or not, but just as soon as we organize to keep swindlers from taking all our earnings then we ourselves begin to question whether the Pope will approve of the scheme.

Good Catholics may organize to skillfully filch the earnings of men and never dream of asking permission from the Pope, but equally as good Catholics may not organize to secure honest pay for honestly performed work without a suspicion that the Pope may not approve of the act.

Cardinal Gibbons visited Rome and explained the mission of our Order, as you will see by referring to the proceedings of the Minneapolis session of the General Assembly. He did not take the A. K. there, and so far as I know he has never seen it. I never visited Rome, and have never been out of the United States except when I visited Canada. I do not know whether the Pope has approved of the Knights of Labor or not, but I do know that he has not condemned it. The Pope did not become a Knight of Labor, and Cardinal Gibbons is not a Knight of Labor.

A man can be a good Catholic, Methodist, Presbyterian, Jew, Turk, or Atheist and be a good Knight of Labor; we deal with questions affecting the welfare of humanity and not those of immortality. Our idea is to teach men how to live by securing for themselves better conditions, rather than practice dying before the time comes.

With best wishes, I remain,

Fraternally yours,

T. V. POWDERLY

Why were all these shafts aimed at me? Those who directed them could not have been animated by a feeling of personal dislike, for they were not acquainted with me. . . . It was not the individual they aimed at, and, perhaps, they were not concerned in what I was doing. The officials of a manufacturing concern, a mining corporation, or a steamship company, men whose interests I may have opposed, might wish to destroy or lessen my influence. If they attacked me because of my opposition to them, they could be charged with doing so for selfish motives. It would look better in the public eye—for them—to have someone apart from their concerns assail me, and who could do so more adroitly —and keep the people looking in the wrong direction so successfully—than a minister of the church, a preacher of religion. . . .

During the month of February, 1892, an industrial conference assembled in St. Louis, Mo. I was authorized to attend and did so. Among the declarations emanating from that conference, was one which aimed at restricting immigration. I had decided opinions on the immigration of that day, and in a letter to my friend Joseph R. Buchanan, I quoted and commented on the pronouncement of the conference in this language:

"Imported pauperized labor beats down the wages" of American laborers is what the industrial platform asserts, and with that subject will the remainder of this letter deal. In a small settlement but three miles distant from the heart of a great city and within sight of the spires on its Christian churches, may be found a number of foreign workmen. Their scantily furnished homes, exposed to the bleak north winds of a chill December day, were uninviting enough when I visited them. Floors without carpets, rooms without chairs or beds. Pallets of straw where mattresses should be and rough boards where tables should stand. Adornment there was none, comfort found no abiding place there, and poverty raised its head in every corner. Inquiry elicited the information that these workmen, who but a short time ago were the inmates of the steerage of some ocean steamer, had been induced to leave their homes and emigrate to this country through false representations. Many of those who came here some years ago can speak the English language tolerably well, they are favored by the superintendents and managers of corporations, construction companies, and coal-mining concerns. When from any cause—that of patriotism or love of country always excepted—these managers or superintendents desire the services of cheap workmen, these English-speaking Italians, Hungarians, Slavonians, Greeks, or Arabians can be bribed to write to acquaintances and friends across the water and induce them to inspire a number of workmen to emigrate to America. . . . The bookkeeper of nearly every coal office or company store has an agency for the sale of steamship tickets, he receives a profit on the sale of each ticket, the steamship company he represents makes a profit on every passenger carried over—he is useful for ballast if for nothing else—the company employing the agent can with safety reduce wages, or displace the well-paid workman with the newly landed immigrant, and as a consequence a standing conspiracy to lower the standard of wages and the level of American citizenship is constantly at work undermining the prosperity of the American workingman. The immigrant is not to blame, he is a stranger, without friends, unacquainted with our language, poor, helpless, starving, and must sell his labor for what is offered to him. He is not in a position to make terms; the employer through him, is enabled to prevent the American workman from making terms and thus secures the services of men who do not know that their labor is worth more than from fifty to ninety cents a day. All through the coal regions this quality of labor abounds, and all through the United States the evil effects of its presence are felt. The needs of the country, the prosperity of her people, or the morals of the community are not considered by those who are directly responsible for the greater portion of the immigration of 1892. In his testimony before the Senate immigration committee, the manager of the Hamburg American Packet line said:

"If immigration is suspended for a year we will simply land our immigrant passengers in Canada. The Canadians will profit by such legislation. Their railroads will get the business which now goes to American roads. Of course the steamship companies will suffer by the change, but they do not propose to give up their business in case Congress tries to stop immigration for a time."

Defiance of authority, of public opinion, of the interests of the American people, was breathed in every word of that paragraph. Cupidity was exalted above love of country or the needs of her people. That sentiment is shared by every other steamship manager who "despises the Republic and endangers liberty" by the dumping of hundreds of thousands of unfortunate immigrants on our shores. Corporate greed is alone responsible for the sweeping tide of immigration now flowing in upon us. That steamship companies may reap a profit, that railroads may carry passengers, that construction and coal companies may obtain the services of some slavish workmen, are the reasons why we must look on while the Constitution of the United States is being translated—and interpreted—into a dozen different tongues. Few of the immigrants will ever own their homes in this country, they cannot earn enough to make the first payment demanded by the land speculator. Every cent they earn must go to feed and clothe them and their families, not one cent can be laid away for a rainy day, and when that day of trouble does come the community must bear the expense of maintaining the poor unfortunate while the corporation which induced him to come to this country engages the services of another—and stronger—man. The steamship dumps its human freight on our shores and takes its profits; the corporation reaps the benefit of the immigrants' presence by having its labor performed for half nothing; the poor immigrant lives but twenty-four hours ahead of the poorhouse, the man he displaces becomes a tramp, and when either one is stricken down the community which is injured, rather than benefited, by the introduction of such an element has to defray the expenses of the poor people who crowd our asylums and houses of charity. When we inquire of the steamship managers why they crowd us, when we ask them to lighten the load, they insultingly tell us that they will land the immigrants in Canada and allow them to find their way across the border. Right here another question looms up, one that we must face and decide in the near future. Why should England have the right to a voice in shaping the affairs of this continent? Why should we not decide what the American people should do without foreign influence or intimidation? I can conceive of no surer way of undermining our American institutions than by loading them down with millions of people who do not understand and, failing to understand, cannot appreciate or care to defend them. Annexation of Canada and the great northwest must sooner or later engage the thought and effort of the people of the United States. We are one people, our interests are identical, our future must blend in one, our every hope and aspiration run in parallel lines, and it is of the greatest importance to both that the artificial barriers which now divide—and annoy—us should be swept away. England may secretly form her alliances to crowd us with the most undesirable of the nations of Europe, we may enact laws to restrict that immigration, but so long as she has the right to stand guard along three thousand miles of our border we are in danger of being subordinated to the wishes of the governments of Europe as expressed through her representatives. Restriction of immigration must be assured and if annexation will aid in the accomplishment of that end, that question, too, must be taken up and solved.

Ponder over the words of that letter. Occupy for a moment the place of a man who would cause workingmen to feel independent, who would thwart the schemes of exploiters of human labor, and you will realize that such a man stood in the way of every grafter who fattened on the proceeds of unrequited toil. Did such as these assail me for what I really did it might focus public attention on their scheming. To assume "the garb of heaven to serve the devil in," they invoked and secured the services of clergymen. Listen to what Tom Fielder, once of the Shenandoah *Herald*, but later of the New York *Times*, said to me: "Don't blame him [referring to a clergyman who had assailed me], he is but a mouthpiece for others. He may or may not know that he is but I do know it. You have offended large interests and they stand back of these drives against you."

The Chicago exposition of 1893 was under discussion at that time. In December, 1892, the American Press Association, through C. C. Hunt, wrote to me for an expression of my views on what conditions in 1992 would be like. In presenting these views I was restricted to "not more than six hundred words."

What I submitted was given wide circulation, and as a natural consequence I was subjected to scathing criticism from church organs, particularly those published by Roman Catholics. I shall let you read what my forecast for 1992 was, and then comment on it:

Three millions celebrated in 1792, 63,000,000 in 1892, and 300,000,000 will in 1992 celebrate the landing of Columbus. They will be educated and refined, for the arts and sciences will be taught in the public schools. Not only will the mind of the pupil be trained but the hand as well, and each child will be instructed in the manual of tools; they will be instructed in the functions of every part of the human system; "man know thyself" will have a meaning in 1992. The economic and social questions of the day will also be taught in the schools, there will be no uneducated persons to act as drags on the car of progress.

The form of government will be simpler, the Initiative and Referendum will prevail and law makers will not be the autocrats they now are, for they will truly register the will of the people, they will not dictate to them as at present. The commonwealth will be organized on industrial lines, labor organizations will have disappeared, for there will be no longer a necessity for their existence. An ideal democracy will stand upon the foundations we of 1892 are erecting. Railroads, water courses, telegraphs, telephones, pneumatic tubes, and all other methods of transporting passengers, freight, and intelligence will be owned and operated by the government; the earnings of these agencies will swell the public treasury; homes will flourish, for they will no longer be taxed. Instead of devoting so much time and money to the erecting of great public structures as at present, the erection and adornment of the home will receive first consideration. Each home will be regarded as a contribution to the wealth and beauty of the nation, the earnings of public concerns will defray the cost of maintaining streets, sewers, water works, and light and heat giving establishments. Cremation will take the place of the present system of burying the dead, the living will be healthier, for the earth will not be poisoned through interment of infection. The contents of sewers will not flow into river and stream to send deadly vapors through the air but will be utilized to enrich the harvest yielding earth. The progress of the lower grades of animal life has been skillfully guided and hastened until we may now assert that cattle and fowl are approaching perfection; in 1992 the same attention will be bestowed on the human race, and instead of rushing blindly forward, increasing and multiplying at haphazard, humanity will knowingly and intelligently advance to higher altitudes. There will be no very rich or very poor, for, long before 1992 dawns upon the world, the industrialists will have learned that the raising of large families is but another way to create slaves to perform the drudgery of the wealthy, and the family will be restricted to the capacity of the parents to maintain and educate. Under such conditions prisons and poorhouses will decline and divorces will not be considered necessary. The system which makes criminals of men and women and at the same time makes millionaires of others will have disappeared, as a consequence the confinement and punishment of criminals will occupy but little of the thought or time of the man of 1992.

I am writing this in February, 1920. Twenty-seven years have passed since the events recorded in this chapter were weaving themselves into the history of 1892 and 1893. Many men have come and gone, many things not dreamed of then have occupied the thought of the people for awhile and gone on toward oblivion.

More stringent laws on immigration have replaced those in force when I wrote that long letter to Mr. Buchanan. More men understand economic conditions than gave heed to them twenty-seven years ago, but selfishness lives, greed thrives, and graft is now known and spoken of as a recognized means of acquiring wealth.

Within the last six months two great strikes have taken place. One was known as the steel strike, the other was called the coal strike.[2] In both strikes workingmen were charged with . . . bolshevism. . . . Hysteria seized a great many, and denunciation of aliens and foreigners generally thickened the air of the United States. We have become accustomed to hearing the term "Red" applied to anyone who expresses a radical sentiment concerning a change in our present method of administering the affairs of government. Men and women alien to our soil and institutions have been deported to a foreign land because their presence among us was inimical to our institutions. I was not on the jury that convicted them, I did not hear or read the evidence on which they were found guilty, and am not, in consequence thereof, competent to say whether they were treated justly or unjustly. I do believe however that if our government deported bolshevists it did not deport bolshevism, and bolshevism will never be deported, abated, or suppressed so long as its parent and original importer remains with us uncurbed, unchecked, and unmolested. The testimony taken before congressional and other commissions bore out all I said in the Buchanan letter as to the methods of stimulating immigration.

Following the writing of that letter, I made a personal canvass of several localities in the hard and soft coal regions. The battle of Homestead had been fought, and I gave some thought, time, and attention to workers in the steel industry. The man-importing industry flourished everywhere and with the sanction of men of wealth and influence known as "captains of industry." Grafters

[2] The bitter and tragic Steel Strike began September 22, 1919, and was finally called off on January 8, 1920. Following an "insurgent" strike in Illinois in August 1919, the post-war coal strike was called on November 1, 1919. In the face of government intervention through the courts, which forced the strike to be called off by the officers of the United Mine Workers' Union, the strikers refused to return to work for several weeks.

of human flesh, bone, and muscle, were engaged in grafting alien stock onto American industry. Duplicity, falsehood, deception, and greed worked double shifts under the never-closing eye of capital as represented in many but not all of the owners of coal mines and iron mills. These men, native Americans for the most part, were the instigators and beneficiaries of the operation of a secret plan of filling and refilling mine and factory with poor, unlettered workmen from crowded Europe. . . .

If an alien imported to this country is a bolshevist, he may be undesirable but he is not a traitor to his country. What shall we call the American who openly, secretly, by himself or through another, connives at, assists, or aids in importing a bolshevist from a foreign land to take the job of an American citizen? Others may call him what they please, I brand him a traitor to our republic. With every boat load of alien bolshevists deported from these shores a brand should be placed on their importers, their aiders and abetters. . . .

I was an agitator, but my agitating was always on and along American lines. I was not opposed to the alien or to immigration, but I did want the immigrant to come of his own free will and accord, with his eyes open and fully aware of what he would, or might, encounter among us.

My forecast for 1992 won for me, when published, a recognition that was quite general but not flattering. Purposely I said that homes would not be taxed in 1992. I wanted to know what people thought of that proposition but they did not tell me. One critic observed that "Mr. Powderly must dislike hard work. The home owner not willing to pay taxes on his home must be an idler so shiftless as not to take much interest in a home." . . .

For what I said on cremation I gained such a generous volume of criticism that a library of scrap books could easily be filled with it. One of the clergymen who wrote me up . . . said: "Mr. Powderly should amend his prophecy by acknowledging that he does not believe he has a soul. In case you are cremated, Mr. Powderly, where will your immortal soul go to?"

That surprising inquiry, and from a clergyman too, perplexed

me for I had always believed that the soul became free from its
earthly entanglement at the departure of breath. . . .

What drew down on my head criticism unstinted, bitter, sar-
castic, and personal was my suggestion that the "family be restricted to the capacity of the parents to maintain and educate."
In this I was "flying in the face of Divine Providence," for was
it not written that we should "increase and multiply" in order to
"replenish the earth"? The greater part of this particular line of
criticism was aimed at me by Catholic clergymen. In much of it I
found more of personal hostility than a desire to set me right, if
wrong. I thought I detected a note of fear that revenue from
church attendance might diminish. I was admonished that when
breath left me, my soul might go where it could fraternize with
the shade of Malthus, and from the opinions expressed as to the
whereabouts of Malthus I judge that he is not confined in a cold
storage plant. A well-known clergyman wrote . . . .

To knowingly, willfully and deliberately frustrate the beneficent design of
Divine Providence in barring the entrance to this world of a human soul is
forbidden by every instinct of God-fearing man. No law human or divine
can be cited to countenance such a practice as Mr. Powderly suggests.
Surely his parents were derelict in not instilling in his mind more of respect
for God's law. Does he not know that God directs the human soul before
as well as after birth and to stay that soul's entry to life and usefulness is a
mortal sin so terrible as to draw down upon the offender the wrath of God.
The human soul must not be touched by the hand of impious man. It shall
not be denied entrance to this world and can not be sent out, or hastened
out of this world except by the will of God. Mr. Powderly had better
confine his effort to his Quixotic onslaught on the so called Reading
Combine.

.   .   .   .

I have never questioned God's direction of the "human soul
before as well as after birth." I have always believed that when
the bodies of men are abused, overworked, and starved until a
stage in human development is reached, where the brute takes the
place of the man, spirituality is dwarfed if not killed, and the
finest, noblest attributes of the human soul are stifled. It was that
stifling process I had to deal with, and I came more directly and
intimately in contact with it than did any of my critics. I came to

believe, and was warranted in that belief by my observation of and experience with the employers of labor, that they did not think about or care whether a worker had a soul so long as he could grind out the daily grist on which the exploiter could realize a profit. The exploiter I have in mind was the average employer of that day, and that his prototype still exists let these words from one of the foremost employers of the present day testify: "We need the strong backs and weak minds from Europe to do our heavy work. The next generation will be too well educated and not strong enough to do it—they will not be as docile as their fathers." . . . If good Christians become shocked at the mere suggestion of regulating the number of children in the family of a poor workingman and raise an outcry against such regulation, why have they not included the rich man in the manifestation of their wrath? I made a quiet but searching inquiry among the wealthy people of three towns, and learned of but two families with more than four children each. . . .

The besetting sin of that day was lust, lust of riches, of ease, of power and social position. The brightest mind that could throw light on a darkened world was obscured beneath the raiment of poverty. The questions: how well does he do his work? does his labor benefit humanity? is he a successful man? were all answered in the negative if it could not be said that he had money, was rich, or was making money. Ambition did not run to serving God or man, but to serving self by getting money. Acquiring wealth became our sole object in life. Instead of money being merely the means of living it was the main object of life. . . . "How can I make the most of the talents God gave me in my life work?" was not asked by the young man starting out in life. "How can I make the most money by it?" was his daily inquiry and thought. The inordinate lust for money was the cause of two-thirds of the crime and corruption of that period. I leave it to present day actors on the world's stage to prove that a still worse condition does not prevail now. Pay as little as you can for labor and get the most you can out of the worker was then the rule. Men became wealthy at a terrible sacrifice, for many ignored, or parted with, the finest and cultivated the meanest, often the basest, qualities of their natures in order to get rich. Did this lust for money, did the questionable practices resorted to to get money by men of small families, receive the wrathful, indignant denunciation that came my way for merely hinting that fewer children among the workers might have the effect of causing wealthy men to stain their hands with honest labor? By no means. Did the precious souls of the children of the poor receive the kind consideration of those who affirmed that: "the human soul must not be touched by the hand of impious man"? Not that I could see. . . .

In this year of 1920 we read that the birth rate of France, Germany, Italy, and what was once Austria has fallen off very much. "The human soul must not be touched by the hand of impious man" is what I was told in 1892. From August 1, 1914, up to and including November 11, 1918, the hands of impious men have pointed a way out of this world, in violation of the will of that God they professed to believe in. . . .

. . . . .

The savage stole up behind his victim, and stabbed him in the back; he scalped him, he burned him at the stake, and we drove him off toward the setting sun after we had taken his land from him—but the savage did not invoke the aid of Almighty God in his cruelty. He devoted no time or talent to inventing new agencies of death or torture, and he left his victim dead, mercifully dead. He was not civilized enough to conjure out of a hellish brain the submarine, poison gas, liquid flame, shrapnel, shell, a seventy-five-mile gun that was intended to destroy humanity by the city-full; he did not invade the clouds to hurl death and destruction on innocent women and children. No! It was left to civilized, Christian man who prayed: "Thy Kingdom come, Thy will be done on earth as it is in heaven," to do all this and gloat over it as for a cycle of time he made this once fair earth a veritable hell.

. . . . .

Some men think they are now engaged in writing the history of that war. They cannot and never will do it. Unless God Himself descends to earth and . . . throws upon the screen of infinity a picture of crushed bodies and brains, of dead, wounded and dying, of mangled men and beasts, of orphaned children, of widowed wives, of all the rivers of blood that flowed from bodies that He, that same God, sent into this world, and from which they should not have been hastened "except by the will of God," its history cannot be told. . . . No history will, or ever can, tell the whole truth of that war; for the historian cannot trace to its lair the wolf of greed, of duplicity, of treachery—of double damned diplomacy that brought it on. The billions of lost, wasted, or squandered dollars may be accounted for or at least enumerated, but the billions lost in untilled soil, in unprovided homes, in wrecked habitations of men, in lost morale among the millions of earth can never be set down in cold, conviction-compelling type. The death rattle of millions cannot be pictured by all the historians of earth. The lost or strayed honesty of men who employ labor and of those who perform labor that would prevent the dumping on the market of the inferior in material and workmanship that all men complain of now cannot be chronicled by any historian no matter how graphic a pen he wields or how skilled or versed in the juggling of words he may be.

How does all this hark back to 1892 and 1893? I was condemned—justly so perhaps, although I do not admit it—for suggesting in 1892 that the number of children in the poor man's family be restricted to the earning and maintaining capacity of the parents. Christian ministers became eloquent in the use of epithets to bestow on one who would lay the hand of impious man on the human soul. . . . They knew what avarice and greed were; they knew that the rulers of earth were bent on conquest and that conquest comes through sacrilege, blasphemy, murder, rape, wholesale butchery of men and women. They could read the signs of the times written in a truckling press that they knew how to interpret. . . . What man among them raised his voice in eloquent, determined protest? Not one. When the magazine was touched off at Sarajevo and the citadels of civilization began to crumble, what man of God raised his voice in intelligent, determined, fearless, impartial, convincing protest? . . .

Dinny Doolin was crossing a stream swollen by a sudden flood, the bridge was old, narrow, and rickety. When he got near the middle he became frightened and halted, scarcely daring to go forward and fearing to turn back. At last he made up his mind to risk it in going on, so he said: "Well, here goes in the name of God—but the divil is not a bad fellow aither." I thought I caught an echo from Dinny Doolin in every fulmination against the iniquity of wholesale murder from August 1, 1914, to November 11, 1918.

And during the war, what happened? Did we not see and hear Christian ministers praying that God would strengthen the arm of the side they were on that it could do to death men on the other side? Were they fulfilling the law of that God who said "Thou shalt not kill"? . . .

Christianity has been under fire ever since that war started; it has, and by many learned men too, been pronounced a failure. They were all wrong, Christianity did not fail. Nothing can fail that has not been tried. Christianity lives, and is as virile and true as when its founder bequeathed it to men as a rule of conduct to follow and abide by. Some Christian ministers have failed, but they have failed because they seldom preached and rarely practiced Christianity. . . .

.   .   .   .

What of the world today? What of our own country in this hour? Morale destroyed or at lowest ebb; faith in those who claim to represent God shattered; confidence in men and government supplanted by suspicion and unrest; grasping greed and avarice ruling the conduct of those who barter and sell. Men tell me the nation has changed from sanity to insanity; that our country is one vast bedlam; that hope of reform is dead; that organized labor and the profiteer stand on equal ground; and that things will continue to grow worse until chaos shall usurp the place of the evils we now face and dread.

.   .   .   .

. . . We are living in a reckless, irresponsible, jazz-band, moving-picture, vaudeville, chocolate-eating, gum-chewing age. To the mentally shortsighted, faith in our government or hope for the future may not be visible, but I believe that out of all our trouble good will come.

I am neither optimist nor pessimist, but having heard prediction that "the country is going to hell" for the last fifty years I refuse to be stampeded or part with my faith in God, my neighbor, or my country. I realize that the present is dark and the future seems hopeless, but in summoning the witnesses who can testify to what happened after the War between the States, particularly during the interim between the panic of 1873 and that of 1907, I can from their lips hear a message of hope and reassurance. Our country is safe, its people are sound to the core; they will restore order, win back lost confidence and clothe the words "government of the people, by the people and for the people" with the raiment of real meaning.

Our trouble is that with the ending of the war we found old forms and formulas dead, dying, decayed, or worthless, and time enough has not elasped for readjustment to brighten in our eyes the vision of future success in traveling forward in the new pathway of "individual and national greatness."

With the death of slavery at the stroke of Lincoln's pen, a system began to take on life and grow to such proportions that it became possible for one man to die poor in 1919 holding fifty millions of dollars in his cold, dead hand, after giving away over three hundred and fifty millions of dollars.[3] He never earned one million of that vast sum; it was not and is not possible for one man alone and unaided to do such a thing through honest labor of hand or brain. Utilizing the brains of other men, taking advantage of competitors, shrewd manipulation of stocks, and the fusing into dollars of the labor of many men in that crucible called the steel industry laid that vast sum in his shrewd, cunning hand. When he passed on, he was eulogized and canonized by public men and in the press, but the means by which he acquired these millions were not dwelt on in sermon, eulogy, or panegyric. My acquaintance with him dated back to Homestead in 1892. I did not know him intimately, but I knew him well. I knew him as one who was personally a good man, a man who liked to do a

---

[3] Andrew Carnegie.

good thing, but wanted the world to know he did it. I speak of him only because he represented in life and activity a system that must give way, a system that cannot live and thrive, if free government is to survive, and I am sure it will.

. . . I read in a morning paper that this man "made millionaires of forty of the men he brought up in the steel business." To make millionaires of forty men, the voice of manly independence was stifled in ten thousand other men. . . . To make forty millionaires and gather together four hundred millions of dollars, the sweat and blood of thousands were poured freely forth in steel mill and blast furnace.

Stand just a little to one side and watch Harry McAleer as he acts as hooker-up before the rail rolls in a Bessemer steel mill. When the eye of the expert steel maker detects the changing colors of the flame spitting from the converter, he shuts off the blast; the huge vessel with its content of seething, molten metal slowly turns on its gudgeons, and the large ingot molds are filled from the mouth of the converter. The ingots are later on run through rolls, reduced in thickness though enlarged as to length. These are cut into pieces, each of which is sufficient to make a steel rail. Harry McAleer inserted one of these reduced ingots between the jaws of the swift revolving rail rolls; it was red hot of course; it went through, becoming larger and thinner as it passed on. Another man, on the other side caught it with his tongs, shoved it to the next and a smaller aperture between the rolls as they were reversed, and it went back longer than before for Harry to hook up and start back on its fiery return journey. It began to take on the form of a steel rail. When it had been started back on its final passage between the rolls, somebody or something distracted Harry's attention, his foot slipped, he stumbled forward, the fiery, jagged end of the rail struck his body, passed through it, carried him forward and left him with his warm life blood pouring out on that heated instrument of torture and death.

They carried him home. A wife suddenly changed to widow met his corpse at the garden gate. Children there were, and these became orphans. Shortly after the funeral the company had need for the house in which that family lived. They were required to move to make room for the family of the man who took Harry's place at the rolls. Fellow workmen paid Harry's funeral expenses; fellow workmen took up a collection for the temporary relief of the widow and orphans; fellow workmen cared for his children for a time, and then the world forgot Harry McAleer and his family. Not one dollar came from that four hundred million fund to erect a home over the heads of Harry McAleer's widow and orphaned children. Millions were devoted to the erection of libraries all over this country and part of Europe, and this one poor, rich man took credit for every dollar so expended. But the names of the Harry McAleers whose labor created every honest dollar of these millions were never mentioned and never remembered.

. . . .

As you snuggle comfortably back in your seat in the parlor car which conveys you from starting point to destination, turn to the stock quotations in the paper in your hand and note the fluctuations of steel as men juggle with it on the exchange. Ponder for a moment over what you are riding, and, if it does not occur to you, let me tell you that you are traveling safely over the blood and sweat of the Harry McAleers of the steel mills. Let me tell you that the cost in sweat and blood of these men is never reckoned in fixing the price of steel; but forget it if you will, overlook it how you may, evade as you please, the steel rail they use in their mock trading passed, in the making, through a crucible tempered with the blood, the bone, and sinew of Harry McAleer.

I am not talking of or for organized or unorganized labor, but [it] is just because labor has not received its fair . . . share of recognition in the making of the wealth and necessities of this country that we have a condition confronting us which approximates insanity. . . .

Such an unhealthy condition of affairs cannot safely continue. It will end when women and men begin to realize that upon each one depends, in a measure, a restoration of the balance necessary to successful coöperation with one another. It will end when we look out on the world from a less selfish standpoint than we now occupy. It will end when we begin in earnest to catch sight of the great truth that we are all of one family, composed of faults and virtues, and that we must be tolerant of faults if we would give the virtues full play. Here we are of all races, we come from everywhere to make a family that has no family tree, a family with no common ancestor, and yet a family that may be traced back to the greatest of all common ancestors—God the Father. We are all children of Him who gave us birth and everything following it to make us happy, contented, prosperous, if we but use His gifts wisely and intelligently. It is because we allowed some to monopolize all the gifts, that there is dissatisfaction, distrust and want in the land. We affect reverence for and belief in God, yet sneer at him who tells us that God gave this earth to all His children, to be used for the benefit of all.

．　　．　　．　　．

I do not blame or condemn that one man for what he did. He but took advantage of the opportunity presented to him to get control of that wealth. The indictment I draw is not one to be called The People vs. Monopoly, but an indictment entitled Right vs. The People for their indifference in permitting wrong to prevail. The ills we complain of are of our own making. We planted the seed and nursed the growth of every evil we suffer from. Let us face the music bravely, acknowledge our error manfully, and determine resolutely to coöperate one with another honestly in future.

From a standpoint within easy distance of the sound and fury of conflicting elements in the American field of economics, with vision unclouded by prejudice, selfish ambition, or personal bias, I can view the processes of industrial adjustment, or readjustment, with a feeling akin to that with which the artisan may regard the various parts of the machinery his hands have helped to fashion as they are being finally assembled and fitted into one perfect, accurately balanced instrument.

Perhaps the great war resulted in bringing all these elements into sharp contrast and conflict at an earlier date than was

scheduled under peacetime conditions, but the conflict was inevitable. The mine was laid, and had been laid for years before
the war began which was destined to explode and shatter the
foundations of the industrial structure in which men labored and
were formerly known as master and servant. It is true these distinctions were not so sharply outlined as they were before the
war of the sixties between the states, but they existed, nevertheless, and for many years after that conflict, the courts rendered
many decisions on the presumption that men worked as master
and servant. The courts did not recognize, and those who were
called employers did not admit, that men whose money was invested in productive enterprise and who gave personal attention
to their business, were workers. No matter how much we may
say about classes and class distinction, there are no classes in
the United States. Men are workers or idlers. I have always refused to admit that we have classes in our country just as I have
refused to admit that the labor of a man's hand or brain is a
commodity. When in the eighties I argued that labor was not a
commodity, my statements were challenged; the law[4] now declares as a truth what I was ridiculed for saying then. . . .

Let me here quote from a letter written by me in December,
1882, to [the] Hon. Abram S. Hewitt, of New York. I had heard
Mr. Hewitt speak at a meeting a day or two before, and my letter
to him, among other things said this:

I infer from your speech that you look on labor as a commodity. True
you did not call it by that name, yet the impression conveyed to me by your
words was that you lumped labor itself with the products of labor. I could,
in what you said, see no differentiation between a bale of hay, a bar of pig
iron, or a sewing machine and the hand or brain labor of the man who
made these things. If that is really your fixed opinion, and I hate to think
it is, you must, in order to be consistent, rate the workman as a commodity
also.

You, as an employer, do not regard your own labor as a commodity.
You plan, contrive, map out, and design. Surely you will not call your
effort a commodity. Whether you care to acknowledge it or not you are a
laborer. Your labor and that of the so called skilled workmen are one in the
finished product. How will you, where will you draw the line?

[4] Powderly refers here to the Clayton Act of 1914, of which section 6 declares that
"the labor of a human being is not a commodity or article of commerce."

You do not call the money you put into your business a commodity, you call it your capital. The labor of the artisan is his capital. These two capitals are united in turning raw material into finished product.

The product of labor is, or may be, a commodity and may be sold or exchanged as such, but until mankind returns the worker to slavery his labor cannot be regarded as a commodity.

As well assert that thought is a commodity, for thought enters into every well performed task of the laborer.

．　　　．　　　．　　　．

Perhaps a day will come when people will stop talking about "classes" in this country. I always refused to be labeled as belonging to a class, and objected to being classified. I always did object to the term "my class." If a man may properly be assigned to a class, how should I be classified? If I am to be classified, to what or which class shall I be assigned and am I privileged to change my classification with every change of activities? I was. in turn a switchman, a car repairer, a trackman, a brakeman, a machinist, a tramp, a locomotive fireman, a locomotive engineer, a foreman in a machine shop, a mayor of a city, a chief of a labor organization, an editor, a writer, an attorney at law, was Commissioner-General of Immigration, and am now a government employee. I was as good a man the day I began work as a switchman as I am now. In which of these callings am I to be classified? Am I to be assigned to a class known under the name of the occupation I follow at date of classification, or shall I be classified as a worker and let it go at that? If so, then who is a worker? I know a man who was a clerk thirty-four years ago and is now a president of a steel company. We have been friends ever since he was a clerk. He now gives all his time and attention to managing the vast concern over which he presides. He regards it as part of his duty to know the economic condition of every man and boy connected with the steel company. He is on speaking and visiting terms with every one of them. He has established libraries, reading rooms, rest rooms, gymnasiums, swimming pools, meeting rooms and lunch rooms for the workers. He has established playgrounds for the children of the employees of the steel company. He meets them all on an equality [*sic*]. He sets a time for them to come to him and talk over such matters as they are interested in; they set a time for him to come and talk with them about improving methods of production. He lays his cards on the table and frankly tells them how his company is financially situated. He tells me he receives most valuable suggestions from the workers, and they tell me they never have to demand increased wages or reduced hours. He has a hall fitted out for their union to meet in, and frequently accepts invitations to meet with them and listen to their debates. He flatly refuses to meet the employees of the steel company in a patronizing manner or on any other plane than as fellow workers. How shall we classify a man of that kind? Years ago that man became a Knight of Labor through my influence, and . . . he still believes in and—what is better—practices the principles of the Order.

The term "master and servant" is dead. The world is accustoming itself to know all as servants, and the word service shall soon take on its real meaning and significance. Out of all the marching and countermarching, out of all the contentions and transitions, will come a fuller, clearer realization of our duty to each other, and our highest duty to each other is service to each other. How this service may best be performed shall constitute the real problem of the future; in its solution toleration must take the place of intolerance, moderation must supplant excess, secret scheming and underhand dealing must give way to open and aboveboard business methods, and the term "love your neighbor" must be clothed anew with the meaning intended when the words were first spoken.

. . . . .

The call of the new day shall be one of service from each according to his ability that all may be served according to their needs. We should begin preparation for this new era by entering the kindergarten of coöperation. Real coöperation has never been tried out to its logical conclusion. It cannot suddenly take the place of the present method of work life; it must be approached gradually, noting failure and success at every step, until the broad-gauge track of coöperation lies plain before us.

. . . . .

I never believed in the wage system and said so. I would substitute for it a system that would relieve the honest laborer of his handicaps and the honest employer of his doubts. You may judge whether I am right or wrong. . . .

. . . Men inspired by lofty sentiments or high ideals, proclaim themselves internationalists and would labor for the remodeling of the world by wholesale. Scattering the little they have to offer over so large a surface leaves none of it visible anywhere.

I once had a neighbor who was so well versed in plant life that he devoted most of his own life to telling others how to raise vegetables. While he was industriously engaged in such altruistic work, he neglected to cultivate a little plot of ground around his own dwelling and the weeds, taking advantage of his inattention, grew luxuriantly all over his garden. I doubt if many were influenced by his preachments. In fact, I believe his effort was largely wasted. Had he taught by example and raised garden truck instead of weeds around his home, he would have accomplished something of benefit for the community. I believe in my own home first, my own country first, and regard it a sacred duty to protect, develop and defend both. Only the man who values and would protect his own home and country first is worthy of either. The man who would defend his own home and country before all others is, of all men, best qualified to defend the home and country of another.

We hear much idle talk about internationalism. Men who do not proclaim themselves internationalists are sneered at by many who call themselves internationalists. I regard that as all wrong— he is the true internationalist who is really and sincerely a nationalist, for no man can truly appreciate a foreign land who does not love and appreciate his own before all other lands. To be so international as to love other countries while remaining indifferent to his own is not the duty of the true American.

I would deal fairly, squarely and justly by all countries, for, above all else, I am an American.

APPENDIX I
THE PHILOSOPHER'S STONE DEGREE

ONLY THE FEW are entitled to it, only the few strive to earn it. It is conferred as a token of appreciation, or reward for distinctive service in the cause of mankind. Badges, crosses, insignias, and decorations of various kinds and designs have, during the ages, been bestowed on men of military training whose deeds of valor have won recognition from the rulers of earth. The decoration now conferred on you is an emblem of peace and not of war. It is only given to one whose love for his neighbor has been exemplified in deeds of loving, unselfish service, symbolic of our Order, and its mission should be regarded by you as binding you to the performance of renewed effort in a cause in which right and duty blend. Every right you claim for yourself entails on you the performance of duty to a neighbor.

You are for the time being a part of the moving power for good on earth. That hate may vanish from, and love rule in, the hearts of men is our hope. Become reconciled to the thought that what we teach will in this hour be called utopian, visionary, and chimerical, but if you, through further effort and example, shall cause one other man or woman to qualify as one worthy of such recognition as you now receive, you will have gone far toward the final coming of "good will among men."

You are now asked to look upon and study this emblem of the Degree of the Philosopher's Stone. We have been taught to believe that what the Philosopher's Stone touches turns to gold. You are asked to substitute the word wealth for gold. Gold may be used as coin, for ornament, and for various uses known to workers in refined metals, but the word wealth embraces gold, all other precious metals, everything of use taken from the earth, and every noble attribute, impulse, thought, and deed of man in a good cause. A wealth of learning, of gratitude, of devotion and ability, may be possessed by a man, but if these are not united with love, the greatest of all is lacking. You are therefore asked to look upon and study the universal side of this emblem. Here you see what is typical of the surface of earth and what it contains. You see a cube, or square, a crystal or triangle, and around them is a band or circle. On the surface you see characters all of which have a meaning far beyond that which they may claim elsewhere. "C. C. C." as tokened here stand for cube, crystal, circle the parts of earth and circle within which it is encompassed. You see a head, a hand and a heart, the principal parts of man; these are represented also by "H. H. H."

The large C at the top betokens the earth's border line, or its circumference, the great circle within which all of earth is encompassed. To the left of the large C is the H larger than the other two. Heart, head and hand is what H. H. H., stand for, but the largest H stands for more than either; it is emblematic of the labor of heart, head, and hand for Humanity. Since the world was young the struggle of progressive men has been to give the heart full play in the councils and plans of men.

The head which you look upon is here called upon to represent eyes that see that which is good, noble, and kind, ears to catch the sound of hope and hear that which is good, noble, and kind, lips and tongue to voice words of wisdom and to counsel all that is good, noble, and kind. Within that head the ever active brain may plan and scheme and contrive, but without the promptings of the heart its plans may be laid in indifference to what is good, noble, and kind. It may contrive in cruelty and consummate in oppression. Therefore the heart with its promptings to all that is good, noble, and kind is here represented. With the head always planning for the good of man, prompted by the heart beating in sympathy with the best aspirations of mankind, the outstretched hand before you will always remain open to give—not charity but justice—for with equal and exact justice prevailing between men charity will be unknown.

Eyes to see the path of duty, ears to catch words of wisdom, lips to voice the love of man, a heart to beat in unison with the best that brain can plan and the outstretched, never-closing hand to aid and assist, protect and defend, the weak and distressed that they may become strong, self-reliant, and useful among men, all utilizing and assisting others to utilize the earth with its cubes, its crystals and its circles for the benefit of mankind, are typified in the emblem you are henceforth to wear as a priceless treasure. Money did not buy it, money could not buy it. Let not love of gain tempt you to part with it.

The reverse side of this emblem shows a level plain on which stands what appears to be a clump of trees. In reality it represents but one tree of many trunks and many roots, it is the banyan tree. When the branches of the banyan tree bend to and touch the earth, they fasten themselves to and take root in the soil, sending upward new, or what appears to be new, trunks of new trees. All are, however, united to and part of one body. This is emblematic of the * * * * *, the growth of which in new assemblies adds strength to the parent body and, though operating and conducting business in a new place, is so united to all other assemblies of the Order of * * * * * as to constitute one complete, harmonious whole. As the growth of each new branch strengthens the tree, so the growth of each new assembly strengthens the * * * * *; injury to one part means loss to all, therefore, it is the concern of all to prevent injustice, counsel kindness, and heal the wounds of the world's cruelties wherever inflicted among men.

As the earth everywhere is for the use of man, this Order is also to be considered his assistant, and it is hoped that through your effort the * * * * * will extend and grow and thrive and flourish until wherever a voice cries out against injustice * * * * *'s will be there to hear that cry and render aid.

APPENDIX II
SECRET CIRCULAR

EXPLANATION OF THE SIGNS AND SYMBOLS OF THE ORDER

*(The Master Workmen will read the following to
their locals at least once in every
quarter, and safely guard it)*

THE GLOBE which we place on the outside of the Outer Veil is the most perfect emblem of the Order of the Knights of Labor. It symbolizes the field of operations of the organization. In selecting this sign, the idea was to keep the Order as closely veiled from the scrutiny of the outside world as the center of the earth is screened from the observation of inhabitants of that planet. Could we but pierce the earth's surface with mortal vision, and scan that part of it from which all things radiate, we would not feel that interest which now attracts us toward it. The mystery surrounding it, the hidden meaning of the Creator in thus guarding from worldly eyes the secrets which philosophers vainly strive to learn and unfold, only cause us to feel it is more wonderful than it really is. In this the purpose of the Creator is to show that though we inhabit the earth, though we may appear to have a knowledge of everything pertaining to the earth and its inhabitants, yet that which constitutes the center of our world must ever be unto us as a sealed book. But only so far as the mystery surrounding it was concerned was the Order of the Knights of Labor to resemble the hidden secret of earth. It was intended that to all men, of all races and of all creeds, should be given the key with which to unlock the Outer and Inner Veils leading to the Order, which, above all others, ultimately leads all men up out of the house of bondage into *"perfect light."* No dream of mortal was ever grander than the aims which men of our Order keep in view. To gather that strength necessary to make a successful beginning, to create a nucleus around which the hopes of toilers everywhere can cling with perfect safety, it was necessary that the early days of the Order should be shrouded in darkness, though darkness was the opposite of the purpose kept in sight in the infancy of the Order, yet that steps should be carefully taken in the gloom of broken hopes, disappointments, heartburnings, and fears which beset the pioneers of other movements was a stern, sad necessity.

The jealousies of men, the ambitions of others, the fears of those who must ever cling to others who are stronger than themselves, were reasons why no outside show of organizing was made on the initial morn of our'existence as an Order. The seed must be carefully sown; the centuries of wrongdoing, of misery and persecution had well nigh broken the hopes of the toilers, hence the necessity for absolute secrecy. To declare the intentions of those who founded the Order openly to the world would only lead to disaster and ruin. Such a proceeding might, in all probability, turn back the index on the dial of progress a full century. Care must be taken, caution observed and nothing done that could possibly lead to failure. All of these things were carefully considered, and the decision reached to keep "profoundly secret everything seen or heard, said or done." If in the spring time of the year, the seed is scattered broadcast over the earth, it is likely to be combatted by the elements. Some qualities of seeds cannot withstand the early frost, the chilling blast, the drenching rain, or the scorching sun; they must be sheltered or perish. It was thus that the Knights of Labor were ushered into being. The opposition of capital, the jealousies of the earth's workers, and the danger that faced such a wide departure from the path of ages rendered it necessary that all things must be done in secret. These elements were to the infant Order as the frosts, the rains, the winds, and the sun would be to the tiny, unprotected seed in early spring time. As the seed is covered over with a thin layer of earth until it has taken root, so was the Order covered until it, too, had secured a foothold. After the seed has taken root, the very elements which would have destroyed it, if left exposed, tend to strengthen and bring it up into strong, active, being. After the Order of the Knights of Labor had established a foothold, then the opposition which would have destroyed it in the beginning became as food on which it grew strong, influential and powerful for the good of mankind.

While the center of the earth is emblematic of the secrecy of the Order, the surface of the earth, the surface of the Globe is adumbrative of the field, the scope of the Order. Its operations will be confined to no prescribed limits except those which bind the earth itself. As the surface of the Globe embraces all countries, so does our Order. All countries are to be the possessors of the blessings which flow from united, organized action on the part of the toilers of the earth.

———————

On entering the vestibule (which we call the anteroom), a small triangular table confronts the intruder. The shape of the table is in itself emblematic of a certain principle, but as that will be discussed further on, the purpose which it serves alone shall claim attention here. On the table a basket full of cards is stationed. The lesson taught the entering member is EDUCATION. The first step on the road to progress is intelligence. That this intelligence may have full play, it is necessary that education be made an auxiliary to the natural attainments of man. The cards in the basket are for the purpose of teaching members that in order to gain admittance to the sanctuary (which we call the meeting-room), the first step on the road to knowledge must be taken. To write one's name is in itself a very simple thing to do, but when we reflect that through the dead and vanished centuries the workers were not permitted to learn to even write their names, we can measure at least a portion of the forward step which has been taken on the road to the emancipation of LABOR. That every member should know how to write his name in full and read the same when written is a necessity. That every member should be forcibly reminded of the duty he owes to himself in acquiring a knowledge sufficient to prevent the evil-disposed from imposing on him, this stimulus is given to the entering member. Two causes combine to inspire the novitiate, to create a thirst for the attainable. The first is pride, for on entering the sanctuary, he desires to do so on an equal footing with his fellow member who can write his name. The second cause is that his eyes are opened, for the first time maybe, to the fact that he is inferior to other men who can write, and a determination seizes him to emulate the example thus set before him, and which other men practice.

The presenting of the card at the Inner Veil indicates that the incomer is acquiring the rudiments of politeness, and inasmuch as the society he expects to find beyond the Inner Veil is better, farther advanced, and in every way preferable to that which he leaves behind him in the outside world, he announces his arrival in a manner which indicates that he approves of and wishes to mingle with that society.

It is to be hoped that the day will come when men of all the nations of earth shall govern themselves; that he who governs shall do so by and with the consent of the governed. That the government of all nations may be properly administered, it is necessary that the governed be educated; therefore, the first step taken in the Knights of Labor is toward that end. This lesson, though simple in itself, is one of the grandest taught by the Order. He who writes his name in full will soon learn to read his name when written. In this way we make it possible for the member to shield himself from the self-seeker and the knave, and when he performs his duty as a citizen by depositing his ballot when selecting a ruler, he has it in his power to do it knowingly and intelligently.

By means of the card we ascertain the qualifications of the member, and in selecting officers for the assembly, we need not perform the delicate task of asking what a member's qualifications are. We know it from experience. Be educated, that you may educate others.

The Lance which confronts the member who knocks for admittance on the Inner Veil signifies "defense." It teaches that, as the lance in the hands of the knight of old was a weapon of defense, so too is the lance of today a weapon of defense to all who shield themselves behind it. It protects no one who remains on the outside. While a "helping hand is extended to all branches of honorable toil," yet the power to defend all branches of toil and all men who toil is not so great as when they are sheltered by the folds of the Order of the Knights of Labor.

The lance of old was used to pierce the armor of the opposing warrior, the lance of today is intended to pierce the armor of greed; the lance of past ages was used to pierce the body of the man who confronted his fellow man as an enemy, the lance placed on the inner wall of the fortress of humanity is intended to pierce the enemy of mankind—IGNORANCE. In no mortal combat can this lance be used but in that combat against the evils to "body, mind, and estate" which "ignorance and greed have imposed"; to dismount the enemy of mankind—"concentrated wealth"; to destroy the power of "the tyranny of capital"; to pierce darkness of mental slavery, this lance is ever ready, and in this work must never rust or tarnish. The point of this lance is typical of intelligence; where this point is thrust, the clouds of darkness roll away as the mist before noonday sun. That this lance may never be turned toward the friends of humanity, the member must first be educated and taught how best to use it for the good of man.

That which strikes the newly initiated most forcibly on entering the sanctuary is that all members, whether they hold positions or not, occupy the same level. This is to indicate that there are no degrees of rank, no upper or lower class—all men are admitted on an equal footing. By this lesson the member is encouraged to work in harmony with his fellow member; he feels that to him all are the same, and in our dealings with each other, this idea must be carried out so far as is consistent with our teachings. If, after the member is taught that he shall share alike with all others all benefits and blessings of the Order, he willfully neglects to perform his duty by his fellow members and remains away from the sessions of the assembly, he of his own accord proclaims that he does not require of other members to "relieve his distress." He voluntarily relinquishes his right to request that "every lawful and honorable means," be resorted to to "procure and retain employment" for him, "and should accident or misfortune befall him," he need not expect of others to "render such aid as lies within their power to give." It is left to the member himself to say whether he will remain on that level to which we uplift him on bringing him into the Order. On entering he becomes the equal of all other members, and no power save his own will can destroy that equality.

If two men join the Order on the same day and continue to attend the meetings of the same every evening, each one shall have an equal right to claim recognition when the second question of the seventh order of business is asked. But if one absents himself from the meetings frequently, and the other attends regularly and promptly, the latter must be accorded the situation if but one vacancy exists.

Another lesson taught by the placing of all members on the one level is that all branches of honorable toil are regarded in the same light by the Order of the Knights of Labor. The laborer, the artisan, the craftsman, and the professional man each has an equal share in the inheritance left to the Order.

The member will notice that at each of the officers' stations there is a symbol. That which designates the Master Workman's station is a Column, three feet in height, the dimensions of which are given in the A. K.[1] The shaft of this symbol is made in imitation of a bunch of rods tightly bound together. It is the "bundle of sticks," which indicates strength. One branch of toil organized by itself may be perfect so far as its power to legislate intelligently on matters pertaining to that particular craft is concerned, but if opposition is met with it falls an easy prey to a stronger power; its sources are of one kind and easily exhausted. In this respect it resembles the solitary stick, which if it is possessed of any native strength at all, or if decay has not set in may resist the power brought to bear on it if taken hold of at but one end and struck against the knee, but if two hands are used and it was then brought forcibly in contact with the knee, it is easily broken. If "a number of sticks," are bound together, the resistance offered to any violent effort to break them is far greater than where one alone is used, and, instead of being broken across the knee, it is the knee which feels the shock the most. One attempt to break a bundle of sticks is sufficient to prevent a second effort in that direction. If all branches of trade are bound together in one Order, the difficulty experienced in overcoming their combined forces is so much greater than that which would be felt in a struggle against one alone that it is the part of wisdom to refrain from making a second attempt. This part of the Master Workman's symbol indicates that "in union there is strength."

But it is not to illustrate what can be accomplished in a struggle against an opposing force so much as to indicate that where the efforts of all are directed toward the one end for the good of all that this symbol was adopted, the cornerstone of the Order being COÖPERATION. The shaft of the Master Workman's symbol is intended to show that the combined strength as well as the united efforts of all are necessary to make coöperation a success.

The base of the emblem is in imitation of coral, as coral was at one time supposed to be the product of the combined effort of the coral animals. It is from this theory that the idea of adopting the base of coral, as being emblematic of the labor of many hands, was conceived. To perfect the union of crafts, the work of many hands is necessary. The coral used to designate

[1]Adelphon Kruptos, "Secret Brotherhood."

the toil of many hands is the Maeandrina, or brain coral. The branch coral is never used in the construction of the Master Workman's symbol.

The leaves used in forming the capital are of three kinds—the cordate or heart-shaped leaf, the reticulate leaf, and the grape leaf. The cordate leaf was selected because of its construction. It was not so much its resemblance to the human heart that recommended it as the manner in which all the cords or fibers of the leaf tended toward the stem on which it grew. In this we find the lesson of all parts of the Order, District or Local Assembly, rendering obedience to the lawful commands of the General Assembly.

The reticulate leaf was adopted owing to the network of fibers and veins that traverses its width and thickness; all parts of the leaf covered and filled. This was to indicate that all parts of the earth should be covered with a network of assemblies.

The grape leaf and the grape itself were chosen partly on account of the symmetry of the fruit, but principally because of the nature of the vine. In the axil of the leaf are two buds; one which develops in the present season, the other retains its strength as a provision for the coming year. The tendrils of this vine are very sensitive to the touch. They are hooked at the ends, and when they come in contact with any object to which they can cling, they at once proceed to twine themselves around it. This is to teach that we should be ever ready to spread the Order into other regions and to cling tenaciously to every opportunity of spreading our principles among men. The adhesion of the vine is in itself typical of the manner in which our principles are planted, for wherever they take root they are seldom displaced.

The capital is surmounted by a human bust. As the head is the "seat of intelligence and wisdom," it is but proper that it should be placed over the emblems of Toil, Coöperation, and Unity. By its will, all things human are directed and managed to serve mankind. It is therefore placed in a position where it can overlook the progress made in reaching the realization of our hopes.

The symbol of the Worthy Foreman is the same as the base of the Master Workman's column. It requires no further illustration than to say it is larger than the base of the column.

The symbols of the other officers are explained in the A. K. in such a way as to obviate a necessity for further explanation. The stations of the officers are significant. The Worthy Foreman is stationed at that end of the sanctuary from which all members enter. The reasons are numerous; he is required to remain at that place in order to make an examination of approaching Knights without disturbing the assembly. The Inside Esquire need not traverse the sanctuary in order to consult him. The Worthy Inspector is stationed to the right and slightly to the rear of the Worthy Foreman. From this position he may examine all cards presented to the

Worthy Foreman, and can perform his duty without asking the name of every member on entering the sanctuary. He has charge of the Master Workman's roll book and on presentation of each card he makes "the proper record" in the same. The Master Workman does not keep his roll book; it is when he wishes to ascertain the exact standing of a member that he examines it.

The Financial Secretary is stationed to the left and slightly in the rear of the Worthy Foreman, in such close proximity to that officer he need not speak above a whisper in acquainting him of the financial standing of an incoming member. When the Worthy Foreman presents a card to the Financial Secretary, that officer immediately looks over his books and states to the Worthy Foreman what the standing of the member is. If the member is not in good standing, if his dues and assessments are not paid up to date, he is informed by the Worthy Foreman to report to the Financial Secretary as soon as he gives the S. of O. No member should be allowed to enter the sanctuary without undergoing this scrutiny. It is an absolute necessity and if faithfully observed no member need be in arrears if he has the inclination to meet his obligations. If the Worthy Foreman, Worthy Inspector and Financial Secretary act in harmony and adhere strictly to their respective duties, all members who are prompt and regular in attendance need make no inquiries as to their standing in the Order, for they will be notified at the proper time if a payment of dues or assessments is necessary. If they are not regular in attendance, the Worthy Foreman, knowing that such is the case, will cause them to be notified before suspension becomes necessary.

When the Master Workman, under the fifth order of business, directs the Unknown Knight to go to the vestibule to make the prescribed examination, he may call the attention of the Assembly to their duty toward the Order and allow them to pay dues, etc., while the Unknown Knight is making the investigation. After the Unknown Knight has ascertained the names, occupations, etc., of the candidates in waiting, he proceeds to the desk of the Recording Secretary and learns whether they were regularly proposed, balloted for and elected. If they are proper subjects for initiation, he announces that fact to the Master Workman in a distinct tone of voice, repeating the names of the candidates. The Master Workman then asks the question beginning with the words "Does any one know cause"; if no objections are made or sustained, the Master Workman then repeats the instruction beginning with the words "Unknown Knight, you will proceed to the vestibule and make the prescribed examination." During all of this time the Financial Secretary may receive dues, etc.

When the Unknown Knight has asked the questions of the candidates and is ready to present them for initiation, he gives the entering signal; when the Inside Esquire attends, he informs him that the candidates are ready for presentation to the Assembly. The Inside Esquire then closes the wicket and announces in a distinct tone of voice that "the Unknown Knight and candidates are waiting." The Master Workman then gives three raps; the members all arise and form a circle, leaving an opening as nearly in front of the Inner Veil as possible; when this is done the Master Workman says: "Admit the Unknown Knight and candidates." The Inner Veil is then opened and the Unknown Knight and candidates are admitted, but not within the circle. As soon as the Inner Veil is closed behind them, the Unknown Knight halts the candidates on the outside of the circle, then taking a step forward he halts in such a position as completes the circle and says: "Master Workman, our friends have satisfactorily answered all inquiries, etc." After the Master Workman has directed him to place the candidates at the center, the Unknown Knight steps inside the circle and to the left of the opening and allows the candidates to come in and proceeds in advance of them, keeping them to his right, toward the center, when at that point he places them in the form of a triangle, and when they are ready to receive the pledge, administers it to them. The remainder of the initiatory exercises are fully explained in the A. K.

THE GREAT SEAL OF KNIGHTHOOD

The base of the triangle (it must be an equilateral triangle), if drawn singly, represents but a single line; this line has a beginning and an end; it was the first part of the seal that was designated, and therefore represents "creation"; to it at either end are attached two other lines, so constructed as to meet at the top, thus forming a triangle; the line to the right represents "existence"; the one to the left signifies "dissolution." Combined, they form a whole, which signifies "humanity" and tell the story of man's birth, life, and death. In the sign language of this part of the seal we are told that as man at his birth is pure and spotless, his existence should be so continued that his death could come at any time and find him prepared to render an account of his stewardship to his Creator.

This sign represents the three elements which are essential to man's existence and happiness, land, labor, and love. The land, from which all of the necessities and luxuries are derived; the labor of man, which produces the fruits of the land; and the love, which furnishes the medium of happiness between all humanity.

These three lines are also emblematic of production, exchange, and consumption. To make production profitable such articles as are produced must be passed into the hands of the consumer. To give the products of one's toil without a fair equivalent would not be in harmony with the principles of equity, therefore they must be exchanged for values, whether these values consist of money or the product of money or the product of another's toil is not material, so long as producer and consumer are satisfied. That production may not cease there must be consumers, who shall give in exchange for such things as man produces either that which we call money or the product of their toil. Here we draw another lesson which our Order teaches its members, that is, that no middlemen are required to carry on the business of the world. What we call profits are not a necessity. If a man produces a pair of shoes and another man is in want of a pair of shoes, they make an exchange of shoes for money, or shoes for the product of labor or labor itself. In this way each one secures the full value of that with which he parts. Acting from this basis, it is not necessary for one man to lay his shoes on the counter of the middleman and pay him for turning them over to the third man. He can perform that duty himself and thus do away with the middleman and save what would be given to him in profits.

The circle which binds together the ends of the lines of the triangle indicates that the bond of unity by which the membership is bound together should be without end; placed on the outside of the triangle it also indicates that all business of the assembly should be transacted among members and for humanity. This circle can be broken from the inside very easily, but from the outside never. If the sentiments of unity and fraternity are properly nourished and cherished among members, unless the elements of disunion, discord, envy, hatred, and ill-will are permitted to enter this circle, it will not be broken from the inside, and it cannot be broken from the outside. A circle of any kind can be forced apart more easily from the inside than it can be crushed in from a power brought to bear on it from without. Therefore if we maintain a solid undivided front toward the enemy, his attack from the outside will in no way injure the "Circle of Universal Brotherhood" by which we are surrounded.

Beneath the base of the triangle and outside of the triangle is a horizontal line; this line indicates that in the beginning the great architect of the universe intended that in their dealings with each other men and women should be guided and governed by that principle which is immutable—JUSTICE. Therefore the line at the bottom of the circle of "Universal Brotherhood" represents justice. Extending outward and upward from the right of Justice we find another line; beautiful in its proportions is displayed the omniscient WISDOM of the Creator, that justice may prevail it is requisite that man should be endowed with wisdom. This line to the right and connecting with the base line is indicative of WISDOM. Extending outward and upward from the left of the horizontal line which bespeaks justice is another line. As the Creator sealed his work with the signet of everlasting truth, so does this line represent TRUTH.

The lines again make a new alliance at the point or summit of wisdom, and extend upward to the left until the end is joined with another line

THE GREAT SEAL

which runs upward from the "Signet of Truth," forming a symmetrical pentagon, being joined above the apex of the triangle; the line running from WISDOM to the left teaches that everything of value or merit is the result of creative INDUSTRY, while the line that extends upward and from the Signet of Truth indicates that the coöperation of all is required to inculcate perfect ECONOMY. Joined together these principles of JUSTICE, WISDOM, TRUTH, INDUSTRY and ECONOMY form the ARCH beneath which we pass on going from the Local to the District Assembly, wherein we are taught while standing beneath the crown of the Arch that INDUSTRY alone produces wealth, ECONOMY only can protect it, TRUTH is the only enduring science, WISDOM the only light to guide, and JUSTICE to rule and govern in all.

The pentagon also represents that inasmuch as we hope by education and organization to secure for the toiler that leisure which rightfully belongs to him, we will work but five of the days of the week; that as all nations partake of the five elements of life, which are SALT, MILK, HONEY, BREAD, and FRUIT, and as to all men the same Creator extended all his blessings, all men of all nations are entitled to admission to this army of PEACE, wherein the sword is beaten into the plowshare, and where neither spear nor sword nor implement of death shall be used forevermore.

The pentagon of the District Assembly also gives forth the lesson that we shall educate our members to utilize the five elements of nature—LAND, AIR, LIGHT, HEAT, and WATER. These elements are essential to the production of the materials that promote the happiness of all. The husbandman must know how to observe the changes of temperature, how the light affects certain plants, when water should be applied to others, and in what manner the air should circulate among them all that he may make the best possible use of the land bequeathed to him by his Creator. Beyond the pentagon we find another circle, from the outside of which rays of light are given out by the lamp of experience, which we have used in passing from Local Assembly to District Assembly, and they now illumine our pathway toward the General Assembly. Outside of the halo of light we see a hexagon, which represents the six mechanical powers which we are taught to use after we have learned to walk in the five avenues of the soul, the God-given senses, SEEING, HEARING, TASTING, SMELLING and FEELING. These six mechanical powers have been used for many purposes, but were given to the world for only one purpose—the good of man. They consist of the LEVER, the PULLEY, the WHEEL and AXLE, the INCLINED PLANE, the WEDGE and the SCREW. These powers are all embraced in the word "Machinery." No matter how many kinds of machinery we find in use they are but a complication of these six powers. In the pentagon we are taught the use of but five mechanical powers, the lever, pulley, screw, wedge, and hammer. The hammer was introduced that the member might be instructed how to weld together the various natures, dispositions, sentiments, feelings, and aspirations by which men are actuated in gaining their ends. The hammer, though not, strictly speaking, a mechanical power, is made use of by all artisans and is therefore introduced.

As improvements are being made every day in the machinery of the world, we assert our right, not alone to these powers, but to the results of man's toil while making use of them.

The hexagon represents not only the five principles of economy, industry, truth, wisdom, and justice, but that of EXPERIENCE as well, and an experience which comes from a knowledge of the conditions and surroundings of the five races of men makes it possible for an organization which recognizes the rights of all of them to partake of its benefits to accomplish more for humanity than any other.

Beyond the hexagon are five points, which represent the FIVE RACES OF MEN. They also represent the FIVE GRAND DIVISIONS OF THE EARTH. From each of these points a distinct race of men looks toward our Order for light. It will be seen that in the Seal of the General Assembly the line of existence in the triangle runs through the Continent of America; it is here that the Order exists and sheds its light today, and it is toward the point from which the Order started that all eyes are turned (looking for the relief, the benefits) ; and toward the Prytaneum that all eyes are directed; around the Prytaneum all hopes of emancipation cling and grow. The words around the pentagon on the Great Seal are "Prytaneum, North America, January 1st, 1878." Their real significance is that the home of the Order was founded in General Assembly, January 1, 1878. "A. K. the 9th," means that it was in the ninth year of the Knighthood that the "home" was founded. At the base of the triangle and to the left we find a small cluster of islands, while the line to the right runs through a continent, this is to convey the idea that though the Order was founded on a continent, yet its aid and light will be extended even unto the uttermost parts of the earth, and until all the inhabitants thereof, the greatest as well as the humblest, will become sharers in the peace and prosperity which shall be dispensed when the Order shall gladden them with its presence. Within the circle of nations we read the motto of the Order "That is the most perfect government in which an injury to one is the concern of all," as it is toward the point at which an injury is inflicted that all should attend, we find, on examining the seal, that it is from that point all eyes are turned, that the best means of repairing the injury may be devised. In perspective from a point opposite the word "injury" it will be seen that the vanishing lines are farthest from the eye, indicating that it is from that point we should look in order to see whereby the injury may be amended.

On approaching the Outer Phylon or Veil of the District we find a blazing sun, the emblem of light and source of life; it typifies "Order" the great law of the universe.

In the center of the Phylacterion, or vestibule, is a small table in shape of a pentagon bearing a basket full of cards; the colors of the cards are red, blue, and gold. In the early history of the Order the delegates to the District were designated as Senior, Intermediate, and Junior, and elected for one, two and three years, respectively, and at the expiration of the Senior's term, his successor became the Junior, the others advancing correspondingly ; the Senior Delegate wrote his name on the gold card, the Intermediate Delegate on the blue card, and the Junior Delegate on the red card. On approaching the Inner Veil, a Shield or pentagon is presented to view with the primary colors, seven in number, through which light is resolved when transmitted through a prism, namely, red, orange, yellow, green, blue, indigo, and violet; these colors converge to the center of the pentagon. Each delegate wears a diploma in color representing the length of his term; on the diploma is the number of the assembly he represents. This is worn on the left breast.

The Representative to the General Assembly on approaching the door of the University or vestibule will find a fountain, on either of which is a column based upon a book, the whole surmounted by an arch. This emblem signifies that the fountain head of the Order from which all laws emanate is based on knowledge, which is represented in the book. The columns represent temperance and education by which the Master Workmen have been enabled to erect the perfect arch, the keystone of which indicates that POWER which comes from intelligent action.

On the door leading into the Prytaneum is a HEXAGON, at the base of which is a PYRAMID beneath a BLAZING SUN. The lesson of this emblem is given on opening the General Assembly.

INDEX

Brumm, Charles N., speaks at Shenandoah demonstration, 330; attitude toward socialism unknown to Powderly, 374

Bryan, William Jennings, campaign for presidency, 296

Buchanan, Joseph R., 141 ff. *passim*; *The Story of a Labor Agitator*, criticism of Powderly, 140; they become friends, 161; letter to, re immigration, 409-11

Burns, Ira H., law student with, 103

Burns, William J., 301

Businessmen, not in sympathy with strikers, 133

Canada, tramp life in winter, 27, 29; Fenian invasion, 175; annexation of, 410

Canals, law re consolidation of, 239

Canavan, Hank, 72

Capital, drives men to strike when public opinion is against them, 170; the fruit of labor, 267, 272; strained relations of labor and, 282

Capitalists, near editor's chair, 173

Carbondale (Pa.), Powderly's parents settle in, 5-6; coal discovered in, 7

Carew, Father Francis, friendly to K. of L., 379

Carlton, Albert A., 152; Powderly's letter to, on closed shop, 315 f.

Carnegie, Andrew, 56 n; Powderly's estimate of, 420 ff.

Carnegie Steel Company, 260

Cars built in Carbondale, 7

Cary, Samuel Fenton, speaks at Shenandoah demonstration, 330; attitude toward socialism, 374

Cassatt, A. J., 238; protest against Reading Combine, 243

Catholic Church, *see* Roman Catholic Church

Catholic priest, disciplined for espousing cause of strikers, 133

Catholic Workingmen's Society of Girardville (Pa.), constitution and by-laws, 330-32, cited, 376; Powderly's comment on, 333; correspondence in Philadelphia *Times* on, 335-37

Cattle Butcher's Assembly, 146

Cattle syndicates, absorption of land by, 223, 224

Central Railroad of New Jersey, 235, 240; subordination to rule of Reading, 237; *see also* Reading Combine

Chamberlain, I. D., letter from Powderly re J. G. White's charges, 404-6

Chautauqua, Powderly criticized by Father O'Reilly for lectures, 367

Chicago, anarchists, 159 n; convention of the Irish race, 180

Chicago, Burlington, and Quincy Railroad, strike of engineers, 165

Chicago exposition (1903), 411

Chicago packers' strike, *see* Stockyards strike

Child labor, 232

Children, kind of education needed, 199 ff.

Christ, an agitator, 38; and the money changers, 264; advice to love your neighbor, 284; clergy as followers of, 378-79

Christians, wrong done workers by professed, 37; recognize kind of commercialism Jesus condemned, 264

Churches, on side of wealth and power, 36, 133; workers exploited for upkeep of, 89

Churchianity, 265, 266

Cigar makers' union, and K. of L., 140; fight against, 140, 142

Circus, 10; flags on tent of, 93

Civil War, 16; veterans, 92

Clan na Gael, 183

Clark, Jack, 10

Class distinctions, 424 f.

Clergy, influenced by rich, 37; Powderly abused by, 39, 95; preach inequality, 60; invited to aid in ridding Scranton of houses of ill-fame, 78; and the Reading Combine, 236, 251; regard calling as a trade to make a living by, 265; failure to drive exploiters from temple of industry, 266; Powderly's conclusions regarding, 328, 365, 378 ff.; many Catholics friendly to K. of L., 379

Cleveland, Grover, Curtin Investigating Committee appointed at request of, 134; effort to restore lands illegally taken by corporations, 222; invitation to Powderly, 224, 230; quoted, 225, 226; offer to appoint Powderly Commissioner of Labor, 230